D1559510

Ritualizing Nature

"We have needed Paul Santmire to write this book. For decades, his has been one of the most important voices enabling us to hold Christian faith and a response to the crisis in nature together. He has always been interested in sacramental and liturgical practice, but now he turns his full attention to the rituals Christians hold and the countercultural, earth-caring ethos they propose. The result is an honest and hopeful proposal. Read this book, and let it help you think again about the importance of the basic symbols your local community enacts. Here is life-giving liturgy for the whole ecumenical house—that is for the whole earth and all of its creatures."

—**Gordon W. Lathrop**, *Lutheran Theological Seminary at Philadelphia, author of* Holy Ground: A Liturgical Cosmology *(2003)*

Ritualizing Nature

Renewing Christian Liturgy in a Time of Crisis

H. Paul Santmire

FORTRESS PRESS
MINNEAPOLIS

RITUALIZING NATURE
Renewing Christian Liturgy in a Time of Crisis

Please visit the author's Web site at www.hpaulsantmire.net.

Unless otherwise noted, scripture quotations are from the New Revised Standard Version Bible, copyright © 1989 by the Division of Christian Education of the National Council of the Churches of Christ in the USA and used by permission. All rights reserved.

Cover image: *Salisbury Cathedral* by John Constable (1776–1837)

Library of Congress Cataloging-in-Publication Data

Santmire, H. Paul.
  Ritualizing nature : renewing Christian liturgy in a time of crisis / H. Paul Santmire.
    p. cm.
  Includes bibliographical references (p.   ) and index.
  ISBN-13: 978-0-8006-6294-3 (alk. paper)
  1. Liturgics. 2. Nature—Religious aspects—Christianity. I. Title.
  BV178.S26 2008
  264.001—dc22

                    2008007911

This book is printed on 30 percent post-consumer recycled content paper.

The paper used in this publication meets the minimum requirements of American National Standard for Information Sciences—Permanence of Paper for Printed Library Materials, ANSI Z329.48-1984.

Manufactured in the U.S.A.

12   11   10   09   08   1   2   3   4   5   6   7   8   9   10

To Laurel

Contents

Acknowledgments

I can mention and thank only a few of those who have taught me and inspired me over the years, without whose support a writing project like this could never have been completed. For more than fifty years, I was mentored in matters liturgical by Henry E. Horn, formerly pastor emeritus, University Lutheran Church, Cambridge, Massachusetts. He was my pastor, teacher, and friend, and also a model for me, both as a liturgical practitioner and a theological interpreter of the liturgy. He joined the Church Triumphant in January 2007. I celebrate his life and his gracious influence on my own life with deep gratitude.

Since 2001, I have especially benefited from the good luncheon counsel of two theological friends of three decades, beginning when we were colleagues at Wellesley College in the late sixties, Clifford Green and Roger Johnson, both of whom read these chapters at various points along the way and made many helpful suggestions. I am indebted to them for their friendship and for their empathetic interest in my work. Jennifer Phillips, a former student of mine and now a gifted liturgical practitioner and writer, also read parts of my manuscript and made good suggestions, and for that help I am grateful as well. I received a number of insightful suggestions, too, for two of my chapters, from members of the Boston Theological Seminar, a faculty colloquium of Boston-area theology schools. I hope I have done justice to those suggestions.

Then, because this book may possibly be the last of what is now a series of four books on the theology of nature, my early preoccupations with this topic come to mind, beginning in 1960 when I began my graduate studies in theology at Harvard Divinity School. I especially remember how difficult it was for me to find a faculty member to oversee a critical dissertation on Karl Barth's theology of nature. It may come as a surprise to people who are theologically conversant today, in this our ecological age, but I was repeatedly told back then, in one way or another, "theologians don't need to be interested in nature." I finally convinced a theologian who was then just in the early stages of what was to be a distinguished scholarly career, Gordon Kaufman, to take me on. Since his theological views at that time differed from mine—subsequently our theological differences have become even more pronounced—I always had to be at my sharpest, even in order to hold my own with such a rigorous and imaginative thinker. Can I say that I am still grateful for that theological baptism by fire? I can—and I am glad to be able to do that in this forum.

Also under the rubric of looking back, I want to express my appreciation to Fortress editor-in-chief Michael West for his kind support and for his willingness to shepherd each of the three books that I have now published with Fortress. I also want to express my gratitude to the entire Fortress editorial staff, who exercised such care with this manuscript.

Finally, for forty years now, I have been accompanied—and often led—in my theological journeys by that bright and strong Eve whom the Lord has so generously given me, my wife, Laurel Oliver Santmire. She has been a true "soul-friend" for me, in a way, I think, that many of the classic Celtic saints would have understood, since such friends—male and female partners included—were an important part of their spiritual milieu. Laurel and I have talked about many theological mysteries during our walks and travels over the years. Amazingly, she also read every page of each of my books and made suggestions before I submitted them for publication. And she loves the liturgy as much as I do. So it is especially important for me to be able to dedicate this kind of a confessional book to her, my lifelong partner and my most patient and insightful spiritual friend and counselor.

Prologue

Come Walk with Me

Following the example of the American transcendentalist Henry David Thoreau, my wife and I have become habitual walkers in recent years, although much more modestly than the Concord, Massachusetts, sage and at some distance from his beloved Walden Pond. One particular route, however, has taken on visionary proportions in my own soul, akin to the intensity of Thoreau's experience with walking, although quite different in character. So I begin this book with this Thoreauvian invitation: come walk with me along the Charles River.

My wife and I often saunter along the banks of the now rejuvenated Charles River in Cambridge, Massachusetts. Its pollution a public scandal for decades, the river has been measurably cleaned up in recent years, so much so that the "Charles River Swimming Club" held its first-ever open swimming race in 2007 in order to boost that group's continuing campaign in behalf of the river. Along the north bank where we walk, there are hidden wooded places where one can remove oneself, somewhat, from the urban setting of cosmopolitan Cambridge. In addition to the wonderful commonplace—the doves, the flickers, the robins, the ducks, the geese, and the seagulls—we have seen the extraordinary: a loon diving and then emerging many moments later to swallow a fish in a gulp; red-tailed hawks soaring high above; an elegant Great Blue Heron standing still in some rushes at the bank; and even, in one halcyon moment, two gracious white swans gliding majestically up the river.

A mélange of people also engage the river happily during the warmer seasons—students in rowing shells, early and late in the day; families in canoes, mostly on weekends; solitary souls in kayaks at virtually any time. On the south bank of the river are many wide grassy spaces and an abundance of shade trees where, on a typical early summer's evening, one can walk in the midst of strollers and joggers and cyclists and those who have come to fish, to picnic, to play, to garden, or to harvest mulberries. Along the way, one can hear a symphony of tongues, what I take to be Spanish, Russian, Haitian, Vietnamese, Armenian, Chinese, and English, among others. The members of this improbable congregation are many colored and of all ages and social classes. People smile at each other and give every appearance of feeling safe and being content. They seem to look after each other, too. On one occasion, when I was doing one of my elderly "power walks," a man about my age, who was sitting on a park bench with a young girl, who must have been his granddaughter, hollered over to me as I labored by: "You're doing fine! Don't get discouraged!" All this appears to me to be a world of peace, in the biblical sense of *shalom*, replete with cultural diversity, a sense of well-being, respectful mutuality, physical security, a welcoming of all the generations, and communion with a natural world that has at least some measure of its own life, free of human intervention.

When I embark on such walks myself, I often have one regular destination, the Episcopal monastery on the north side of the river, one of the homes of the Society of Saint John the Evangelist, which came to Cambridge in 1870. There I am blessed to be able to kneel in prayer anytime during the week and often to participate in moving liturgies, like the Great Vigil of Easter Eve, in the gracious 1936 basilica-style Chapel of St. Mary and St. John, whose massive but elegant granite structure commands the riverfront at that point. That the chapel's inner, mammoth wood roof beams were once part of a bridge over Boston's Mystic River only heightens my own fascination with the charged spiritual and liturgical drama that daily emerges in its midst and deepens my own engagement with its Charles River setting all the more.

That pilgrimage through those different places—the worlds of the loons and the swans, of the ordinary folks of many nations at peace, and of the community of faith gathered in hope for its Eucharist and other rites—is for me a kind of mundane mystical journey. For me, the worlds of the still, wild woods and the people's park and the quiet yet songful basilica all inform each other inseparably, and all bespeak God's presence and the promises of God for the whole creation.

It so happens that I also read the witness of the Scriptures in a like manner, as celebrating all those worlds. Which is no accident, because the liturgy, after all, hands me the Scriptures every week and has done so ever since my parents promised at my baptism to put those Scriptures into my hands. This they did chiefly by their devout participation in the liturgy, with me and my siblings in tow when we were children, which impressed me enormously. Now when I read those Scriptures, I encounter that very vision of God's will for our world: nature, human community, and church in differentiated and dynamic harmony, with the church called to celebrate and to embody the vision of divine *shalom*, of peace with justice, which is God's ultimate purpose—which is to say, God's *eschatological* purpose—for the whole universe. The biblical promise of God's last things (*ta eschata* in Greek, hence our word *eschatology*) and the inreach of those last things into my present experience has been very real for me, for many years.

I use the much-abused language of eschatology here because it is so important to me. Hence, I will try to be as clear as I possibly can be. I am not talking here about being "raptured" up to heaven with a few other believers, there to await the destruction of the earth. On the contrary, in the Bible the city of God comes down to earth (Rev. 21:2) to be established in the midst of "a new heaven and a new earth" (Rev. 21:1). Nor do I have access to any kind of timetable for the arrival of that new city in the midst of that new heaven and new earth. That is not for us to know, as the Bible also says (Acts 1:7). Eschatology is the witness to the future arrival of the consummated creation, when God will be all in all (1 Cor. 15:28), a thought that I can give voice to only with hesitation, since now if we see that future of God at all, we only "see through a glass darkly" (1 Cor. 13:12). On the other hand, that future of God has arrived and does arrive on earth ahead of time, as it were. Paradoxically, it arrives before it arrives, finally. It arrives powerfully in the life, death, and resurrection of Jesus Christ, and then, mediated through him by the power of the Spirit, in the life of the church, which is the body of Christ. The future of God arrives here and now, when it does, as a "foretaste." The technical theological language is that that future of God arrives "proleptically."

All this is a deep mystery. In faith and in hope, sinful mortals like we who are members of Christ's body believe we can live, by the inspiration of the Holy Spirit, in that future world here and now. Indeed, with the eyes of faith and hope given to us in the body of Christ, we believe that we can see signs of that future world, as our eyes are illuminated by the Spirit, now and again, around us. This is the faith and this is the hope that, when it is so given to me, leads me to see those many fragmentary signs of *shalom* as I walk along the Charles River.

So be assured. I am well aware that when I saunter along that river, alone or with my wife, I am seeing the world through rose-colored glasses. Or, better, in the apt image of John Calvin, I am seeing the world through a biblical lens, which I have been taught to use in the community of faith and hope. This means that I am seeing the world primarily in terms of its divine promise, to be consummated when the end of all things arrives, when the day of the new heavens and the new earth, in which righteousness dwells, dawns, as announced by the Bible. The world I see reflects "the last things" of God's purposes, a vision given to me in fragments as one who partakes in the body of Christ, here and now.

But the actual world where I walk is not only a world of eschatological peace, realized in fragments, here and now: it is also a world that is thoroughly broken and pervasively polluted and rampant with violence. On some hot summer days, the Charles River may be permeated with an explosive growth of an algae that can be highly toxic to humans and animals, in response to which authorities suspend all boating, which casts the idea of swimming in the river also into serious doubt. Along the shores of the river, Japanese knotweed, an invasive, bamboo-like perennial that forms dense thickets, is choking the life out of many native plants everywhere. Such occurrences remind us that the interconnectedness of our earth has sometimes deadly dimensions as it deals with the stresses and strains in our time. A fenced-in, gone-wild acre that I pass at one point in my walk once held a military arsenal's storage area; it leeched toxic chemicals into the river for many years and is still off-limits to the public. The terrors of war come to mind every time I notice it. Moreover, one dare not walk along the Charles unguardedly at night for fear of assaults, or worse. So the rejuvenated river itself and its sometimes peaceful environs is by no means that ultimate river that flows through the City of God, for which Christians long when they sing, "Shall We Gather at the River?"

Further, I am very much aware that even an imperfectly restored Charles River is today an exception, compared to many rivers of the world, depleted or poisoned as they are. I understand that a peaceful, multiethnic, multigenerational, and multiclass early-evening stroll in a riverside park is today an exception compared to the experience of most of the people around the globe whose early evenings are filled violence, strife, and hunger. I know that even quiet prayers or an exquisite liturgy in a gracious chapel can mask ecclesial corruption (painfully apparent in recent years to those of us who live in the Boston area, where stories of priestly sexual abuse seem to know no end). Indeed, I could fill the remainder of this book with stories of the evils of this world, some of which I will catalogue in my review of our global ecojustice crisis in the next chapter.

In such a world, dominated by the principalities and powers of evil, I am compelled to ask, How can I sustain that eschatological vision that so enchants my soul? How can I "walk the walk" of that vision of peace as well as "talk the talk" of that vision? How can anyone? These questions set the stage for the explorations of this book. I invite the reader to walk with me each step of the way.

Partners for the Journey

This personal, "confessional" approach—as I will presently identify it—to the theological journey before us is as a matter of course informed by a variety of theological partners, past and present. I want the reader to know at the outset that the story of walking along the Charles that I have just narrated is by no means idiosyncratic. Many others have gone before me. Their insights have consciously, and no doubt unconsciously, shaped my own encounter with the world of nature.

An example: the following statement by the Christian ethicist James Nash gives voice, instructively and discursively, to a range of theological convictions that have helped me to see what I have seen in my walks along the Charles. Nash allows that "the expectation of universal or cosmic redemption" in eschatological terms is "a necessarily vague vision of the consummation of *shalom*." On the other hand, says Nash,

> Ecologically, this vision gives ultimate meaning and worth to the cosmic ecosphere. It is the confirmation of nature's ultimate value to God. Nothing is any longer valueless or meaningless or irrelevant. Every living creature counts for itself and for God ultimately. This perspective stands in judgment on anthropocentrism. If the natural world as a whole will participate in God's redemption,

then all things must be treated with respect in accordance with divine valuations, and all living creatures must be treated as ends in themselves—not simply as means to human ends . . ."

Then Nash concludes, pointedly: "This vision of cosmic redemption causes enormous confusion in our current use of ethical language and our understanding of the breadth of ethical obligations. The confusion will not soon end . . ." But, as Nash states, this vision has its own power:

In the midst of the moral ambiguities of creation, we can experience only promising signs—not the full harmony—of the New Creation, the Peaceable Kingdom. The very fact that eschatological visions are necessary precludes romantic illusions about historical possibilities. Nevertheless, the vision represents the ultimate goal to which God is beckoning us. Our moral responsibility, then, is to approximate the harmony of the New Creation to the fullest extent possible under the constricted conditions of the creation. The present task of Christian communities . . . is to anticipate and contribute to the promise of ultimate liberation and reconciliation in human communities and with the rest of nature.[1]

The questions with which I begin these explorations have precisely to do with this kind of eschatological vision that is so important for everything else in the midst of our broken world. How can this vision be engendered? How can it be sustained? How can it be lived?

PART ONE
NATURE, LITURGY, AND THEOLOGY

1

The Making of a Theme:
Ritualizing Nature

My walks along the Charles only set the stage for the explorations that are to follow. I therefore want to take some time in this early chapter to be more specific about what has prompted me to write this particular book and why I have chosen to proceed as I have, all in order to convey to readers as forcefully as I can why I think that a book like this is urgently needed at this time—beyond those reasons that are so profoundly existential for me and for many others. I also need to explain right at the start what I mean by my title, which is not exactly a media sound bite nor even a theme that most people conversant with theology will recognize.

I am writing, in the first place, in response to a grassroots surprise concerning the theology of nature, as will be immediately apparent. I am also writing in response to what I—and many well-tutored scientists and countless other thoughtful analysts—consider to be a severe global crisis that is now engulfing our planet. Throughout, moreover, I am writing in hope to respond to what I consider to be the social system of "Death" that is currently wreaking havoc on God's good earth and on the beloved poor of God, thereby threatening the end of nature as humans have known it for millennia.

This book, too, is a theological response to all of the above, in the form of what I like to think of as a confessional voice. Finally, and most to the direction of our explorations, this book is a venture in confessional theology that has a very specific focus. This book examines *the liturgy* as a form of ritual. It then contemplates nature in relation to that particular ritual. But before I consider these important preliminary matters, I must say as explicitly and as clearly as I possibly can what I mean by *ritualizing nature.*

What Is "Ritualizing Nature"?

Those new to theological discussions as well as those conversant with theological issues will probably be perplexed by the title of this book. Some may even be put off by it, not just because ritual is not exactly a household word in our culture, but more so because in some contexts ritual has negative connotations (more on this in chapter 3).

I could wax prosaic, at this preliminary point, and leave it at that. I could say that the lead words of my title, *Ritualizing Nature*, mean that I am committed to interpret the world of nature as seen from the context of the chief ritual of many churches, the liturgy. In other words, in this book I will not investigate nature in itself (whatever that might mean), but nature as claimed and celebrated by Christian ritual. With this approach, moreover, as will quickly be apparent to some, I am presupposing that "nature" is not the exclusive preserve of what we commonly think of as the natural sciences. I hasten to add, however, that the ear of any theologian who discusses nature must be attuned to those sciences, especially to the disciplines of ecology, evolutionary biology, and cosmological physics.[1]

Ritualizing nature, then, means standing within the cultural world of Christian worship and seeing what one can see as one contemplates the world of nature from that standpoint. Not everything one sees from that perspective, to be sure, will be helpful. That, indeed, is why Christian ritual must be renewed, as we will presently see. But, for better or for worse, that is the standpoint of this book, whence come my major theological presuppositions. That is the existential location that gives me my angle of vision as I contemplate nature.

This explanation of my title will hopefully suffice for some, at this preliminary point in the discussion. But I think I can do better, before I have said anything more, with a personal story. This story is prosaic in its own way, since—in Christian circles known to me—it so familiar.

I have fond memories from my childhood of the annual Christmas Eve candlelight service, the "Christ Mass." That was a charged time for a young boy—staying up so late for the midnight liturgy and anticipating the gifts under the tree the following morning as well. It was all the more exciting for me when the lights were turned off and the huge throng in the nave was hushed in total darkness. All, especially young children, would then expectantly wait for their candles to be lighted by acolytes making their way through the midst of the great congregation. Soon, what had then been a world of charged darkness was ablaze with hundreds of lights.

In the warm glow of those lights, I would then climb up to stand on the pew so I could catch a glimpse of the crèche at the front of the sanctuary, where the infant Jesus lay with Mary and Joseph, where shepherds knelt and cows and donkeys watched. And I could marvel, too, at the cascading red or white poinsettias that had been amassed around that crèche. What had been for me some moments of uncertain silence—especially because of my childhood fears of the dark—was then transfigured even more, beyond the visions of the crèche and the poinsettias, bathed in the beautiful candlelight, with exuberant song: "Joy to the world, the Lord has come. Let earth receive her king. . . . And heaven and nature sing! And heaven and nature sing!" The peace of that holy night was announced, too, in so many words. Year after year at those midnight liturgies, I heard, from the voice of the prophet, that the lamb will lie down with the lion and that a little child shall lead them (Isa. 11:6), and from the Gospel, about "peace on earth" and good will to all (Luke 2:14).

The excitement I experienced as a child in such ritual moments was palpable. Did those moments of joy and well-being with the whole earth, with the animals at the crèche and with the powers that be everywhere, then have the effect of shaping—*ritualizing*—my experiences of the world of nature more generally? I believe that they did, however subliminally, along with other great liturgical festivals, like Easter. Easter liturgies always announced to me, even in my imperfect childhood hearing, the renewal of the whole earth, suggested visually by the scores of lilies in the chancel. What else gave birth to my longstanding joyful engagement with the wonders of God and nature and my deep-seated hope for peace with nature? Why else have I always, even as a child, been so eager to consider the lilies of the field in all their glory?

But the plot of that childhood Christ Mass story is not the whole story. As a young theological student, early on I discovered that my own fascination with those Christmas Eve liturgies, in particular, was only a prosaic recapitulation of one great poetic act of inspiration centuries before. I was astounded to learn that that celebrated lover of nature, Francis of Assisi, was the one who had more or less *invented* the drama of the crèche, with living animals, at a Christ Mass, outdoors, in the midst of the darkness of a great cave lit by candles or torches or both. Still later, after much more study, I became convinced that, in so enacting the crèche drama in the context of that Mass, Francis himself had been ritualizing nature. Indeed, it can be argued that, for Francis, love of nature is inextricably bound up with that crèche drama in the Christ Mass. That is the greater story that I will attempt to tell in this book.

Come with me, then, and see how the liturgy ritualizes nature, for those whose faith is shaped by that liturgy. See how the liturgy is, for members of the household of faith, what Peter Berger calls "the sacred canopy" of hope for the whole creation. See how the liturgy embodies, for the faithful, the great story of the history of all things, a metanarrative that is a comedy—in the classical sense of the word, as used by Dante in the fourteenth century—not a tragedy. Hence, anyone who, in faith, enters into the liturgy and whose mind and heart is shaped by that practice, can have hope for the whole creation. This is an audacious claim, of course, especially in our late-modern or postmodern world that excludes or even ridicules the very idea of a metanarrative.[2] But this is the challenge every Christian theologian must face in these times. So I join with a whole host of others, many of whom have borne the heat and burden of the postmodern day long before I began to write this book.[3]

A Grassroots Surprise

In what sense is this book a response to a grassroots surprise—and what is that surprise? For more than three decades, I have been addressing Christian student groups, parish Bible classes, denominational assemblies, ecumenical retreats, conventions of church outdoor-ministry leaders, students and faculty from both environmental and religious studies departments, seminary audiences, and gatherings of environmental activists. In all of those contexts, I have again and again encountered committed Christians, from all walks of life, who have been surprised!

In many of those settings, likewise, I have also been engaged by "serious seekers," people who have been alienated from the Christian faith at some point in their lives but who have longed to find a way back, or others who have begun to explore for the first time whether the claims of the Christian faith might make sense for them. These seekers, typically, have been even more surprised! The same holds for some critical environmentalists in my audiences who had not entirely given up on the Christian faith.

The surprise on the part of many was to hear this claim: *the Christian faith has something of profound importance to say about nature and human life in nature.* It's not that some of us have not been proclaiming this truth from the bell towers, so to speak, for many decades. But good news sometimes travels slowly. And good news can sometimes easily be resisted. Why? First, because Christianity in the modern West—notwithstanding important exceptions—has been *pervasively anthropocentric* (*anthropos* being the Greek word for "human"). It has focused on human needs and aspirations, not on nature together with humanity. In the same spirit, Christianity has also frequently been *captive of the modern industrial worldview,* shared by the advocates of both Marxism and capitalism, that regards nature merely as "the means of production." As a result, in the modern period many Christians have rarely, perhaps never, heard nature talked about in sermons in their churches. Second, the good news of Christianity's ecological vision has been resisted because highly vocal critics of the Christian tradition, many of them with legitimate and passionately held concerns about environmental degradation in our time, have again and again announced that Christianity is "ecologically bankrupt." That these critics have often not told the whole truth, or that their criticism has sometimes been exaggerated, at times even unhistorical, is another matter. The point remains. No wonder so many grassroots Christians and others, too, have been surprised to hear a different story!

This is that different story. It comes in two parts. First, historic Christianity has generally been of *two minds* regarding nature, the one ecological and, as it were, nature friendly, the other what can be called spiritualizing or anthropocentric and therefore neutral with regard to nature or even, sometimes, anti-nature in character.[4] Second, in its ecological expressions, historic Christianity has been shaped, on occasion, by *a form of worship that has been profoundly nature friendly.* This claim has elicited the most surprise from my audiences—too good to be true, many have said. But it *is* true. My purpose in this book is to establish that truth for all who have eyes to see.[5]

A Severe Global Crisis

This book is not only a response to a grassroots surprise; it is also a response to a severe global crisis. And herein lies a story, too.

Reinhold Niebuhr, the great Christian ethicist of the last century, was known for what was called his "Christian realism." Yet not just ethical discourse but *all* Christian reflection must be realistic, which is to say, truthful. Strangely, however, Christians in our era have often found ways *not* to tell the whole truth. They have found many, often powerful, ways to announce the truth of the gospel of Jesus Christ, but they have not been nearly so zealous about finding ways fully to enunciate the truth about the world that Jesus Christ was sent to save. Call this a failure of imagination or a theological parochialism, but we can no longer afford to be captive to that habit of mind. Christians today must be radically realistic, radically committed to telling the whole truth, because nothing less than the future of the world God sent Jesus Christ to save—more specifically, the future of life as we know it on Planet Earth—is at stake. Hence, I ask the reader to stay with me in the following paragraphs, even though—or precisely because—they are full of bad news about the world in which we live.

The account that follows, I want to emphasize, is not, strictly speaking, scientific writing. I believe, however, that in all essential respects it is accurate. Although I do not provide a citation for every statistic cited, much of the information I have gathered here comes from the World-watch Institute's *State of the World* volumes and their bimonthly *Worldwatch* magazine. In addition, among countless monographs on the crisis, the 2004 work by James Gustave Speth, *Red Sky at Morning: America and the Crisis of the Global Environment* merits special attention.[6] Overall I have gathered these findings from a variety of reliable sources, according to the canons of good journalism. But good journalism, for our purposes here, is more than enough. Schematic as it is, the overall picture that emerges is shocking. This truth is almost too much to bear.

Today citizens of this planet are being threatened by a pervasive, global environmental crisis that will not go away, however much defenders of the status quo try to assure us otherwise. Something is radically, perhaps fatally, wrong with the way we humans are now living on the earth. The very life-support systems of our planet and the lives of all living creatures, especially human creatures, more especially those millions and millions of human creatures who live in poverty, are at risk. The threat of global warming, in itself, can make any sensitive soul shudder.

But such threats just add to a peril of much longer duration. In 2007 the *Bulletin of the Atomic Scientists* moved its "Doomsday Clock," which it created in 1947 to warn the world of the dangers of nuclear weapons, two minutes closer to midnight. The clock then stood the closest to midnight since 1984, at the height of the Cold War between the United States and Russia. "We stand at the brink of a second nuclear age," said the *Bulletin*, made all the worse by the "dire threat to human civilization" posed by global warming.

Global Warming

Are we that close to Doomsday? Consider the following facts. In 1910 there were 150 glaciers in Glacier National Park; today there are fewer than thirty and they have shrunk; in thirty years all these glaciers will, in all likelihood, be gone. The same story is true, all the more so, for the glaciers and permafrost of the Arctic region: a 2004 study discovered that the average amount of sea ice in the Arctic has decreased by about 8 percent in the preceding thirty years, resulting in the loss of an area larger than Texas and Arizona combined. By 2006 that kind of trend had increased, dramatically, according to two separate studies by NASA. One of those studies, by the Jet Propulsion Laboratory of California, indicated that Arctic perennial ice, which typically survives summer melting, shrank by 14 percent in just one year, between 2004 and 2005, reducing that ice conglomerate by an area almost as large as Turkey.

As a result of this kind of melting, waters around the globe are rising. Louisiana, for example, even before Hurricane Katrina in 2005, was losing twenty-five square miles of coastal wetlands a year to the encroaching waters of the Gulf of Mexico. The threat of escalating damage from disasters such as hurricanes is increasing, moreover, due to rising seas and warmer waters that may increase the intensity and destructiveness of future storms. Both are effects of global climate change, according to former *Worldwatch* magazine researcher John Young. More generally, rising waters around the globe threaten the livelihoods of one hundred million people who live within three feet of the mean sea level, a threat of devastations that is already taking its toll in the impoverished nation of Bangladesh, where salinity intrusions into groundwater are radically reducing water available both for drinking and for agriculture, and in some Arctic regions, where those most affected by the encroaching waters are indigenous peoples. In the Atlantic Ocean, the Gulf Stream—the "ocean conveyor belt" that sends cold waters from the Arctic southward in the depths of the ocean waters, thereby creating a sucking effect on warmer southern waters, pulling them north on the upper ocean surfaces—is slowing down and could stop, thus exposing areas such as the United Kingdom to radically colder weather, with unknown effects on human food production and energy consumption in those regions. To the south, the world's largest rain forest, the Amazon River basin, which contains nearly a quarter of the world's fresh water, was struck by a devastating drought from 2000 to 2005, the most severe since records have been kept, beginning one hundred years ago. Studies published in the journals *Nature* and *Science* attribute this kind of catastrophic development, in significant measure, to the severe weather patterns and the temperature increases, which have been unleashed by global warming. A 2006 study, overseen by a scientist from the Scripps Institution of Oceanography, concluded that global warming is in all likelihood also responsible for increasingly destructive wildfires in the western United States in the preceding two decades. Another 2006 study, by Great Britain's leading climate scientists, working with supercomputer modeling for the Hadley Centre for Climate Prediction and Research, told a profoundly disturbing, longer-range story: one third of the earth's land masses will be desert by the year 2100, if current trends continue.

Some less publicized trends are no less troubling. The English-based scientific association, the Global Canopy Programme, stated in 2007 that the destruction of equatorial rain forests, by slashing and burning, results in far greater global carbon emissions than those caused by planes, automobiles, and factories combined. One day's deforestation, said the group, is the equivalent of a day's carbon footprint of the eight million people living in New York City. What other destructive climate-change trends are likewise out of sight and out of mind?

The social and economic ramifications of global warming may be enormous. A report prepared for the U.S. Department of Defense in 2003 entitled "An Abrupt Climate Change Scenario and Its Implications of United States National Security" warned, according to Michael T. Klare of Hampshire College, that "global climate change is more likely to result in sudden, cataclysmic environmental events than a gradual (and therefore manageable) rise in average temperatures." The onslaught of rising sea levels, huge storms, and extensive dust-bowl effects "would trigger pitched battles between the survivors of these effects for access to food, water, habitable land and energy supplies." The report noted that "violence and disruption stemming from the stresses created by abrupt changes in the climate pose a different type of threat to national security than we are accustomed to today." A number of scholarly observers have opined, in this regard, that threats of the next major war in the Middle East will in all likelihood arise regarding scarce water resources, not shrinking oil supplies.

The second 2007 report of the International Panel on Climate Change projected all these trends well on into the twenty-first century, with even more sobering conclusions, that is, if major changes affecting the climate are not made very soon. By 2030 global-warming-related illnesses such as malaria will be out of control in some areas. By 2080, 1.1 to 3.2 billion people around the world will face water shortages and two hundred to six hundred million people could be hungry. By 2080, likewise, some one hundred million people's communities could be flooded by rising sea waters.

How much of this global climate change is caused by excessive human demands on the earth's biosphere and how much by causes that are beyond human control? Some, most notably those who speak for institutes funded by the energy industry and other corporate interests, argue that there is disagreement among scientists themselves about the matter and that therefore it is "too early" to plan for serious changes in our economic institutions, governmental policies, and consumer priorities.[7] While it is true that individual scientists can be found who will argue that global warming is, for the most part, driven mainly by "natural" rather than human causes, the great majority of scientists who write for refereed scholarly journals, and the scientific community more generally, as it speaks through professional associations such as the National Academy of Sciences and the International Association of Meteorology and Atmospheric Sciences, are mainly in agreement: the trends toward global warming, many of them accelerated in recent centuries, even recent decades, are significantly driven by human interventions in nature, particularly industrial activity and changing land-use patterns.[8] The fourth report of the U.N.'s Intergovernmental Panel on Climate Change, with representatives from more than one hundred countries, stated forcefully that there is at least a 90 percent chance that human-caused emissions are the main factor in warming since 1950. But, even allowing for some scientific disagreement about scope of human causation of global climate change, common ethical sense—called, technically, "the precautionary principle"—impels us to do whatever we can justly do, without delay, both individually and systemically, to reduce human contributions to global warming. Which is to say: better be safe than sorry.

Or, more to the same point, in biblical perspective: better be just than just unsure. According to the World Health Organization, the impact of climate change and related environmental disruptions, as Noah J. Toly has observed, "already claims the lives of 150,000 people every year, a tragedy faced by a population consisting largely of poor children in Africa, Asia, and Latin America." Toly argues that we moderns in the West have made a "god" of technology and are willing to make human sacrifices to it. This is his thought-provoking conclusion: "While [ancient] Israel was prohibited from offering its children as burnt sacrifices to Molech, our technological society stands ready to offer our neighbors, children, grandchildren, and God's good creation as burnt sacrifices to Mammon in the fiery furnace of earth's future climate."[9] In response to this situation, what are Christians and other people of good will to do? To walk by on the other side, like the priest and the Levite in Jesus' parable of the good Samaritan?

Other Disturbing Facts on the Ground

Beyond the threats of global warming, the situation is even less cheering, as the mere mention of other "facts on the ground" indicates. Think of the global threats to life-sustaining biodiversity, the mounting exhaustion of soil, fossil fuel, food, and fresh-water resources around the world, the rising rates of atmospheric pollutants everywhere, the input of vast amounts of toxic chemicals into the world's ground-water systems and oceans. The U.S. Environmental Protection Agency estimated in 2004 that 630,000 children are born each year in the United States with levels of mercury that put them at risk for learning disabilities and neurological disorders. Due to the run-off of fertilizers into and through the Mississippi River, the Gulf of Mexico now has a totally dead zone in one area the size of the state of New Jersey. Further to the north, stresses from polluted rivers and invasive species threaten to trigger an ecological breakdown in the Great Lakes, on which more than thirty million people rely for drinking water.

Around the world, the news about the earth's water systems is even more disturbing. In China, according to several news sources summarized in *Grist* magazine,[10] the Yangtze River, the third longest in the world, is "cancerous" with pollution, mainly industrial waste and agricultural run-off. Experts project that up to 70 percent of its water may be unusable, especially for drinking, by 2010. In the mid-1980s, the river supported 126 animal species; in 2002, it was home to fifty-two species. In 2005, the Chinese government declared the Yellow River, the country's second longest, too polluted to provide drinking water. Some three hundred million Chinese do not have access to safe drinking water. But water pollution in China and elsewhere is by no means the only problem related to water.

Nonsustainable usage of water is perhaps of even greater concern. The ecologist Paul F. Bente Jr. has pointed out that in China, a nation that is home to more than 20 percent of the world's population, renewable water supplies support only half the people. China is therefore mining aquifers that will take thousands of years to recharge. Water demands for agriculture have so used up lake waters in China's Gianghou Plain that only three hundred of one thousand lakes still exist. Fish species have dropped from one hundred to only thirty. So it was no surprise to hear, in a story about a 2006 report by China's Environmental Protection Agency that "overgrazing, logging, and loss of ground water turn nearly a million acres into desert every year [in China], displacing millions and cutting the global food supply." Soon, 40 percent of China could turn into scrubland, according to the report.

Similar trends are in evidence in many other places. The Aral Sea, in central Asia, was once the fourth largest inland water body in the world. Since 1960, it has lost three-fourths of its water and contracted to half its size. Lake Chad, once the second largest lake in Africa, has shrunk from ten thousand to one thousand square miles. The lake's fisheries have collapsed. Animal life in the area has been decimated. Closer to home, and little noticed by the public, as James L. Hecht of the University of Denver has observed, the Ogalla Aquifer, which runs 1,300 miles from South Dakota to Texas, is being used up eight times faster than nature can refill it. Yet ever-expanding economic development in much of that area continues unabated and is even celebrated by the likes of the popular *New York Times* columnist David Brooks as a sign of the vitality of American society. And everywhere, for a variety of reasons, unchecked economic forces are, in effect, undercutting the United Nations' mandate that "the human right to water entitles everyone to sufficient, affordable, physically accessible, safe, and acceptable water for personal and domestic uses." Everywhere, water is increasingly being commodified, sold for a profit to those who can afford to pay. Since 1990, three corporations have gained control over the water supplied to almost three hundred million people in all regions of the earth, according to a report in *Sojourners* magazine. Water industry profits globally are nearly one trillion dollars a year, 40 percent as large as oil industry profits. At the same time, according to Water Partners International, more than a billion people around the earth do not have access to clean water and 2.4 billion do not have adequate sanitation. That agency keeps a grim tally of the numbers of people who die from water-related diseases. It reaches at least 13,500 every day. In contrast, the rich minority in the world mostly have all the clean water they want for drinking and sanitation. The average American uses forty gallons a day, compared to the billion of the poorest of the world, who use, on average, 1.3 gallons of water a day per person.

Other related ecojustice issues of profound concern also confront us. A 2006 international study by well-known marine scientists, published in *Science*, projected the progressive disintegration of entire marine ecosystems, leading to an ecological collapse of all commercial fishing globally by the year 2048, if current trends of overfishing continue. This, in a world already plagued by massive food shortages for the poor.

More generally, it is simply not acceptable, morally, for a few of us to prosper in a world where 1.2 billion people live on less than a dollar a day—what the United Nations calls "extreme poverty." Also according to the United Nations, thirty thousand children die every day of preventable illness and malnutrition. Behind such troubling facts is the even starker truth about global income distribution: a 2006 study by the UN Development Institute revealed that 2 percent of adults command more than half of the world's wealth, while the bottom 50 percent possess just 1 percent. Nor is it morally acceptable for us to live in a world where, as the United Nations estimated in 2005, as many as fifty million people could become "environmental refugees" by 2010, due to increasing rates of drought, deforestation, and declining soil fertility, all of which could be exacerbated by global warming.

The morally shocking correlative of these sobering global circumstances is the huge over-consumption of the earth's resources by so-called first-world nations. One example: the Intercommunity Peace and Justice

Center of Washington state calculated that the energy *wasted* in the year 2001 in the United States by not recycling aluminum cans could have met the electricity needs of homes in Chicago, Dallas, Detroit, San Francisco, and Seattle for one year. U.S. energy consumption generally is the least efficient of all developed nations. And the high technology that the U.S. economy constantly fosters requires inordinate energy investments. The Sears Tower in Chicago uses more energy in twenty-four hours than an average American city of 150,000 or an Indian city of more than a million. Another striking example of waste is the development of the bottled water industry. Currently in the United States, seventeen million barrels of crude oil go into these totally unneeded and hyper-expensive products each year (the same amount of oil would power one million U.S. cars a year). Eighty percent of these bottles end up in landfills, where they will last one thousand years. No longer does the American nation live by the motto "waste not, want not," as during the Great Depression. Now it is "want much, waste more." In the United States and other first-world countries, we not only commandeer the majority of the world's resources, we innocently or arrogantly squander many of them in the process.

Again, it is not morally acceptable that the remaining great wilderness areas of this planet, from the rain forests of the Amazon to the old growth forests of the Tongass in Alaska, are now being attacked and increasingly decimated by the forces of human greed. Nor, likewise, is it morally acceptable that so many of our fellow creatures who have no voice in human affairs—the animals—are being subjected to such cruel and inhumane treatment on such a wide industrial scale, much of it for the sake of cheaply feeding the insatiable American appetite for Big Macs and Kentucky Fried Chicken. That hundreds of species of likewise voiceless vegetative creatures—consider all of them, along with the lilies of the field—are being wiped out every year is also a moral scandal. According to a 2006 report by the United Nations Convention on Biological Diversity, humans have provoked, in the last five hundred years and with increasing frequency in our time, the sixth major extinction event in the history of the earth, the worst spate of extinctions since the dinosaurs were wiped out sixty-five million years ago. Perhaps the most dramatic and also most revealing example of all this destructiveness is what is benignly called "mountaintop removal" in areas such as Appalachia. In search of coal to satisfy what is even more benignly called "U.S. energy needs," mining corporations level whole mountains, fill valleys with often poisonous debris, destroy entire human communities, and wreak death on innumerable other animals and plants in the process, not to speak of defacing the grandeur of the mountains and the valleys themselves.

A System of Death and a Posture of Hope

How could all this be happening? Has not our planet gone through a "green revolution" and has not our own society, in particular, witnessed, at all levels and from many constituencies, innumerable calls for the "greening" of just about everything? Is it not the case that some global corporations and even some oil company executives, in particular, are now seeking ways to alleviate the effects of global warming? And did not California, boasting one of the world's largest economies, impose real limits on the emission of greenhouse gases? Wasn't it heartening, too, in 2007 when the documentary *An Inconvenient Truth,* featuring former Vice President Al Gore, won an Academy Award, and Gore himself won the Nobel Peace Prize for his work on climate change? The news at that time was full of stories about political initiatives to combat global warming, as well.[11] Then there are many cheering human-interest stories such as the news about Boston Harbor—once a dead zone for fish and a political joke for the nation, and today a destination for anglers—especially important for people like me, who live nearby. Such reports of individual and regional environmental turn-arounds could be multiplied, and the press typically makes much of them.

The Principalities and Powers of Death

But things overall, by any careful analysis, keep getting worse, above all because of the phenomenon of global warming, but also because of other troublesome "facts on the ground" (as detailed above). The whole earth seems to be in the iron grip of destructive forces, by all reasonable estimates. A system of ecologic Death seems to be driving the affairs of human history in our time (I capitalize "Death" in contexts such as this one, since Death in these instances is more than biological "death"; it is a cultural and existential matter as well). Notwithstanding all the best efforts of well-intended people to address the global ecojustice crisis, our planetary society seems to be dominated by what Paul Tillich called "the demonic" or by what some early Christians thought of as "principalities, . . .

powers, . . . world rulers of this present darkness, . . . spiritual hosts of wickedness in heavenly places" (Eph. 6:12 [RSV[12]]). Strange words, perhaps, in the context of an America that prides itself in scientific rationality, ever-increasing productivity, technological know-how, and trust in human ingenuity. But perhaps this era of global disintegration and destruction can only be described by strange words. The demonic? Principalities and powers?

Use of the construct "the demonic" has fallen out of favor in Christian theology, since Tillich gave it currency in the middle of the last century. This is curious, since the trends to which he was pointing have, if anything, only increased in their virulence. Indeed, what Tillich said of the demonic in his analysis of the cultural, political, social, and spiritual fragmentation at the apex of the modern period, circa 1950, sounds chillingly prescient of such trends today, now flourishing exponentially, in our postmodern era of ecological, social, political, and spiritual disintegration:

> It is not an exaggeration to say that today man experiences his present situation in terms of disruption, conflict, self-destruction, meaninglessness, and despair in all realms of life. This experience is expressed in the arts and in literature, conceptualized in existential philosophy, actualized in political cleavages of all kinds, and analyzed in the psychology of the unconscious. It has given theology a new understanding of the demonic-tragic structures of individual and social life.[13]

Obviously, in a short study like this one, such forces in human history can only be mentioned, not fully described and analyzed. In this respect I must defer to the work of others, like Tillich and Walter Wink.

Wink has suggestively explored the relevance of the biblical theme of the principalities and powers in his study *Unmasking the Powers: The Invisible Forces That Determine Human Existence*[14] and in other works. Wink has argued in various contexts that the world in which Christianity first took shape, along with parallel religious developments in Judaism of the time and the expressions of the then-emergent religion of Gnosticism, was enormously oppressive for vast numbers of people. The profound encounter many had in that era with the macerating forces of Roman might then came to expression in the popular mind and heart in thoughts and teachings about invisible principalities and powers. Those invisible "demons," for the people of that era, were, in Wink's view, "an authentic revelation of the actual spirituality of the massive political and social institutions that bestrode the Roman world . . . , [which] required the sacrifice of human beings to the system."[15] Wink writes in a summary statement,

> What Gnostics, Christians, and pagans . . . shared in that period was a common awareness of spiritual forces that were impinging on them through the massive institutions that had supplanted the world of the city-state and the ethnic kingdoms. They could not yet in most cases identify the institutional sources of their distress, but they were able to isolate those forces, as it were, by projection, and to fight them "in the air" as a way of winning some measure of freedom from their power.[16]

Wink tells us that "Only three religions—Judaism, Christianity, and Gnosticism (the latter two in many respects children of the former)—attacked the idolatry of the Empire and its suffocating controls. The Jews actually fought, repeatedly. The Christians resisted, non-violently. The Gnostics withdrew, invisibly."[17]

A more extended account of "the demonic" and "the principalities and powers" would also have to focus on the contours and the depths of human sinfulness, in addition to Tillich's and Wink's general discussions of the matter. A good place to begin that particular kind of exploration would be with the classic works of Reinhold Niebuhr, most comprehensively his two-volume study *The Nature and Destiny of Man: A Christian Interpretation,* and, most concentrated on sinful human institutions and their power, *Moral Man and Immoral Society: A Study in Ethics and Politics.*[18] Niebuhr believed that the forces of human sinfulness were heightened exponentially as human institutions themselves grew in magnitude. Although he did not develop a theology of "the demonic" the way Tillich did and would not have been comfortable with the language of principalities and powers as Wink has explored such meanings, Niebuhr might well have agreed with Tillich and Wink that there is a demonic aura surrounding human institutions and that that power grows as those institutions themselves grow in magnitude and might.

Naming the Powers?

Given how the language of the demonic has faded in Christian theology, how can we begin to name these invisible powers in order to develop a planetary consensus against them? One critically important way, already suggested by Wink, is to take a fresh look at the dominant economic system that currently has the world in its grips. A number of critical thinkers, like economist Herman Daly and theologian John Cobb, have begun to do just that by analyzing the much-discussed phenomenon of "globalization" and by positing instead a vision of "the common good."[19] Ethicist Cynthia Moe-Lobeda has explored "the disabling of moral agency by the prevailing paradigm of economic globalization" and has proposed instead "the enabling of moral agency" by a new vision of humans' relationship with the God who indwells creation.[20]

Social critic David Pfrimmer has instructively focused his attention particularly on the form of globalization called "the Washington consensus." "This form of globalization," he explains, "with its reliance on an open market that relentlessly pursues economic growth and development, has had a most pervasive impact on people, communities, societies, and even our way of thinking." Pfrimmer identifies three facets of globalization, thus understood, that he believes are driving societies further and faster in the direction of self-destruction: "treating the environment as an externality, privatizing aspects of the ecological commons that should remain public, and the commodification of elements of earth community that should remain beyond market transactions."[21] By this he means: (1) that the powers that be today do not count the costs of pollution or the exhaustion of resources, as they measure growth; hence they take no account, for example, of the New-Jersey-sized dead zone in the Gulf of Mexico or the depletion of aquifers, when calculating farm profits; (2) that the same global system encourages and then justifies those in power when they ravage wilderness areas—by mountaintop removal, for example—for the sake of their own short-term financial gain; (3) that the same system, again, allows blessings of this earth, intended for all, like water, to be more and more monopolized by the powerful in order to maximize their own wealth.

Ethicist Larry Rasmussen has set these trends in historical perspective, which confronts us with a still more sobering picture of our global society. Globalization, he observes, as it makes its impact on human communities and the biosphere, itself has been underway for centuries, in three waves, beginning with colonialism, moving through its twentieth-century development phase, and taking the form in our time of free-trade global capitalism. These waves, he writes, "have always been transformative, and sometimes destructive, of life-forms themselves, together with the ecosystems that comprise their lifelines and matrix." Further, "the waves of globalization continue to institutionalize the conquest of nature as the key to progress, just as they continue to live off nature's capital for the sake of human well-being, rather than off nature's income only." Rasmussen's perspective is as sobering as it is because it is so understated. He is here pointing to huge and infinitely complex, so it seems, centuries-long global trends that are like a tsunami in their collective effects on humans and on the biosphere, before which even the most inspired of human efforts to change things seem to be minuscule indeed.[22]

But whether we are in a position now, on the basis of this kind of brief analysis, thus to name the invisible forces that seem to be wreaking so much havoc on our planet, there can be little doubt that our global society *is* currently drifting, if not racing, toward the abyss of Death, ecologically. We know what many of the poisonous effects are, for sure, even though we may not be ready, at this point, to name names: to identify convincingly what causes those effects.

The Death of Nature?

This is the truth about the world in which we live. Ours is a time when we can anticipate *the Death of nature*—as humans have known the world of nature for millennia—as a real possibility, if some far-reaching global changes are not made very soon. Thus, the widely respected Christian environmentalist Holmes Rolston III wrote in 1996 that because of human factors and failings,

> . . . nature is more at peril than at any time in the last two and a half billion years. The sun will rise tomorrow, because it rose yesterday and the day before; but nature may no longer be there. Unless in the next millennium, indeed in the next century, we can regulate and control the escalating human devastation of our planet, we may face the end of nature as it has hitherto been known.[23]

Some, like the well-tutored Christian critic Bill McKibben, who published a book with the title *The Death of Nature* in 1989, believe that Death, thus understood, has, in effect, *already* occurred.[24]

This is the point before us here: once certain irreversible ecological trends take over, the damage to the earth's biosphere itself will be *irreversible*. Therefore, as a 2005 statement of the National Council of Churches of Christ appropriately and urgently said: "To 'renew the face of the earth' (Ps. 104:30) is, in fact, the moral assignment of our time, comparable to the Civil Rights struggles of the 1960's and on-going efforts to control weapons of mass destruction in a post-Hiroshima world."[25]

Hence, the phrase "in a time of crisis" appears as a matter of course in the title of this book. This is not the first time, to be sure, that I have lifted up these words for readers to see and to ponder. My first book in 1970 had the subtitle *Nature, God, and Ecology in a Time of Crisis.*[26] But I had no idea back then what those words of warning could and would mean three or four decades later. If only we could return to the relatively untroubled days of the "crisis" that was beginning to unfold circa 1970! Sadly, however, we are now in the midst of a much more ominous—and possibly calamitous—era. The trends that some of us identified as a mounting crisis four decades ago have in our time become much more entrenched and, in some respects, have multiplied geometrically in their portent.

Today, soberingly, it does make existential sense to talk about "the Death of nature," as distinct from "merely" cataloging a number of serious threats to nature's diversity and integrity and related threats to the quality of human well-being on the earth—a catalog that was serious enough in itself in 1970. Especially with the menacing clouds of global warming looming on our horizon, ours is a global crisis that approaches biblical proportions in its severity, particularly with regard to the terminal tragedy that could befall many of the already impoverished millions on this planet. It is not too much to say that, even though some otherwise sophisticated observers today choose to live inside a capsule of innocent obliviousness, ours is a time of apocalyptic uncertainty.[27]

The Ambiguities of Apocalyptic Language

True, talk about crisis and all the more so thoughts of a coming apocalypse is sometimes cheap and, in that respect, dysfunctional. We all know about "prophets of doom" who have cried wolf once too often! Soberingly, however, the issue here is not that talk about apocalyptic uncertainty is misguided, for it is not. The issue is that the currents of dysfunctionality, given with our global crisis, run deeper than the apocalyptic picture of our world bequeathed to us by such scientific, economic, and theological analysis. Much more serious is the cloud of what might be called environmental and existential nihilism that hovers at the edges of the American mind in these times of crisis. This is the belief, in the language of the streets, that the world is going to hell and there is nothing anybody can do about it. Signs of this kind of nihilism are all around us.

It comes to expression in a religious garb in the immensely popular "Left Behind" series of novels by Tim LaHaye and Jerry B. Jenkins, which celebrate (the correct word) the violent destruction of our planet and the heavenly escape or "rapture" of a few righteous souls.[28] It also can be seen in a variety of secular works of fiction that depict valiant bands of survivors traveling to other planets and leaving the earth to its own uncertain future, if not its complete destruction. Or, in its bleakest and perhaps most sophisticated form, it can be seen in Cormac McCarthy's widely celebrated 2006 novel *The Road*, a story of two survivors trapped on a dying planet in a time of nuclear winter where rape, torture, murder, pandemics, and even cannibalism are rampant.[29] Films also have not only picked up such dark themes but sometimes have wildly dramatized them for the movie-going masses. For example, Alfonso Cuaron's 2007 film *Children of Men* shows a bomb-pocked police state in Britain in the year 2027, where everything is going up in flames and where, with but one exception, there are no longer any children. As a character in Michelle Huneven's 2003 novel *Jamesland*—a story about a fragmented and isolated collection of characters heroically getting by in a bland but macerating contemporary California subculture—mused, as he pondered coyotes from the hills devouring the local cats: "Hope, when you thought about it, was a lousy, vile, traitorous emotion. A flimsy web of wishful nonsense spun in desperation to hold reality at bay."[30]

Hovering behind such expressions of environmental and existential nihilism is the sometimes beautiful but finally grim picture of "the starry heavens above" (Immanuel Kant) and the "billions and billions of galaxies" (Carl Sagan) constantly proffered to us by contemporary cosmological physics. A single, colorfully illustrated, science-section news report from the *New York Times* will illustrate how depressing this picture can be. This was the bold headline of the front-page spread: "From Space, a New View of Doomsday: How Mysterious Dark Energy Might Blast the Universe Apart." The new scientific proposal, banally called "the Big Rip," is the latest of four theories about the universe's "path to oblivion," a projected cosmic cataclysm estimated to happen thirty-five billion years after the big bang (in contrast to the hitherto theorized fifty-six or sixty-eight billion years, or an indefinite movement toward some final "big chill" or total collapse).[31]

Such reports are very much a part of the everyday experience of thoughtful citizens of our postmodern world. Such reports also regularly provide support for a kind of anti-sacred canopy for our culture, which, in turn, relentlessly, if silently, foster readings of the whole universe as meaningless. This is the picture we see: we who are doomed to die exist on a little spec of cosmic dust, called Planet Earth, in the midst of an unimaginably vast and alien cosmos, all of which is doomed to die. A character in John Updike's short story, "The Accelerating Expansion of the Universe," gave voice to the sentiment: "We are riding a pointless explosion to nowhere. Only an invisible, malevolent anti-gravity, a so-called Dark Force, explained it."[32] Call this the canopy of cosmic nihilism. It meshes all too smoothly with the more publicly visible expressions of environmental and existential nihilism that focus on the future of life on earth.

A Posture of Hope

I would not be writing this book, however, if I were any kind of a nihilist, anymore than medical researchers in their right minds would take on new and arduous projects if they believed that nothing they could do would ever make any difference. And much more: in common with Christians throughout the ages, when it is given to me, I have what can be called a hope beyond hope. Think of the hope that informs these pages elliptically, therefore, as having two foci, as being both penultimate and ultimate. Such a hope frames for me all this legitimate, but profoundly disquieting talk about global crisis and apocalyptic uncertainty.

Penultimately, I believe, there *is* hope if the human species generally, and a whole variety of human communities in particular—among them religious communities—resolve with a due sense of urgency to make changes about the way we humans are currently living on the planet and then honor that resolve with sustained political engagement. More particularly, now is the hour, as never before, for the ecumenical church to get its own house in order: so that the more than two billion Christians around the world, and especially those many millions who live in the United States who could influence our nation's policies for the better, can be more of a force for healing the earth and for championing the cause of the downtrodden everywhere.[33] Perhaps one small theology book like this one can, and hopefully will, help with that in-house process of ecumenical renovation, for the sake of our earthly home (the Greek word for home is *oikos*, also the root of "ecology" and "economics") and all creatures who dwell therein.

Hopefully, too, this kind of commitment to ecumenical theological renovation, as it is rooted in acts of public witness by the whole church, will then contribute to that larger global movement for which Thomas Berry has called. This, in Berry's terms, is the "Great Work" of humanity that is urgently needed in our time, arduous and lengthy as the project will undoubtedly be, involving a plethora of global communities and constituencies as it will necessarily have to do: the envisioning and the establishing of a truly just and beautifully viable earth community.[34]

An amazing variety of human communities are already at work around the globe, often behind the scenes, in behalf of this Great Work. From the UN Rio Conference in 1992 to this very day, global institutions have invested sizeable human and material resources in behalf of addressing our earth crisis. Many of these energies have been crystallized by the Global Earth Charter initiative.[35] Think tanks like the Worldwatch Institute have had enormous influence. Meanwhile, millions of communities and organizations have been laboring for years at the grass roots in the struggle to heal the earth and to respond to the needs of the poor. There is evidence that the oft-quoted maxim of the pioneering French ecologist, René Dubos—"think globally, act locally"—has now been established as a practice in every region of the earth.[36]

Signs of partnership in behalf of the Great Work on the part of a number of religious communities are also coming into view.[37] And a promising proposal for encouraging representatives from a variety of religious traditions to work together pragmatically in behalf of nature and the poor is already on the table—a proposal that steers around the question whether divergent truth claims on the part of many religions will allow them to develop a single vision of what is religiously mandated in this time of crisis.[38] Others, like Larry Rasmussen, have been exploring what it might mean for religious communities to transcend their own particular traditions, while yet speaking from within the context of a single tradition, in order to develop a global earth ethic that could find support well beyond the traditions of historic Christianity.[39] Sizeable grassroots energies in behalf of ecojustice issues have also been invested by American religious communities, in particular, supported by coalitions like the National Religious Partnership for the Environment, launched in 1993, and the Eco-Justice Working Group of the National Council of Churches, founded in 1984.[40] Such signs around the globe are surely promising.

Notwithstanding such good signs, however, the theme before us is critically important: to encourage and to help the ecumenical churches, especially those that take the liturgy as a historic given, to renew their worship, precisely in order to make possible more meaningful, more effective, and more passionate Christian participation in the quest to accomplish the Great Work of our time. In this respect, Rasmussen is surely right when he observes that a "significant work for Christian communities for the foreseeable future is adapting their major teachings and practices—the 'deep traditions' of Christianity, together with its reading of Scripture—to the task of revaluing nature/culture together so as to prevent their destruction and contribute to their sustainability." I propose to do this, focusing on liturgical practices, both by making a break with the theological past and by preserving essential theological trajectories—to use Rasmussen's terms—in behalf of lending support to the Great Work of our time.[41] This, I believe, is a venture in penultimate hope.

Beyond this measured hope for the here and now, I also have, when it is so given to me, an ultimate hope for the then and there: for the whole earth and indeed for the entire cosmos, notwithstanding the apocalyptic severity of our current earthly crisis and predictions of an ultimate cosmic catastrophe by most cosmological physicists. This is my hope beyond hope. This ultimate hope makes the penultimate hope that I sometimes am given for the here and now worthwhile and keeps it alive and flourishing, when I am so blessed by the power of the Spirit.

I read somewhere years ago that during World War II in France, when the resistance movement against the destructive power of the occupying Nazi troops encountered setbacks, even when that movement suffered the most demoralizing of losses, it was typically the Christian members of the movement who showed up the next day to renew the struggle. If true, that was as it should have been. For those French Christians' primal hope was for a coming day when there would be an ultimate victory over violence and injustice on earth and an ultimate renewal of the whole creation. This hope beyond hope freed them to invest their lives, faithfully and passionately, but in a measured and constant way, here and now, in the struggles for peace and justice and renewal of human life in this world. In the same spirit, Martin Luther once remarked that if he learned that the world were going to come to an end tomorrow, he would plant an apple tree.

That is the spirit that has driven me to write this book, notwithstanding all the sometimes apocalyptic uncertainties of these times. I am seeking to do, as best as I can, what the writer of 1 Peter enjoined first-century Christians always to be ready to do, to give an accounting of the hope that is in them (1 Peter 3:15).

A Confessional Voice

I have chosen to give expression to that hope here with a confessional voice—in two senses. First, I write as a kind of personal testimony, as the reader will already have discerned. I already have asked the reader to walk with me along the Charles River, where I have witnessed signs of eschatological peace, made real for me as I have participated in the liturgies of the monastic chapel of the Community of St. John the Evangelist.

I will also invite you to join me in visits to other memorable worship settings in my own history, in South Africa during the apartheid era, in a wilderness center in Washington State, and in my own inner-city congregation in Roxbury, Massachusetts. I will beckon you to come with me, too, as I enter the world of the great and glorious cathedrals of the medieval era and think there about the sometimes tumultuous theological experiences of Martin Luther. Likewise, I will ask you join me in a "walk-through" of the liturgy itself, beginning with a baptismal entrance, continuing with an encounter with proclamation of the gospel and its affirmation, moving through the table fellowship of the Eucharist, and finally being sent forth to witness and to serve. At the end, I will ask the reader to join me in exploring some of the habits of faith that the liturgy forms in those who claim it as their own, standing in awe of nature, serving nature, and building human community in partnership with nature. At every turn of this journey of mind and heart, I will speak personally.

But this book is also confessional in a second sense. Confessional theology, in my view, is an existential first-person address, but I also take it to be an authoritative churchwide discourse that narrates and celebrates "the mighty acts" of the "God of grace and God of glory" in the creation, redemption, and consummation of all things, acts made known in the gracious self-communication of God to us in God's Word. This kind of narrative theology takes the Scriptures as its chief norm (*norma normans*), on the one hand, and the creedal tradition of the church as its secondary norm (*norma normata*), on the other hand, all with a view to addressing the missional needs of the church in any given time and place.[42] Since such an approach to our theme may not be familiar to all readers, however, I want to make an effort here to view it in historical perspective.

Confessional Theology in Historical Perspective

The classical example of the first-person kind of confessional voice—first person even in an autobiographical sense—would be St. Augustine's *Confessions*. A good example of the second usage of the term, in perhaps its strictest sense, would be *The Apology of the Augsburg Confession* penned by the sixteenth-century reformer Phillip Melanchthon. Dietrich Bonhoeffer's *Letters and Papers from Prison*, on the one hand, and his *Sanctorum Communio: A Theological Study of the Sociology of the Church*, on the other, would be more contemporary illustrations of the same two kinds of confessional theology—or, perhaps better, the same two *emphases* of confessional theology. I instance these classic examples not to claim their self-authenticating authority for my own reflections by association, but to illustrate what kind of theology I am aspiring to write.

I understand confessional theology, more particularly, whatever its form or emphasis, as reflection that interprets the symbols of the church's ritual life—what might be called the church's "Nicene inheritance," with reference to the ecumenical creed with that title[43]—in constant conversation with the church's chief authority, the Scriptures (the *norma normans*) and the witness of the theological tradition (the *norma normata*). Confessional theology is interpretive (hermeneutical), in other words, before it is constructive. As a reflective, typically narrative undertaking, confessional theology "tells the story" of the mighty acts of God in terms that hopefully speak to people who are caught up in the sometimes turbulent currents of contemporary American life. Confessional theology, understood in this sense, is one reflective step removed from the church's ritual life, yet intimately and self-consciously bound up with it. It is an articulated expression of the theology that, in principle, anyone can encounter who enters into the world of Christian ritual itself and also, wherever necessary, a critical response to that theology. There are other approaches to theological method, of course.

Even to speak of "theological method" is an undertaking fraught with theological peril. There are as many theological methodologies as there are theologians. And, on occasion, discussions of theological method have degenerated into what has been called "methodolatry." So it is understandable, if not fully defensible, when even preeminent theologians (such as Stanley Hauerwas) sometimes emphatically refuse to talk about method at all.

If I were to pursue the matter beyond what I have said here, I would want to begin with the distinction that Paul Tillich made between what he called "kerygmatic theology" and "apologetic theology." The first, for Tillich, is the theology that explicates the meaning of Christian symbols in their own terms (that is, explicating "the message" or the *kerygma* of the church). The second is the kind of theology that "answers" questions implied in the culture of any given era, entering into the categories of thought of that culture and, insofar as possible, shaping the theological response in terms of those categories. The latter was Tillich's own "method of correlation." In Tillich's own mind, Karl Barth was a prominent example of a kerygmatic theologian, while he, Tillich, was, in his own terms, an apologetic theologian.

The method of this volume, which I have called "confessional," falls under the rubric of the first of Tillich's two types, the kerygmatic. In some contexts, I think, the two terms, confessional and kerygmatic, can be used interchangeably. But I prefer "confessional" because it is both more concrete and more accessible to most readers.

I would further want to distinguish between two kinds of kerygmatic theology (Tillich did not address this distinction directly), *primary kerygmatic theology*—that is, the language of the Christian ritual and of the piety and the proclamation embedded in that ritual—and *secondary kerygmatic theology*, which I would understand to be the narrative explication of the symbols given in the discourse of primary kerygmatic theology, in conversation with the Scriptures and the creedal traditions of the church—"faith seeking understanding" in that sense. This kind of theology, at its best, is surely imaginative (think of the way that Augustine's *Confessions* and his *City of God* have powerfully claimed readers throughout the ages), but it is also fundamentally hermeneutical. It interprets symbols given in the received tradition. It does not construct new symbols (assuming for the moment that such an enterprise is even possible; Tillich, for one, held that theologians cannot construct new symbols).

Sometimes these two types of theology have been opposed to each other (Tillich, notwithstanding his theological categories, sometimes did this in practice). I see no reason to do that. Rather, in the spirit of Rabbi Gamaliel in the book of Acts, I would prefer to see both types of theology flourish, for the sake of enhancing the fragile and fragmentary Christian witness to the mystery of God. It is even conceivable that practitioners of these two kinds of theology might, on occasion, learn from each other! The life of the church has been enriched, surely, by the works of both Tillich (the "apologetic") and Barth (the "kerygmatic"), although they distanced themselves from each other.

To be *both* a kerygmatic theologian and an apologetic theologian at the same time, moreover, *may* be possible. Tillich thought that only two thinkers in the history of Christian thought had achieved this kind of a methodological synthesis, Augustine and John Calvin. But, apart from such monumental achievements (if, indeed, Tillich was right), most theologians, in my judgment, should probably aspire either to be good kerygmatic theologians or good apologetic theologians. That is challenge enough in itself for even the most inspired among us. In any case, the confessional option is the one that has most often commended itself to me.[44]

The Bible, the Witness of the Tradition, and the Newspaper

As these explorations in confessional theology unfold, the reader will encounter constant references to the Scriptures and to the theological tradition, all in the context of a reading of the signs of our times, symbolized by the newspaper. I want to prepare the reader for this kind of confessional adventure.

Confessional theology takes the primary authority of the Bible as a given. This explains why this book includes a number of extended discussions of biblical texts, like Genesis 1 and Genesis 2 in its last two chapters, as I seek to interpret what the liturgy has meant and what it can mean today. This is also why I will lead the reader early on to encounter the liturgical experience of the church in the first and second centuries, for that was the era in the church's life that both carried the traditions that were finally brought together in the canonical New Testament and that was itself self-consciously carried by those traditions.[45]

I could, of course, say much more about the authority of Scripture for the kind of confessional method I am adopting. If I were to do that, I would want to begin by observing that the authority of Scripture itself has a center, the gospel of Jesus Christ. As Luther once observed, the Scriptures are the cradle of Christ. But the question of biblical authority is much more complex than I can indicate here in a way that could begin to do justice to the questions in the minds of both nonspecialists and specialists. In short compass, I can do no better than quote, with agreement, the theological summary statement by Carl Braaten:

> The Holy Scriptures are the source and norm of the knowledge of God's revelation which concerns the Christian faith. The ultimate authority of Christian theology is not the biblical canon as such, but the gospel of Jesus Christ to which the Scriptures bear witness—the "canon within the canon." Jesus Christ is the Lord of the Scriptures, the source and scope of its authority.

But the Bible does not stand alone for confessional theology, notwithstanding its standing as the primary authority. The reader will perhaps also have noticed that, right from the start, in addition to the primary authority of the Scriptures, I have taken the witness of the classical theological tradition of the church as an indispensable, albeit secondary, authority—that is, the church's "Nicene inheritance." This expression refers to the testimony of the creed by that name, in particular to its witness to God the Father, Creator of all things visible and invisible, to the divinity and humanity of Jesus Christ, and to the life-giving power of the Holy Spirit, as that testimony is carried and celebrated by the church's worship throughout the ages. I would then want to signal what I take to be the authority of the church's creedal tradition by paraphrasing Braaten's statement this way:

> The church's creedal tradition is the secondary source and norm of the knowledge of God's revelation that concerns the Christian faith. The ultimate authority of Christian theology is neither the biblical canon as such, nor the creedal tradition as such, but the gospel of Jesus Christ to which both the Scriptures and the creedal tradition bear witness. . . .[46]

Yet, for the confessional theologian, the Bible and the creedal tradition of the Church cannot be left to stand alone. As Karl Barth once memorably stated (or as he has often been so quoted), the theologian is one who carries the Bible in one hand and the newspaper in the other. In fact, Barth's own practice presses that image to the breaking point. For, Barth in effect imagined—surely in his *Church Dogmatics*—that the theologian is one who carries both the Bible *and* the confessional books of the church in one hand, and the newspaper in the other. But the point here is not Barth's image but his commitment to read the newspaper. That was—and is—a confessional commitment. The left hand must know what the right hand is doing. Confessional theology always, whether implicitly or (preferably) explicitly, addresses the public and private issues of the culture of its own time.

Thus, in a sense, Barth's entire monumental theological achievement in his voluminous *Church Dogmatics* was founded on his own participation in the Confessing Church in Germany in the 1940s, which, in the name of the gospel of the Risen Lord Jesus Christ, stood up in public protest against the demonic claims to power by the Nazis. Likewise, in the same sense, Luther's own monumental theological achievement was founded on his own revolt against the theopolitical dominance of the papacy in the sixteenth century and the poisonous fruits he believed that produced in the lives of the faithful, whom he believed had been robbed of the certainty of salvation by the papal establishment. In the same spirit, confessional theologians today must confront the destructive dominance of the principalities and powers of our era, which have put in peril the very future of human life on God's good earth and have particularly marginalized the poor of the earth almost to the point of no return.

These are the methodological thoughts, then, that are in my mind for the journey we are about to undertake: seeking to narrate the cosmic story of the God of grace and God of glory, and doing so with the acknowledgment of the primary authority of the Scriptures, the secondary authority of the creedal tradition of the church, and the urgencies of the historical context in which we find ourselves today—as those authorities and that context press themselves upon my own mind and heart, as an enthusiastic participant in the church's liturgy.

Terms of the Discussion: Liturgy and Nature

As we embark on these explorations, we are faced with a number of powerful concepts, some of which I have already employed, and all of which must be clarified at the outset, in order to avoid serious confusion, among them: ritual, liturgy, and nature. Lest these explorations be bogged down in some terminological morass, I propose a definitional short-cut that I believe will facilitate, not block, our explorations. I will regard "liturgy" and "nature" as the two generic constructs in this study, in terms of which all other related constructs will be understood.

I will address the meaning of liturgy in the next chapter. Suffice to say here that when I am talking about ritualizing nature, I concretely have in mind the historic Christian liturgy as a major expression of Christian ritual. Likewise, when I use the term *worship*, unless otherwise qualified, I will also be thinking of the liturgy. This is not to suggest that the liturgy is the only valid form of Christian ritual or Christian worship. It is rather to identify concretely the focus of these investigations.[47]

Nature is something else.[48] The term resists definition. It is akin to "time," as Augustine once observed: he knew what it is, he said, until someone asked him to define it. The historian of ideas Arthur Lovejoy once identified dozens of definitions of the word nature, and there are probably more. The term nature also has a complicated and sometimes ominous—as in social Darwinism—set of cultural meanings, which often becloud its usage.

"Nature" is one of the most "mythic" of the words in our Western vocabularies and, since that fact has been so little understood, that has meant that "nature" (or "Nature") has also been fraught with powerful social meanings that have themselves, in turn, been even less understood, often to the disservice of both humanity and the world of nature. A prime example of this process has been the modern image of nature as a machine. If nature is a machine, how else should we relate to it than by using it for our own purposes and before too long abusing it? Is not use a machine's raison d'etre? Whose interests are served, moreover, by defining nature as a machine?[49]

Given the ambiguities of the term, the respected French sociologist of science Bruno Latour resolved never to use the word. With due regard for all this uncertainty, I am going to assume that what might be called a commonplace understanding of the term will suffice at this point, as long as readers are aware that this is how we are proceeding. By "nature" I mean first something very much like the commonly used expression "the natural world." But not just the natural world, thus identified. I understand nature to encompass "fabricated nature," as well as "wild nature" and "cultivated nature." Or to put the matter more sharply, nature encompasses what has lately come to be called "the *built* environment" as well as "the environment." Of course, understanding nature in such a manner has its limitations, since the human body is very much part of "nature" (it is not self-evidently wild or cultivated or fabricated nature). Given these ambiguities, therefore, for many years I have been working with a related theological definition of nature, which is probably the best rendering for purposes such as ours here. Despite its ring of abstractness, for definitional purposes only, I prefer to understand nature as "the material-vital aspect of God's creation," what the Nicene Creed calls "all things visible."

Throughout this study, moreover, I will also be using a family of familiar words whose meanings sometimes overlap with nature thus understood: earth, cosmos, and universe. "Earth" I will take in the common sense of our planet and its biosphere. "Cosmos" I will understand to refer to the whole material-vital world of nature, including the earth, with the weight of the meaning falling on the vastness of extraterrestrial reality. But note well: the reader should be prepared to hear this familiar term employed *theologically*, akin to the usage of the term nature. Thus, I will later refer to the "cosmic Christ," who, according to biblical testimony and traditional Christian teaching, is the agent of God's creating and redeeming. Then one last term for our consideration here: "universe," in my usage, means the same as "cosmos."

With the term *nature* thus sufficiently identified, if not fully defined, we can turn to consider the meaning of the term *liturgy*. This will put us in touch with the animating center of this book's argument.

2

Counterculture, Simplicity, Ecstasy: Liturgy at First Glance

What kind of rite is the liturgy? If we are to find a way to grasp how nature can be ritualized by the liturgy, we need to have a baseline of understanding about what the liturgy is. Likewise, if we are to take the measure of the cognitive dissonance that hovers over and around the effort to bring liturgy and nature together (a phenomenon I will discuss in the next chapter), it will be most helpful to work from that same baseline, in order to be in a position to come to terms with the dissonance itself.

To identify satisfactorily what the liturgy is would probably require a book in itself. One recent scholarly account of the liturgy's history in the West took 747 pages to describe and analyze Christian liturgical practices in their many historical expressions.[1] Some studies of individual liturgical topics have been of similar magnitude. A recent, major liturgical theology by Gordon Lathrop was published in three volumes.[2] Our considerations here, however, will necessarily have to be brief and schematic. To this end, I will look at the liturgy descriptively from three perspectives: how it functions, what forms shape its functioning, and how the functions and the forms are held together in the experience. I will suggest that the liturgy (1) functions to form a counterculture (2) by the agency of simple ritual forms, (3) as that forming and those forms are united in an experience of communal ecstasy.

In proposing this first glance at the liturgy, I have used the expression to "look at the liturgy descriptively" deliberately, to convey that I am undertaking what, in more technical terms, can be called a phenomenology of the liturgy: contemplating in this central Christian rite what any observer who has eyes to see can, in principle, see. I will probe more deeply into the theological substratum of these phenomena in subsequent chapters.

The Counterculture of the Liturgy

Consider first the *function* of liturgy. Sometimes the most accessible way to grasp the meaning of something is to assess "what it does." Think then of the liturgy *as a ritual for countercultural community formation.* When it is practiced according to its historic intentionality, the liturgy is not "mere ritual" that tends to support the status quo, by default, if not self-consciously. It is community-building ritual, for the sake of what are perceived to be God's universal purposes of peace and justice, over against the sinful violence of this world.

The contemporary theologian who has explored the countercultural and communal dimensions of the Christian faith and its liturgical praxis of peace and justice with more acclaim than most is Stanley Hauerwas.[3] But Hauerwas's work has been subjected to legitimate criticism, not so much for his emphasis on the church as counterculture, but because Hauerwas, for all his protests to the contrary, seems to opt for a kind of "sectarian" withdrawal from the world of politics, rather than encouraging an active and strategic engagement with that world, in the name of peace and justice.[4] Further, while Hauerwas frequently acknowledges the importance of the liturgy, he has not written extensively about the liturgy, its history, or its ritual dynamics.

Perhaps the most influential voice in the whole discussion of the church as a counterculture has been that of George Lindbeck, especially through his widely read and frequently translated volume, *The Nature of Doctrine: Religion and Theology in a Postliberal Age.*[5] For Lindbeck, "Religions are seen as comprehensive interpretive schemes, usually embodied in myths or narratives and heavily ritualized, which structure human experience and understanding of self and world."[6] As Lindbeck explains:

Religion cannot be pictured in the cognitivist (and voluntarist) manner as primarily a matter of deliberately choosing to believe or follow explicitly known propositions or directives. Rather, to become religious—no less than to become culturally or linguistically competent—is to interiorize a set of skills by practice and training. One learns how to feel, act, and think in conformity with a religious tradition that is, in its inner structure, far richer and more subtle than can be explicitly articulated. The primary knowledge is not about the religion, nor that the religion teaches such and such, but rather how to be religious in such and such ways.[7]

Strikingly, however, as one of Lindbeck's most friendly critics observes, Lindbeck "fails to account for the fundamental role that liturgy always plays in the recovery and internalization of the Christian faith."[8] In this respect, Lindbeck's argument can be strengthened when read in conjunction with the perspective of David S. Yeago, who argues instructively that the liturgy is indeed formative of the church as a counterculture.[9] Yeago writes,

> The apostolic proclamation of salvation is . . . relentlessly corporeal and public. . . . The mission of this community is therefore not fulfilled when something happens only in the heart, in the private inwardness of those it reaches; its aim is rather something that must happen out in public, out in the bodily world; the building up of a new people, whose life together is witness to the claim that the Crucified makes on the whole world, who likewise struggle together to submit their own bodily lives in the world to that lordship.

The theologian who has most carefully explored the historical dynamics of the church's liturgy as a counterculture is Lathrop, particularly in his landmark study, *Holy Ground: A Liturgical Cosmology*.[10] Lathrop, whose works I will cite often in this book, sees the church as a countercultural community that claims symbols by acknowledging their brokenness and that stands over against the world around it, even as it celebrates the goodness of the world generally and the God-given place where the church finds itself, in particular.

While I could probe the work of these thinkers more deeply, here a single example of this kind of countercultural communal functionality must suffice in order to illustrate this highly complex phenomenon. What does it mean when the officiating priest, in preparing the table for the sacramental meal, typically called the Eucharist, adds *water* to the sacramental *wine*? This simple act could be interpreted as "mere ritual," a practice that in one way or another—because of its apparent cultural irrelevance, if nothing else—reinforces the status quo. Think, in this connection, of Karl Marx's dictum that "religion is the opiate of the masses." Seen from a Marxist perspective, pouring water into wine could easily be regarded as one more idle gesture that keeps people thinking about some other, spiritual world and keeps them from addressing the ills of this world. But what I want to show now is that this alleged idle gesture *originally* functioned to help establish and to announce a new countercultural community of peace and justice, which, in turn, was understood to be a sign of hope for the whole world.

Mixing water with wine was a traditional practice in ancient Greek society, at least since Homer's time, for the purpose of reducing the inebriating impact of the wine and also presumably to make more of this relatively scarce drink available. Thomas Aquinas surmised that Jesus himself drank wine mixed with water, a practice which Thomas thought was customary in Jewish society of Jesus' time. Much earlier, we meet an oft-cited reference to the practice of mingling water with the sacramental wine in the writings of the second-century Christian leader Justin Martyr, but without explanation.[11] Not too long after Justin's time, however, this mingling of wine and water in the eucharistic cup or chalice was given a symbolic interpretation, which perhaps had hovered around the practice in Christian circles from its inception.

The practice of mixing water with the wine typically has been regarded to be a symbolic act that recalls the crucifixion account in the Gospel of John, where we read about a Roman soldier piercing the side of the dying Jesus with a spear whence came *blood and water* (John 19:34). So Christian traditions have suggested throughout the ages that the "blood of Christ," identified with the wine of the Eucharist, fittingly has water mixed with it in order to recall the crucifixion as John portrayed it. That interpretation is attested throughout the church's history and survives in many churches in our own time, sustained mainly by official teaching and the weight of traditional usage (the sixteenth-century Council of Trent decreed that any celebrant who does *not* mix water with the wine for the Eucharist should be excommunicated!). Other, biblically inspired, symbolic interpretations of that mingling were also developed in the course of time. But this apparently routine symbolic act *originally* announced revolutionary meanings, which Justin himself may or may not have understood and which subsequent ecclesial interpreters evidently did not generally know.[12]

This was the setting.[13] In the earliest Christian communities before and during Justin's time (ca. 100–165), "liturgy" was understood to be "the work of the people." That is what the Greek word *leitourgia* meant. And this early Christian "people" or "assembly," called the *ekklesia* in Greek (usually translated as "church"), was a radically countercultural community.[14] It was a culture of its own, to begin with; it was not a free-floating "message" of some kind that only later became involved in one or more different kinds of cultures around the Mediterranean basin.[15] In this communal context, in keeping with the practices of Jesus, who shared table fellowship and associated with sinners, prostitutes, lepers, and many other marginalized "people of the earth," the earliest Christian assemblies themselves were constituted by persons of many and diverse social classes. Paul indicates this also in his first-century letter to the Galatians (3:28): the poor as well as the rich, women as well as men, Gentiles as well and Jews, slaves as well as the free. Paul, or a close follower of his, thus thinks of the Christian assembly as a place where walls of hostility are broken down by the reconciling peace of Christ, in this instance between Jews and Gentiles: so that Christ "might create in himself one new humanity in place of the two, thus making peace, and might reconcile both groups to God in one body through the cross, thus putting to death that hostility through it" (Eph. 2:15-16).

And the communal norm that publicly was intended to shape the interactions between members of these egalitarian communities was self-giving love, as Paul indicated memorably in 1 Corinthians 13. We meet the same kind of thinking in the book of Acts, where Luke reports that the early Christian community shared all things in common, insofar as any had need (Acts 2:44-45). This ethos of love, moreover, was by no means exclusively or even chiefly a local matter. Early Christian literature, as a matter of fact, was distinctive, perhaps even unique, in its accent on caring for members of other Christian assemblies all around the Mediterranean basin.[16] These early Christian communities thus differed radically, in intent if not always in fact, from the pervasively powerful institutions of the Greco-Roman world of that era, which were rigidly hierarchal, socially segregated, often parochial, and typically dominated by powerful, wealthy, and sometimes ruthless male oligarchs.

Remarkably, in the midst of *that* hierarchical Greco-Roman society, on the first day of the week, Sunday, it was the practice of members of *those* egalitarian Christian communities to bring with them from their own social settings the basic elements for their common, eucharistic meals—the bread and the wine. This was part of "the work of the people." But the very poor among those members typically could not afford to bring wine. So *they* brought water (which, according to cultural mores, was perfectly appropriate). That water they poured into the large, common chalice, mingling it with the wine from the others, so that, in the end, there was then only one offering. All social, political, and cultural distinctions were thereby countermanded and transfigured. All the people of the Christian assembly were then, by virtue of their individual offerings, as Paul also said to the Galatians, "one in Christ Jesus." Thus, what for Christians today is often merely a routine act of traditional symbolism—biblically rooted, to be sure, but not of major ritual importance—was for those early Christians a profound and revolutionary public acknowledgment of a new kind of egalitarian society and a new kind of hope for the whole world.

It was also a robust sign, for those early Christians, of their willingness to stand apart from the dominant society of their time, *no matter what the cost*. The book of Revelation is only the most dramatic expression of the early Christian consciousness that the Christian "way" was the way of the Lord, the way of suffering. The Gospel of Mark is full of such reminders as well, especially evident in Jesus' rebuke of Peter, "Get behind me, Satan!" (Mark 8:32), when Peter had objected to Jesus' teaching about Jesus' own sufferings and death. Persecution loomed around the corner for many Christian communities and overtook more than a few of them. The very fact that the prayers of early Christian assemblies, perhaps already in the first century, came to be directed to "the king of the universe" reveals much. Their meals, as Gordon Lathrop has observed, "took place in a distressed social situation, full of military oppression and apocalyptic longing. The prayers at meals could be seen as an interior, religious response—even as a protest—to the horrors of that other [king], the one who ruled the Roman empire."[17]

An Ecological Counterculture

Perhaps the most striking characteristic of the liturgy in its earliest expressions, for our purposes here, was precisely the theological opposition to the then-current Roman attitudes toward *nature* that those earliest expressions of the liturgy presupposed. The worshiping communities of early Christianity were in fact, in addition to everything else, *an ecological counterculture*. Such terms, of course, belong to our era. Still, these terms point us to a set of cultural and theological assumptions that early Christian assemblies seem to have taken for granted. New Testament scholars Robert Jewett and Barbara Rossing have shown as much in their respective studies of Paul's theology in Romans 8 and the vision of the book of Revelation.[18]

Roman society at the time of Paul and the seer of Revelation presupposed a widely held vision of nature that had been most memorably articulated for that culture by the eighth-century B.C.E. Greek poet Hesiod. The ancient poet had projected a cosmic vision of a world that had a history of three ages. It began with a golden age, a time when the earth produced richly and when there was no violence. That age then gave way to silver and bronze ages, according to Hesiod, in which war and the devastation of nature became increasingly commonplace. In 44 B.C.E., the young Roman emperor Augustus, seizing the moment of the appearance of a comet, drew on the traditions of Hesiod in order to announce that *a new golden age* of prosperity and peace with nature was about to emerge. The great Roman poet of Augustus's time, Virgil, provided in turn a kind of "messianic" interpretation for the Hesiodian line of thought, focusing on the emergence of a new ruler who would himself inaugurate a new golden age. So Virgil wrote in his *Fourth Eclogue* in words that were soon taken to refer to Augustus, given Virgil's later support for the emperor:

> But for you, child, shall the earth untilled pour forth. . . . Uncalled, the goats shall bring home their udders, swollen with milk, and the herds shall fear not huge lions. . . . The serpent, too, shall perish, and the false poison-plant shall perish. . . . The earth shall not feel the harrow, nor the vine the pruning-hook; the sturdy ploughman, too, shall now loose his oxen from the yoke.[19]

Virgil later identified the messianic figure of his *Eclogues* with Augustus explicitly, in his enormously influential epic poem, the *Aeneid*.

Such themes were widely known in Roman society of that era and were celebrated in many works of sculpture and on coins, as well as in prose and poetry. With this, the imperial propaganda of the era championed both the peace that the Roman emperor(s) allegedly had brought to the Mediterranean world, the *Pax Romana*, and the great fruitfulness of the earth, whose abundant harvests came flowing into the great city of Rome and which were directly attributed to the pacifying rule of the emperor(s). So the second-century Greek orator Aelius Aristides celebrated "the arrivals and departures of ships [in Rome, that] never stop. . . . So everything comes together here, trade, seafaring, farming . . . all the crafts that exist or have existed, all that is produced or grown."[20] The peace and fecundity of the new golden age had arrived—according to the imperial propaganda.

But the ecological and human truths of that era were far different "on the ground" than the picture portrayed by the imperial propaganda of those times. As most of the impoverished and oppressed population of the empire well knew, Rome was in fact a violent, war- and slave-driven culture, which presided over the devastation of the very world of nature that its own propaganda so lavishly celebrated. The great riches of Rome, celebrated by writers like Aristides, were claimed at a violent price, the ravaging of agricultural lands and the forests far beyond Rome. This is the context in which the well-known but widely misunderstood critique of "Babylon" (that is, Rome) in Revelation must be understood, as Rossing convincingly argues: "Revelation's critique of Babylon's prostitution is not sexual but is directed metaphorically against Rome's exploitative trade and economic domination." Likewise, when Revelation refers to the famous apocalyptic "beast" of the end times as hating "the whore" of Babylon (the Roman Empire), by making that whore "desolate and naked" (Rev. 17:16), the reference is ecological: the seer of Revelation is pointing to ecological catastrophe, to Rome's wide-reaching and violent deforestation and plundering of the lands around the Mediterranean.

Over against the human and ecological destructiveness of Rome and its lord and king, Caesar, both the seer of Revelation and the apostle Paul proclaimed the advent of a radically different kind of messianic figure, Jesus, who they believed came to inaugurate a truly new era of genuine peace and justice and the renewal of nature, an era to be consummated in the end times.[21] This is the significance of Revelation's climactic announcement about the coming eschatological world that the "sea will be no more" (Rev. 21:1). Rossing shows that the primary meaning of this text is economic and social, and, by implication, ecological, because the sea, for the seer of Revelation, was a metaphor for the destructive and exploitative powers of Roman trade, predicated as it was on ruthless military might. With the consummated rule of Jesus as the Lamb of God, moreover, Revelation depicts a new city of justice and peace, the New Jerusalem—an eschatological golden age, as it were—where the needs of all will be met "without payment" (Rev. 21:6, 22:17). The brutalizing and devastating world of Roman trade will have come to an end. And that new city will be established, says the seer, on a gloriously renewed and abundant new earth, under the canopy of new heavens. The rule of the cosmic Lamb, Jesus Christ, will have made all things new.

The apostle Paul, in his letter to the Romans, was addressing the same Roman world that the seer of Revelation took as a given, according to Jewett.[22] This was dramatically apparent in Romans 8, Jewett argues, where Paul writes:

> I consider that the sufferings of this present time are not worth comparing with the glory about to be revealed to us. For the creation waits with eager longing for the revealing of the children of God; for the creation was subjected to futility, not of its own will but by the will of the one who subjected it, in hope that the creation itself will obtain the freedom of the glory of the children of God. (Rom. 8:18-21)

According to Jewett, Paul's reference to the whole earth "groaning in travail" (8:22) should be read not only as hearkening back to the Genesis story of the fall of Adam and Eve, when God was said to curse the ground because of their sin, but also with reference to the particular devastation wrought on the earth, its peoples, and other creatures of nature by the destructive ways of Roman power.[23]

More particularly, Paul's reference to the groaning creation was intended to announce that the world of Rome was far from the idyllic world portrayed by imperial propaganda. Paul believed, furthermore, that the struggling early Christian communities, not Caesar and his legions, would themselves process through the world in peace, not in violence as did Caesar, and thereby make possible the establishment of the reign of Christ and the renewal of all things. For that kind of peaceful triumph, Paul maintained, the whole beleaguered world of nature waited in hope, even as it had so long been groaning in travail under the weight of the principalities and powers of that age.

Paul thus shared with other Christian visionaries of the apostolic era, like the seer of Revelation, the radically countercultural conviction that, with the coming of Christ, not Caesar, and with the witness of the people whom Christ had called together and sent forth in peace, not by the power of Caesar's legions, a new age of cosmic justice and renewal had dawned and would be consummated as soon as Christ concluded his reign on earth (1 Cor. 15:28). For this cosmic consummation, Paul hoped passionately and labored fervently, as Jewett concludes: "Paul does not hope for 'redemption from the body,' or as the peculiar singular reference to "body" [in Romans 8:23] seems to suggest, for a resurrection of the body in some individualistic sense of being detached from the creation and its corruptibility, but for a socially transformed corporeality within the context of a transformed creation that is no longer subject to corruption."[24]

The End of the Ancient Theology of Sacrifice

In its earliest expressions, the liturgy was also profoundly countercultural because it presupposed the rejection of the then-reigning theology of sacrifice in the Roman world and that world's attendant public processionals, bloody cultic practices, and widespread celebration of violence. Gordon Lathrop has convincingly and insightfully explored this point in his book *Holy Things: A Liturgical Theology*, whose complex argument I will try to summarize here (with page numbers from that work in parentheses).[25] Lathrop explains,

> We know that the cultic killing of animals and the cultic presentation of agricultural products played a primary role in the religious conceptions and world-order of the late antique Rome. . . . [It] can be asserted that sacrifice was regarded as binding the city and the people into a whole with each other and with the gods, all of them together witnesses at the killing and guests at the bloody table. Sacrifice sustained the civic order, bringing rank and wealth to public expressions that were paid for according to the ability of the principal sacrificer. . . . Sacrifice was the central ritual act of late antique society, bearing and sustaining a conception of the world, including the gods, into the heart of daily experience. (143–44)

Sacrifice was, in other words, the *mythos* that undergirded the whole Roman culture of war and violence.

Lathrop points out that Christian writers, surrounded by this culture of sacrifice, passionately rejected the idea of ritual killing, drawing on language from the Greek philosophical critique of the cult as well as from the Hebrew prophets. As a result, Christians were as a matter of course brought into "deep political and social conflict with representatives of the prevailing order" (144). In this connection, Lathrop focuses on the works of Justin Martyr, to whom I have already referred. "Justin," says Lathrop, "readily admits . . . that the Christians do not sacrifice, the grounds on which they are accused of atheism. In fact, [Justin] revels in the rejection of ritual killing. He argues that the true God needs no such 'gifts,' and that so to waste the creatures of God is to be ungrateful for creation" (145).

Justin projects his argument, further, in terms of a *metaphorical reversal*, as Lathrop explains. Justin states that the Christian "processions and hymns"—a phrase popularly used in Justin's time to refer to Roman sacrificial events—are in fact something quite different. Justin points to the meal of the Christian assembly, to the thanksgiving over the meal, and to the food that is given away to the poor when the meal has been concluded. Which was Justin's way of saying that *the Christian sacrifice is in fact no sacrifice*. "It is as if we," says Lathrop, "living in a culture full of warfare . . . , taking warfare for granted, not even knowing a purpose for warfare anymore, would say, 'These prayers we pray, these meals we eat, this food we give away, they are our "warfare." . . . All other warfare is utterly wrong'" (146). This was Justin's point: "The tradition of Christians is to offer food not to the gods but to the poor and, with thanksgiving, to themselves. This is our ritual of sacrifice" (147). Justin is maintaining, then, that "the only sacrifice the Christians have, the pure sacrifice, is no sacrifice at all. It is a meal, a sharing of food, in thanksgiving" (150).

Behind this argument on Justin's part, according to Lathrop, is a different kind of theology that is predicated on the conviction that the meal of the Christian assembly is—*a gift from God*: ". . . [The] Christian doing of Eucharist is the pure offering simply because Jesus Christ gave it and because the people, now forgiven, have been made a priesthood to receive it. Indeed, receiving this gift is what it means to offer this sacrifice" (150–51). Compare this with the *do-ut-des* piety of the Roman sacrifices ("I give so that you [the gods] might give [to me]"). Christians, in contrast to the Roman practice, do not give something to God in order to gain something; Christians receive and give thanks for the divine gift.

This theology of the divine gift is, in turn, integrally related to Justin's understanding of the cross of Christ, Lathrop observes. Although Justin develops no "theology of the atonement" to explain why Christ had to die on the cross (later writers would address this question in many and diverse ways), it is clear that Justin understands that, whatever else it may mean, the divine act on the cross is itself the primal gift, which Justin understood also by way of metaphorical reversal. The cross, too, "is sacrifice that is no sacrifice, but rather the end of ritual killing" (154). Although Lathrop does not explicitly draw the contrast here between the Roman world of violence and the new Christian culture of peacemaking, it is clear that that is what is on his mind. This, along with the theology of the divine gift: "Both cross and meal are nothing that is given to God, but rather they are the merciful, restorative gift of God to us" (154).

Thus, the early Christian rejection of the Roman practices of sacrifices is yet another salient instance of how that community's ritual life was profoundly countercultural, in this case over against the violence of sacrifice and the *mythos* of violence that that sacrifice presupposed. Once more we see vivid testimony to the culture of a new peaceable kingdom established by "the Prince of Peace" (Isa. 9:6; cf. Luke 2:14) squarely in the midst of the violence of the *Pax Romana*.

The Liturgy's Ambiguous Countercultural Promise

New Testament scholars generally believe that the book of Revelation and letters like Paul's to the Romans were written for presentation to early Christian communities that they might be read in the midst of their liturgies. So we can easily imagine that those very communities which mixed water with wine, in order to announce the countercultural message of God's inclusion of all peoples within the church in equity and harmony, also were shaped by profoundly countercultural convictions, like those of Revelation and Romans 8, that rejected the humanly and ecologically destructive *Pax Romana* of Augustus and his successors as these communities celebrated the work of a remarkably different kind of king, Jesus the Messiah, and his promise of redemption and consummation of the whole creation in eternal peace and justice.

Readers of this volume who are new to "the liturgy" as a construct, then, and who may have had little or even no existential exposure the liturgical worship, must first have ears to hear and eyes to see, if the argument of this book is going to make any sense to them. Rightly heard and rightly seen, this ritual "work of the people" potentially carries within it enormous, transformative social and cultural power.[26] It is not "mere ritual."

A paradigmatic case in point, beyond the apostolic era, is the revolutionary peace-ethic of St. Francis in the thirteenth century.[27] Francis was a champion of the vision of the peaceable kingdom *par excellence*. In a time when the Crusades were a—perhaps *the*—driving agenda of Western Christendom, Francis was dramatically silent about such things. Instead of preaching in behalf of the crusading spirit, as the saintly prophet of love, Bernard Clairvaux, had done in the preceding century, Francis himself made a pilgrimage to visit the Sultan, in the name of the peace of Christ. Francis's much celebrated love of nature, moreover, rightly seen in the context of Francis's own life, was his enactment of life in the eschatological peaceable kingdom, the time when the lamb will lie down with the lion, according to biblical prophecy. And one can argue that all this—the ethic, the vision, and indeed his spirituality—was integrally related in Francis's own life with his daily (whenever possible) participation in the Eucharist, where he encountered the humble, peaceable Christ. Francis brought all these things together in the summary statement he made about his life, his mission, and his vision, in the Christ Crèche Mass toward the end of his life (as noted in the preceding chapter).

On the other hand, after the era of Constantine in the fourth century, when the church was established by fiat as *the* religion of the Roman Empire, the liturgy was transformed into the public cult of the political order in many locales, and in that respect it tended to lose its countercultural power, as the church struggled to maintain its identity in a new cultural and political world.[28] In that era and in ensuing centuries in that kind of milieu, it was easy at times for the liturgy to function as "mere ritual," and for the revolutionary dynamics of acts like mixing water with the wine and for radical hope for the whole creation to be forgotten, notwithstanding strong countervailing trends.[29] For our purposes here, however, the point is to illustrate how the liturgy originally *did* function, how it sometimes *has* functioned, as in the case of Francis, and arguably still *can* function—as a countercultural, community-forming ritual, for the sake of peace and justice and ecological hope.[30] This is the ambiguous countercultural promise of the liturgy. I will return to such thoughts in chapter four.

Some postmodern critics of Christian ritual practices, to be sure, have claimed that the idea of a countercultural liturgy is a contradiction in terms, since the liturgy, by their definition, is essentially "cultural," that is, the agency of the powerful, above all in the West. The very term *ordo*, which I will circumspectly be using in this book to refer to common features of the historic liturgy, sounds heavy and authoritarian to some, akin to the German *Ordnung*. Be that as it may, that dispute, in my view, cannot be adjudicated finally by any scholarly argumentation. Readers will have to make a decision themselves on the basis of what they encounter in actual liturgical praxis in a variety of settings. Hence my emphasis in this book is on engaging the liturgy at its best (see especially chapter 3).

Still, there is a good, if not finally conclusive, response to the postmodern critics, which Gordon Lathrop has ably stated:

> To the question of "whose *ordo* this is," I answer that the ecumenical *ordo*, like all Christian matters, can be used badly, as a tool for the advancement of disguised power. But when bath, word, prayer and table are indeed allowed to stand next to each other in strength, mutually reinterpreting each other, bearing witness to the God of the gospels. . . , then what is privileged will not be any clergy or any denomination. What is privileged will be rather the actual location, the biblical Christ, and the call to faith, to worldly reorientation and to wider communion. The many cultures of humanity are welcome to sing their own songs, use their own local languages and signs, and find their own critical reorientation of this cultural material in doing this local *ordo*. Among those cultures will be the remarkably mixed cultures, the post-colonialist cultures, which mark so many of us in the current world.[31]

The Simplicity of the Liturgy

What, then, did that "work of the people" look like in practice? Early Christian assemblies, strikingly, were not "cultic," as moderns usually think of such things. Most of the words used for "worship" in first-century Hellenistic culture were not used of first-century Christian assemblies by Christians themselves. Early Christians gathered for a meal, during the course of which they remembered the death of Jesus by partaking of bread and wine, accompanied by prayers of thanksgiving. Readings from the Scriptures and of letters (such as from Paul), interpretation of the same, and prophetic utterances were also part of this mix.[32] The revolutionary "work of the people," which I have been highlighting, originally was, and throughout the Christian centuries has been, *a relatively simple set of ritual practices*, rooted in first-century Jewish gatherings for teaching and preaching and in the fellowship meals over which Jesus himself had presided, and received by the faithful throughout the centuries as having been inaugurated, essentially, by Jesus himself.[33]

Scholars have debated about how that relatively simple set of practices evolved in the early church. About this much there is agreement: early Christian worship practices that we know about were not designed by a theological committee, as it were, nor did they somehow drop from heaven for early Christians to adopt as a completed project. Those practices *did* evolve and evolved differently in different places. Further, there is much that we do not know about early Christian worship. Our best knowledge is fragmentary. Yet as those practices come into view in the data available to us, they do seem to fall into place in a kind of "shape" or "pattern" or, to invoke a similar term preferred by Gordon Lathrop, an "order" (Latin: *ordo*). Such interpretive ideas are themselves contested by other scholars,[34] but there does seem to be significant evidence in early Christianity and in ensuing centuries of *a few common ritual elements* in a variety of settings.[35] I will use the word *ordo* on occasion, for convenience's sake, to refer to these ritual elements but always with that generic sense. The history of the liturgy is a history of great diversity, not a history of a single, fixed "order of worship," of the kind that one might encounter printed in a modern hymnal or promulgated in a papal statement.

This is the picture that the available data present to us in early Christianity: an assembly of the baptized, gathered usually on the first day of the week, Sunday, for the sake of prayer and praise, hearing and celebrating the Word of God (in Scripture and in preaching), offering of gifts, and participating in the meal of thanksgiving (the word *Eucharist* is from the Greek word for thanksgiving), an assembly whose members would then disperse into the world to continue to express the countercultural identity they shared in those actions. These ritual actions might flow in a variety of sequences, and, at any given time, a single action might overlap or even merge with another.

An early, illustrative example of these actions can be found in the writings of Justin Martyr, summarized, as follows, by Lathrop:

Gathering in one place
Reading of scriptures by a reader
Homily by the presider
Standing prayers
Setting out of the food of the Eucharist

Great thanksgiving by the presider and the amen

Distribution of the food of the thanksgiving and sending to the absent by the deacons

Collection for the poor deposited with the presider sometime in the course of the meeting.[36]

Many Christian communions today practice a form of liturgical worship that is continuous with such practices. The current worship books of Roman Catholic, Lutheran, Episcopal, United Presbyterian, and United Methodist communions reflect those practices, as do major Orthodox traditions. The forms differ widely, of course, but the underlying actions are basically the same for all these traditions, whatever their cultural or historical locations and whatever they call this chief rite, the Mass, the Eucharist, the Divine Liturgy, Holy Communion, the Sacrament of the Altar, or the Lord's Supper.

A modern version of the same set of practices, obviously not identical in detail with Justin's narrative, also cited by Lathrop, is found in the American Episcopal *Book of Common Prayer:*

The People and Priest

Gather in the Lord's Name

Proclaim and Respond to the Word of God

Pray for the World and the Church

Exchange the Peace

Prepare the Table

Make Eucharist

Break the Bread

Share the Gifts of God[37]

Yet another version of that set of practices appears in what might for some students of the traditional liturgy seem to be an unexpected place. In recent years, a new kind of Christian community has appeared in significant numbers in the United States, the so-called emerging or emergent churches. These are independent churches, many of them with an affinity with evangelical traditions, some of whose leaders consider their congregations to be "postevangelical" and, strikingly, "postmodern."[38] One such independent congregation, Jacob's Well, in Kansas City, which attracts about one thousand people each week to its various services, describes its own worship (on its Web site) in words that very much reflect the historic liturgical practices we have already reviewed:

Singing
Call to Worship
Greeting
Preaching
Communion
Offering
Benediction[39]

Such practices have been given expression in countless settings throughout the centuries, from quiet, small, and modest gatherings in the catacombs of ancient Rome to, in our time, elaborate, musically effusive, and architecturally monumental midnight masses with overflowing crowds on Christmas Eve in St. Peter's, Rome, broadcast around the world. Sometimes their intrinsic, transformative, and countercultural power has been released, as they have simply or even ornately unfolded. At other times, however, especially since the era of Constantine, that contrariety has been restrained or even repressed. In this book, we are poised to explore how that power might more creatively and regularly be released by the practice of those few simple ritual actions and done so in a way that makes an impact on today's world with healing and hope for the sake of peace and justice for all creatures.

The Ecstasy of the Liturgy

How does all this hold together *experientially*? What is the spiritual energy that courses through the members of the worshiping assembly and that calls forth their countercultural, communal formation for the sake of peace and justice as they participate in the simple *ordo* of the liturgy? I will give a first-hand account of my own experience of being swept into and claimed by the liturgy presently. Here I can only sketch the outline of an answer to ponder, lest I leave readers with the mistaken impression that the liturgy is only a kind of sociological functionality, important as that is, characterized by a few regularly repeated ritual actions, repeated perhaps by rote, historically essential as they appear to be.

Call the experience of the liturgy, when it is true to its historic origins, *the experience of communal ecstasy*. The word *ecstasy*, as Paul Tillich often pointed out, means "standing outside" (*ek stasis*) oneself. It was an experience that Tillich found throughout the history of religions, in the arts, in mysticism, and in some forms of speculative philosophy. Tillich may have learned to talk about ecstasy in this way from his own Lutheran tradition, having grown up spiritually in the company of what he thought of as visionaries like Martin Luther. This, for example, was Luther's image of Adam in the garden of Eden: "Before the fall, [Adam was] created in such a way that he was, as it were, intoxicated with rejoicing toward God and was delighted also with all the other creatures. . . ."[40] In a word, for Luther, Adam lived in worshipful ecstasy.

I am using the word *ecstasy* here not just in terms of an individual's experience, however, but in the more specific sense *of standing outside oneself as part of a larger body*, in this case the church, called by the Apostle Paul "the body of Christ." A mundane secular example is a crowd at a sporting event, whose members, mainly unknown to each other, become as "one body" during the course of the event, when they cheer the home team on to a close and exciting victory. Another commonplace example would be the audience at a moving concert of classical music, which spontaneously stands and cheers, as "one body," when the last note of the concluding symphony has sounded. In experiences such as these, the whole is greater than the sum of its parts. Individuals in some very real psychic sense are drawn outside of themselves and stand together, as "one body." So it is with the liturgy.[41] As you participate in the liturgy, by the grace of God, according to the liturgy's own canons, you stand outside yourself as you stand with your brothers and sisters in the same assembly. The language of Paul, therefore, who thought of the church, as we have noted, as the body of Christ, is particularly apt in describing the liturgical experience.

An In-the-Body Experience

The reference to "the body" here is deliberate. The communal ecstasy of the liturgy presupposes physically interactive engagement. A crowd at a baseball game, to cite a related mundane example, not only will cheer spontaneously when a player hits a home run; its members, or at least most of them, will as a body jump up to their feet as they cheer. In the same vein, at some sporting events, members of the crowd will initiate what sports insiders know as "the wave." Some people in one section of the stadium stand up, with their hands up and waving, and then sit down. In rhythm, section after section of the stadium successively does the same. Individuals who participate, as most do, are swept up into this human wave, bodily, and, as a result, become as one body, as the wave rolls around the stadium. Likewise for the liturgy. This was most visible perhaps in the early Christian rite of "the kiss of peace," during which members of the assemblies reconciled themselves to each other with that physical embrace. Practice of this rite was minimized in later centuries, but it was revived in the form of "sharing the peace" in a number of liturgical churches in the twentieth century and now has found a permanent place in many assemblies in our era.

In light of such practices, Mark Searle has observed, more generally: "Liturgy is uniquely a matter of the body: both the individual body and the collective body. From the viewpoint of the individual, liturgy requires bodily presence and a bodily engagement that includes, but is by no means confined to, verbal utterances." Even what may appear to outsiders to be "mere statements," recitation of a creed, for example, are, as Searle notes, "almost invariably ritual 'performances,' that is to say, preformulated acts of praise, petition, repentance . . ." Through such actions, verbal and nonverbal, Searle points out, "the collective body acts corporately and affirms its corporate identity, while the individual participants temporarily subordinate their individuality to the constraints of the joint undertaking."[42]

Lamentation and Exultation

This kind of communal bodily motion in the liturgy is characteristically driven by two powerful emotions, which, as a matter of course, take on a nearly infinite number of variations, depending on the cultural location and the historical circumstances of any particular liturgical celebration. Call them *emotions in motion*. These emotions give expression to the community's most rudimentary faith, as it understands itself to be identifying, bodily as well as spiritually, with the death and resurrection of Jesus: *lamentation* and *exultation*. The root affections of this identification are grief and joy.[43] These are the chief emotions that course through the body of the faithful during the liturgy, in one way or another, drawing people outside themselves, binding them together in ritual acts as one body.

The linguistic roots of the word *lament* are profoundly physical, having to do with wailing, akin to the sounds of a loon screeching or a dog howling. The mourning practices of traditional societies, with the prescribed times for grieving and even sometimes with enlisted official "wailers" involved, also come to mind. In a liturgical context, the wailing of the Christ figure on the cross is always also implied—"My God, my God, why have you forsaken me?!" (Mark 15:34)—when the theme of lamentation comes to the fore in any liturgical context. All these nuances are brought together and transfigured in some of the church's great liturgical music, such as Mozart's *Requiem*.

The word *exultation* also suggests profoundly physical nuances. The word is derived from the Latin expression "leap up" (*ex salire*) and suggests meanings such as rejoicing, being glad, being in high spirits, or glorying, as in a time of victory. I am thinking generally about the embodied rising up of the community to rejoice. I have already pointed to the mundane examples of how this happens with a crowd at a sporting event. But I also want to explore, more particularly, in the context of the liturgy, exultation as an expression of the communal *voice*, either in unison or in dialogue.

Rising to sing is a familiar ritual act in many liturgical churches, an act sometimes given additional ritual expression in bodily motions such as dance steps or clapping during the singing. But the prayers, especially the traditional "collects," which have been shaped by the rising voice of the people, and so "collected" over the centuries, often themselves vibrate, as it were, with the same kind of corporeal sensibilities, reminiscent of the strings of a violin under the bow. Liturgical prayers typically invoke, as Geoffrey Wainwright has said, "rhythm, parallelism, balance, word pairs, contrasts, biblical echoes, archetypal ideas, and the discreet use of affective language."[44] Public liturgical readings from the Scriptures may have many of the same qualities, above all, the ritual reading of "the Gospel," sometimes "performed" in the midst of an elaborate procession. As the Gospel is dramatically announced, the people may bow and also make the sign of the cross on their foreheads, lips, and hearts. Prayers and readings are themselves, on occasion, literally chanted, which highlights a vocal physicality that they already have as ritual enactments. Even the sermon, in a liturgical setting, can and, at its best, does take on a embodied, performative quality, where didacticism is again and again transfigured by those same prayerful elements that Wainwright cites. To this day, preachers from a variety of liturgical and cultural settings sometimes report how their sermons catch them up with enthusiasm (from the root, *en theos,* "in God"), as they are performed with dramatic gestures along the way, sometimes even with the impulse to jump up and down. On the other hand, the wrenching sounds of lamentation sometimes also shape the prayers and the readings and the proclamation, especially when the liturgy of the day is a requiem Mass. At such times, the preaching fittingly honors the cadences of the lamentation with a deep solemnity.

Both these emotions in motion, the lamentation and the exultation, are expressed dramatically in the church's prayerbook, the book of Psalms, which has itself extensively and intensely shaped the church's liturgy and its devotional life throughout the centuries. First the *lamentation,* words heard from the lips of Jesus on the cross, to which I have already alluded: "My God, my God, why have you forsaken me? . . . Yet you are holy, enthroned on the praises of Israel" (Ps. 22:1, 3). A similar voice: "In my distress I called upon the LORD; to my God I cried for help. From his temple he heard my voice, and my cry to him reached his ears" (Ps. 18:6). Second, the *exultation*: "Come, bless the LORD, all you servants of the LORD, who stand by night in the house of the LORD! Lift up your hands to the holy place, and bless the LORD" (Ps. 134:1-2). Or this: "Make a joyful noise to the LORD, all the earth. Worship the LORD with gladness; come into his presence with singing. Know that the LORD is God. It is he that made us, and we are his. . . . Enter his gates with thanksgiving, and his courts with praise. Give thanks to him, bless his name" (Ps. 100:1-4).

Notwithstanding the fact that many New Testament writings were thoroughly shaped by the joys that arose in the immediate aftermath of the resurrection experiences, we meet a strong witness to the pervasiveness of lamentation as well. Although we have no direct reports about the response of the disciples to what is traditionally thought of as Jesus' institution of the Eucharist "on the night before he was betrayed," we surely would be remiss if we did not assume that this text presupposes emotions of deep despair and a sense of impending doom on the part of the disciples that night. The first generation of Christian assemblies, likewise, for all their exaltations, were also "well acquainted with grief," particularly with threats of persecution and death.

We see the realities of their lamentations reflected, indeed, in one of the most hopeful testimonies found in the New Testament, in the concluding chapters of the book of Revelation. The writer of that visionary work was in all likelihood a "prophet," whose calling was to preach during the liturgies of various assemblies. His book was apparently intended to replace his personal presence in a variety of assemblies (in settings, presumably, which he could not visit); it was to be read during the liturgy (Rev. 1:3).[45] In his climactic testimony, when he announces that "the home of God is among mortals," that God is dwelling with them (Rev. 21:3), he directly addresses what must have been the wrenching feelings of lament that those stricken or at least deadly threatened followers of the Crucified must have carried in their hearts, when they gathered in their assemblies. God, says the prophetic seer, "will wipe every tear from their eyes. Death will be no more, mourning and crying and pain will be no more, for the first things have passed away" (Rev. 21:4).

Yet as even this text suggests, the mood of lamentation in those assemblies typically was overwhelmed by another: vibrant exultation. This is nowhere more vividly attested in the New Testament than in the words of Paul (or of a close disciple of his) traditionally thought to have been directed to Christians at Ephesus, witnessing to a kind of spiritual intoxication of joy in the liturgy: "Do not get drunk with wine, for that is debauchery; but be filled with the Spirit, as you sing psalms and hymns and spiritual songs among yourselves, singing and making melody to the Lord in your hearts, giving thanks to God the Father at all times and for everything in the same of our Lord Jesus Christ" (Eph. 5:18-20).

Still, the Cognitive Dissonance

Undoubtedly, much more could be said about this central rite in the lives of many churches, the liturgy, beyond highlighting its countercultural, community-building functionality, describing its basic, simple elements, and pointing to its ecstatic experiential communal matrix. But I hope that in this respect, for our purposes at this point, "less is more," and that those who encounter the following discussions of the liturgy as explorations of new territory will herewith have heard in these reflections, as if in an overture, some chords that resonate.

Keep this countercultural work of the Christian assembly in mind, in any case, as we proceed: gathering for prayer and praise, word, offering, and meal, and departing. And constantly recall that these simple community-forming practices come alive, when they are so inspired, with deep and moving experiences of embodied, communal ecstasy.

Still, the prior question I have identified must be addressed without delay in our explorations here, startling as this may sound to some Christians, especially those who treasure the liturgy. *Why bother?* For as soon as we think about *the liturgy* and then the liturgy *together with nature* these days, we do indeed find ourselves in a world of cognitive dissonance.[46]

3

The Cognitive Dissonance: Liturgy and Nature

How can nature be ritualized by the liturgy? That is the question I am exploring in this book. But this begs another, critically important question. Does the question itself make any sense? It is like searching for a bridge over troubled waters. Such a search is one thing, but to search for a bridge that does not exist is another. Before we proceed any further, therefore, it is necessary to confront the cognitive dissonance that hovers around our theme. In this chapter, I will consider first that dissonance as it pertains to the liturgy itself and, second, how that dissonance casts the idea of any meaningful theological interpretation of nature into doubt.

Why Bother with the Liturgy?

The first form of our theme's cognitive dissonance is suggested by the question, Why bother with the liturgy? This question is profoundly existential. It emerges from the turbulent currents of contemporary American culture. It has to do with what is perceived to be a fundamental clash of ideas and intuitions about the deepest kinds of personal and public meaning in our world.

Consider the following exchange between two bright, young, cohabiting surgeons on the popular TV show *Grey's Anatomy* that aired during one recent December. He, an African American, wanted to set up a small Christmas tree in their apartment. She, an Asian American, objected, provocatively claiming, "I'm Jewish." Then she explained that she had had a Jewish stepfather. But far more important, she said, was that she perceived herself as having no religious convictions whatsoever. He, in turn, evidently wanted to find some middle ground, some pluralistic position that would take into account a variety of religious traditions, like Hanukkah or Christmas, or even cultural traditions like Kwanzaa, which would thereby bring them closer together. So he explained to her, in words like these: "For me, a Christmas tree isn't something *religious*. It's something *spiritual*."

An art writer for the *New York Times*, Ken Johnson, recently expressed the same kind of thinking, albeit in a more sophisticated form, in the *Harvard Divinity Bulletin*.[1] The son of a Congregationalist minister, Johnson says he lost his faith after he left home for college. Institutionalized religion, with its doctrines, its rites, and its hierarchies of authority, no longer made any sense to him. What he did not lose, however, "was a fascination with all things magical and mysterious." Things that "come under the heading of 'spiritual,'" he says, have always attracted him. Now a self-proclaimed atheist, he has turned to the world of *art* to find meaning in life. For him, "art serves the same purpose for society that dreaming does for the individual." Good art reveals, for him, what might be called the sacredness of all things, however unverifiable that quality of our experience of the world might be. In this sense, Johnson states, "the spiritual mission of art" is to "create divinity." By this he means that art can make available "a psychological energy of great value and utility to individuals and to whole societies." This is the transcendent function of art, in his view: art "creates energies in the psyche that seem and feel supernatural." One could even imagine this sophisticated art critic participating wholeheartedly in the Christmas Eve Mass in Rome. But he would do that, according to the canons of his own belief system, only as an aesthetic experience that itself "creates divinity," not as a religious ritual that is predicated on communion with the self-disclosure of a gracious God, not as something "religious" in that public, traditional sense.

These two examples reveal some deeply rooted features of American culture today. In recent years it has become commonplace for people of varied faith backgrounds and experiences to distinguish between "religion" and "spirituality," typically in order to reject the former and to affirm the latter.[2] Religion, in this sense, usually means what is sometimes called "institutional religion," that is, legally recognized public bodies, with their own clergy, moral codes, teachings, and rites. The Roman Catholic Church would be a good example of what "religion" means, in this popular, cultural sense. You can *see* this religious body and *know* what it stands for. The Roman Church is a city-state in its own right, in Italy. It has vast holdings of buildings, land, and other tangible assets around the world. It is governed by a visible clerical hierarchy, which seeks to enforce publicly attested doctrinal teachings and moral codes for the sake of all its members. Many Catholics today, as a matter of fact, even Catholics critical of their own tradition, are quite comfortable with the thought that, whatever else it is, theirs is a highly visible "religion" in this popular, cultural sense.

"Spirituality," in contrast, is typically understood, again in a popular cultural context, as a private and interior faith or deep feeling on the part of individuals. This individual faith, moreover, is usually not considered to be dependent on the clergy, moral codes, teachings, or rites of any organized religion. A classic American example of this point of view is the thought of the nineteenth-century champion of radical individualism, Henry David Thoreau.[3] Thoreau is still widely venerated for his refusal to submit to what he thought of as "the dirty institutions of men [sic]" and particularly for his rejection of so-called institutional religion in favor of a faith—influenced by his studies of Asian religions—that he created by his own interior inspiration and on the basis of his own encounter with what he thought of as the wilds of nature, professed in his still widely read classic, *Walden*. Given his rejection of institutions, on the one hand, and his radical individualism, defined by his encounter with nature, on the other, Thoreau remains an invisible, if not self-consciously affirmed, patron saint of American culture to this day. The figure of Thoreau, in this sense, hovers powerfully, if not explicitly, over my examples of the TV doctors and the art critic. Thoreau's was the way of spirituality, in our popular sense, *par excellence*.[4]

The same kind of Thoreauvian sensibility appears to shape many of the beliefs and practices of those who devote themselves to New Age spiritualities.[5] While these spiritualities sometimes find a place for rituals of various kinds, frequently involving the world of nature, they appear to be highly eclectic and privatized. And they often seem to be self-consciously developed in opposition to the public, communal rites of established churches.

Because of the longstanding popularity of what might be called such Thoreauvian spiritualities, many readers may well experience cognitive dissonance from the outset, asking themselves, How can *liturgy* be conjoined with nature? For them, liturgy has to do with the "rites" of a particular "institutional religion" that has defined theological doctrines to which all participants must adhere. How narrow! How parochial! How weighed down, to the point of suffocation perhaps, by traditions from the past! Isn't liturgy so much "going through the motions" or merely "hocus pocus" (a term that is in fact a slur on the words of institution in the Eucharist, "this is my body": *hoc est corpus meum*)?

Nor does it help when some parish liturgies appear to be rites of futility themselves. Both old hands and newcomers of any persuasion can quickly sense that the life has gone out of some of these liturgies, by the absence of real congregational participation or by the pedestrian pace of the leadership and the music, not to mention sermons or "homilies" that give little evidence of real engagement with the Word of God and that help to explain why the word *preachy* has become an epithet in our society. The eminent Dutch theologian Edward Schillebeeckx tells this story starkly: "'What's the use?,' I heard a twelve-year-old girl say in the United States after a Sunday Mass, which struck me, too, as pretty well meaningless, with its accompanying banal talk on video tape. Even though it was all conducted precisely and punctiliously according to the official precepts, there was no bond with the communicants, no inspiration, just a vacuous routine."[6] Sometimes liturgical practitioners are their own worst enemies.

Spirituality, on the other hand, according to the same way of thinking, has to do with the freewheeling inner quest of the individual, often in encounter with the wonders and the beauties of the awesome wilds of nature, although sometimes in response to the powerful claims of art. How often, indeed, have even people who consider themselves to be Christians remarked to their friends or to their clergy: "I get so much more out of communing with God at the seashore than I do coming to church on Sunday"? Anecdotal evidence suggests that more than a few American Christians harbor such thoughts deeply in their souls even as they dutifully pull into their church parking lots on Sunday mornings in vehicles sporting bumper stickers that say, "I'd rather be fishing." Likewise, many people regularly seek out highly charged aesthetic experiences, such as encountering Van Gogh's *Starry Night* or hearing Bach's B-Minor Mass, for the spiritual experiences that most move them. In contrast to these aesthetic heights, thoughts of participating in the seemingly banal rites of a nearby parish church have little or no appeal.

Such is the cognitive dissonance of our theme, in one form. Religion and its ritual expressions sometimes seem to have very little to offer, while nature and spirituality have a widespread and often captivating appeal. Why therefore would anyone concerned with nature and spirituality seek to cultivate any serious interest in liturgy?

Considering the Liturgy at Its Best

Without defending all that passes for "institutional religion" in the United States, with all its allegedly "dead rites" derived from the past and its spiritual banalities, I do want to suggest here that there is more than one way to deal with this cognitive dissonance. True, many Americans, including not a few Christians, have responded to that dissonance by rejecting the liturgy and claiming the spirituality of nature as their own. But there is a much more compelling alternative, I believe. That is to take a fresh look at the historic liturgy itself as practiced in its best expressions today, rather than focus on the liturgy as imagined in its most conventional, or even its most suffocating, expressions. The English theologian and Bible translator J. B. Phillips once wrote a book entitled *Your God Is Too Small.* I want to suggest to readers who are experiencing cognitive dissonance with the theme of this book, because its lead idea is the liturgy: *Your liturgical experience is too small.*

Let me take you to a different place, then. Let me show you what the liturgy looks like in some of its best expressions. In my own experience, the liturgy has indeed been a revolutionary community-building and life-transforming experience, akin to the communal ecstasy that drove the life of early Christian communities as they mixed the water with the wine and saw visions of a new heavens and a new earth.

Where did *I* come from? I have always been, for better or for worse, what William James called a "once-born" soul. I grew up theologically and spiritually and in every other way with the classical liturgy of the ecumenical church as the beginning of every week and as the festival matrix of great seasonal celebrations, Christmas and Easter being chief among them. The liturgy was the air that I breathed, without thinking much about it. Sometimes when I was a child my parents had to drag me to church, to be sure. On other Sundays, particularly in times of crisis or times of passage, I entered into what I can only think about of as mystical moments of divine encounter, mediated through the figure of Jesus, who was very real for me, even as a young boy. I remember kneeling silently at the communion rail with my father at my grandfather's funeral in the late 1940s, the first death I had ever experienced. I remember being overpowered and embraced by a comforting presence at the moment when the officiating pastor offered me the bread and said, "the body of Christ, given for you." I also remember being "carried away" with tears, as the congregation majestically sang hymns like "Now Thank We All Our God."

But sometimes you have to travel far away in order fully to understand where you have been standing all along. Such has been my experience with the liturgy. Here is an account of two of those revelatory journeys. When I am finished with these narratives about far-away places, I will then lead the reader full circle, to the city in which I happen to live.

Southern Africa

In 1987, the congregation I was serving sent me on a month-long pilgrimage, with a racially mixed group of laity and other clergy from my denomination, to visit and to support and to learn from fellow Christians in the black Lutheran churches of South Africa and Namibia.[7] Coming at the height of the apartheid crisis, it was a journey fraught with some dangers. Along a back country road in Namibia, for example, our VW van had to detour around a gaping crater in the road in front of us. Just the day before, a large landmine had exploded directly beneath a pick-up truck, blowing that truck and its driver high into the air. We could see fragments of the vehicle scattered all around the crater as we slowly drove by. But our fears, such as they were, were nothing compared to the joys we experienced worshiping with our brothers and sisters in those churches, under those circumstances.

On more than one occasion, we sang together Luther's rousing hymn, "A Mighty Fortress is Our God," as well as several great hymns of South African heritage. At such times, we outsiders vividly experienced the liturgy of the church as both a spiritual fortress and a spiritual force sending us forth to engage God's world, especially the lives of the oppressed, of whom there were many in those regions. The members of those all-black congregations had to deal with all the trials and tribulations of the heinous apartheid system, the systematic oppression, the poor schools, the wretched living conditions, the meager supplies of food and medicine, and above all the shootings or the middle-of-the-night abductions of church members by the police or other collaborators paid and sent by the government. Many of those Christians were also tacitly or sometimes actively involved in the resistance movement against the apartheid system, and thus put their lives at risk every day.

Notwithstanding all that, they sang their praises vibrantly and celebrated their Eucharists with an enthusiasm that I had never before witnessed. As they clapped their hands and danced in place, the joy was palpable, virtually sweeping us outsiders off our feet. Those liturgies sometimes went on for two or three hours, and then the people danced some more, out the front door and into the streets, still singing and clapping, all under the watchful eye of the secret police. The spirit of hospitality in those churches was also overwhelming. Members of those congregations purchased fine foods that they could not afford so that they could prepare banquets for those of us who could afford so much more. It has been said that the church is always at its best under persecution. Be that as it may, that encounter with the liturgical worship of those South African and Namibian congregations was a kind of conversion experience for me, once-born soul that I was. I went home to my own inner-city, multiracial congregation in the United States inspired to throw myself into our liturgical celebrations all over again and driven to engage the principalities and powers of this age all the more.

Holden Village

Compare another journey into the church's liturgy, in a markedly different setting. Beginning shortly after the year 2000 and several times thereafter, I was invited to give lectures to a community that I had heard about and admired from a distance for many years, Holden Village, in eastern Washington state. I have always been an advocate for the ecumenical church's outdoor ministries in the United States, having long before concluded that their immense resources, extensive access to church members both young and old, financial backing, imaginative and committed staff, and, above all, ecological location offered the mission of the American churches often unappreciated and never fully realized riches. But Holden Village, as I have continued to experience it over the years, is something else, more than and different from many other outdoor ministries of the church, even some of the most excellent among them.

Holden Village is a remote, year-round Christian center for renewal, reachable only by boat along gorgeous, mountain-lined Lake Chelan. The center is actually a former village, nestled in the heart of the towering Cascade Mountains, thirteen miles up from the lakeshore into those heights, accessed by a single, winding road with several hairpin curves. Originally, the village had been built for staff and workers at a huge copper mine, which was a prime supporter of U.S. military needs during World War II. Gargantuan piles of tailings from that mine still form a kind of toxic reminder of the environmental aftershock that many modern industrial interventions in nature have caused. The surrounding mountains and wilderness areas bespeak their own message of divine beauty and mystery. Each year the village attracts more than seven thousand people for a range of studies of church renewal in that magnificent setting. The village produces its own hydroelectric power and recycles many of the materials it uses. It lives on food that is mostly produced by farmers in that region or on the basis of fair-trade products from elsewhere.

Those who participate in the life and studies of the village include not only a year-round resident community but also university students and faculty, professional theologians, clergy, and laity from many walks of life. The community is intentionally multiracial and multicultural and welcomes persons regardless of ethnic background or sexual orientation to its membership and leadership. Further, although it is far removed geographically from so-called civilization, Holden Village has consistently highlighted educational and experiential ministries focusing on what are now called ecojustice issues, particularly addressing the challenges of contemporary urban life. One program initiative, for example, brought numbers of recovering prostitutes to the village from Seattle so that they might explore their own strengths and gifts, and draw on the rich theological and spiritual resources of the Holden community, in order to build support networks and to learn how to hope for a more sane and fulfilling future for all creatures and especially for themselves.

So many ministries, moving in so many directions from this ecumenical center! How does it all hold together? For Holden Village, the center *does* hold and the center does indeed renew and energize. That center is the classical liturgy of the ecumenical church, adopted and adapted with many fitting variations, inspired by the village's diverse human community and its thought-provoking and inspiring location, next to the tailings and surrounded by the mountains. Call this liturgy the generating center.

From the rich baptismal celebrations with abundant waters to the moving eucharistic liturgies, sometimes "oriented" to that place, by asking worshipers to pray facing first east, then south, west, and north, during the liturgy, Holden Village acknowledges and announces and participates in the groaning of the whole creation and the divine promise of a new heavens and a new earth, in which righteousness dwells. Holden's rich, global hymnody and its stirring liturgical music more generally make an already charged worship experience all the more electric for all who participate.

If my own journey to South Africa and Namibia was a kind of conversion experience for my once-born soul, my participation in the life of Holden Village over the years has been nothing less. Countless thousands of those who have been shaped likewise by the liturgical center of that village community, and who now serve as leaders in the ecumenical church throughout the country and as theological, spiritual, and moral leaders in their own fields, would readily say the same.

Roxbury

But I do not want to leave the reader with the impression that one must travel to exotic-sounding locales such as Southern Africa or Holden Village in order to encounter the compelling vitalities of the liturgy. All I, for one, have to do is to show up any Sunday at my own parish church, Resurrection Lutheran Church, in inner-city Boston! There I am blessed with a kind of weekly conversion experience. A stalwart community center for Swedish immigrants a century ago, this church is recapitulating that history these days with different kinds of minority peoples. Resurrection is now a thriving African American congregation in the heart of Boston's most famous, and still in many ways most troubled, black neighborhood, Roxbury. The congregation's history has positioned it, in addition, to aspire to be a multiethnic community. Not a "historic black church," yet with a mainly black membership, the congregation is seeking to reach out to Boston's growing Hispanic community, as well as to welcome Africans and North American whites and a variety of immigrants from the region.

Resurrection is committed to the standard but still critically important inner-city ministries that address the urgent needs of low-income people, both those who are members and those in the surrounding community: the food pantry, the after-school program, the summer ministry for children, the Family Support Center, the adjacent halfway house for residents who are mentally ill. But the congregation also has been a leader in fostering the growth of the Greater Boston Interfaith Organization, which has valiantly addressed low-income housing issues, the plight of Haitian nursing-home workers, and, in coalition with others, the needs of the five hundred thousand people in Massachusetts who at the time had no health insurance. Such ventures portray the public face of the congregation.

But if anyone were to ask most members of Resurrection to speak of their church, they would almost surely first tell enthusiastic stories about what they would consider to be the heart of the congregation's life, its worship. Call it evangelical catholic worship with a global beat. The *ordo* of the classical liturgy is always there, especially the good biblical preaching and the reverent and passionate eucharistic celebrations. The music is vibrant and multicultural, from Bach to Taizé, from gospel to Asian and Latin American and Finnish, and offered with the help of many instruments, from a traditional pipe organ to a gospel band, from the elegance of a solo flute to the solemnity of an Asian gong. Lay liturgical deacons from the congregation play a pivotal role in liturgical leadership, from powerful readings of the Gospel to devout incensing of the table, the ministers, and the people. Youth regularly participate as liturgical leaders, too, as lectors, crucifers, and book and offering bearers. The prayers of the people and the passing of the peace sometimes seem to go on forever, yet timelessly in their own way, as members of the congregation, young and old, audibly offer their petitions and reach out eagerly to embrace one another with Christian affection. Before you know it, this two-hour liturgy is over. And you have been sent home, renewed in body, mind, and spirit.

Running through this powerful liturgical experience, like blood through the body, is a flow of interpersonal ministry. The imprisoned for whom the congregation prays are known personally to many congregation members. The prayers for people who have lost their jobs are for people known personally to many congregation members. The applause for youth who have graduated from high school, called to the front of the congregation to be recognized, are for people known personally to many congregation members. The prayers for the grieving often give voice to a profound communal grief, as when on one Sunday the congregation prayed for the director of its after-school program, whose daughter had been murdered and her body burned and discarded in a nearby public park. In this communal matrix of sharing, passing the peace is thus much more than sharing a cordial greeting with friends. It can be a wrenching, grieving experience—or a tearfully joyful celebration. Likewise, when the congregation recites the Lord's Prayer together during the Eucharist, when everyone in the congregation reaches out to hold the hands of neighbors, that touching is often the power of deep consolation, one member to another, and also the power of ecstatic praise, as all lift up their hands—neighbors lifting up the hands of those so burdened that they could not lift them up themselves—saying together, "For thine is the power and the glory, for ever and ever. Amen."

The Liturgy Alive and Well around the World

I could multiply the number of such stories, first from my own experience of forty years as a pastor and teacher and worshiper in the ecumenical church, but all the more so from a variety of other witnesses. Ethicist Larry Rasmussen undertook a sabbatical year's liturgical journey of his own, around the globe a few years ago.[8] He visited liturgically centered Christian communities, all of them involved not only in renewing the church but also committed resolutely to championing the causes of social and ecological justice. He participated in the life of:

1. Congregations of the African Earthkeeping Churches in Zimbabwe, which celebrate and plant trees in barren regions of that country with a passion;

2. A Catholic monastic community of women in the Philippines whose members are working with downtrodden forest laborers. These women make it a practice not only to mark the stations of the cross but also, in a processional trail around their monastery, to celebrate the stations of our unfolding cosmos, from the big bang to the birth of the earth and then finally to the emergence of the promised new heavens and the new earth;

3. A Russian Orthodox congregation in Alaska that has merged native lore about the salmon and their rivers with its baptismal practices; and,

4. In the spirit of the classical Celtic saints, the Protestant community of Iona, on the northerly island of that name, in Scotland, which was founded both to encourage contemplation of nature and service to the urban poor.

Not to be forgotten, likewise, is the motherhouse of all post–World War II church renewal centers, the ecumenical community of Taizé, in eastern France, whose music, spirituality, global hospitality, and ministry to the poor has inspired thousands and thousands of Christians of every walk of life, all over the world, especially the young among them, for several generations.[9] In the spirit of the earliest Christian assemblies, which mixed water with the wine and saw visions of a new heavens and a new earth, all of these impressive centers of church renewal and social and ecological engagement have been deeply sustained and profoundly inspired by resolutely, imaginatively, and joyfully practicing the ecumenical church's liturgy, each one adapting that liturgy, as has happened throughout the ages, to its own setting and to its own particular theological, spiritual, and missional needs.

All of which is to say, emphatically, that the ecumenical church's liturgy today, in its best expressions, bears no resemblance to that caricature so widespread in contemporary American culture, which presupposes that liturgy belongs to the effete and often dead milieu of so-called institutional religion, in contrast to what are perceived to be the free-flowing vitalities of the spiritualities of individuals, particularly in their communion with the august mysteries of nature or in their encounters with the great creations of human art. On the contrary, liturgical worship in the ecumenical church today, in its best expressions, is alive and well, flourishing and vital. It is profoundly countercultural, in many ways, not unlike the community-forming "work of the people" of the earliest Christian assemblies. It is fundamentally accessible, in its underlying simplicity, in many places and several traditional settings around the world. It is experientially electric, binding individuals from many walks of life and many cultures together in ecstasy, as one body. Of that I have no doubt, both on the basis of my own experience and as a student of liturgical renewal for the past four decades.

Hence, there need be no necessary cognitive dissonance reverberating from this book's focus on the liturgy. The ecumenical church's liturgy today is not dead but living, in its best expressions. Indeed, it is not only living, sometimes with amazing power, but it stands at the vital center of many communities of church renewal and social and ecological engagement, in the United States and beyond. It is *the* center for these communities—a center that, contrary to Yeats's nightmare, really does hold.

Nature and the Cognitive Dissonance

Since when do Christians care about nature? That is the question at the core of the second form of cognitive dissonance we must address. As we have just seen, readers unfamiliar with the life of the ecumenical church in our era could easily assume, on the basis of widely held cultural presuppositions, that the *liturgy* of the church is of no viable significance today (first form of the dissonance), and thereby they would be *wrong*. Yet the same readers might just as easily assume, again on the basis of widely held cultural presuppositions, that the ecumenical church has nothing of significance to say about *nature* (second form of the dissonance), and those readers would to some degree be *right*. Indeed, the charge that historic Christianity, especially in the modern period, has been ecologically bankrupt has its own legitimacy, though it is a simplification and in some respects a distortion.[10]

We can approach the matter this way. If, again, we think of the example of Thoreau, we see a thought-world that richly celebrates the interpenetration of spirituality and nature. Is a thought-world of this kind essentially beyond the pale of Christian theology? Is there such a thing as a viable *theology of nature* in the Christian tradition? Most of those Americans who follow in the paths of Thoreau would be hard pressed to answer in the affirmative. Christianity as a religion of nature? The very idea runs against the grain of our culture. Even some influential Christian writers, like Matthew Fox, have made this kind of critique their own.[11] Hence, readers who are also aware of the Christian tradition's ambiguous history with nature will likely also experience cognitive dissonance with our theme, liturgy and nature, in this respect as well. A glimpse at modern ecumenical theology will show how this kind of cognitive dissonance is, to some degree, justified.

The Eclipse of Nature in Modern Ecumenical Theology

Sophisticated theological reflection about liturgy and spirituality is ancient and well attested in every Christian epoch. And, traditionally, both have been closely related, so much so that one could think of a liturgically shaped faith, on the one hand, and a liturgical spirituality, on the other, even on the part of some of those who have most distanced themselves from "civilization" in general and from gathered ecclesial communities in particular, such as recluses, itinerant preachers, or those who have sought to adhere to the traditions of the so-called Desert Fathers. Expressed in another way, the classical faith of the church's liturgy has profoundly shaped the lives of the church's spiritual masters. The life and faith of Francis of Assisi is a good example of that kind of unity between liturgical faith and spiritual practice. But the ecumenical church's historic approach to *nature* in the modern era has been something else.

Substantive theological reflection about nature, while in evidence at various points in the classical Christian tradition, has indeed had a checkered history, as I have shown in my study, *The Travail of Nature*. In the modern era, moreover, especially in Protestant thought, substantive theological reflection about nature largely fell by the wayside. The theology of nature was widely left to nature-romantics, thinkers like Thoreau and a range of popularizing, often sentimentalizing, poets and artists. Christian theology in the modern era, especially in its Protestant expressions, was mainly preoccupied with human existence. It was, in this sense, thoroughly *anthropocentric*.

Since the emergence of the global environmental crisis in the second half of the twentieth century, however, one would have anticipated that the spirituality of nature and the theology of nature—or what can be called ecological theology—would have very soon taken on an urgent importance as a major theme in the ecumenical church's theological discussions and spiritual practices. But it did not. Anyone who chooses to review the unfolding of ecumenical theology in the last century and on into our own—especially as it has been practiced in official circles, such as the World Council of Churches (WCC)—will quickly discover that ecumenical theology has been preoccupied with other things.[12]

Until very recently, likewise, advocates of doctrinal or liturgical renewal generally have had very little to say about ecological themes. That apparently has seemed to most of them to be outside their purview, either because it appeared to them mainly to be a matter of ethics or perhaps because it appeared to them to be heterodox, an expression of what might be taken to be neopagan or New Age nature worship or spirituality. Similarly, for the advocates of church growth or liberation praxis, until very recently, interest in ecological issues has often appeared to be a self-evident threat, even an aberration, a theological concern that would distract people from what for these advocates are the primary evangelistic or social justice issues of our era.

Within official ecumenical circles, such as the WCC, theological reflection on nature has been sidetracked by the fault lines that emerged between groups captivated by different interests. One group, which for shorthand purposes I identify as "centripetal," appeared to be most interested in the inner dynamics of the church (such as sacramental theology); the other, which I call "centrifugal," was most concerned with the relationship of the church to the world around it (such as discussion of the impact of technology). For much of the second half of the twentieth century, moreover, when nature *was* discussed in official ecumenical circles, nature was regarded in instrumental terms at best, as having no meaning in itself. Thus, one of the preparatory papers for the WCC's 1966 Conference on Church and Society stated:

> The biblical story . . . secularizes nature. It places creation—the physical world—in the context of covenant relation and does not try to understand it apart from that relation. The history of God with his people has a setting, and this setting is called nature. But the movement of history, not the structure of the setting, is central to reality. Physical creation even participates in this history; its timeless and cyclical character, as far as it exists, is unimportant. The physical world, in other words, does not have meaning in itself.[13]

In retrospect, we can indeed think of these trends as representing the eclipse of nature in modern ecumenical theology.[14]

So it no surprise that even one of the most famous WCC mottos, still widely hailed in ecumenical circles, "Peace, Justice, and the Integrity of Creation," a theme that *sounds* so comprehensive, was *suspect* right from the start. Why? Because the phrase "the Integrity of Creation" was added to "Peace" and "Justice" as a kind of afterthought in WCC discussions and then quickly sidetracked in ensuing deliberations, if not totally forgotten, in favor of concerns that were perceived at the time to have been "more pressing."

Nor did it help substantively when some of the few theologians who did discuss nature in ecumenical contexts typically did so in ways that were essentially focused on God in relation to human needs and aspirations or humanity's primary status in the greater scheme of things. In this respect, the 1978 WCC study by the orthodox ecumenist Paulos Gregorios, with the revealing title, *The Human Presence: An Orthodox View of*

Nature,[15] was representative of a general set of assumptions in that era. For Gregorios, "humanity has a special vocation as the priest of creation, as the mediator through whom God manifests himself to creation and redeems it." In this schema, nature has mainly, if not exclusively, instrumental meaning: "Nature itself is in fact the stage, complete with the actors and props among which man is placed." Gregorios's approach, soberingly, is still representative of the thought of major orthodox theologians today.[16]

The same kind of anthropocentrism was also evident, at least implicitly, in the work of other ecumenical thinkers of this era who did attend to nature but who did so mainly under the rubric of "stewardship," a construct that, notwithstanding its popularity since that time nor denying its value, compared to many inherited patterns of thought and practice, presupposes that nature is to be defined, essentially, as the object of wise and just *human* use.[17] This perspective was articulated forcefully in 1973 in the WCC study book by Thomas Derr, *Ecology and Human Need*.[18] Other ecumenical thinkers in the same period also addressed nature but mainly for apologetic purposes, as the object of scientific study or technological development, under the rubric of the "religion and science dialogue" or in response to the then rising influence of technology in industrialized societies. Their intent was not so much to project a theology of nature but a theology of *the human* that would not contradict, or that was not contradicted by, the findings of the natural sciences or the imperatives of modern technology.

Along the way, moreover, those very few who *did* address ecological issues substantively and nonanthropocentrically in ecumenical discussions generally were received in those contexts with polite indifference, if not outright hostility. Call these ecological theologians "the forerunners," who, until very recently, were mostly excluded from the mainstream of modern ecumenical theology. This was particularly evident in the response to forerunner Joseph Sittler's prophetic address in 1961 to the WCC assembly in New Delhi, where he called for the projection of a "cosmic Christology" as the church's response to the widespread and ever-increasing desecration of nature.[19] Due to this theological shunning, ecological theologians in the ecumenical community have had to labor for many decades as if on the other side of a de facto theological fault line of substantial proportions.

The Emergence of Nature in Recent Ecumenical Theology

This situation has now begun to change across the width and length of the ecumenical community, thankfully, signaled by the publication of a number of works by eminent, ecumenically recognized scholars. After a long gestation period, biblical studies has now given birth to a new and powerful paradigm for approaching nature in the Bible, signaled by perhaps the single most important study of its kind, Terence E. Fretheim's *God and World in the Old Testament: A Relational Theology of Creation.*[20] Fretheim demonstrates that, contrary to the received paradigm of twentieth-century biblical studies, the theologies of the Bible, especially of the Old Testament, presuppose and celebrate God's purposes with the whole creation, not just with human history. A liturgical theology like Gordon Lathrop's *Holy Ground* now addresses not only centripetal themes, in this case liturgical praxis, but also the centrifugal challenges of justice and mission, *and* holistic ecological issues.[21]

Likewise for liberation theologies like Leonardo Boff's *Cry of the Earth, Cry of the Poor* (1997).[22] Boff's ecumenically Catholic theology unites many concerns, internal church renewal, external justice commitments, and holistic ecological themes. Larry Rasmussen has been deeply but critically involved in WCC discussions of these matters. On his own, he has made the case for "an evolutionary sacramentalist cosmology" in his widely heralded study *Earth Community Earth Ethics* (1997).[23] Evangelical theologians, whose churches have taken missionary praxis to be their chief raison d'être, have also begun to join in the discussion of ecological issues, as is evidenced by the foundational declaration of the Evangelical Environmental Network, "On the Care of Creation" (1994) and works like Stephen Bouma-Prediger's *For the Beauty of the Earth* (2001).[24] More broadly, a coalition of American evangelical leaders issued a theologically sophisticated and scientifically informed statement on global warming, "Our Commitment to Jesus Christ Compels Us To Solve the Global Warming Crisis" (2006), published as a full-page advertisement in the *New York Times*, a statement that received extensive media coverage.[25] In 2008, forty-four leaders of the conservative Southern Baptist Convention, the largest Protestant denomination in the United States, issued a statement expressing concern about climate change and imploring its members to take on this cause, on biblical grounds. Ecumenical bodies themselves have also begun to address the challenge, in a holistic way, such as the aforementioned 2005 statement, "The Earth is Sacred," by theologians of the National Council of Churches, USA, myself among them.

Similar changes have also begun to appear in Roman Catholic and Orthodox circles. In significant measure, these communities have been shaped in the modern period by what can be called centripetal concerns. Beyond this, however, the Catholic Church has significantly engaged itself, centrifugally, with modern political and cultural issues, above all through papal social teachings and through some of the declarations of the Second Vatican Council in the second half of the last century. But recently both Catholic and Orthodox communions have begun to address more holistic ecological issues publicly and with authority.

Thus, among Roman Catholics, Pope John Paul II issued a message for the World Day of Peace in 1990, "The Ecological Crisis: A Common Responsibility."[26] Individual Catholic theologians, such as Denis Edwards, especially in his 1995 study *Jesus and the Wisdom of God*,[27] have also entered the discussion. Systematic theologian John F. Haught has focused his attention on the theology of nature, with particular reference to evolutionary thought, most notably perhaps in his 1999 study *God After Darwin: A Theology of Evolution*.[28] The U.S. Catholic Conference has devoted significant attention to issues of ecology and justice, too, as is evidenced in the 1996 volume *"And God Saw That It Was Good": Catholic Theology and the Environment*.[29] Pope Benedict XVI himself has added his voice to this discussion, most audibly in 2007 when, at a Vatican conference on climate change, he declared that global warming and abuse of the environment more generally are against God's will and that Catholics especially must much more eagerly "respect creation," while "focusing on the needs of sustainable development."[30] The Pope took a similar message to the United Nations in 2008 when he urged that "international action to preserve the environment and to protect various forms of life on earth must not only guarantee a rational use of technology and science, but must also rediscover the authentic image of creation."[31]

On the Orthodox side, at least one strong voice has been heard publicly concerning these matters, the Ecumenical Patriarch Bartholomew.[32] In a 1997 address he condemned exploitation of the natural world in the strongest terms, as "a sin."[33] He returned to this theme in an address to the WCC in Porto Alegre, Brazil, in 2006, which focused on global water needs. Water, he said, should never be treated as private property. Indeed: "indifference towards the vitality of water constitutes both a blasphemy to

God, the Creator, and a crime against humanity."[34] Other Orthodox leaders have also added their voices to this discussion.[35]

Behind all this, a cadre of mostly solitary explorers, whom I have called the forerunners, has for some time been probing these mostly unknown regions, most notably the American Lutheran Joseph Sittler and the American process theologian John Cobb, whose names I have already mentioned, and the German Reformed theologian Jürgen Moltmann.[36] Feminist theologians, above all Rosemary Radford Ruether and Sallie McFague, have made substantial contributions along the way,[37] as has the ethicist James Nash, whose theology we have already met in these pages, with his groundbreaking 1991 book, *Loving Nature: Ecological Integrity and Christian Responsibility*.[38] In 1981, moreover, John Cobb and the Australian biologist Charles Birch produced a significant study of the gradations of value in nature, *The Liberation of Life: From Cell to Community*, laying the groundwork for a discriminating ethical bonding with creatures in the whole scale of life.[39] I have been a participant in these discussions myself for more than thirty-five years, beginning with my 1970 study, *Brother Earth: Nature, God, and Ecology in a Time of Crisis*. These works, as well as the contributions of many other thinkers, have helped prepare the way for explorations such as our own in this book.[40]

Beyond the Cognitive Dissonance

In retrospect, then, I have offered a twofold response to the twofold cognitive dissonance that hovers around our theme. First, I have argued that the liturgy of the church is alive and well and indeed flourishing, as a simple, countercultural, and community-forming ritual of substantial proportions, in its best expressions, in our time. Liturgy is by no means necessarily an effete and dysfunctional rite that can only work, by default if not by intention, to reinforce the injustices and the banalities of the status quo. Second, I have proposed that the eclipse of nature in modern ecumenical theology and practice need no longer have the effect of keeping the church in the dark, because that eclipse itself has begun to fade, both at the level of church praxis and because of the influence of those whom I have called the ecological forerunners.

Much work, however, remains to be done. While recent developments have signaled the ending of the eclipse of nature in modern ecumenical theology, it is evident that the mind and heart of the whole ecumenical church has yet to be converted so as to embrace a vision of nature that is ecumenical in the broadest sense, not just encompassing all the churches, nor even just the whole inhabited earth, but indeed the whole cosmos. What is required for our churches in these times is *a single vision* that integrates theological reflection about nature in all its dimensions into the mainstream of ecumenical thought and worship practices, thereby uniting the centripetal, the centrifugal, and the holistic perspectives. *Ritualizing Nature* is intended to take us one small step forward toward the realization of that goal.

PART TWO
THE LITURGICAL ASSEMBLY

4

The Heart of the Matter:
The Liturgical Assembly

I have invited the reader to come with me on my walks along the Charles River and to see fragments of a vision of eschatological peace with nature and the poor of the earth. I have said that, for me, the only way to sustain that kind of vision, and to live it in deed as well as in word, is to enter into the liturgical practices of communities like the Society of St. John the Evangelist, along the river. The liturgical practices of such communities can ritualize nature for those whose lives are shaped by those practices, notwithstanding the cognitive dissonance that sometimes has hovered around liturgical practices and Christian concerns for nature at various times.

I now ask the reader to pause with me along the way, for an inner adventure. Think of it, perhaps, as a theological discussion that could take place intramurally, within the walls of that monastery. In this chapter and the two that follow, I intend to explore some complex historical themes, focusing on early Christianity, on cultural and theological trends in the high Middle Ages that can be traced into our own time, and on the sometimes turbulent theological world of Martin Luther in the sixteenth century.

Why this inner adventure? Those who do not remember the past, according to the familiar aphorism of George Santayana, are condemned to repeat it. I underline the obvious corollary: those who *do* remember the past are liberated to learn from it. And this is a situation that cries out for historical understanding and for thoughtful learning. In my decades-long experience with the theology of nature, I have observed that even some of our foremost theologians have not fully grasped the significance of the historical materials to which I will be calling attention here.

In this chapter, I will ask the reader first to consider the importance of *the assembly* (*ekklesia*, often translated as "church") in New Testament times and later, communities like that monastic chapel assembly along the banks of the Charles. I will then explore, in more detail than previously, the significance of the ritual process that forms that kind of assembly—the liturgy itself. I will argue that the assembly is the *sine qua non* of the Christian faith, that without which there is no biblically shaped Christianity. And I will maintain, in turn, that the liturgy is that rite which makes the assembly what it is in liturgical churches.[1] For these communions, in more technical language, *the liturgy is the assembly's mode of identity formation.*

In service of these intramural explorations, I ask readers to bring with them that descriptive (phenomenological) image of the liturgy which I identified in chapter 2 and to measure it against the historical and theological data I will be highlighting. See the liturgy as that sacred canopy which identifies a countercultural community of *shalom* in the midst of a world of violence and exploitation. See it, too, as fundamentally a simple rite of word and praise and meal. Yet see the experience that holds it together as one of communal ecstasy, which expresses itself variously, depending on the circumstances, as lamentation or exultation, grief or joy. Finally, see this liturgy situated in a particular place, say, Southern Africa or Holden Village or Roxbury, perhaps in the Episcopal monastery along the Charles River. Or call to mind neighborhoods in first-century Jerusalem or Ephesus or Corinth or Rome.

In the Beginning Was the Deed:
The Liturgical Assembly's Formative Role

One of the great theologians of the last century, Paul Tillich, devoted much of his attention to correlating "the Christian message" with the questions posed by the modern era. This was a heroic undertaking on Tillich's part, and we may still learn much from his method and even more from his own theological vision. But in so defining his method, Tillich made an unexamined assumption, which theologians in our century have more and more come to question: that Christianity is most fundamentally "a message." For Tillich, this message is the heart of the matter.

It is understandable that Tillich would have made this assumption. Did not the Gospel of John announce, "In the beginning was the Word" (John 1:1)? Were not the apostles commissioned to "preach the gospel" to every nation (cf. Matt. 28:16-20)? Did not the great theologians of the church, like Augustine and Thomas Aquinas, preoccupy themselves with interpreting that gospel Word as the mind or the *Logos* of God revealed? And did not the magisterial reformers of the sixteenth century, above all one of Tillich's historic mentors, Martin Luther, maintain passionately that the "proclamation of the Word" is the heart of the Christian faith? Further, was not much of nineteenth-century Protestant theology driven by many of the same concerns that so captivated Tillich, to correlate the claims of the Christian message with the findings of modern science and philosophy, and, in response, to reformulate those Christian claims, especially in light of a new kind of historical study of the Scriptures?

Since Tillich's time, however, historical research itself has given us a much more complex picture of Christian origins than was available to him; and the scientific study of religion has also broadened and deepened our understanding of the phenomena of human religion more generally. To map these developments would take us too far afield, but it is important to note their significance here, at least in a schematic way, as we seek to understand why and how the Christian assembly, not the Christian message, is the heart of the matter.

Christian Origins and the Assembly

As far as Christian origins are concerned, what can be called the new scholarly interpretation can be summarized this way: "in the beginning was the assembly."

With this formulation, I pass by a complicated theological debate: Which came first, the chicken or the egg? Which came first, the proclamation of the gospel or the community that embodied and so proclaimed the gospel? Obviously there would have been no Christian assemblies scattered around the first-century Roman world had there been no ambassadors to carry the "good news" to new places. But the aim of those ambassadors was to call together communities to hear and to respond. And the gospel presumably would have been soon forgotten in those places, apart from the lives of those communities.

Instructively, Karl Barth once remarked that there is no such thing in the New Testament as Jesus without the people of God, and no such thing as the people of God without Jesus. Analogously, I think, there is no such thing as the proclamation of the gospel without the community that hears and responds, and then carries that proclamation further. And there is no such thing as the Christian community without the proclamation of the gospel. Consider also the comments of Robert Jenson: "The most concise statement of the Gospel is 'Jesus is risen!' There is no strand or stratum of New Testament witness which cannot be derived from this sentence. This is the news with which the first witnesses crisscrossed the Mediterranean world to create the church." It is also noteworthy that Jenson almost immediately observes that the proclamation "Jesus is risen!" is meaningful "only within the traditions of Israel's history and faith."[2] Which is to say, again, that the proclamation and the—tradition-bearing—community always belong together. They are inseparable. Luther emphatically stated this point already in the sixteenth century. The preached Word, Luther remarked, "cannot be without God's people, and conversely, God's people cannot be without God's Word."[3]

The reason I am stressing here that "in the beginning was the assembly" is not to deny that proclamation and the community go hand in hand, but to stress precisely that: there is no such thing as "the Christian message" abstracted from the Christian community, where that message finds its home and its base. There is no "naked gospel." There is only an "enfleshed gospel" in the community.

An illustrative New Testament story is that of the women visiting Jesus' tomb after the crucifixion. They are told by the angelic messenger, "'He has been raised from the dead'. . . . So they left the tomb quickly with fear and great joy, and ran to tell his disciples" (Matt. 28:7-8). The formation of the community of believers is always the goal of proclamation. Even more telling is the dramatic story of the appearance of the risen Jesus to the two disciples along the road to Emmaus. They do not recognize him, even as he expounds the Word of the Scriptures to them. Teaching about the promises of God and their fulfillment from the Word is not enough. It is only in the communal meal of the two disciples with Jesus, in the breaking of the bread, that that Word that was proclaimed to them along the way comes home to them and is recognized as such (Luke 24:13-35).

Gordon Lathrop has identified "the assembly" as the chief symbol of the church, and he is probably right.[4] The term itself was rich with cultural meanings in its first-century context.[5] "Assembly" did not refer to a cultic gathering, nor to a private association or club; other Greek words were used in those contexts. Rather, as Lathrop explains, "*ekklesia* was especially the name of the assembly of all the free, male citizens of a Greek city-republic, gathered to decide matters in the city." Christians took over this public construct but transvalued its meaning. The members of Christian assemblies were men and women, slaves and free, not just free males. Christians also extended the scope of the construct to include all believers gathered everywhere, not just those in a particular city. Christians thought of themselves, literally (Lathrop's translation), as "all the assemblies of the nations" (Rom. 16:4), even as the whole "assembly of God" (Gal. 1:13). In this respect, Lathrop observes, the word *assembly* surely carried "an excess symbolic meaning, beyond the voters' meeting of the Greek city, more than could be indicated by Hellenistic social vocabulary."

It appears that that kind of "excess symbolic meaning" of the assembly had been shaped, for Christians, by biblical meanings carried by some of the traditions of Judaism of the time. The content of the construct "assembly," as compared to its form, depended in significant measure on the Hebrew word *qahal*, commonly translated *ekklesia* in the Greek version of the Old Testament, the Septuagint. That word in the Old Testament, in turn, was used to refer to symbolically significant places and events, like the gathering of the people at Mount Sinai. By New Testament times, it had also been shaped richly with nuances of eschatological hope: that God would once again reconstitute God's people, with all the blessings of a fecund land and with justice in that land, and that the people—the *qahal*—would then dwell in *shalom*. Most likely, Lathrop explains, these eschatological meanings were what was being symbolized in the early Christian usage of the word *ekklesia*:

> Against all appearances, Christians believed, God's final times have dawned in Jesus Christ, in his cross, his resurrection, and the faith which is through him. Because of Jesus Christ, surprisingly, sinners and outsiders and gentiles have been called into the assembly of God, joined to the royal priestly people whose task is to declare the truth of God in the world. Through Jesus Christ, as a sign of these last times, the Spirit of God has been poured out upon all the assembly—not just the leader and elders and prophets—to enable them in this task. The local meetings of Christians then actually are the beginning of "the assembly" of biblical hope.

Lathrop points to the testimony of the letter to the Hebrews as an expression of this kind of understanding of the "assembly," a public body, inclusive of all stations and sorts of people from many nations, defined by its eschatological vision that itself is dependent on the hopes of the ancient people of God:

> ... you have come to Mount Zion and to the city of the living God, the heavenly Jerusalem, and to innumerable angels in festal gathering, and to the assembly [*ekklesia*] of the firstborn who are enrolled in heaven, and to God the judge of all, and to the spirits of the righteous made perfect, and to Jesus, the mediator of a new covenant, and to the sprinkled blood that speaks a better word than the blood of Abel. (Heb. 12:22-24)

The eminent New Testament scholar Helmut Koester has summarized this kind of approach to early Christianity, highlighting the early church's continuity with Jesus himself, as follows:

> In the earliest understanding of the continuity with the historical Jesus, neither the report of Jesus' miracles nor the transmission of his sayings was constitutive. Rather, the new understanding of the significance of Jesus' celebration of common meals in anticipation of the "messianic banquet" and the story of his suffering and death provided the constitutive elements for the self-definition of the community as a new nation and of its claims to eschatological fulfillment of the hopes of all people.[6]

This eschatological shape of early Christian faith—anticipating the final realization of the reign of God, when all nations, along with the whole creation, would be redeemed—also helps to explain the remarkable ethos of openness that was apparent in the communal life of early Christian assemblies. While persecution was a constant threat and sometimes a reality, these assemblies typically did not hide behind closed doors, as it were, akin to the practices of some of the mystery religions of the time that functioned like secret societies. Rather, Christian assemblies placed a high value on welcoming the stranger, honoring the teaching of Jesus thoroughly in this respect: "I was a stranger and you welcomed me" (Matt. 25:35). So Paul, while urging the assembly at Rome to "love one another with mutual affection," also urged the faithful there to "extend hospitality" (Rom. 12:13). The letter to the Hebrews likewise urged Christians not to "neglect to show hospitality to strangers" (Heb. 13:2). Eschatology clearly inspired the early Christian practice of hospitality at least as much as the early Christian practice of mutual love.[7]

A Familiar Text in Point

What can be called this formative New Testament eschatological consciousness of the early Christian assembly is evident even more strikingly in a text that has historically been regarded as the "great missionary text" of the New Testament, understood especially in the modern era as the mandate to "take the gospel to every nation," Matthew 28:16-20:

> Now the eleven disciples went to Galilee, to the mountain to which Jesus had directed them. When they saw him, they worshiped him; but some doubted. And Jesus came and said to them, "All authority has been given to me. Go therefore and make disciples of all nations, baptizing them in the name of the Father and of the Son and of the Holy Spirit, and teaching them to obey everything that I have commanded you. And remember, I am with you always, to the end of the age."

Jesus is here depicted as gathering the community of the end times, just as he had previously gathered the twelve disciples during his earthly ministry, signaling that his mission from God should be understood as the birth of a new Israel and its twelve tribes, thus fulfilling the ancient promises of God to Israel, from Abraham to the recreation of the whole world. The end-time reference, to be sure, is hidden here. It all depends on how the interpreter reads the reference to the disciples going "to *the mountain to which Jesus had directed them.*" There is substantial evidence that this is not merely a geographical reference, if it is that. Rather, this is an allusion to the mountain of then-current Jewish eschatological expectations.[8] Texts such as Isaiah 25:6-10 very much shaped the mind of Jewish eschatological expectation in those days:

> On this mountain the LORD of hosts will make for all peoples a feast of rich food, a feast of well-aged wines. . . . And he will destroy on this mountain the shroud that is cast over all people. . .; he will swallow up death forever. . . . It will be said on that day, Lo, this is our God; we have waited for him, so that he might save us. . . . For the hand of the LORD will rest on this mountain.

When first-century Jewish Christians would hear about Jesus meeting the disciples "on the mountain," therefore, they would take it for granted that this is the mountain of the end times.[9]

Matthew 28:16-20 is, therefore, in fact, an eschatological church establishment text, not a verbal proclamation text, as such. It is not primarily about the launching of "a message." It is primarily about the formation of a community, about "making disciples" in all nations by incorporating newcomers into the community of faith through baptism and by helping them to grow into this communal faith: by teaching them all that Jesus commanded, everything with the sure and certain knowledge that the risen Christ dwells in the midst of the community itself, to the end of the age, where its members worship him. And the commands from Jesus that this community is to follow, according to Matthew, surely included not only the mandates of texts like the Sermon on the Mount (again, the reference to the mountain) but also Jesus' culminating eucharistic admonitions, regarding the bread and the cup (Matt. 26:26-28)—"Take, eat; this is my body" and "Drink from it, all of you"—this, in the context of communal hymnody (cf. Matt. 26:30).

Paul's Vision of the Liturgical Assembly

A similar kind of focus on the gathered eucharistic community is dramatically evident in the letters of Paul. The apostle has long been regarded as the great exemplar of Christian missionary praxis. Following his conversion, did he not "preach the gospel to all nations"? He most certainly sought to do so. But recent Pauline studies show us that the way Paul accomplished his mission was not primarily by preaching and then *moving on*, although he surely did preach (even on Mars Hill in Athens, according to the Lukan account). Paul responded to his apostolic calling primarily by preaching or teaching and then *staying on*. His primary apostolic purpose was to establish assemblies of faith, in the then known world, from Asia Minor to Spain. To this end, Paul apparently brought his own community of co-workers with him on his missionary journeys, as many as forty, sufficient to form an assembly in any given locale, in which he could then incorporate converts before moving on to establish yet other assemblies.[10]

Recent Pauline studies have also established that the vision that inspired Paul and which he preached and taught in those assemblies was much more comprehensive than most modern Christians have thought and taught.

Modern Christians, especially those who have self-consciously stood in the tradition of Martin Luther, have taken it for granted that Paul's chief message was, as Luther had so passionately argued, "justification by faith alone." The validity of Luther's reading of Paul is not generally in dispute, surely not in this book. The issue here is the scope of Paul's vision.

This discussion was set in motion by the seminal essay of New Testament scholar Krister Stendahl, "Paul and the Introspective Conscience of the West." There Stendahl argued that, while Paul set forth a theology of grace—the heart of which Luther was later to affirm in terms of sixteenth-century issues—Paul's own perspective was cosmic, world-historical, and communal, not primarily individualistic.[11] Luther's primary question was: How can I find a gracious God? Paul's question, I venture to say, was more something like this: How can we be faithful to the righteous acts of God, who has called together a New Israel of Jews and Gentiles, in order to consummate the eschatological victory of God?[12]

"Two millennia ago," theologian Douglas Harink writes, summarizing those recent trends in Pauline studies, "the risen Jesus Christ invaded the world of a Jewish rabbi named Paul, destroyed the cosmic order as he knew it, incorporated him into a 'new creation' and conscripted him for a mission that extended through the Roman Empire and to the ends of the earth." In response, Paul's mission "created communities of faithful comrades . . . called to a life of harmonious solidarity." Essential to Paul's community-establishing mission was his conviction that in Christ God had broken down all the ancient walls of separation and hostility between slave and free, male and female, Jews and Gentiles. "To these God-created communities," Harink concludes, "Paul wrote letters in which he reiterated the good news of God's justice and power in Christ, and instructed the members in a way of life commensurate with that news."[13]

Those assemblies, to be sure, had to struggle to establish their God-given identity as communities of the end times. This was particularly true, in Paul's experience, regarding the sometimes combative relationships between Christian Jews and Christian Gentiles, a theme that preoccupies Paul's letter to the Romans. But divisions between rich and poor also claimed Paul's attention. This was dramatically evident in one interchange between Paul and the Corinthian assembly (1 Cor. 11:17-33). Some, presumably the affluent, who had the leisure to do so, were in the habit of arriving early for the assembly's eucharistic meal, and they ate and drank to their hearts' content, even to the point of intoxication, while others, presumably the poorer members whose days were filled with hard labor, arrived later and had nothing to eat. Meanwhile, the first group paid no heed to the needs of the second. Paul condemns that first party as failing to embody their own identity as members of the church of Christ. "Do you show contempt for the church of God," he asks, "and humiliate those who have nothing?"

The issue here for Paul is sustaining the egalitarian and self-giving life of the community established by the equalizing and self-giving work of Christ himself. Paul then illustrates this essential theme by recalling Jesus' own institution of this meal: "This is my body that is for you. Do this in remembrance of me" (1 Cor. 11:25). The point? That the life of the Corinthian assembly should always be shaped by the self-giving life of Christ: "For as often as you eat this bread and drink this cup, you proclaim the Lord's death until he comes" (1 Cor. 11:26; see also Phil. 2:5ff.). Then Paul concludes with reference to this egalitarian assembly where love is supposed to reign supreme (see also 1 Corinthians 13), an assembly that for Paul is "the body of Christ": "For all who eat and drink without discerning the body, eat and drink judgment against themselves" (1 Cor. 11:29).

This Pauline interchange with the Corinthian assembly is revealing in a number of ways. First, in the words of Gordon Lathrop: the earliest Christian communities were "meal-keeping assemblies."[14] They encountered the risen Christ "in the breaking of the bread" (Luke 24:35). Such meals had a rich cultural meaning of their own in those times, as Lathrop points out. They were held in houses, typically in the largest available room, in keeping with social practices of that era. Christian meal-keeping assemblies were also shaped by memories of Jewish meal practices, above all with the self-conscious understanding of those Jewish gatherings that the meal was taken before God; hence the insertion of prayers and some forms of praise. Of even greater import for Christians, according to Lathrop, was their memory of the meal practices of Jesus himself, to which we have already alluded, meals that were thoroughly eschatological in character. They were meals of the end times.[15] They were also radically inclusive meals, as we have seen and as Lathrop emphasizes: "Unlike the Hellenistic Jewish feasts, the feasts of Jesus welcome 'the many' to participation in these [eschatological] signs. He ate and drank with sinners. 'Forgive us as we forgive,' he also taught his disciples to pray. If meals were indeed signs of God's coming day, then Jesus welcomed sinners to life-giving participation in that day."[16] This helps to explain Paul's passionate rebuke of the wealthy members of the church at Corinth, who had lapsed into what for them were typical social practices of the day, leading to the marginalization of the poor.

It also helps to explain Paul's focus on the primacy of the communal "body" in his vision of God's work in the world. More traditional interpretations of this text have focused—mistakenly—on the notion that one group of Corinthians did not have the proper understanding of the "real presence" of Jesus Christ in the sacramental bread and wine. The problem Paul is addressing here, however, and often in his letters, is, in modern terms, more sociological than doctrinal. It has to do with how the body of Christ is in fact embodied as a community of the end times, rather than whether its members have correct theological understandings.

Liturgy as the Assembly's Mode of Identity Formation

Our theme here—"in the beginning was the assembly"—becomes still more plausible as the best available approach to interpreting Christian origins when we consider trends in the scientific study of religion more generally, particularly the study of ritual. Ritual, according to many leading phenomenologists of religion, is what establishes human community generally.[17] Ritual is not what humans do in order to express other things, such as their theological ideas or their myths or their power relationships or their fears. Counterintuitive as this may sound to modern ears, this is the idea: *ritual creates and sustains* the ideas and values and myths, the power relationships and the fears, not the other way around. In this sense the dark aphorism of Goethe's *Faust* is aptly bright for us here, as a further refinement of our theme: not just "In the beginning was the assembly," but more particularly, in Goethe's words, "In the beginning was the deed."

Émile Durkheim offered a classic example of this kind of thinking in his 1912 book, *Elementary Forms of Religious life*.[18] In that work, Durkheim described the reaction of a group of Australian aborigines to a death. When the death was announced, many members of the community began to scatter widely, howling and weeping, some doing physical harm to themselves. Such acts were not spontaneous expressions of grief, accordingly to Durkheim, but highly ritualized forms, patterns of behavior handed down from generation to generation. Those who felt no grief themselves thus felt pressure to behave in conformity with the feelings of the truly bereaved. In this way, ritual forms had the effect of creating a grieving community, rather than the other way around, as most moderns would typically assume.

More recently, in the same vein, the work of the anthropologist Clifford Geertz has been widely influential.[19] From his perspective, there is no generic religion experience—let us say, an encounter with "the Holy" (Rudolf Otto)—to which all humans have access. Rather, all religious experience, according to Geertz, is dependent on the cultural context in which people find themselves. Hence, Geertz memorably proposed the theoretical thesis that religion is "a system of symbols which acts to establish powerful, pervasive, and long-lasting moods and motivations in men by formulating conceptions of a general order of existence and clothing these conceptions with such an aura of factuality that the moods and motivations seem uniquely realistic." That "system of symbols" which acts so powerfully to establish religious expression is inculcated, as others have maintained, including various followers of Geertz, by ritual.

Erik Erikson, for one, argued from the perspective of developmental psychology that ritual generically is the human mode of identity formation.[20] The parent, for example, who enters the room where the infant has just awakened and who smiles at the infant, morning after morning, day after day, is engaging in a ritual that inculcates what Erikson called "basic trust." The infant does not develop basic trust and so does not appropriately enter into the processes of psychological maturization, according to Erikson, apart from such rituals. Many other scientific students of ritual have drawn similar conclusions about its creative social functionality.[21] Also, many of the now widely celebrated works of George Lindbeck, whose works we have already encountered, have pointed in the same direction.[22]

In the Beginning Was the Liturgy

With this glance at the new perspective of Christian origins before us, then, and mindful of developments more generally in the scientific study of religion concerning the formative power of ritual in human life, we are now in a position to assess the import of the liturgy—its socio-theological "thickness"—in order to identify as clearly as possible its formative power. "In the beginning was the assembly"? Yes. But, much more particularly now: "In the beginning was the *liturgy*." Liturgy, we may say, is the mode of identity formation of the assembly, as the community of the end times, for those churches that practice the liturgy.

I want to explicate this point now in terms of the mission of the church, suggested by our reflections about Matthew 28:16-20: the mission of the church is first and foremost *to be the church, ritually.*[23] The mission of the church is not first and foremost evangelism or ethics or even both together. This admittedly is an un-American thought. In America, mission has characteristically been interpreted pragmatically in the past hundred years, as the church at work in the world, witnessing to the gospel, ministering to the poor, announcing the claims of God's justice, entering into the struggles for the liberation of the oppressed. But none of these essential patterns of discipleship can be created or sustained *ex nihilo.* The *doing* of the church flows from the *being* of the church. The works of the church emerge from the grace received by the church. The life of faithful discipleship grows from the rich soil of faithful communal ritual. The church at work is totally dependent on the church at worship. Worship is the way the church inculcates the eschatological vision of *shalom* in its members. In our liturgical churches, every Christian spirituality, every Christian environmental ethic, every Christian political ethic, every Christian individual ethic, and every Christian evangelism initiative presupposes the generative matrix of the liturgy of the church, for better or for worse.[24] If a theological pun be permitted, this is the gospel truth: you will indeed know them by their moral fruits, but all the more so you will know them by their ritual roots.

It is therefore sobering to have to notice that more than a few of the church's traditional liturgical practices—and, presumably, many of its "contemporary worship" practices as well—have been thoroughly shaped by a theology that is seriously deficient. Those practices have been shaped from within by a sometimes beautiful but, in the end, parochial spirit that has had the effect of prohibiting the liturgy from embodying the fullness of biblical testimony. That inner meaning has been constituted by a hierarchical anthropocentrism and an indifference, even a hostility, toward the natural world, to the disservice of the church's teaching and practices regarding nature. In the next chapter, I will identify this kind of theological anthropocentrism by invoking an architectural metaphor. Call this historical phenomenon *the ambiguous gothic vision.*

5

The Ambiguities of the Gothic Vision: The Theology of Ascent

Few have ever walked into a great gothic cathedral without at first standing still, awestruck by the vision: the narrative richness of the towering west facade and its entrances, the carvings both inside and out giving tangible testimony to the creatures of nature, the effulgence of light everywhere inside, the soaring heights, the sometimes subtle, sometimes brilliant colors of the stained glass, the simple but often elegant contours of the high altar, and much more. To walk into a great gothic cathedral is to walk into a world apart, a world of dazzling and overpowering beauty and sanctity.

The great gothic cathedrals may seem to be a world apart from the world in which we live, and in a sense they are. But it is precisely in their strangeness, as well as in their magnificence, that they have much to teach us. They are a theological genome, as it were, that, once decoded, can help us to see the traditional teachings of the church and its traditional liturgical practices in a new light. We will see that that genome, notwithstanding its overwhelming beauty, has some serious structural faults—faults that have influenced generations of worshipers, even to our own day, particularly with disservice to their encounter with nature.[1]

The Triumph of Ascent and Mastery

The cathedrals were designed, indeed, to be a world apart: a world that luminescently, harmoniously, and powerfully proclaims the mystery of divine truth, insofar as that truth can be grasped by sinful mortals. German art historian Erwin Panofsky instructively juxtaposed the high gothic cathedrals with the great systematic and synthetic works of philosophy and theology produced by the leading theologians of the medieval era, the *Summae*, constructed by geniuses such as Thomas Aquinas.[2] "In its imagery," Panofsky explains, "the high gothic cathedral sought to embody the whole of Christian knowledge, theological, moral, natural, and historical, with everything in its place and that which no longer found its place, suppressed." Further, and again like the *Summae*, Panofsky argues, the high gothic cathedral represented a vast and harmonious and hierarchical arrangement according to a system of homologous parts and parts of parts.[3]

We know what that system of harmonious arrangement was. It was the metaphysical and metapoetic vision of the Great Chain of Being—identified classically in modern times by Arthur Lovejoy's study with that title.[4] The power of this vision can be illustrated with reference to the story of what was perhaps the single most influential gothic structure of the medieval era, the abbey church of St. Denis in France, which the eminent Abbot Suger of St. Denis envisioned in the twelfth century.[5] Suger was a champion of the metaphysics and the metapoetics of the Great Chain of Being.

As Otto von Simson tells us, the abbey of St. Denis itself owed its influential ecclesiastical position to the fact that "it preserved the relics of the saint and martyr who, in the third century, had converted France to Christianity and was hence revered as the patron of the royal house and of the realm. But this St. Denis was held to be identical with an Eastern theologian who was one of the great mystical writers of the early Christian era and, in fact, of the Christian tradition."[6] This Denis has come to be called, for reasons that need not concern us here, the Pseudo-Areopagite or, more simply, Dionysius the Areopagite. With reference to the thought of this Dionysius, George Duby comments, "Suger designed St. Denis as a monument of applied theology."[7]

The works of Dionysius, available to Suger in translation and beloved by him, above all the *Celestial Hierarchy*, depicted the vision of the Great Chain of Being in all its fullness. In those writings, Suger found a majestic testimony to the effulgence of light and to both of the principles we saw Panovsky identify, a comprehensive representation of the rich and manifold fullness of created reality and an arrangement that was harmonious and hierarchical.

For our purposes here, what is important is not any of the details of this story or any particular gothic cathedral but what can be called *the gothic vision*, which enshrined the metaphysics and the metapoetics of the Great Chain of Being. That was a vision of reality which extended from sheer matter or nonbeing at the nadir, through gradations of being—mineral, biological, human, and angelic—to pure spirit or God or "the One" at the apex.

Fatefully, in this hierarchical vision, the line that divided matter from spirit was believed to run through the human creature, who, as body, it was believed, is matter and who, as soul, is spirit. Some scholars have talked instructively about a "spirit-matter dualism," in this connection. In one respect, the human creature is on the side of the angels; in the other respect the human creature is on the side of the animals. But what is critical for the unfolding of the vision is this: within the whole biophysical world, the human creature is the only creature with spirit. Herein lies the grounds for this vision's anthropocentrism, over against the whole material creation. For, in effect, the only material creature that is finally important in the greater scheme of things is the human creature. In biblical imagery, according to this way of thinking, only Adam and Eve and their redeemed progeny, no other earthly creatures, have an *eternal* destiny.

Here we touch on the ambiguity of the gothic vision. In my study *The Travail of Nature*, drawing on the work of Arthur Lovejoy, I identified two fundamental metaphors that this hierarchical conceptuality presupposes, the metaphor of *ascent* and the metaphor of *descent*.[8] When this hierarchy is viewed from below, as if one were standing at the base of a great mountain, the metaphor of ascent dominates. Here the spirituality drives the soul to ascend up to the spiritual One, high above, and to leave the world of matter behind, as if one were climbing a mountain to contemplate the sun. In contrast, when the hierarchy is viewed from above, as if one were standing at the peak of a great mountain surveying the surrounding valleys below, the metaphor of descent predominates. Here the spirituality drives the soul to contemplate and to identify itself with the descending of God or the One, the overflowing of the divine, to encompass and embrace the whole of the spiritual and material universe.

As Dionysius depicted the Great Chain of Being, more particularly, there were *two major movements* in the hierarchy: first, the overflowing movement from God extending to the fullness of created beings below; second, the movement of return of the many to the One, toward union with the eternal world of pure spirit above. The theme of light dominated Dionysius's two-movement vision, as George Duby eloquently explains:

> At the core of the treatise was one idea: God is light. Every creature stems from that initial, uncreated, creative light. Every creature receives and transmits the divine illumination according to its capacity, that is, according to its rank in the scale of beings, according to the level at which God's intentions situated it hierarchically. The universe, born of an irradiance, was a downward-spilling burst of luminosity, and the light emanating from the primal Being established every created being in its immutable place. But it united all beings, linking them with love, irrigating the entire world, establishing order and coherence within it. And because every object reflected light to a greater or lesser degree, the initial irradiance brought forth from the depths of the shadow, by means of a continuous chain of reflections, a contrary movement, a movement of reflection back toward the source of its effulgence. In this way the luminous act of creation brought about of itself a gradual ascension leading backward, step by step, to the invisible and ineffable Being from which all proceeds.

This vision, Duby concludes, was to be the key to gothic art, "an art of light, clarity, and dazzling radiance. . . . and Suger's abbey church was its prototype."[9]

It was the metaphor of ascent that drove the gothic vision. That is indicated dramatically by the gothic heights themselves, pointing to salvation above. The gothic cathedral surely offered representations of the world of nature below and sometimes richly. But it was the second movement of the great hierarchical flow of reality that most fascinated the theologians and the mystics of that era: the ascent to heaven, leaving the world of nature behind. The great Thomas Aquinas would leave no doubt about this ascent: salvation, the return of the many to the One, the ascent of souls to God, meant that nature as we know it, the world of trees and mountains, animals and oceans, would be abrogated. On the last day, there will be no new creation of *all* things, according to Thomas, only spiritual beings.[10]

In this kind of gothic setting, the meaning of the *liturgy* could move only in one direction finally, to accent the ascent of the soul to God, and the abandonment of the material world. The way for this implicit, if not always explicit trend had been prepared for centuries by those, such as Pope Gregory the Great in the sixth century, who viewed the Eucharist as the gateway to heaven: "What right believing Christian can doubt that in the very hour of the sacrifice [of the Mass], at the words of the priest, the heavens be opened, and the quires of Angels are present in that mystery of Jesus Christ, that high things are accomplished with low, and earthly joined to heavenly, and that one thing is made visible and invisible."[11]

Yes, imagery from the creation was carved into the very stone of the cathedral buildings, preachers and teachers could on occasion talk about the glories of the material-vital creation, and poets like Dante could celebrate them.[12] And both the mystics and the common folk of faith could see the glories of the creation illustrated in the cathedrals, as worshipers were bathed in the descending light. But the gothic vision brought with it, of course, the fascination with the light of heaven, the eternal light of God, and of the return of the soul to union with the selfsame eternal light above. So, we may imagine, when in the eucharistic rite the celebrant uttered phrases to the people such as "lift up your hearts," both he and they knew exactly what he really meant, as he stood at the high altar behind the rood screen, facing the east wall with his back to the people, dwarfed by the immense heights of the cathedral and defined by the effulgence of the light coming in from above: salvation is above, removed from this world of matter.

The way for this trend had also been prepared by the increasing exclusion of laity from the Mass during the Middle Ages, symbolized by the construction of sometimes monumental cathedral "rood screens," great walls that separated the nave, where the laity gathered, from the chancel, where the priests functioned. "This [exclusion of the laity] involved a change in the understanding of the Mass," as Martin R. Dudley explains, "which was seen no longer in its fully ecclesial context, the celebration of the people of God united with Christ, but in the context of human need, in which the Mass was offered for someone, living or departed, and the act of offering well might be limited to the priest and a server."[13] One striking example from the later Middle Ages, in the years just before the Reformation in Germany, described by Helmar Junghans, illustrates this long-standing trend: "The Castle Church in Wittenberg (dedicated in 1503 and completed in 1509) included nineteen side altars, at which—including the high altar—nearly 9000 masses were sung or read in 1519 alone."[14] The Eucharist thus became for many laity in the West an instrumental rite, a mechanism for moving someone, living or dead, closer to heaven above.

What was thus announced in terms of architecture and liturgical practice was strongly reinforced by developments in spirituality during the gothic era. This story begins with how the great St. Augustine was read in those times. Was it, as it were, horizontally or vertically? Was it in terms of his vision of creation history, unfolding epoch by epoch "on the ground," and consummated by the coming of the new creation of all things, when God would be all in all? Or was it in terms of his teaching about the journey of the individual soul seeking to be at rest in God above? It apparently was the latter.[15] As Barbara Nolan concludes, regarding early medieval commentators, in particular: "[for them,] the possibility of mankind moving progressively in time toward total spiritual perfection and knowledge during . . . [the last epoch of creation-history] was overshadowed by the emphasis on the individual soul moving with great difficulty out of time toward its own eschaton. The visionary approach to God was personal and vertical rather than social and historical."[16] She quotes the highly influential Scottish mystic who flourished in Paris, Richard of St. Victor (d. 1173), to illustrate how this way of thinking fascinated many in this era:

> By the greatness of wonder, the human soul is led above itself, irradiated by divine light and suspended in wonder before the greatest beauty. So vehemently is it shaken by bewilderment that it is utterly torn from its foundation. The more it is cast to the depths in contempt of self by comparison with such beauty— shaken by its desire for the highest things—so much the higher and faster will it be raised into the sublime and carried above itself like a lightning flash.[17]

Nolan points out that Abbot Suger himself held similar views of the spiritual life, which he expressed artistically not only in the Cathedral of St. Denis but also in his work on the Chartres Cathedral. In his writings, Suger described himself "as ascending to a quasi-temporal state of cognitive suspension between earth and heaven" where he could "enjoy the sensible beauty of human artistic creation," and then, through it, "rise to that higher world of the spirit" symbolized by the gothic heights.[18]

That there were a variety of other trends in medieval worship and spirituality, in addition to the theme of ascent, can be taken for granted. Above all, the church moved emphatically to safeguard and indeed to celebrate the idea of the real presence of Christ in the eucharistic elements on the altar, the descent of the Savior into "the flesh" of the bread and the wine.[19] But such emphases by no means undercut the dominant theology and spirituality of the gothic era. The Eucharist in that epoch was nothing if it was not a means of grace by which people of faith could be freed for their heavenly ascent, above and beyond the world of created matter. This movement of gothic thinking was dramatically illustrated by Dante in his *Divine Comedy*. Glorious as the created universe was for Dante, the end of the whole journey for the pilgrim of faith was ascent to the immaterial heavens and the vision of God.[20]

If matter was thus left behind—or below—by the dynamics of the gothic vision, that should not be taken to mean that it was of no interest to the powers that be of the gothic era. On the contrary, the anthropocentrism of the gothic vision brought with it, and probably was also fostered by, a burgeoning new kind of cultural engagement with nature, in terms of scientific empiricism and technological mastery.[21] This was reflected in the art of the era. "The emergence of gothic art," Lynn White Jr. explains, "reflects a fundamental change in the European attitude toward the natural environment. Things ceased to be merely symbols, *rebuses, Dei vestigia* [figures, traces of God], and became objects interesting and important in themselves, quite apart from *man's* [sic] spiritual needs."[22] The architectural complexity and huge scale of the great cathedrals themselves were dramatic expressions of this new confidence in understanding and mastering nature.

The two trends actually appear to have been one: the spiritual rising above and the mundane quest for mastery. The more the faithful aspired to transcend matter in order to be with God above the heavens, the more they also, in this era, engaged themselves with the earth below as "mere matter," as a world at their disposal, as an "It." This was not yet the spirit of domination of the modern era, by any means, but it undoubtedly set in motion cultural and economic forces that would prepare the way for the aggressive scientific and technological trends of modernity.

The Legacy of the Gothic Vision

How much has the gothic vision of ascent persisted in later eras? The half-life of this vision has been remarkable. Centuries after the era of the gothic cathedrals has passed, in a time indeed when many of those grand structures in Europe have become more like museums than vital centers of liturgical and spiritual practice, the way of seeing the world that they represented persists with enormous strength.

The gothic vision of ascent surely seems to have shaped forcefully those theologies and spiritualities that have taken the metaphysics and the metapoetics of the Great Chain of Being as a datum of life and thought, particularly in some of the traditions of Roman Catholicism.[23] The great and highly influential Catholic visionary of the twentieth century, Pierre Teilhard de Chardin stood in this tradition. He projected the same kind of spiritualizing picture of the end times as Thomas Aquinas did, in the tradition of Dionysius. Teilhard's spirituality, likewise, was predicated on a vision of the soul's ascent to God. Revealingly, Teilhard liked to think of the evolutionary movement of the whole cosmos as "a cone." For Teilhard, the whole cosmos is evolving onwards and upwards toward a purely spiritual fulfillment in God, when the world of matter will have fallen back into nothingness. And more: Teilhard celebrated human mastery over nature with what was perhaps, for a theologian, an unprecedented enthusiasm and confidence.[24]

The eminent Catholic theologian Louis Bouyer, an influential figure both in the twentieth-century liturgical movement and in the ranks of those who participated in the Second Vatican Council, also drew on the traditions of the Great Chain of Being conceptuality to interpret both the Eucharist and the cosmos as a whole. While he did not maintain as sharply as Teilhard did that matter would be abolished in the end times or that matter should chiefly be the object of human mastery, Bouyer made the hierarchical, spiritualizing schema of Dionysius his own. The cosmos, for Bouyer, is "basically angelic."[25] The realm of the angels is what links the sensible world to God.[26] Further, Bouyer seems to hold that the human creature (somehow) mediates the visible creation to God, through the Incarnation: "All creation tends toward man, all mankind tends toward Christ, and in turn Christ, as he has revealed himself to us, tends to unite with all mankind, and through it with the universe."[27] In the end times, for Bouyer, it is as if the sensible world is to be virtually swallowed up by the human world.[28] "When the last of the elect have been absorbed and conformed" to the mystical body of Christ, Bouyer tells us, then Christ will have reached his "cosmic fullness . . . , then Christ will have reached maturity in all his members, and his own Parousia [his Second Coming], the event toward which this entire growth had been straining, will finally take place."[29] There is no testimony here that reflects the biblical promise of a new heaven and a new earth, no images of the lamb lying down with the lion, no visions of a peaceable kingdom for all creatures. The consummation of all things, according to Bouyer's vision, seems to have left the vast material creation behind, except for the human creature. It is out of sight, out of mind, much as it was for Teilhard.[30] Throughout his study, *Cosmos: The World and the Glory of God* (from which I have been quoting here), Bouyer is nothing if he is not a champion of the Dionysian language of descent and ascent, with the accent clearly falling on the latter as it did for Teilhard.

The gothic vision of ascent also appears to have persisted more generally, beyond this kind of Catholic witness, in a variety of Christian traditions, above all in the form of the architectural and spiritual emphases on the experience of *the heights* in worship and in piety. In many forms of Christian worship and prayer, the language that God is *high above* is taken for granted and reinforced continually with hymns and preaching and prayers, even in the midst of church buildings that, externally, have little resemblance to historic gothic styles. Thus, one of the most popular Christian hymns in the U.S. today, written by the Grammy Award winning singer, Donnie McClurkin, is "Lord, I lift your name on high." This hymn a has found a place in the worship of many American churches across the denominational spectrum, from Evangelical to Catholic.[31]

The popular language of spirituality in our churches today reflects this theme, too. Many devout American Christians cherish the ideal of finding a "mountaintop experience" or, in language borrowed from the psychologist Abraham Maslow, a "peak experience." Even a work of sophisticated historical analysis of eucharistic prayer in the Reformed tradition, by Ronald P. Byars, bears the title *Lift Your Hearts on High*, with no apparent awareness of the historical ambiguities of this theme.[32]

With these liturgical and spiritual tendencies, many American church buildings, surely those designed in a neogothic style but others as well, have self-consciously or unconsciously been constructed to *block out* the world around them, much as the historic cathedrals' towering walls and elegant stained-glass windows had been designed, in part, to create a world apart. In American settings, however, the wonderful imagery of the created world that so enhanced the interiors of many medieval cathedrals is mostly missing. Hence, the architectural break between the created world and the realm of the church's worship is all the more pronounced.

Such trends are still more apparent in much, although not all, of the architecture of the "megachurches" that began to dominate the world of American Protestantism toward the end of the last century. Thus "The Chapel on Fir Hill," built in 1970 in Akron, Ohio, is essentially—notwithstanding its rustic name—a large auditorium that seats 1800 and is totally separate from the wider world of nature. It has no windows nor any other interior signs of the natural world anywhere. It is a perfect setting for singing "Lord I Lift Your Name on High," which, as a matter of fact, is often sung there. This megachurch story could be duplicated many times over. In such tangible ways, the traditional theme of ascent is being reclaimed in our own time by American Protestants, even in settings radically different from the Gothic.

One of the most dramatic examples of the same kind of architectural trend—although indebted to European Catholic traditions rather than American Protestant sensibilities—is the Chapel of the Cross at Pacific Lutheran Theological Seminary in Berkeley, California, designed and built in the middle of the twentieth century. Its location is stunning, set upon a hill overlooking the Golden Gate Bridge and San Francisco Bay. In a promotional essay, the seminary's president calls potential applicants' attention to that vista and also observes that "deer wander on the campus and occasionally we are visited by a magnificent blue heron." But none of this can you actually *see* when you enter the Chapel of the Cross! Its walls are monumentally thick, in the style of Le Corbusier, with tiny slats for windows. There, set upon a hill, overlooking one of the great cities of the world, positioned in the midst of vistas of natural beauty, this particular building does not permit worshipers even a glimpse of that magnificence.

True, a number of American-designed church buildings, of varying degrees of aesthetic quality, have been constructed "in the wilds" or with clear-glass visions of the world around them in the last fifty years. The huge Crystal Cathedral in Garden Grove, California, with its towering all-glass walls on every side, is one example. Another is the Dio Padre Misericordioso, an extraordinary neighborhood church built in 2003 in a nondescript suburb of Rome, designed by the American architect Richard Meier. Suffused with Meier's signature all-white coloration, internally and externally, with three dramatic, cantilevered arches defining the building, which are connected by abundant glass, this graceful structure allows the influx of abundant light and also, from within, an easy vision of the surrounding community, which the church was built to serve. E. Fay Jones' widely hailed Thorncrown Chapel, built in 1980, in Eureka Springs, Arkansas, is also worthy of mention here. Essentially a pilgrimage chapel set in a forest but large enough to hold three hundred, this soaring wood structure provides ample space for glass so that those who are inside can have a kind of seamless experience of the surrounding and overarching trees outside. Notwithstanding such architectural achievements, however, the point here is to underline the remarkably strong persistence of the gothic spirit of ascent structured into a variety of architectural forms in our own time.

In the modern era, this accent on God above and the concomitant tendency to block out the created order as a realm worthy of contemplation in itself has been undergirded in Protestant circles, sometimes powerfully, by some forms of Reformed theology that are heirs of the tradition of Calvin. These theologies have celebrated the *ascension* of the risen Lord to the right hand of God in the heavenly heights and indeed even accented *the absence* of the risen Christ in the here and now, in order to reinforce the theme of his heavenly sovereignty.[33] This kind of theological accent on the ascension of Christ has, in turn, at least in its popular American expressions, gone hand in hand with the broader cultural trends that Max Weber called the "spirit of capitalism," which were, and are, predicated on a thoroughgoing commitment to the mastery of nature for the sake of productivity.[34] Weber called this phenomenon the "desacralization of nature." In this respect, not without some historical irony, modern American Protestantism has tended to be the captive of the traditional gothic vision of ascent, undoubtedly in ways that many Protestants themselves have little understood.[35]

Then there is a somewhat more subtle but perhaps even more powerful historical trend that has pushed the American Protestant mind and heart in the same direction. Hovering in the background, sometimes only scarcely visible behind the historic gothic vision, has always been a much more insidious theological and spiritual force, which can be called the spirit of Gnosticism. This is the religious worldview which holds that the material order is purely evil and that human beings contain within themselves sparks from an otherworldly, spiritual divine Being, not the Creator of this world, whose sparks are entrapped in the human body as in a prison.[36] Augustine himself was a captive of this way of thinking, in his years as a Manichee, and then later opposed it vehemently. Both St. Francis and Thomas Aquinas opposed this way of thinking, which had emerged in their era in the movement of the heretical—as Francis and Thomas thought of them—Catharii.

Gnosticism employs the metaphor of ascent in an extreme fashion. In its various expressions, Gnosticism proclaims that salvation means rising above the material world to seek union with the totally spiritual One above, because the material world, including the human body, is evil. With the Gnostic spirit, moreover, goes a radical individualism, or at least that has been the tendency, since what matters most for those who are taken by this religious worldview is the liberation of their own souls, that is, the divine spark within.

The American literary scholar Harold Bloom has argued provocatively that Gnosticism has become *the* American religion, predicated on the deep-seated American cultural commitments to radical individualism.[37] This is not the place to review Bloom's argument. But that argument does have implications for our discussion here, if it is correct, in part or altogether.[38] Insofar as American Christianity has become the captive of radical individualism, which has been particularly attractive to Protestants, American Christianity may have become vulnerable to, if not totally made the captive of, the Gnostic spirit.[39] Think of the "Me Culture," memorably called the "Culture of Narcissism" by Christopher Lasch, promulgated and sustained by mass advertising in our era: what really matters in this world is my peace of mind, my comfort, my security, my freedom to drive whatever I want to drive and to eat whatever I want to eat and to consume as many resources as I want to consume and to believe in a "god" that I want to believe in. Spiritually, likewise, what really matters is my own sin, my own conversion, and my own soul. Other realities, social and ecological, do not even appear on the screen of the Me Culture.

How much has American Christianity become the captive of the Me Culture? Witness the widespread emphasis at the Protestant grass roots on having a "personal relationship with Jesus Christ," to the exclusion of almost everything else, and, more generally, on a wide variety of spiritual self-help therapies. Much popular Protestant preaching is driven in the same direction: it focuses on the individual's conversion or on the individual experience of the forgiveness of sin, often under the advertised slogan, "We will meet your needs."

Surely important in this context, too, is the growing interest on the part of popularizing scholars and among some circles of Christians in Gnosticism itself as a "new" spirituality. A recent example of this phenomenon was the publicity splash produced by the release of the *Gospel of Judas* in 2006, a bona fide Gnostic writing that may have its origins in the second century.[40] Of considerable interest to historians who specialize in the religious life of that period in the West, the launching of that document was intended to garner much more than scholarly attention and indeed to undergird prior commitments to foster Gnostic spirituality in a contemporary form, over against what has been perceived by such popularizers to be the dominant, even suffocating, orthodox traditions in the West. Thus, one of the advocates of the *Gospel of Judas* stated enthusiastically: "Following our own star is an idea that is as relevant today as it was back then. Rather than cast out the betrayer [Judas, therefore], we should look more deeply for the goodness inside ourselves."[41] Thus, a spirituality which is founded on the notions that the whole of nature, including human bodies, is evil, that everything material was created by an alien, evil "god," and that the great spiritual challenge of our time is to find a way to release the divine spark that is trapped within our bodies, is more and more celebrated as the hottest item on the consumer shelf of new spiritual commodities.

Quite different in content but remarkably similar in form is the popular theology of the "Left Behind" series of novels, by Tim LaHaye and Jerry B. Jenkins. These immensely popular novels claim the authority of the book of Revelation but actually present a radically Gnostic theology in form. They envision the salvation of a very few, who are to be "raptured" to salvation above, and a hell-and-brimstone destruction of this "evil earth" and all its inhabitants here below. I was shocked to learn at a mainline Protestant conference center, not too many years ago, that a sizeable minority of attendees at that particular conference was avidly reading those novels. These rank-and-file Protestants had mistakenly assumed, how or why I am not sure, that those novels were a modern retelling of the witness of the book of Revelation.[42]

Insofar as American Christianity has been taken over by this kind of radical individualism, whether in its consumerist or its apocalyptic forms, it has become the captive not of the gothic vision as such, but of the gothic vision exaggerated to the point where it has become something much more radical, akin to the Gnostic spirit. No wonder that a popularly marketed Gnostic spirituality appears to be so attractive, at least to some. No wonder, too, that the preaching of the church sometimes seems to fall on so many deaf ears. If people sitting in the pews care only about rising above the matrix of their own social and ecological worlds, in behalf of uplifting their own souls and serving their own physical and psychic well-being, it stands to reason that even the best preachers and teachers today cannot touch them with biblical texts that have to do with social justice and the love of nature.

Be that as it may, it is necessary for us to be on our guard against such trends, even in their relatively benign gothic expressions, lest they consciously or unconsciously be allowed to infiltrate the theology that undergirds American liturgical practices and thereby inculcate among the faithful habits of thought and action that presuppose the inferiority and, often, the final annihilation of the material world and that validate the legitimacy of the aggressive mastery of nature. If the liturgy is indeed the assembly's mode of identity formation, and if that identity formation of the faithful is in fact spiritualizing, fundamentally alienating communicants from nature, how are the faithful today to be shaped so that they can engage the world of nature with love and care and wonder and gratitude, and even learn how to "commune with nature" in its own right?[43]

Which leaves us with this question: Can the liturgy, insofar as it has been thus shaped by the gothic vision, be renewed? Is there a theology available which can transfigure liturgical practices in a way that will claim and inspire the faithful to engage all the creatures of God's good earth and indeed the infinite reaches of God's good cosmos with love and care and wonder and gratitude? I believe there is, what I call the *theology of descent*.

6

A Revolutionary Vision of Divine Immanence: The Theology of Descent

Given the influence of the gothic vision, both directly and indirectly, on the practice of worship in the Christian churches ever since the founding era of the great gothic cathedrals, and given the ambiguities of that vision, it will be instructive to turn to a very different kind of theological thinker, who took issue with the Great Chain of Being conceptuality— Martin Luther, in the sixteenth century. Seen against the background of that conceptuality, Luther's vision was revolutionary. In breaking away from what I have called the gothic vision, Luther also took passionate issue with the whole idea of the ascent of the soul to God. Hence, the vision he bequeathed to us can instructively be called the theology of descent.

For Luther, God is always "God with us," immanent in our world, immediately active in the world of creation where we live, on our level. More particularly, for Luther, God is always "God with us"—Immanuel— in the person of the Savior, the Word of God incarnate, Jesus Christ. The whole of Luther's theology, in this respect, might well be read as a commentary on the words of the prophet Jeremiah: "Am I a God near by, says the LORD, and not a God afar off? . . . Do I not fill heaven and earth? says the LORD" (Jer. 23:23).[1] Luther is, in this sense, a champion of divine immanence in the creation and this makes it possible for us, in conversation with him, to entertain the thought, in faith, of the sacrality of nature.

Divine Immanence and the Sacrality of Nature

I avoid the word *sacred* at this point, in favor of *sacrality*, for a reason. In Luther's thought, there is never any suggestion that nature is divine, whether in the form of pantheism or panentheism (more on such terms presently). And "sacred" tends to suggest that nature is divine in some fashion, as in the expression "encountering the Sacred." On the other hand, Luther has a rich understanding of the presence of God in nature and of the openness of nature to God. Historians of Christian thought sometimes suggest that the Latin expression *finitum capax infinitum*—"the finite is open to the infinite"—is a hallmark of Luther's thought, and that is true. This is what I mean to suggest by the expression "the sacrality of nature" in Luther's theology. "Sacrality," then, specified as openness to God, has what might be called a lowercase theological clarity.

The same cannot be said for an alternative way of speaking about the same matters that is now fashionable in some theological circles, the language of "sacrament." That is why I also have self-consciously chosen not to invoke the idea that nature is somehow "sacramental," as a key to interpreting Luther's thought in this context, although the idea of the sacramentality of nature is "in the air" in *our* era, and it might be tempting to employ it, in order to make Luther's thought more accessible to twenty-first-century Americans.[2]

Of the numerous theologians who have chosen this nomenclature, Elizabeth Johnson's usage seems to be both representative and revealing.[3] On the one hand, I completely agree with the point she is making when she invokes the language of sacrament. This is her illuminating vision, using the term *sacrament* where I would prefer to speak of *sacrality*:

Contemplative appreciation of the glory of God flaming out in the natural world, undergirded by the theological notion of created participation in uncreated being, gives rise to the realization that the world itself is a revelation and a sacrament of revelation: revelation, because the invisible grandeur of God can be glimpsed and known experientially in the splendor of the universe, its balance, complexity, creativity, diversity, fruitfulness; and sacrament, because the mystery of divine, self-giving presence is really mediated through the riches of the heavens and the earth. Participating in the glory of God, our whole planet is a beautiful showing forth of divine goodness and generosity. By being simply and thoroughly its magnificent self, it bodies forth the glory of God that empowers it, being as it were an icon. And, in keeping with such a theme of glory, this carries with it a note of promise. Pervaded and encircled by the glory of God, nature's beauty, intricacy, wildness, richness, order, and novelty are a sacrament of hidden glory not yet fully revealed.

On the other hand, the problem with the construct of sacramentality used this way, in my view, is that it brings, as it were, too much uppercase symbolic meaning to this particular discussion, making it therefore confusing and thus weakening Johnson's point. Johnson seems to understand "sacrament" more as a history-of-religions category than in theological terms—a kind of *mysterium tremendum et fascinans* (Rudolf Otto) experience, which it is, or can be.

But "sacrament" is also much more particular in meaning. Theologically speaking, "sacrament," as I understand its historic meaning, is the visible Word (Augustine) of the Gospel of Jesus Christ. "Sacrament" in Luther's mature thought has a very particular meaning, referring to the communication of "the forgiveness of sins, life, and salvation" through the real presence of Jesus Christ, in an I-Thou relationship with believers in the liturgical assembly. "Sacrament" thus is integrally dependent on the particularity of the incarnation, as announced by the Fourth Gospel: the Word that was in the beginning and that was God, through whom all things were made, became flesh and dwelt among us, and we beheld his glory (John 1:1-3, 14). All that rich, personal particularity is missing from believers' encounter with the glory of God in nature, overpowering and inspiring as that encounter with God in nature is, or can be.

If this is the case, as I believe it is, then the construct of sacramentality applied to believers' general encounter with nature will, in the end, leave them with a sense that they have not really encountered nature as God has intended them to do, because their experience of nature—though profoundly rich and pervasively charged with their encounter with God's glory—is not, finally, sacramental in terms of what they know as sacramentality in the liturgical assembly. Where, one may ask, is the forgiveness of sins, life, and salvation and the personal communion with Jesus Christ in my encounter with the starry night?

Then there is the possibility of unanticipated consequences of this kind of thinking, such as the following experiential corollary. It could happen, under the influence of the history-of-religions imagery, that believers might be led to step back from, even to devalue, the rich particularity of the sacraments in the life of the assembly, settling for something much different, a kind of general encounter with "the Holy" in the Eucharist, for example. Where then would they receive "the forgiveness of sins, life, and salvation"? Where likewise would they encounter the real presence of Jesus Christ who addresses them personally?[4]

A further problem with the language of earth as sacrament arises in other expressions of the conceptuality, beyond Johnson's carefully construed discussions. Thus, as Rosemary Radford Ruether understands the "sacramental tradition of Catholic Christianity," for example, the "visible universe is the emanational manifestation of God, God's sacramental body. God is incarnate in [it] as the cosmic body of the universe, although not reduced to it."[5] This pan-incarnational view of God and the singular metaphor of the world as God's body I regard as highly problematic, since I see no warrant for it either in the Scriptures or in the classical theological tradition.

Hence, I prefer to allow the construct *sacramentality* to keep its particular and profoundly historic theological meaning, and to introduce a less charged term here, *sacrality*, in order to unveil and to celebrate the very kind of experience that Johnson is referring to in her exposition and which writers like Ruether, I believe, are also seeking to identify and indeed to celebrate. I think Luther's perspective on this matter should be respected, both in order to affirm the theological richness of the sacraments in the life of the church and also in order to keep that theological richness from being watered down into some vague kind of spiritual experience that offers believers no personal communion with Jesus Christ.

This is not to suggest that our experience of God in nature, seen from Luther's angle of vision, must somehow be vague. On the contrary, nature *is* sacral, as Luther views such things, and that means that nature is vividly and overwhelmingly and profoundly charged with the glory and mystery and power of God. That indeed is the primary point. Luther's vision of things is first and foremost about *God*. It is theocentric. To say that nature is sacral, then, from the perspective of Luther's thought, is correct. But Luther's understanding of the immanence of God in nature has its conceptual weight in another place, in his understanding of *God's* presence, rather than his view of the openness of *nature* to God.

Luther, in effect, canceled the second movement depicted by the Great Chain of Being conceptuality in its Dionysian form, the return of the spiritual creatures to God, a fact that even some of the best interpreters of

Luther have not fully realized.[6] He counseled his followers to "shun like the plague that 'Mystical Theology' of Dionysius . . ."[7] For Luther, although he was not wont to express the point this way, only the descent of the One to the many is real. More to the point, the world where the Creator is known is horizontal, not vertical. For Luther there is no divine hierarchy. The Creator is continually overflowing into the created world: the Creator is in, with, and under all things, immediately present, not high and lifted up at the apex of some grand Chain of Being, far removed from this world:

> It is God who creates, effects and preserves all things through his almighty power and right hand, as our creed confesses. For he dispatches no officials or angels when he creates or preserves something, but all this is the work of the divine power itself. If he is to create it or preserve it, however, he must be present and must make and preserve his creation both in its innermost and outermost aspects.[8]

For Luther, likewise, the Redeemer is continually overflowing, as the risen and ascended Lord, into the whole created world. In this respect, as in every other for Luther, the Creator and the Redeemer are one. In this respect also, for Luther, the metaphor of descent, which I identified earlier, shapes everything else, his thought both about creation and about redemption.

How much, in Luther's view, the Creator is *known*, and how much the Redeemer is *known*, in, with, and under all things, on the other hand, is another matter. Luther sometimes offered differing responses to such epistemological questions. That God *is* with us, however, immediately and intimately and overpoweringly with us, both as Creator and as Redeemer, of that, for Luther, there can be no doubt. This is a typical utterance:

> God is substantially present everywhere, in and through all creatures, in all their parts and places, so that the world is full of God and he fills all, but without his being encompassed and surrounded by it. He is at the same time outside and above all creatures. These are all exceedingly incomprehensible matters; yet they are articles of our faith and are attested clearly and mightily in Holy Writ . . .[9]

Luther's approach to worship can be described in similar terms. Call his view the liturgy of "God with us." In this respect, Luther's understanding of the chief sacraments of the church, baptism and Eucharist, is most revealing and therefore most helpful for our own explorations. We will approach these critically important points obliquely, by way of conversation with the voices of traditional sacramental theology.

The Cosmic, Enfleshed Word

To this end, two historical clarifications are necessary. First, since the time of Augustine, a variety of theologians—for typically sound theological reasons, particularly in the context of post-Augustinian reformation theology—adopted his affirmation that the sacraments are "visible words." To view the sacraments this way appealed to many, since it appeared to be a congenial way to support Luther's approach to the sacraments, which was shaped by his theology of the Word. Robert Jenson has therefore entitled his highly regarded study of the sacraments, *Visible Words*, with substantive as well as historical appropriateness.[10]

But when we speak this way, it is important to recall which "Word" we are identifying. This is the Word of "God with us," God in the flesh in Jesus Christ. This, further, is the selfsame Christ proclaimed by the Pauline writer of Colossians, the Christ "in whom all things hold together" (Col. 1:17) and the Christ who makes peace with all things by the blood of his cross (Col. 1:20). This is *the cosmic Christ,* who is the inaugurator of the new creation, the One who draws all things to himself, and the One who restores every person of faith to his or her rightful relationship to the Father and to the plan of the Father to unite *all things* in him.[11]

The cosmic Christ. The pioneering ecological theologian Joseph Sittler lifted this up as a theme in its own right in the mainstream of modern ecumenical theology in 1961.[12] This was Sittler's way of recapturing the New Testament witness to Christ in the letter to the Colossians concerning Christ as the agent of God in the creation, redemption, and consummation of the world. Luther took this New Testament testimony to Christ for granted, as the following statement from a sermon on John 1:3—"All things came into being through him [Christ], and without him not one thing came into being"—indicates:

Christ is the man who brings forth something visible from that which is still invisible. Thus through him heaven and earth were produced from that which was invisible and nothing, and were rendered visible. And it is Christ the Lord, who was present at the time of the creation of all things not as a mere spectator but as a coequal Creator and Worker, who still governs and preserves all and will continue to govern and preserve all until the end of the world. For he is the beginning, the middle, and the end of all creatures.[13]

But this vision of the Word made flesh as the cosmic Christ has tended to be underplayed, even obscured at times, in reformation traditions after Luther's time. All too often the idea that the sacraments are visible words has been taken by default, if not consciously, in a different sense, not as the presence of the cosmic Christ. This leads us away from Luther's rich theology of divine immanence and therefore away from contemplation of the sacrality of nature. During Luther's lifetime, as a matter of fact, theological trends were emerging that would "frame" the construct of visible words in ways quite different than Luther did. Some took the idea of the sacraments as visible words, in those days and thereafter, to mean the proclamation of the word of doctrine, rather than the mediation of the Word made flesh. That critical shift of nuance already appears to have been underway in the sixteenth century in the appropriation of Luther's sacramental theology by his ardent champion, Phillip Melanchthon.

As a result, for some Protestant traditions, the sacraments have tended to become illustrations of an idea, dispensations announcing the unmerited grace of God perhaps, but basically understood as rites that God has instituted for the sake of simple, even illiterate souls in order to teach them about what God has revealed more directly in God's written or proclaimed Word, in immediate revelations to the soul, or by the dogmatic authority of the church. So we must state resolutely and affirmatively that the sacraments of baptism and Eucharist, as "visible words," are indeed sacraments of the real presence of the cosmic Word made flesh.

The Omnipresence of the Risen and Ascended Christ

The second clarification has to do with the theology of the divine immanence, from the perspective of faith, and finally with the possibility of affirming the sacrality of nature. I am referring to Luther's theology of *the ubiquity of the risen and ascended Christ*. We have already encountered this theme in Luther's commentary on John 1:3, concerning the agency of

Christ in the history of creation. This teaching has been something of an embarrassment to even the most enthusiastic of Luther's interpreters.[14] It has scandalized many others.[15] Nevertheless, Luther described the divine immanence in the whole creation in highly sophisticated, dialectical terms, distinguished by his maximal use of spatial pronouns—for example, his often cited phrase about God's presence being "in, with, and under."[16]

Further, Luther understands space paradoxically: first and foremost as *God's space,* a theological fundamental that Karl Barth may well have learned from Luther even as he was at the same time rejecting Luther's sacramental theology in other ways.[17] Luther's theological depiction of space is first and foremost a description of *God's* inscrutable space, then the world's. So Luther can readily suggest that the whole of the Godhead is present in the baby on Mary's lap. He can make the same affirmation about a grain of wheat! God's space is not limited by the space of this world. On the contrary, God's space dwarfs, indwells, overwhelms, and embraces the space of this world:

> For how can reason tolerate it that the Divine majesty is so small that it can be substantially present in a grain, on a grain, over a grain, through a grain, within and without, and that, although it is a single Majesty, it nevertheless is entirely in each grain separately, no matter how immeasurably numerous these grains may be? . . . And that the same Majesty is so large that neither this world nor a thousand worlds can encompass it and say: "Behold, there it is!" . . . His own divine essence can be in all creatures collectively and in each one individually more profoundly, more intimately, more present than the creature is in itself; yet it can be encompassed nowhere and by no one. It encompasses all things and dwells in all, but not one thing encompasses it and dwells in it.[18]

In the same paradoxical spirit, Luther was wont to quote the saying attributed in his day to the ancient mystical philosopher Hermes Trismegistus: "God is the circle whose center is everywhere and whose circumference is nowhere." For Luther, the fullness of God is before our very eyes, as it were. It is not to be sought in some supra-sensible "beyond" or "above."

With this approach to God's space and God's paradoxical presence in, with, and under all the creatures of this world, Luther in effect set himself apart from other major trends in Western theology that addressed these matters and from the expression of those trends in our own era. This can be signaled, in theological shorthand, by invoking generic constructs that are familiar in theological discussions today: atheism, deism, theism, pantheism, and panentheism. None of these terms really "works" for explaining Luther's thought at this point, in my view, including theism and panentheism, which would be the most likely candidates, as I will explain.

Obviously, Luther is not an atheist or a deist (the latter meaning essentially that God creates the world like a clock and lets it run on its own, without "interfering" with the world). Nor, clearly, is Luther a pantheist, a term meaning that God and the world are fundamentally indistinguishable. The world is world, for Luther; it is not God. In this respect, for Luther, there is what in modern theology (Søren Kierkegaard, the early Karl Barth) would be called an "infinite qualitative difference" between God and the world. Or, more pointedly, in the same modern categories, for Luther, God can be said to be "Wholly Other," even as God is also "Wholly Near."

Some have been inclined to call Luther a panentheist, which could be appropriate, depending on how that word is defined. But the term probably should be avoided when interpreting Luther's thought. Typically, for the panentheist, "the world is *in* God"—*pan-en-theos* (all in God). Further, for the panentheist, that preposition "in" is *the* defining and often the only word invoked. It often seems to be taken literally, too, in order to declare that that is where the world is, in fact: in God, something akin to an unborn infant in the womb. Luther is at the other end of the metaphorical spectrum. He insists that we must use *many pronouns*, that no single one can viably give expression to God's relationship with the creatures. Also, Luther does not approach the theology of divine immanence from the direction assumed by many panentheists, and suggested by the word itself, how the creatures relate to God, whether *the creatures* are inside or outside of God. Luther's approach is theocentric, in terms of God's space. The question is how *God* relates to the creatures and in this respect, for Luther, God is in, with, and under—and above and behind and around and so forth—all creatures.

This leaves us finally with the thought that Luther must be a theist. But that term is problematic in this context, too, if the word is understood as it often is used in theological discussions today: showing us a picture of God above time and space, ruling all things in transcendent majesty, perhaps through angelic intermediaries (the mature Augustine), perhaps by his inscrutable will (Calvin, at times), perhaps by God's Spirit (Calvin, at times). If that is what theism means—God, above time and space, ruling—then Luther is not a theist. While Luther insists that God is working powerfully in all things, Luther attests to the descent of God, here and now, within the world of space and time. To express the matter sharply: there is no all-defining "above" for Luther. The only God we know, in Luther's view, is the God we know here and now, in, with, and under all things. We do not know the "there-ness" of God, only the "here-ness" of God, as God discloses Godself to us.

Rather than depending on such constructs as theism and panentheism, for example, to explicate Luther's thought in this respect, therefore, we are best advised to stay focused on the particulars of his thought. Then we will see how clearly and how sharply he distinguishes God from the creation, on the one hand, yet how richly and how powerfully he depicts the presence of God in, with, and under the whole creation and indeed every individual creature. Which is to say: it is preferable to let Luther's theology speak for itself, as much as possible. And speak powerfully it does, most concretely regarding the ascension of Christ.

When Luther states, concerning the ascension of the risen Lord to the right hand of the Father, that "the right hand of God is everywhere" (*dextera Dei ubique est*),[19] the Reformer is merely (!!) giving his rich theology of the divine immanence what is for him an appropriate christological concreteness. Since God the Father, for Luther, is, as a matter of course, in, with, and under all things, so is the ascended Son of God. This christological qualification of the divine immanence then makes it possible for Luther to carry through his program of accenting the descent of the God who is our Immanuel, with specific reference to sacramental theology. For Luther, the same God who was and is in, with, and under all things is also fully present in the child on the lap of Mary, and therefore is also fully present in the waters of baptism and in the bread and the wine of the Eucharist, and so known by the faithful, whenever those sacraments are administered according to the selfsame cosmic Word.

Now this surely does not mean that everything that Luther said is defensible or that he said everything that needs to be said.[20] Two themes, in particular, must be addressed, if we are to claim his vision of divine descent in our time in a way that will be theologically fruitful: first, regarding the logic of Luther's theology of the ubiquity or omnipresence of the risen and ascended Christ and, second, regarding what I will call its full existential value.

The Theology of Descent and the Omnipresence of Christ in Retrospect

I have already pointed to the difficulties some followers of Luther and many others as well have had coming to terms with his theology of the ubiquity of the risen and ascended Christ. Although this issue may seem esoteric to some, even "counting angels on the head of a pin" to others, huge theological issues are at stake here. Indeed, how we address them will have profound ramifications for how we think about and practice the liturgy and how we encounter the world of nature.

Some of the questions directed at Luther's thought in this respect are surely legitimate, particularly from the perspective of theologians speaking from Calvinist traditions.[21] If the humanity of Christ is omnipresent, they ask, does not this mean that that humanity is, in effect, destroyed? The image suggested by such questions is this: that the humanity of Christ is, as it were, decimated, exploded, as if it were like the dust emerging from a volcanic eruption, now drifting as particles in air currents around the globe.[22] But, if anything like that were to be asserted, the result would surely be destructive to the faith: one cannot be in communion with particles of Christ, as it were; one can only be in communion with the whole Christ. But that kind of questioning reflects a misreading of Luther's intentions at this point, although scholars could presumably find individual utterances of Luther where his intentions are not so clearly expressed.

Luther's distinction here is subtle but clear. He presupposes the omnipresence of the "Father Almighty," who is attested in the creeds. Next, so the logic of his thought unfolds, Luther affirms that "the right hand of God is everywhere." It then follows, for Luther, that when the risen Christ ascends to the right hand of God, Christ ascends to that particular place, where he remains unchangeably located, as the whole Christ. Now, *that place* where Christ sits enthroned is omnipresent, according to Luther. So it is not the humanity of Christ that is omnipresent, technically speaking, it is the right hand of God. The whole Christ sits at the right hand of God, wherever that right hand is—and that is everywhere. Only this way can Luther affirm as consistently and as passionately as he does that in the Eucharist the believer is in communion with the whole Christ, thus encountering "God with us," Immanuel, then and there, really present in the administration of bread and wine.

There is an analogy here, for Luther, with the incarnation of the Son of God. The eternal Son of God is united to the man Jesus, here on earth, born of the virgin Mary. The humanity of Jesus embodies or enfleshes his divinity, here on earth: the Word becomes flesh (John 1:13). One does not have to rise to heaven to encounter the divinity of Jesus. For Luther, the person of Jesus Christ should not, indeed cannot, be divided. Faith always encounters the whole Christ here on earth. Likewise, there is a "sacramental union" in the Eucharist, according to Luther. The whole Christ is fully present, really present, then and there, in, with, and under the bread and wine, and not somehow constrained to remain in heaven.

Behind this entire conceptuality is Luther's highly suggestive and powerful understanding of the omnipresence of God itself, which we have already considered. Luther self-consciously—and almost exuberantly— claims *that the only way to understand the presence God is to invoke the language of paradox.*[23] Luther does this, as we have seen, by maximizing the use of prepositions: not only "in, with, and under" (as his followers later codified his utterances in this respect) but many others. This, for Luther, is the only way sinful human creatures can begin to affirm anything meaningful about the mysterious presence of God and the unfathomable ways of God. It appears, then, that those who question Luther's theology of the ubiquity of the risen and ascended Christ, should first come to terms with—or not, as they may wish—Luther's paradoxical language about God's presence generally.[24] That seems to be the underlying issue in this case. When that is dealt with in Luther's terms, then there really will be no viable theological reason to raise questions about the human nature of Christ being decimated or exploded or otherwise marginalized.

This is the experience to which Luther's teaching points us: when I stand at the table of the Lord with my hands extended receptively, and the priest places the eucharistic bread in my hands, saying, "the body of Christ, given for you," I am then and there, in faith, in communion with the whole Christ, my good shepherd, who has come there and then to my finite, existential lostness, to commune with me and to invite me, in the power of his Spirit, to commune with him. At that moment, Christ is closer to me than the priest who offers me the bread, closer, indeed—to invoke Augustine's comparably paradoxical language from another context—than I am to myself. As I stand at the table, in other words, I am not somehow beamed up to heaven in the Spirit, to be with Christ in some heavenly heights, far above our mundane world, where he sits at the right hand of the Father in eternal glory. This is the critically important sacramental legacy of Luther's theology of descent.

For Luther, the real presence of Christ in the Eucharist, in other words, is real. Christ is not *dialectically* present, as some theologians say; Christ is *really* present. David F. Ford, for example, holding to a Calvinistic ascent theology, maintains that Christ is present *and* not-present in the Eucharist.[25] And Ford rejects Luther's ubiquity theology on the grounds that Luther does not attest what Ford thinks of as the "eschatological tension" in the Eucharist. Ford here apparently conflates two different sets of ideas. For Luther, Christ is really present in a tree, let us say, or in the sacraments, but Christ is only *accessible* to us when Christ discloses himself to us by his Word and when we hear that Word in faith. Luther's ideational framework, then, is this: *a real presence that is inaccessible or accessible.* For Ford, when Christ is present, Christ is also absent. So, for Ford, there is a real presence and a real absence. Not so for Luther. Luther also holds that Christ will come again in glory and will make all things new. But the Christ who will so publicly claim his lordship in the eschaton, for Luther, is the same Christ who is really here, in these times, exercising his lordship in hidden ways and known only to the faithful to whom he discloses himself in the "Means of Grace," that is, by Word and Sacrament.

Is there any reason, then, why not to claim that legacy for our own purposes in interpreting the Scriptures? Did not the risen Christ who "ascended far above all heavens" do so "so that he might fill all things" (Eph. 4:10)? Is not the risen Christ, who, as Paul teaches, reigns throughout the cosmos (1 Corinthians 15; Colossians 1), really present at any time and any place in baptism and Eucharist? Is he not really present, as he promised, wherever two or three are gathered in his name (Matt. 18:20)? And is this not the same *invisible* Christ who appeared *visibly* to Mary at the tomb and to Thomas behind closed doors? According to Luther, in keeping with the witness of these biblical themes, the faithful do not have to ascend to God in order to commune with God. The Holy Spirit, according to Luther, mediates the ascended Christ to believers, here and now, on our level, as happened to the community of the first witnesses of the Resurrection.

In light of these considerations, the theological burden of the proof would seem to rest squarely on the shoulders of those Christians who would minimize or reject Luther's theology of the ubiquity of the risen and ascended Christ. In this respect, as in many others, Luther's theological affirmations seem to have been not only appropriate, but commendable interpretations of the witness of the Scriptures. In so doing, Luther in effect transvalued the gothic vision of ascent. For Luther, both with respect to creation and redemption, and in particular with regard to liturgical practice, descent, not ascent, is the vision that shapes every theological affirmation, from beginning to ending.

Encountering the Omnipresent Christ and the Sacrality of Nature

All this discourse about the risen and ascended Christ may indeed be the foundation of Luther's theology of descent, but what difference does it make, if any, beyond the sacramental life of the church? To use the language of William James, What is the "cash value" of this kind of discourse? How does it matter existentially in the totality of my experience? Call this, in terms better than James's, its "full existential value." For now, this is what I would like the reader to envision: that the believer, whose life is shaped by the liturgy, can encounter the omnipresent Christ in nature and so gain or recover a compelling sense for the sacrality of nature. I want to develop this thought now by invoking a conceptuality that I first suggested some years ago.

In my 1968 *Journal of Religion* article, "I-Thou, I-It, and I-Ens," I proposed a fresh way to describe human relatedness, in conversation with the thought of Martin Buber, classically expressed in his little book, *I and Thou*.[26] Drawing here on the conceptuality that article proposed should allow us to grasp, in some measure, the full existential value of the believer's relationship with the ubiquitous Christ.

In an appendix of *I and Thou*, Buber considered the thought that one can have an I-Thou relationship with a *tree*! An I-Thou relationship, as Buber described it in its essentials, is a relationship of mutuality and reciprocity and respect between two persons. An I-Thou relationship, in Buber's view, is, more particularly, a *spoken* relationship, a verbal communicating between respectfully listening persons. Herein lies the challenge, for Buber, of interpreting the relationship with the tree that so concerned him. Buber poetically described his encounter with the tree. That encounter is respectful. It is not objectifying, the way Buber thought an I-It relationship with a tree would be. According to the canons of an I-It relationship, one would have to have viewed the tree as an object that was useful for some human purpose, perhaps for providing fuel or for functioning to purify the atmosphere. One would have had no problem, moreover, with the idea of cutting down the tree. But Buber encounters the tree as an end-in-itself, as a genuine other, not as an object. Buber also considers human relationships with animal companions. Such encounters, said Buber, also can have qualities akin to an I-Thou relationship: mutual respect and even reciprocity. But they are not, said Buber, I-Thou relationships, since they lack the essential reality of speech. Those relationships are "at the threshold of speech," said Buber. But Buber never gave a coherent answer to the question posed to him by his encounter with the tree, as Buber himself admitted.

Keeping with the flow of Buber's analysis, can we not think of *a third type* of human relatedness, an I-Ens relationship (drawing on the Latin for "being," *ens*)? For example, Joseph Sittler once observed that the King James translation of the words of Jesus, "*Behold* the lilies of the field," is much to be preferred to the Revised Standard Version translation, "*Consider* the lilies of the field." Sittler explained:

> The word "behold" lies upon that which is beheld with a kind of tenderness which suggests that things in themselves have their own wondrous authenticity and integrity. I am called upon in such a saying not simply to "look" at a nonself but to "regard" things with a kind of spiritual honoring of the immaculate integrity of things which are not myself.[27]

Sittler believed that Jesus himself was an heir of ancient Hebraic apperceptions of nature, according to which nature, as it were, has a voice of its own (nature praises God) and is worthy of our highest contemplative respect, as indicated by the English word *behold*.[28] The great American nature writer John Muir, whose vision of nature was deeply shaped by the sensibilities of Calvin's thought, himself thought of nature as the theater of God's glory. This kind of encounter with nature can suggestively be called an I-Ens relationship. An I-Ens relationship is akin to an I-Thou relationship in almost every respect—on some occasions even a kind of reciprocity can be identified—except that there is no speech, no verbal communication between the I and the Ens.

This conceptuality can serve us well as we seek to identify what can be discerned about the full existential value of our theme, the ubiquity of the risen and ascended Christ. Luther invoked the latter theme implicitly in terms of an I-Thou relationship. For Luther, the believer encounters the whole Christ *in the Word* addressed to the believer, which, for Luther, is the real presence of Christ for the believer. In the preached Word and in what Luther thought of as "the mutual conversation of the brothers and the sisters," as well as in the Eucharist of the church, Jesus Christ is really present for the believer. In these ways, for Luther, Jesus Christ speaks to and with the believer, and the believer responds. It would take us too far afield to explore Luther's sacramental thinking in depth at this point, but it is worth mentioning that Luther considered the encounter of Christ with the believer to be so real that Luther could imagine a so-called "unworthy eating" of the sacrament by *unbelievers*. In this case, for Luther, the really present Christ addresses the unbeliever, but then Christ is rebuffed, as, let us say, one spouse can address another and be rebuffed. The fact of the rejection by the "Thou" of the communication initiated by the "I," however, by no means contradicts the fact that the relationship between the two is an I-Thou relationship.

More generally, Luther addressed these same issues with a technical theological distinction: Christ, said Luther, is always there, anywhere. But in the proclamation of the church and in the mutual consolation of the brothers and the sisters and in the sacrament of the altar, Christ is there *for me* (*pro me*), since Christ addresses me there with his Word. That is where we should seek Christ, said Luther, where Christ speaks his Word to us, not more generally, where Christ does not speak his Word to us. In addition, while Luther could celebrate the wonders of God in the created order, in the birth of a child, for example, or in what for Luther was the miracle of a grain of wheat, Luther tended to look at the world of nature as a whole as the realm of the hidden God alone. And that sometimes meant, for Luther, that the world of nature is dramatically an expression of God's wrath.[29]

I consider Luther's treatment of the ubiquitous presence of the risen and ascended Christ to be an underdeveloped theme in his thought. Luther drew on that theme, especially in his disputes with Huldrich Zwingli about the real presence of Christ in the Eucharist, in order to undergird Luther's own sacramental realism. But, thereafter, Luther more or less let the ubiquity theme fade to the edges of his thought. With the availability of the I-Ens conceptuality, however, and in response to the needs of our own time, championed first and foremost by Joseph Sittler, who announced the need for a "cosmic Christology," we do not have to remain satisfied with Luther's reticence about the ubiquitous Christ beyond the life of the Christian community.

I obviously cannot address all the facets of such a cosmic Christology in this context.[30] Here I want to underline chiefly the existential dimension of this cosmic Christology, how believers may think of themselves encountering the ubiquitous Christ beyond the pale of the Christian assembly and beyond the context of relationships with other believers at any time or place. That means beyond the milieu where the Word is proclaimed and embodied and made visible. Hence, when Luther says that "God will not deal with us except through his external Word and sacrament,"[31] I want to say yes—and no.

A humble but telling example can set the stage for this kind of expansion of Luther's vision. From my summer home, I look out the window at the garden some distance away. There I see my wife of more than forty years engaged in caring for the garden, weeding, fertilizing, thinning, transplanting. I am surely graced with an I-Thou relationship with her at the dinner table and in other intimate settings. But as I contemplate her in the garden, this is not an I-Thou relationship, as such. There is no speech. There is no communication. She is not even aware that I am contemplating her in the garden, so there is no reciprocity in the relationship. Yet I surely do not view her as an object at that moment, as an "It," as someone who is working so that I can have food on my table, for example. I contemplate the beautiful sight of her so engaged with those plants and with the soil and her caring. Without so much as a word to her or from her, I love her all the more as I see her working there, as I also remember our other times of intimacy, when we do speak to each other, sometimes placidly, sometimes intensely. I give thanks to God for this vision, for the freedom we have to enjoy our garden together and for her patience with my own sometimes blundering efforts to care for the garden. I also give thanks to God for the freedom God has given me, in trust, to step back from that, to me, pristine scene and to let it be: that I do not feel compelled narcissistically to begrudge her that caring for the garden. At that moment, as I contemplate her in the garden, I am in an I-Ens relationship with her— although that would quickly change if I were to go out to speak with her, as I often do. That would then be an I-Thou relationship.

It is an imperfect analogy, as are all analogies. But it allows me to speak confessionally also about my relationship with the tree. As one who is sometimes gifted with faith, when I contemplate the tree, I not only see the tree, but with eyes of faith I also see the presence of Jesus Christ. This is the very Christ with whom I personally commune in the Eucharist and who personally addresses me in the proclaimed Word and who personally cares for me through the works of mercy of my brothers and sisters in Christ. True, Christ is not present there, in, with, and under that tree, *for me*. Christ does not feed me spiritually or address me to forgive my sins or to console me through that tree. But, seeing with the eyes of faith, I know that *he is there*, caring for that tree in some way appropriate to its treeness (as Tillich often spoke about trees), and in some way appropriate to its particularity. Christ is really there, invisibly, I know in faith, much as my wife is really there, visibly, in the garden. And more so, of course. For the same risen and ascended Christ whom I encounter invisibly in an I-Ens relationship in, with, and under that tree, is also the One "in whom all things hold together" (Col. 1:17). My point is, *nature is sacral to me* when I am gifted in the Spirit to experience it so, because nature is where I encounter the same Christ whom I know personally, by grace alone, in the midst of the assembly.

To be sure, this way of thinking about encountering Christ in, with, and under the tree must be regarded as preliminary at this point. For the world of nature is not only my peaceful encounter with the tree, as Buber envisioned it. It is also my very particular and indeed terrifying encounter with an oak tree in the foothills of the White Mountains, in southwestern Maine, that was hit by a lightning bolt near where I was walking once, a bolt that split that huge tree in half, reminding me of the foolishness of being out in a thunderstorm, where I easily could have been killed. Nature does have a dark side, after all, and is pervaded with death and violence. Is it the case, then, that, when that lightning hit that oak tree, *Christ* was there? Am I proposing that?! I am. But I am also proposing that much more must be said if that kind of statement is to make real existential sense for believers. I will return to this discussion more than once in ensuing chapters.

Thoughts for Further Discussion

By way of concluding the present discussion of the theology of descent and as a prelude to forthcoming chapters on liturgical renewal and habits of faith, I want to make five observations. These comments will allow us to step back and take stock of the argument of this book thus far, with regard to one major theme, and also to identify some pregnant implications of that argument, which will show that the argument itself brings with it a suggestiveness for other areas of theological and spiritual exploration.

The Christological Focus of This Book in Perspective

First, under the rubric of taking stock, I want to make a candid and necessary qualification about the argument of this book thus far—and to its conclusion. This study is, and it will be to the very end, *a work in progress*, perhaps in many ways, but surely regarding one theological fundamental, its *christological focus*.

The liturgy and the theology that has informed the liturgy throughout the ages has been and is thoroughly and self-consciously *trinitarian*. Baptism is as a matter of course enacted "in the name of the Father and of the Son and of the Holy Spirit." Eucharistic prayers often, although not always, have had a trinitarian structure. The classical hymnody and creedal utterances of the church are richly trinitarian, as in the liturgical confession, "Glory be to the Father and to the Son and to the Holy Spirit, as it was in the beginning, is now, and ever more shall be so." The liturgy ends with the people being sent forth with the blessing of the triune God.[32] But our explorations of the theology of descent thus far have necessarily focused chiefly on the figure of Jesus Christ, God with us, our Immanuel, on his incarnate life, his cross, his resurrection, and his ascension. This, in turn, has led us to seek ever more particularly to discern the scope and meaning of the cosmic omnipresence of Jesus Christ.

Why this particular focus?[33] In my judgment, if nature is to be ritualized according to the canons of the liturgy, the christological basis for that ritualization must be firmly and explicitly established.[34] Otherwise the whole argument could falter or even fail, theologically. So in this case, it is a question of first things first and also of first things spoken with sufficient depth to do them justice. I will defer to readers to judge, once they have finished the book, whether this christological focus has in fact allowed them clearly to see what the ritualization of nature can mean, when viewed in this perspective.

Even if this approach accomplishes that end, however, this book will still have to be regarded as a work in progress because of its trinitarian incompleteness, if for no other reason. This approach will not allow us to explore the full trinitarian richness of the liturgy, even though I am pre-supposing throughout the works of the Father and of the Spirit, as well as the works of the Son, in the metanarrative of creation, redemption, and consummation.

Consider, for example, the importance of understanding the works of the Holy Spirit. The traditional reading of Genesis 1:2 depicts the Spirit as hovering creatively over the world-coming-into-being in the very beginning. The psalmist knows the Spirit as the One who is the agent of God's creativity and who renews the earth (Ps. 104:3). The Spirit is regularly depicted in traditional theological discussions as the Life-Giver, the Comforter, the Advocate, the Flame of inspiration, the Creator. In the second century, more particularly, Irenaeus gave expression to the works of the Spirit, alongside those of the Son, by suggesting metaphorically that the Spirit and the Son are "the hands" that God used and continues to use in creating and redeeming the world. This prompts the question, In our day, how should we understand the cosmic works of the Spirit in relationship with the cosmic works of Jesus Christ?

My response is that there is much for preachers and teachers and theologians of the church to say about the Trinity and about the mission of the Holy Spirit, in particular, in the context of the theology of nature.[35] Yet a theological trap has ensnared many Western Christian theologians, that is, the tendency to reduce pneumatology to almost nothing. Students of Western trinitarian theology are generally agreed that this tradition has frequently trended toward a kind of *functional binitarianism*, focusing as a matter of emphasis on the Father and the Son sometimes almost to the exclusion of the Spirit. Paul Tillich diagnosed this trend as reflecting a distrust of charismatic gifts on the part of those in authority. The freewheeling inspirations of the Spirit are difficult to control! Paul already had to contend with such issues in his own time, as is evident in 1 Corinthians 13, where he sought to "test the spirits" with the criteria of faith, hope, and love, the greatest of these, he said, being love. Liberation theologians have often made much of the kind of point Tillich was proposing, contrasting the Spirit-filled life of the first generation of Christians and its spiritual democracy that gave voice to the poor as well as the rich and to women as well as men with the development of an established, male-dominated episcopacy in later generations. Theological binitarianism, in that perspective, was the result of a kind of power-grab by an elite which sought to solidify its own position by banishing spontaneity and democracy.

There are important exceptions to this generalization, of course. The trend toward binitarianism in the West has by no means been universal. One counterexample is the balanced trinitarian theology of the mature thought of John Calvin, where the role of the Spirit has its own intrinsic importance. Still, the overall historical trend *is* noteworthy. It is reflected in traditional Christian art in the West, for example, as that art has depicted the Trinity: the Father and the Son are typically presented vividly, while the Spirit sometimes seems to be peripheral, typically represented with the tiny image of a dove hovering above the other two "main characters." I do not want this book to be read as yet another expression of that kind of functional binitarianism. For this reason, also, I am emphasizing that this book must be considered to be a work in progress.

Implications for Enriching the Spiritual Life with Christ

Second, does not the way of thinking I am proposing in this book about the ubiquitous Christ, who is present here and now in the liturgy and indeed throughout the whole creation, *also* make it possible for us to have a much more engaging *spiritual life with Christ*, wherever we may be? Consider the spirituality that comes to expression in this English adaptation of the powerful traditional Celtic song, "St. Patrick's Breastplate":

> Christ beside me, Christ before me,
> Christ behind me, king of my heart;
> Christ within me, Christ below me,
> Christ above me, never to part.

Or this, from the great spiritual, "I Want Jesus to Walk with Me":

> When I'm in trouble, Lord, walk with me;
> When I'm in trouble, Lord, walk with me;
> When my head is bowed in sorrow,
> Lord, I want Jesus to walk with me.

Is it possible for me to imagine that at night, as I am walking alone on a dark road, perhaps burdened by the cares of this world, Christ is *really* walking with me? Could this thought then replace the more familiar modern theological notion that in the midst of such an experience it is *as if* Christ were walking with me? Could it be, more particularly, that Luther's reading of the ubiquity of Christ prepares us most helpfully to grasp what the classical Celtic saints and the African saints of the slavery era actually experienced, as their faith came to expression in testimonies such as these?[36]

During the time when I was most energetically engaged with the challenge of writing this book, my wife and I found some time to be away in rural, southwestern Maine, where we garden, under her guidance. One morning I awoke and soon discovered that something was wrong. I could not wake her. It turned out that she had suffered a stroke. She went into a coma for many hours. I was sure that we had lost her. And I waited. I have no idea why some people die or become profoundly disabled in such circumstances, and why some do not. As a pastor, I have been at the side of countless souls in such circumstances, many of whom died or were seriously disabled. And that is the kind of outcome that I expected, frankly. But after hours that seemed to have no end, and with superb medical care in two different hospitals, she opened her eyes and started to talk. Subsequently, she recovered fully.

This ordeal comes to mind here, because of what happened to me in midstream, when I was feeling that there was no hope for her to survive. A dear friend of mine of many years showed up in the emergency room in the rural hospital where my wife had first been taken. I told him the whole story, and then I threw my arms around him and began to sob. He held me until I stopped crying. In subsequent weeks, it dawned on me what had happened in that emergency room, as my wife lay in a coma. That was not just my dear friend embracing me in the midst of my distress; that was Christ Jesus who is always within me, below me, above me, never to part. But I needed that visit from the outside, by my friend, in order to reveal to me the One to whom I have always belonged. Experiences such as these over the years have made it all the easier for me to take seriously the theological vision of the ubiquity of Christ Jesus.

Implications for Understanding Christ's Presence with the Poor

Third, and also regarding a related theological and spiritual attractiveness of the christocentric argument I have been making: Does not this way of thinking about the ubiquitous Christ, present here and now, likewise make it possible for the biblical thought of *Christ's presence in and with the poor* to come alive existentially in a new way? Particularly, the powerful parable of Jesus recorded in Matthew 25:31-46, where we hear, in part: "for I was hungry and you gave me food, I was thirsty and you gave me something to drink, I was a stranger and you welcomed me, I was naked and you gave me clothing, I was sick and you took care of me, I was in prison and you visited me" (vv. 35-36). Is it not possible, with our theme of Christ's ubiquity in mind, to think of the *real presence* of Christ among the poor, suffering with them, empowering them, liberating them? Need we be satisfied with a reading of such texts as merely powerful *metaphorical* statements?

For thirteen years I served an inner-city congregation in one of the poorest neighborhoods of what was then the fourth poorest city in the nation, Hartford, Connecticut. For the welfare mothers with whom I worked, the presence of Christ in their lives was not a question for theological discussion. It was a matter of survival. I often encountered in those days one disappointment after another, one more failed struggle with a landlord and the rats and roaches in his or her apartments, one more pregnant teenager with no hope, one more experience of a newborn dying scarcely before he or she could breathe, one more Vietnam veteran dead or near-dead on the streets, lost to his family due to alcohol abuse and despair and his post-traumatic stress syndrome. And I encountered all this, and more like it, with a feeling of deep futility, frustration, anger, and, at times, hopelessness. But numbers of those welfare mothers were beautiful believers. However much they were shaken, broken, exploited, and bereaved, their "walking with the Lord," as they thought of it, never ceased to inspire them. And I, who could easily have lost all my faith, had I been in their places, saw Christ in their faces. Such experiences point us to the junction where the theology of nature and the theology of liberation not only meet but meet as allies. But this kind of discussion must be reserved for another place.

Implications for Discussions of Historical Evil

Fourth, what does an existential reading of Christ's omnipresence raise for the discussion of the "theodicy" issues that have emerged, understandably, with such urgency and fervor, in this era "after Auschwitz"? Horrible as the thought of Auschwitz is, as a matter of fact, that camp is also the symbol of the evils of an entire era. Looking back on the last one hundred years, from happenings like the trench warfare of World War I to the Holocaust and Hiroshima and Nagasaki and Biafra and the killing fields of Cambodia, Jürgen Moltmann, the great proponent of the "theology of hope," poignantly wrote: "What we suffered in the twentieth century, and are still suffering, is an apocalypse without hope, extermination without justification, pure pleasure in torture, rape, and murder."[37] In our era, we know the "theodicy question" (justifying the ways of God)—"How could God let the Holocaust happen?"—perhaps more trenchantly than many other eras have known it.[38] But, whatever the era, the profundity and impenetrability of the question remains the same. It probably can never satisfactorily be answered, short of the dawning of the eschaton. On the other hand, it may be possible to invoke the image of the cosmic Christ in order to help Christians to address the theodicy question at least in a fragmentary way, by helping them to envision God suffering, through Christ, with the godforsaken and those being murdered, in the midst of the unimaginable horrors of evils like the Holocaust.[39]

It was not until I was a college undergraduate, astoundingly, that this whole matter devolved upon my soul. I remember the year, it was the fall of 1954. I was sitting in a course on modern German history. The instructor began to speak about the horrors of the Holocaust and about the complicity of many "good Germans" in that catastrophe. He also showed brutal photographs of some of the camps, when they were being liberated. I, a young man of proud German heritage, on my way to becoming a pastor and teacher in the church of my forebears, had, shockingly, never heard of the Holocaust before! I slumped in my chair and began to weep, as silently as I could, so as not to disturb the hundred students or so in that lecture hall.

That moment of wrenching discovery has been with me ever since. I have heard several friends and acquaintances tell stories like this, too. I and countless others have never stopped asking the question, Where was God in those dark and demonic days during World War II? But a good pastor once said to me, even as he told me of his own grief that would not subside, that in those days, as in every other epoch, God was *on the cross*. I have never forgotten those words. This is why I dare to suggest that the confession of the omnipresent Christ, suffering with the afflicted everywhere, is worth pondering anew, in the midst of our grief over the shrieking evils of this world. This kind of broken image, which is surely not for interfaith discussions with our Jewish brothers and sisters but only for cautious exploration among the members of the assembly, might have some scintilla of meaning for the theodicy discussion among Christians.[40]

Implications for Reclaiming the Witness of the Great Gothic Cathedrals

Fifth and finally, regarding a particular internal issue that emerges from the foregoing discussion of the gothic vision: As we think how the theology of descent can and should so thoroughly be allowed to transvalue the gothic vision, *what about the great gothic cathedrals themselves*? To put the question sharply and perhaps ungratefully: If, as I have argued, the theology of *ascent* and what might be called the mystique of the gothic heights should no longer shape the Christian mind and heart, of what use are those magnificent soaring cathedral structures anymore? Are they now to be regarded, perhaps like the pyramids, as beautiful but no longer living testimonies of a bygone age? By no means.

Think of John Constable's striking 1825 painting *Salisbury Cathedral, From the Bishop's Grounds* (a representation of which is found on this book's cover). Is that magnificent church structure in the painting any less compelling because we now see it, with Constable, in perspective, from a distance, framed by cathedral-like trees? If what we know of God in the assembly in the power of the Spirit is that the descending and overflowing goodness of God fills all things, and that the resurrected and ascended Christ is likewise in, with, and under all things, should we begrudge God's generosity for overflowing not only upon that cathedral and its assembly with the descending light of God's glory, but also upon the surrounding human city and its "landscape?" Are not those trees charged with the glory of God?

Is the beauty of that cathedral and its assembly in its civic and natural settings any less, moreover, if we allow our imaginations not only to see that much, but also some of the wild regions of the earth, beyond the placid image of Constable's painting and beyond the shores of insular England—such as the vast and tempestuous seas, attested powerfully by J. M. W. Turner in his painting from the early 1840s, *Stormy Sea Breaking On a Shore*? Turner himself, strikingly, wrote a poem about the winds of an ocean storm "howling the wild west with boisterous sweep" as they

"Lash the rude shore that rising from the deep . . . Presents . . . A Power supreme on the upmost stones."[41]

And still more. Is the glory of that great cathedral in Salisbury and its assembly diminished at all, if, in addition to seeing everything else, the wild seas included, we also search with our eyes at night to contemplate, hovering all around and beyond that cathedral, the infinitely expanding spheres of the heavens, as Vincent Van Gogh's much-revered, but still profoundly moving 1889 painting, *Starry Night,* leads us to do, where we see the high steeple of the church virtually drowned by that brilliant night? Cannot the eyes of the cathedral assembly, enlightened by the descending light of God, thus in faith *see through* the walls and the towers and the roofing of that magnificent cathedral to contemplate a much more encompassing cosmic vision, as the prophet Isaiah did, in the midst of the ancient Temple, when he proclaimed, "Holy, holy, holy is the LORD of hosts; the whole earth is full of his glory" (Isa. 6:3)?

The reader may wish to keep this thought of *the spiritual transparency of the reclaimed gothic cathedral* in mind, as we now begin to explore how the assembly that dwells in such charged spaces and the central rite that it there enacts, the liturgy, can be renewed by the theology of descent.

7

Baptism, Proclamation, Offertory: Framed by the Theology of Descent

Even if, on a good day, I, for one, can experience intimations of eschatological peace as I saunter along the Charles River, how can I sustain that experience in a world that, sadly, seems to have run amok so thoroughly? Even more, how can I live that experience, in deed as well as in word? For people like me who are struggling to believe and to live faithfully, it all depends on entering into the midst of assemblies like those I have described—along the Charles, in Southern Africa, Holden Village, or Roxbury, among others.

But that, frankly, is not enough—in practice. The liturgical practices shaping such assemblies, must *themselves* be renewed, if eschatological hope is to be sustained and fostered and if nature, in particular, is to be ritualized in peace by that same hope. This, then, is the very practical question before us in this chapter and the next. How can liturgical practices be shaped in order to embody and indeed to celebrate eschatological peace for the whole creation?

I will suggest that it all hinges on letting the theology of descent frame our liturgical practices, since the liturgy is the assembly's mode of identity formation. The image of framing is appropriate here. I will employ it in terms of the theory of "root metaphors," fundamental metapoetic, even subliminal, cognitive lenses that reveal and define a field of knowing.[1] The root metaphor before us here is the image of descending a mountain, which I have called discursively the theology of descent. This theology encourages us to envision God cascading down, like a mountain river, into all things, binding them together and calling forth growth. It points us to God, working the divine purposes in, with, and under the whole creation. What, then, does the liturgy look like when we let it be framed by this lens?

Obviously, our explorations of the liturgy in this context will have to be probative, rather than conclusive, since we are here concerned with the vital heart of the assembly's life. The scope and practice of the assembly's liturgy are just too much for us to explore thoroughly in the space available to us. My purpose here, therefore, will be to say enough to indicate how the practices of the liturgy can be shaped so as to incorporate themes pertaining to God and the whole creation, to nature as well as to human history and the history of the church, all framed by the theology of divine descent, with the ultimate goal being to make it possible for the faithful to ritualize nature. In these considerations, I will, for convenience's and relevance's sake, work with those ritual elements (that aforementioned *ordo* of the liturgy) that are in evidence in many, if not all, liturgical churches today.

I will begin by considering *baptism* as the entranceway to the liturgy and then explore the *rite of the Word or proclamation*, which is the first major movement of the liturgy itself, and next the *offertory*, which responds to and recapitulates that first movement. In the following chapter I will consider the *Eucharist* and *the sending*, attending every step of the way to implications of this ritual process for our encounter with nature, whether it be with the lilies of the field, the farms that bless us with the fruits of the earth, the architecture of our church buildings, the streets of our violent cities, or the cosmic conundrums of dark matter.

Baptism and Gathering in a Cosmic Setting

The ancient church testified to the cosmic meanings of baptism in numerous ways, especially in the architecture of baptisteries.[2] Often those freestanding structures were designed to image-forth the whole cosmos, with domed ceilings, for example, representing the heavens. Their octagonal shapes, moreover, told the story of the universal history of salvation, for all who had eyes to see. The "eighth day" of creation, was, for the ancient Christian mind, the day of the resurrection, the restoration and the perfection of the whole creation, first shaped by the Creator through a history of seven days.

Recent church architecture has tended, properly, to move in the direction of restoring that kind of cosmic symbolism for the baptismal font, through the introduction of living waters in some magnitude, by the incorporation of cosmic imagery on the font and its setting, with the placement of appropriate plants adjacent to the font, and by the location of fonts near or at the center of the public liturgical action.[3] Some fonts have been constructed large enough for immersions or submersions, "large enough to drown in," as liturgical scholar Richard Giles has pointedly observed. All of which encourages a reaffirmation of biblical motifs, from the waters of chaos and death to the waters of deliverance and renewal of the earth, focusing on and illuminating believers' dying and rising with Christ. But generally, it would appear, those suggestive architectural expressions have not been maximized as they might have been in any architecturally consistent fashion in our era. Still, what cannot be accomplished in structures that cannot be rebuilt, or instituted in new structures, for all manner of architectural or financial reasons, can surely be accomplished in the baptismal rite itself, with the ample use of water, with a baptismal prayer of cosmic amplitude, and with other appropriate liturgical enactments, such as enhanced musical settings.

The celebratory baptismal prayer offered in the *Lutheran Book of Worship* offers us one good verbal expression of these ritual meanings.[4] Notwithstanding certain limitations, in particular its muted eschatological witness, this is a powerfully suggestive cosmic prayer. It celebrates "the mighty acts of God" in creation, redemption, and consummation, culminating with its understated but evident witness to the gloriously universal reign of God that is yet to be fully realized. The heritage of this prayer is ecumenical. It stems from Luther's memorable "Flood Prayer" of 1523, which was also adopted by Huldrich Zwingli in 1525 and by Thomas Cranmer in the 1549 *Book of Common Prayer*.[5]

> Holy God, mighty Lord, gracious Father: We give you thanks, for in the beginning your Spirit moved over the waters and you created heaven and earth. By the gift of water you nourish and sustain us and all living things.
>
> By the waters of the flood you condemned the wicked and saved those whom you had chosen, Noah and his family. You led Israel by the pillar of cloud and fire through the sea, out of slavery into the freedom of the promised land. In the waters of the Jordan your son was baptized by John and anointed with the Spirit. By the baptism of his own death and resurrection your beloved Son

has set us free from bondage to sin and death, and has opened the way to the joy and freedom of everlasting life. He made water a sign of the kingdom and of cleansing and rebirth. In obedience to his command, we make disciples of all nations, baptizing them in the name of the Father, and of the Son, and of the Holy Spirit.

But anecdotal evidence suggests, sadly, that even in congregations that do have access to baptismal prayers of such cosmic plenitude, the use of those prayers is minimized—often for reasons of "saving time." Thereby the salvation brought by the One who has saved all of time is minimized and marginalized, in favor of other atheological and mundane concerns.[6]

Would that the church of our time could hearken back to the days of the great bronze-based pools of water placed centrally in the ancient temple precincts of the Hebrew people, where issues of chaos and cosmos, nonbeing and being, death and life, were evidently at stake. Would that the church could set aside creatively envisioned, centrally stationed (in the "Welcome Center"?) baptismal spaces, akin to the freestanding baptistries of old that were shaped and permeated by cosmic symbolism. Would that worshipers would be encouraged to touch the waters and make the sign of the cross whenever they enter, and to give knowledgeable consideration to baptism by immersion or even submersion for themselves or their children. Would that church musicians today could be encouraged to create dramatic works for the sake of baptismal liturgies, giving expression to the cosmic plenitude of the death and resurrection of Christ: works that tell of cacophonic thunder and lightning, reminiscent of Psalm 29, and also of the halcyon harmonies of the whole creation, reminiscent of Psalm 104. Would that priests and pastors could have the liturgical imagination to find ways to draw on such creations in order to enhance baptismal liturgies, precisely for the sake of saving time.

Some congregations and their pastoral leaders have found a way to move toward this kind of rich baptismal ritualization by instituting or reemphasizing the importance of the traditional Easter Vigil. That rite tells the whole history of creation, salvation, and consummation with lavish biblical readings and dramatic baptismal themes, culminating in a eucharistic celebration which is explicitly and thoroughly rooted in that grand narrative.[7] In the Easter Vigil, when it is announced, "He is risen!" the participants know, or can know, the resurrection of the Lord as the fulfillment and the consummation of the whole divine plan, purpose, and providence, and understand baptism in that setting, as well, as tangible incorporation into that divine history.

But baptism, however important it is, by no means stands alone. It is the doorway to the entire liturgy. It is the way through which people proceed to gather for Word and meal. In ancient Christian times this sacramental reality was literally enacted, as those who were baptized on Easter Eve in the Vigil then made their way from freestanding baptistries into the sanctuary to participate, for the first time, in the full liturgy. Over time, to be sure, a range of other ritual practices has grown up in place of this, the most fundamental entrance rite. In recent years, however, under the influence of the movement for liturgical renewal, the baptismal focal point of all entrance rites has rightfully been reemphasized, not only by the placement of fonts in prominent public places but by the literal use of the font to allow worshipers to touch the waters upon entering the sanctuary and to make the sign of the cross, reminding themselves of that baptismal passageway into the liturgy. Some assemblies, as we will see concretely in a moment, literally begin their liturgies with the people gathered at the baptismal font. Baptism, thus, in addition to everything else, means the gathering of the faithful, to proclaim and acclaim the Word and to celebrate the meal.[8]

The Cosmic Word:
Narrating the Whole Gospel Preferentially

From the earliest times in the history of the church known to us, the liturgy has been a composite rite. By a historical process that is even now, after more than a half-century of meticulous study, not fully understood, scriptural and prayer rites, similar to practices in Jewish synagogues of the time, were adjoined with the meal rites that the early Christian assemblies inherited from the circle of disciples around Jesus. These meal rites were also shaped, in some measure, by the meal practices of the Hellenistic and Jewish cultures around them. The composite word-and-meal rites were, as a matter of course, also set in a ritual milieu of hymns and other utterances of prayer and praise. So in the letter to the Ephesians, the Pauline author wrote: ". . . be filled with the Spirit, as you sing psalms and hymns and spiritual songs among yourselves, singing and making melody to the Lord in your hearts . . ." (Eph. 5:18-19).

Here we take the time to review the ministry of the Word in the liturgy, a subject under-regarded by some liturgical practitioners, given their understandable eagerness to explore the rich meanings of the Eucharist. I am particularly interested in the countercultural and cosmic scope of this ministry, although I must acknowledge, too, that this is a ministry that does not always flourish in practice. It is easy to caricature the state of preaching in American liturgical churches today.

The caricature derives from the tendency in some liturgical churches to downplay the import of proclamation, for a variety of reasons, resulting in the degeneration of preaching. The sermon becomes a "homily," spiritual instruction for the soul or ritual instruction about the liturgy or mission instruction about reaching out to the unchurched or moral instruction about some good cause. Further, good and solid biblically inspired proclamation takes time. But pragmatic, on-the-go American worshipers often assume that time is one "commodity"—a telling thought—that they do not have enough of. Hence, there is pressure on preachers from their congregants "to get to the meat of things"—an expression I have heard on numerous occasions—that is, to the Eucharist itself. Sometimes pressure is even brought on the preacher to cancel the sermon, say, if there is "too much music" on any given day (for instance, if the liturgy of the day is a Rutter mass, with much choral music).

Popular writers about the art of homiletics bring an additional kind of pressure to bear on preachers. These writers point out that the attention span of our TV-dominated era is no longer than a few minutes. Hence, preachers are told in so many words to speak as briefly as possible. In response to such demands, some preachers experiment with "different ways to reach people," as quickly and as dramatically as possible. They leave the pulpit and wander around the sanctuary, for example, talking eyeball to eyeball with congregants in their pews, and in so doing sometimes call more attention to themselves than to the Word they are proclaiming. Or they tell stories, from literature, TV, films, or, more often, from their own experience, with the result that the congregants may well remember those stories well and perhaps be moved by some of them, while the biblical point of the stories they may or may not even recall, never mind take to heart.

Perhaps most seriously, numerous preachers today seem to have succumbed to the "triumph of the therapeutic" (Philip Rieff) in American society. This culture centers on the conflicted individual. What matters is whether this individual can find "healing" or "wholeness." With this trend, traditional ideas of sin, grace, and discipleship give way to the idea that what is of value is the healing and the self-realization of the individual. Christians whose lives have been so shaped by this culture then, as a matter of course, approach the preacher with the question, "Can you meet my needs?"

American preaching, as a result, especially in Protestant circles, where the individual and his or her direct converse with God has long been a high, if not the chief, value, has been sorely tempted, at least since World War II—and probably since the emergence of revivalism as a dominant force in American life—to focus the individual's self-perceived needs, chiefly, if not exclusively. From a Norman Vincent Peale fifty years ago to the still flourishing ministry of a Robert Schuller at the turn of our century, numerous American preachers have been preoccupied with offering individual "positive," self-help, and self-improvement strategies to their congregants (and TV audiences) for coping with the stresses of modern life. That this very focus of American preaching has sometimes been cloaked more recently, especially in more liturgical churches, in the guise of the quest for a new spirituality, has not radically altered such trends.

This caricature is valuable, insofar as it helps to set the vocation of the American preacher today in clear relief. And it is clear to me, on the basis of many travels around the country and of frequent opportunities to hear preachers in a variety of settings, that significant numbers of American liturgical preachers today are eager, not to say desperate, to avoid the caricature and, instead, to heed their calling. What is that calling? I want to highlight two indicators of that calling that are particularly important in the context of our explorations here: to guard the counterculture preferentially and to tell the whole, cosmic story.

Preaching the Word:
Guarding the Counterculture Preferentially

Not for nothing did the ancient prophet say to the religious establishment of his own time, with reference to the great rituals of the Temple, addressing the people in the words of the Lord: "I hate, I despise your festivals, and I take no delight in your solemn assemblies. . . . Take away from me the noise of your songs; I will not listen to the melody of your harps. But let justice roll down like waters, and righteousness like an ever-flowing stream" (Amos 5:21, 23-24). Preaching, when it is biblical, frames the liturgical life of the assembly within those parameters. Preaching, when it is right, reminds the assembly of its countercultural heritage, how it is an equalitarian community that from the very beginning mixed water with wine and saw visions of a new heavens and a new earth, how it is a single-minded community that from the very beginning had one Lord, and rejected all the totalizing claims of the lords of this world. Preaching, when it is faithful, announces that everything in the life of the assembly must be tested by the divine demand for justice for the poor and the oppressed.

This mandate has been clarified and reenforced in our time especially by Latin American liberation theologians, although it is as ancient as biblical prophecy, as the words of Amos indicate; and it is as solidly traditional as the claims of Catholic social teaching during the last one hundred years also show. In its most concise form, this mandate is called "the preferential option for the poor."[9] This does not mean that the gospel is not good news for all, although that is what the "elder brothers," as in Jesus' parable of the prodigal son, sometimes prefer to hear. On the contrary, all are offered the forgiveness of sins, life, and salvation (Luther), those who are near, like the elder brother, and those who are far, like the prodigal son. The preferential option for the poor simply means that the assembly always stands on the side of those who have been excluded from their fair share in the commonwealth of God's good creation, the downtrodden, not the powerful, for their need is the greatest: in keeping with the Magnificat of Mary, recorded in Luke: "My soul magnifies the Lord, and my spirit rejoices in God my Savior. . . . His mercy is for those who fear him from generation to generation. . . . He has brought down the powerful from their thrones, and lifted up the lowly; he has filled the hungry with good things, and sent the rich away empty . . ." (Luke 1:46-55). This means, further, that the assembly, when it is true to its countercultural heritage, gives its highest priority to "hearing the voice of the voiceless" and making that voice its own, in worship and in every act of public witness.

It is critically important for preachers in America today self-consciously to keep the option for the poor in mind as they proclaim the gospel, first for what I take to be the obvious reason that many American assemblies today are gatherings of people who are rich, by any reasonable global standards. But more to the point with regard to the theology of nature: this is one of the most ideologically charged themes of our time.[10] Nature has functioned in American history in significant ways as a great escape mechanism for the wealthy. "Getting back to nature," whether in terms of contemplating the wilderness or of finding a tranquil place in some idealized agricultural setting or gated community, has functioned to keep Christians' (and others') minds and hearts away from confronting the plight of the poor and the homeless and the polluted in our society, especially in urban areas.

At the same time, many American Christians have found it easy to succumb to an ideology of human domination over nature, as well, blessed by an ideological reading of the biblical theme of dominion. The result has been that they have, by default, supported the degradation of nature and the resultant dispossession or poisoning of the poor which frequently accompanies that kind of degradation. Especially when it comes to discourse about nature, therefore, preachers who serve the renewed liturgy must constantly be willing to speak the hard words of biblical prophecy, to say no to injustice as well as yes to nature. In this respect especially, they must constantly guard the "counter" of the assembly's countercultural liturgy. They must preach preferentially.

Preaching the Whole Story: The Cosmic Word Made Flesh

Of course, announcing the yes of the gospel is the end goal of all preaching. Preachers will, as a matter of course, be eager to "tell the old, old story, of Jesus and his love," as the hymn of our forebears says, and do so in a way that overcomes many, if not all, of the aforementioned obstacles. They will do this, hopefully, not only with great gifts and deep understanding but with what might be called an appropriate evangelical stubbornness. They will indeed implicitly, if not explicitly, honor the theological conviction of Martin Luther that proclaiming the Word of God communicates the *real presence* of Jesus Christ, the same real presence that the assembly encounters in the Eucharist. This is Luther:

> When you open the book containing the gospels and read or hear how Christ comes here or there, or how someone is brought to him, you should therein perceive the sermon or the Gospel through which he is coming to you, or you are being brought to him. For the preaching of the Gospel is nothing else than Christ coming to us, or we being brought to him.[11]

In the I-Thou relationship of preaching, the hearer encounters the real Christ, who arrives to grant the hearer what Luther also refers to, as we have seen many times, as "the forgiveness of sins, life, and salvation."

But good preachers will also do more. The proclamation of the Word is also an I-Thou encounter between the preacher and the *community*. "Preaching," Gordon Lathrop instructively writes, "is an assembly-based event. . . . It is an expression of the faith of the assembly, in communion with the faith of the whole church, spoken for the purpose of grounding the community once again in the faith."[12] This means that when the preacher tells "the old, old story of Jesus and his love," he or she will also tell the community's story about the love of Jesus which is the fulfillment and the consummation of all God's ancient promises, which story the community itself is called to proclaim and to embody.

What is needed today, therefore, if the liturgy is to be renewed according to the canons of the theology of the descent of God, particularly in terms of the omnipresence of the risen and ascended Christ, is not only the proclamation of the Gospel to individuals in the community but the proclamation of the Gospel to the community itself: that is, telling the *whole* old, old story. Call this holistic narrative preaching. Following the example of Paul, this kind of preaching recapitulates the entire biblical story, from creation through redemption to the consummation of all things, in every sermon, at least implicitly.[13] It may be as simple as announcing that "Jesus is risen."[14] It may be as complex as exploring Paul's proclamation in Romans 8:22 that "the whole creation is groaning in travail." But however simple or however complex, for this kind of preaching, the burden of proof is on the shoulders of the preacher to be able to say, if asked, and to say with conviction and knowledge, how his or her particular sermon on any given day illuminates the whole biblical narrative, from Genesis to Revelation, for the people.

Moreover, good preachers will be particularly mindful of eschatological meanings that are the capstone of holistic narrative preaching. To that end, exegetical and theological riches abound in our day. What were a relatively few insightful studies of biblical eschatology only a few years ago, and what was a relatively new "school" in eschatological theology during the second half of the last century, has now grown to be a commanding theological movement in our time.[15]

The Word of the Sermon and the Word in the Liturgy

To be sure, the sermon does not stand alone. The universal vision of God-with-us in creation and redemption and consummation of the universe must be narrated throughout the entire liturgy. This narration takes the concrete form of the proclamation of the cosmic Word of God, in, with, and under those ritual actions that are the formative sacramental ministrations of the church's life, baptism and Eucharist, as well as in those focal moments that are given over to preaching the selfsame Word. In most classical expressions of the church's liturgy, indeed, virtually every word is a word from Holy Scripture. Hence the whole liturgy is one grand proclamation of the Word of God.

In these times of ecological and social disruption, however, the classic narrative flow of the liturgy should not simply be allowed to "take care of itself," as it is handed down from generation to generation, however replete it might be, and is, with testimonies from the Word of God. There is ample evidence, indeed, that the Scripture texts that have been traditionally read as part of the church's yearly liturgical cycle, have typically *not* been chosen to give voice to the universality of the cosmic faith celebrated by the Scriptures: to announce the God who is always God-with-us, in the creation and consummation of all things, as well as in human redemption.

Today's liturgy therefore urgently requires imaginative interventions on the part of its theological and pastoral leaders—hopefully in concert with many ecumenical partners. Some have already experimented, for example, with the introduction of a "creation-cycle" of lectionary readings during four to six weeks of the Pentecost/Ordinary Time season of the church year, typically during the fall (in the northern hemisphere), highlighting harvest themes wherever appropriate and overlapping the feast day of St. Francis.[16] Prophetic texts, which bespeak the renewal of both society and nature, and which especially highlight new creational blessings for the poor must as a matter of course, also, be part of this renewed lectionary. Likewise for the prayers of the people: liturgical leaders attuned to these issues will make sure that the whole narrative which they proclaim in their sermons and which is made more vivid by strategic and sensitive revisions of the lectionary will also be reflected when the assembly prays. Why not so shepherd the prayers of the people so that every Sunday at least one petition addresses, in some manner, the groaning of the whole creation and the trials and tribulations of earth's biosphere in particular?[17]

But much still depends on the faithful labors of those called to proclaim the gospel. Unless the preachers of the church persistently and imaginatively and forcefully tell the cosmic story of faith in their sermons and in their teaching, the whole case for a liturgy that is ecologically and socially formative, according to the cosmic Word of God, could easily be lost.[18] The faithful need to hear the whole biblical story told and retold in this manner so that they can see with new eyes the ministrations of the cosmic Word of God in their own midst, especially in the sacraments of baptism and Eucharist, and know, too, that it is Christ himself who addresses them in the proclaimed Word. Then, hopefully, they will also realize that that very Word of God is addressing them in all the particular proclamations of the cosmic Word which the liturgy announces.

No less important, that proclamation must announce to the members of the assembly, implicitly and explicitly, that, when they go forth from the gathered community to witness to the gospel and live according to it where they find themselves during the week, they are not going forth into some alien, godforsaken world. They are, to be sure, going out into a world dominated by the principalities of Death and destruction, against which they will be unable to stand, by their own strength. But they can be encouraged to depend on Christ to go before them and to be where they are going before they arrive. United with Christ, by the power of the Spirit, they can be promised they will discover that they are in truth going forth into *God's* good creation, where they can encounter the very same Jesus Christ whom they encountered in the Word and in the Eucharist also in their weekday experience, in, with, and under the impoverished neighborhoods or the affluent high-rises where they live or work, or in, with, and under the vision of the rainbow that on a given day seems to hover miraculously over a troubled city.

The Proclamation and the Acclamation of the Cosmic Word

While the details of the origins of the composite word-and-meal rite are still somewhat obscure, it is possible to discern an underlying rationale, theologically, for what finally emerged in the early Christian centuries and beyond in the *ordo* of the liturgy that we have already discussed. This process of discernment will lead us, in a certain sense, "beneath the texts" that reveal the constellation of ritual elements to us. This is a process of "faith seeking understanding" (*fides quaerens intellectum*), a kind of theological reflection self-consciously familiar in the theological tradition at least since the time of Anselm in the Middle Ages. I want to pursue that process now, specifically with regard to the "word" moments of the composite word-and-meal rite of the earliest Christian assemblies.

My presupposition is that the preaching and the teaching of the Word in those assemblies always took, in intention, if not in fact, the form of an I-Thou relationship between the preachers and the other members of those assemblies.[19] It is relatively easy to make this assumption, notwithstanding the absence of a range of data about Christian preaching in the first century, its practitioners, its audience, and its settings, once we recall, with Alexander Olivar, that "it is likely that the New Testament sprang from early Christian preaching rather than the other way around."[20] Hence, while we can surely learn some things from the "sermons" we have in Acts (more perhaps about Luke's purposes and Luke's theology), we can, in principle, learn much more about early Christian preaching, by inference, from the New Testament as a whole. Thus, an I-Thou form of communication is already evident in the theology of friendship attested by the Gospel of John, where Jesus speaks of his disciples as his "friends" (John 15:15). The same kind of theology is announced by Paul in his letter to the Galatians, when he rejects hierarchical (I-It) relationships, and proclaims that all, slave and free, male and female, Jew and Greek, are one in Christ Jesus (Gal. 3:26ff.). Behind all this lies the practices of Jesus himself, as they are attested in the New Testament.

Jesus' characteristic mode of public communication, as we know it in the Gospels, was parabolic, a kind of teaching that was projected in order to elicit a personal response. And while his self-proclamation was powerful, as the Johannine "I am" sayings show (for instance, "I am the bread of life," John 6:35), that self-proclamation always remained dialogical, as the great confessional text of Peter in Matthew indicates. Jesus asks Peter who people say that he is for a reason: "Who do people say that I am?" (Matt. 16:13). Jesus evidently wants Peter to entrust his life to Jesus personally. Jesus is asking Peter to offer himself unreservedly to him as the Messiah. But Jesus will not do this arbitrarily or heteronomously (Tillich), as if Jesus were some alien, authoritarian other. He will not, in effect, make any disciple into an "It." Jesus always speaks to others as "I" to "Thou." The capstone of this New Testament theology of relationality, is surely Jesus' proclamation in the Gospel of John, already referred to, about his friendship with the disciples: "I do not call you servants [Gk.: slaves] any longer, because the servant does not know what the master is doing; but I have called you friends . . ." (John 15:15).

Nor should we overlook the wealth of information that we have about the relationship between Paul, in particular, and the assemblies to which he wrote with such passion and, often, with such intense affection. These were letters that were intended to be read in public ecclesial gatherings, as if Paul were standing there himself. While they presuppose what might be called a certain dialectical shrewdness, insofar as they praise intended hearers, perhaps in order to soften their hearts so that they will all the more eagerly receive the message communicated, Paul's address to those assemblies was surely shaped by the canons of friendship, too, as in 1 Corinthians 15:58: "Therefore, my beloved, be steadfast, immovable, always excelling in the work of the Lord, because you know that in the Lord your labor is not in vain." Likewise for the picture of early Christian community life that Paul communicates in 2 Corinthians 13:11-12: "Finally, brothers and sisters, farewell. Put things in order, listen to my appeal, agree with one another, live in peace; and the God of love and peace will be with you. Greet one another with a holy kiss. All the saints greet you."

If the ethos of friendship, rather than domination, was supposed to shape everything else in the early Christian assembly, and if, more particularly, the relationship between the proclaimer and the other members of the assembly was assumed to be, as a matter of course, an I-Thou relationship (and there is no reason to think that it was anything else), then we can gain some insight into those early Christian word rites, because we know something about the nature of I-Thou relationships. According to the canons of I-Thou relationships, the address of an I to a Thou typically elicits a response, appropriate to the address. Hence, we can surmise that that originating *proclamation* of the Word typically elicited an *acclamation* of the Word, by the hearers. Which, of course, in a certain sense is to state the obvious, since it appears that those word rites were typically set in the context of hymns and songs of praise and even charismatic utterances. For this reason, theologians in the twentieth century like Emil Brunner and Karl Barth typically thought of the proclamation of the Word in terms of "Word and response" (*Wort und Antwort*). Or call it, underlining terms that I prefer: *proclamation* and *acclamation*. Luther himself had set the stage for such affirmations with his own theology of the Word in worship. So the reformer once observed, at the dedication of a new sanctuary, that

Christ himself speaks to us "through his holy Word and we respond to him through prayer and praise."[21]

These reflections, however, as faith seeking understanding, could be misleading, apart from a further clarification. The canons of the I-Thou relationship, especially as they were identified by Buber, presuppose that that kind of mutual relationality, coming to expression in speech, is always *embodied*. Not for nothing did Buber himself write a short poetic essay entitled "Brother Body." Further, the Hebraic inheritance in the earliest Christian assemblies was strong. While many of the members of those assemblies lived in a Hellenistic culture that presupposed a thoroughgoing body-soul dualism—even to the point, as in some forms of Gnosticism, of a dualism that denigrated the body entirely—early Christian communities of which we know appear to have presupposed a view of the human that was strongly shaped by Old Testament traditions, which took the human body with utmost seriousness.[22] Hence, the early Christian emphasis on the resurrection of the body was a nonnegotiable confession of faith for those communities. So Paul could as a matter of course invoke the images of the liturgy, and urge the Roman church: ". . . by the mercies of God, to present your bodies as a living sacrifice to God, which is your spiritual worship" (Rom. 12:1).

In our quest to grasp something of the underlying theological logic of the early Christian community's word rites, therefore, we will have good reason to presuppose that the I-Thou communication of proclamation and acclamation in that community was a communication that presupposed and indeed accented the bodily dimensions of both the speaking and the responses. I want to identify some implications of these findings now, with regard to that ritual action of response on the part of the worshipers traditionally called "the Offertory."

The Offertory as Embodied Response to the Cosmic Word Made Flesh

The great German philosopher of history G. W. F. Hegel once uttered this aphorism: "The owl of Minerva does not take to flight until the dusk has come." Which is to say: we cannot understand historical trends of which we are a part; but we can understand historical trends, retrospectively, once they have run their course. I have suggested above that such retrospective understanding of the word rite of the liturgy is possible. Although the *ordo* of the liturgy in its earliest expressions was fluid in character and multiformed, the method of faith seeking understanding can allow us to grasp *why* the liturgy evolved as it did, at least with regard to some of its major features. The fact that the word rite came to be followed, over the centuries of liturgical history, by "the Offertory" on the way to the eucharistic meal, I believe, is one of those instances.

This was the underlying liturgical logic: The Word announces the gospel, that Jesus is risen, in fulfillment of God's original intentions for the whole creation and in order to inaugurate the coming of the new creation, and that, as a result, those who believe now receive "the forgiveness of sins, life, and salvation." The Word, as the address of an "I" to a "Thou," then as a matter of course elicits a response from those hearers who believe, and since the Word itself communicated hope and peace for the whole world and the forgiveness of sins, life, and salvation for all who hear it, that response of those who receive it in faith is, as a matter of course, *gratitude.*

Concretely, therefore, the underlying liturgical logic elicits this ritual sequence: the proclamation of the Word in the liturgy is followed by the Offertory of the people, according to the pattern of address and response (*Wort und Antwort*) or proclamation and acclamation. The Offertory, according to this logic, is a profound act of thanksgiving on the part of all the people.

Picture this. In response to the proclamation of the gospel, the people sing hymns of thanksgiving and confess the faith of their hearts in a great ecumenical credo such as the Nicene Creed. The people also give thanks to God by giving of themselves, sharing themselves, as they greet one another in peace. Soon the floodgates of thanksgiving are opened in the form of a procession that flows through the midst of the people toward the table of the Lord. Those in the procession carry gifts that are given by all, the bread and the wine, the first fruits of God's good creation, financial gifts from all the people to support the life and mission of the assembly, food perhaps offered in thanksgiving for the bounty of the good creation and to be shared with the poor, even gifts reflecting the particular thanksgiving of members of the assembly, a painting perhaps or a sheaf of poems. Such a procession might be led by dancers from the assembly, offering their bodies as a living sacrifice to God, recalling the testimony of the apostle Paul (Rom. 12:2).

Something like this picture of the Offertory can be witnessed in many assemblies today. But our ecumenical churches did not arrive at this fullness of self-offering in the Offertory without considerable soul searching. It is especially important for liturgical leaders to understand this sometimes painful process of growth in liturgical celebration, so that the end result can be more firmly established. Hence, I want to review some moments in the history of the Offertory itself so we can better consider the promise it holds for us.

The Offertory as a liturgical enactment has had an uncertain and, in some ways, a peripheral history. In the second century, the anti-Gnostic bishop and theologian Irenaeus relates giving of "first fruits" of the material creation to Jesus' institution of the Eucharist, and then comments, presumably with the Gnostic rejection of the material order in mind: "the Lord instructed his disciples to offer first fruits to God from his own creatures, not because God needed them, but so that they themselves might not be unfruitful or ungrateful."[23] But Irenaeus, unfortunately, does not develop those thoughts at length. Notwithstanding the absence of any thorough theological rationale, however, by the time of the late-patristic church in the West, according to Robert Jenson, the practice of the Offertory itself had developed richly: "The Offertory was a splendid event. The people brought their gifts in kind: bread, wine, and produce. From these, sufficient bread and wine were taken for the supper; the rest was later distributed to the poor."[24] A mosaic on the floor of the fourth-century Basilica of Aquileia in northern Italy shows that these gifts were sometimes rich and elaborate indeed: grapes, wine, birds, fruit, wool, oil, honey, olives, cheese, silver, and gold.[25]

By the late Middle Ages, however, Jenson observes, since so-called private masses came to be the dominant form of the Eucharist, there was no one to bring gifts! So the Offertory more or less was pushed to the margins. And that process then influenced public masses, in turn. As a result, the Offertory became dysfunctional or it was swept up into a sacrificial theology of merits, announced in the late Middle Ages by then current forms of the eucharistic prayer.[26]

This was the phenomenon against which Martin Luther reacted so vehemently, the influx of the theology of merits into the heart of the Eucharist. Luther also reacted strongly, as Frank Senn observes, against the Offertory because it had become "the occasion for the paying of mass stipends for votive masses that would be offered for the benefit of the living and the dead."[27] This is why Luther once called the Offertory "that total abomination"![28] On the other hand, Luther was not an ideologue about the matter. While he rejected the late medieval approach to the Offertory, he by no means rejected the theological importance of offering as an element of the liturgy. Thus, at one point he asks: "What sacrifices, then, are we to offer?" This is his answer: "Ourselves, and all that we have, with constant prayer . . ."[29] And more specifically, regarding the eucharistic elements: "For the bread and wine are offered beforehand for blessing in order that they may be sanctified by the Word and by prayer, but after they have been blessed and consecrated they are no longer offered, but received as a gift from God."[30]

In ensuing centuries, numerous Protestant theologians took Luther's rejection of the Offertory for granted, while not attending much to Luther's thoughts about the importance of the offering of the faithful. Given these developments, and the marginal character of the Offertory in the history of the liturgy more generally, a number of liturgical theologians in recent years have argued that the Offertory should be abolished, either on the grounds that it is redundant and therefore superfluous, in light of the eucharistic prayer that is to come, or because the whole idea of the Mass itself as a sacrifice—offering anything to God—is suspect.[31]

In the last century, however, especially in the wake of the ecumenical movement for liturgical renewal, a number of Protestant communions have found ways to reintroduce the Offertory. In the American context, where churches are self-sustaining financially and not supported by the state, liturgical leaders have as a matter of course wanted to find a way to integrate the practice of "free-will offerings" into their worship practices. As a result, the historic accent on "collections for the poor" tended to be directed to a now, in this respect, reconfigured Offertory. And a new theological conceptuality took root in many communions, lifting up the need for members to give tithes for the sake of supporting the mission of the church and in order to respond to the needs of the poor. Countless books and pamphlets and sermons have been written and preached, therefore, announcing this new theology, under the rubric of "stewardship."[32] On the other hand, that trend has itself brought with it its own problems, particularly in money-conscious, middle-class American churches. A new kind of financial meritocracy has sometimes crept in the back door in Protestant communions especially, even as the meritocracy of works righteousness had been pushed out the front door.

Offertory practices today thus seem to be highly problematic, both in terms of their ambiguous history and their multivalent contemporary forms. The theological motives of those who seek to diminish the importance of the Offertory are, as those motives are typically given written expression, worthy of serious respect.[33] Still, it would be a great loss to the ecumenical church if the Offertory were to be abolished across the board or left to drift by itself, so to speak, without firm theological direction, for two reasons. First, the Offertory is, as we have seen, integrally related to the proclamation of the Word. To excise the Offertory would be to excise the appropriate ritual response to the Word of grace: thanksgiving. It would likewise undercut the I-Thou character of the proclamation-acclamation event. If the people cannot bespeak the gratitude in their hearts in response to the Word, sooner or later they will stop taking the Word to heart. Then it may happen that the Word, however powerfully proclaimed, will sail right over the heads of many hearers.

Second, the Offertory, rightly construed, can help to keep the liturgy rooted in the creation, reflecting both Irenaeus's anti-Gnostic insights and Luther's theology of the descent of God. This kind of emphasis on the offering, more particularly, can honor both the theology of the omnipresence of God and the ubiquitous Christ that so thoroughly shaped Luther's thinking and his rigorous accent on the free grace of God, while, at the same time, rejecting Luther's own rejection of the Offertory itself. Instructed by Irenaeus and the late-Western patristic example more generally and by Luther's own positive regard for the theme of offering, and then laying hold of the liturgical logic of the Offertory as a response to the proclamation, the Offertory, as an act of thanksgiving, can now and should now be celebrated, rather than denigrated. The Pauline theme of presenting our bodies to God as a living sacrifice, which is our rightful (we may translate) worship, suggests the promise of this way of thinking.

The Promise of the Offertory

This is the promise of the Offertory.[34] Claimed by the gospel, by the "hearing of faith" (Gal. 3:2), I rejoice that I am now a new creature, in hope and peace, and I give thanks. Restored to my rightful relationship to God, through Jesus Christ, in the power of the Spirit, I can now see the good creation in a new way, as Luther says:

Now if I believe in God's Son and bear in mind that he became man, all creatures will appear a hundred times more beautiful to me than before. Then I will properly appreciate the sun, the moon, the stars, trees, apples, pears, as I reflect that he is Lord over and the center of all things.[35]

So I am deeply grateful for this new world that I have received, through Jesus Christ, and I respond by offering my whole self to God, as the Spirit inspires me to do. I join with all other believers and "with the whole company of heaven" and with all the unfallen creatures of nature in their great song of praise of the Creator. I have nothing to offer to God, but I nevertheless offer myself and everything that I hitherto thought was mine to God. And, as I join with other members of the assembly, who are doing the same, the result can be a symphony of praise, a dance of thanksgiving, the deepest poetry of our souls. For *everyone* has something to offer.

Modern ears may not hear the radicalness of this claim. The minds and hearts of Protestants, in particular, have been shaped by the theology of the "priesthood of all believers" and American Protestants, still more particularly, have been deeply influenced by a pervasive and, some would say, problematic culture of individualism. Hence, Protestants, especially in America, tend to take it for granted that *everyone* has something to offer. But this kind of Protestant ethos more often than not masks profound divisions of race and class and gender. In the early Christian assemblies, in contrast, as Bernd Wannenwetsch reminds us, "worship includes in full participation all the representatives of the debased household: women, slaves, children, artisans, and so on—a reconciliation of hitherto unreconciled groups and realms of social life."[36] So, as Wannenwetsch explains, "it was all-important that every individual believer would bring forward his or her own oblation (offering). This implied a certain eucharistic 'egalitarianism' which was not only the result of the equality of reception (all share in the same gift) but was already indicated by a particular equality of action. . . ." Thus, "the have-nots of the papal school of orphans in Rome were not hidden away but brought the water that was to be mingled with the wine, while the bishop would not only offer all oblations on behalf of the whole body but also had to bring his own personal offering."[37] The Offertory thus was for the early church a tangible expression of the conviction that the whole liturgy is "the work of the people" and, as such, an expression, here and now, of life in the world to come.

The Offertory in contemporary practice can comprehend many things, including: confessional offerings of faith, in the words of the Apostolic or Nicene Creeds; communal offerings of prayer, incorporating the voices of all the people, wherever possible; sharing of the peace with brothers and sisters in Christ; offering of the "first fruits" of the creation, as Irenaeus suggested, in the forms of bread and wine and also, *mirabile dictu,* money.[38]

Money is a highly charged subject in most American congregations, so it is wise for us to consider it directly, although only a few words will have to suffice here. This "filthy lucre," the love of which is the root of all evil, has been made clean by the justifying grace of Jesus Christ. This money I bring, with others, into the center of the assembly as an offering to God, signifies that "the earth is the LORD's and all that is in it" (Ps. 24:1) that there is no such thing as something that belongs *to me.* This offering thus stands over against what my own culture has taught me to think of as "my money." The idea of me owning anything, as a matter of fact, whether it be property or money or anything else—or some other human being!—is an expression of my sin, not any divine mandate.[39] God has created me to be, not to have; to live, not to accumulate; to care, not to possess; to share, not to hoard. The good earth on which I am blessed to live is the commonwealth of my Creator and Redeemer, intended by this God as a blessing for all creatures, not just for a privileged few. It is a sinful act, an expression of will-to-power, to say or think "this is mine." The Offertory announces that truth as the underside of the people's expressed gratitude, since "every generous act of giving, with every perfect gift, is from above . . ." (James 1:17). The people thereby give thanks for all the gifts that they have received and all the gifts that they *will* receive.

That kind of future reference must be underlined. For it qualifies everything else. Some New Testament scholars have suggested, in this respect, that the proper translation of the petition for bread in the Lord's Prayer is eschatological: "Our bread for tomorrow give us today."[40] As the proclaimed Word brings the new creation of the end times close to the people here and now, so the people live, by anticipation, in that new creation, here and now, in response to the Word. This is why some congregations, like my own in Roxbury, have taken to "milling around in joy" during the passing of the peace, as playful children of the end times, and why they rightfully resist directives from anyone, however authoritative, to be more "serious" or "more respectful" at this point, as if they were always destined to be well-behaved, middle-class adults, rather than children of God. In a dramatically countercultural mode, the faithful, in offering their bodies to God as their rightful sacrifice, thus live in a world of eschatological sharing.

This is what the Offertory procession, in particular, announces powerfully. As that procession makes its way to the table, with all the people looking eagerly on, with representatives of all the faithful carrying bread and wine, the first fruits of God's good creation, which will become manna from the end times for all who feed on it, and other food and gifts for distribution to the poor, and money to support the mission of the assembly, perhaps led by dancers and surrounded by both instrumental and vocal songs of thanksgiving, the whole assembly "leans into" the end times and is, for that moment, a harbinger of the coming peaceable kingdom of God.[41]

8

Eucharist and Sending:
Framed by the Theology of Descent

With the people gathered, having entered through the baptismal passageway, and the Word thus proclaimed and acclaimed, it is time for the meal and then, finally, for the sending—all this framed, once again, by the theology of descent.[1] It is instructive, at the outset, to ponder the ritual movement to the meal, in particular, in order better to grasp the full meaning of the Eucharist, the central moment of the liturgy, and its particular ritualizing of nature. A renovated Episcopal cathedral in a historic American city tells this story visually, perhaps more powerfully than words could do.

The Ritual Movement to the Eucharist and Its Existential Logic

The Philadelphia Cathedral is a large Romanesque structure, rebuilt in 1906, following a fire, in the style of an early Christian basilica.[2] The bishop's chair and the seating for the priests (the presbytery) are against the east wall, not at the altar, signaling the role of those liturgical leaders as first among equals (*prima inter pares*), thus highlighting *the assembly* as the primary liturgical actor, rather than the priestly leaders. Recently the whole sanctuary space was imaginatively redesigned (completed in 2002), in order to accent the focal points of the whole liturgy. A large baptismal font stands before those who enter the building. Although both the pulpit/lectern (ambo) and the table are moveable, each one typically occupies its own distinct but prominent place in the sanctuary. This makes possible a "liturgy on the move," a liturgy that is designed itself to highlight the theme of "journey."

This is no insignificant architectural and liturgical achievement. Why? In the wake of the Reformation, preaching more and more became *the* central, meaning-giving action of the liturgy. Luther himself was inclined to think of the church building as a "mouth-house" (*Mundhaus*). Many of his followers took that theme for granted, while they did not always also carry forth the richness of Luther's sacramental theology. Calvin and his disciples were even more emphatic about the centrality of preaching, a theological motif which was given architectural expression in the Reformed tradition by the construction of central, elevated pulpits that towered over what were then to become much smaller tables for Holy Communion below.

In the wake of that trend, Protestant worshipers tended to become passive auditors, a phenomenon that was accented when pews were introduced. The primary Protestant posture in worship came to be sitting, a posture that was interrupted mainly when congregations stood (if they did) to sing hymns. This, in turn, had the effect of minimizing worship participation by the whole self, *the body*, as well as the mind and spirit. In some Protestant traditions this trend was further accented when the practice arose of administering the sacramental elements to the people in their pews. This, finally, had the effect of repressing bodily participation in many expressions of Protestant worship to the extreme. These developments, in turn, made it necessary to address the bodily discomforts of sitting too long on hard wooden pews. In this respect, the body seemed to be "getting in the way" of attentive listening. Hence, cushions were added. The end result of all these developments, in Protestantism, was what can be called the "theatricalization" of worship in the twentieth century, if not before, when church buildings were constructed as vast, comfortable auditoriums and any notion of bodily movement was totally suppressed. This had the effect of suppressing the natural in worship, too, since the body, as I have emphasized, is of course very much a part of nature.

The introduction of the possibility of genuine movement by the people during the liturgy, as in the case of the Philadelphia Cathedral, is therefore an event of considerable importance, as far as our theme is concerned. It frees the body to become a full participant, as it were, in the liturgy and thereby also gives a boost to the more general dynamics of the renewed liturgy and its ritualization of nature.

The kind of bodily movement envisioned here, importantly, should not be thought to be some kind of random exercise. Subliminally, if not self-consciously, these bodily movements are eschatologically shaped. They reenact the pilgrimage of the people of God throughout the ages toward the eschaton. They suggest that the people of God in our aeon of creation history are always a people "on the way." As one of the designers of the Philadelphia Cathedral, Richard Giles, observed more generally about the significance of congregational movement from font to ambo to table:

> Movement in . . . [this] liturgical sense . . . [involves] the whole assembly moving together from one liturgical act to another. This essential element of movement in liturgy, engaged in week by week, can be a powerful symbol of our life-long journey of faith. Movement is the hallmark of a community which knows that it has not arrived, but is in transit, discovering God not at the end of the journey, but in the journeying.[3]

At the Philadelphia Cathedral worshipers typically gather around the font for the entrance rite. Then they move to the space around the ambo. Finally the whole congregation processes to the center of the nave and gathers around a freestanding table for the Eucharist. There the presiding priest enlists the participation of the entire congregation in the words and ritual acts of the Eucharist, so that the theme of *prima inter pares*, priestly leadership *with* the people, is carried through in this climactic setting, too.

There appears to be *an inner existential logic* to this liturgical movement in the Philadelphia Cathedral, which perhaps can be identified with a simple, mundane illustration. Imagine being invited to a dinner party by someone whom you know is a gracious host. You are not sure who else will be present, but you trust the host to care for such things. You arrive with high expectations and perhaps some anxieties, since you may be uncertain about whom you will meet or what you will hear or how you will choose to respond. You are warmly welcomed at the door by your host, who leads you into her living room and introduces you to other guests who have already gathered. Soon after you have entered, perhaps to your surprise, you find that you are easily and eagerly communicating with the other guests, sparked by your host's imaginative and sometimes dramatic conversational interventions. In due course, you find a way to thank your host for inviting you, and she thanks you, in turn, for the house gift you carried with you to that dinner party, perhaps a bottle of wine, even a loaf of bread that you baked at home. That living-room gathering takes on a timeless character for you. You have been accepted as a member of that congenial gathering. You have been addressed personally by other guests and you have responded personally. So you are deeply grateful to be there.

But suddenly your host interrupts the conversations, and invites all to come into her dining room. There you see a table, simply prepared, with candles and modestly arranged flowers, which another guest brought as a gift to the host. In due course, after your host has said the blessing, you all begin to eat together. You share the platters of food with one another. This is a feast indeed! You smile at one another. The conversation at the table takes on an energy of its own. And everyone has a voice. At one point, one of the guests excitedly announces that she is pregnant, and everyone applauds. At another point, after the conversation had shifted to people's concerns about their jobs, another guest quietly confides to all that this has not been a good week for him. He has been "down-sized," he says, and he is not sure what is to become of his life. Others offer expressions of care and support, and there is silence for several moments, too deep for words.

Throughout, thanks to the good communication earlier in the living room, and the engaging mood at the table, you discover that in some real sense you have been communing with the host and with all the other guests. This communing, you realize, subliminally if not directly, is something more than the communication you all shared in the living room, important and gratifying as that was. This communion at the table is a kind of intimate sharing. For that moment, as you eat and drink together, you are embraced and bound together by some intangible peace and love, which probably people only think about consciously later, on their way home, if at all. Most guests, on their way home, will carry a spirit of warm gratitude in their hearts and savor that spirit, perhaps not being totally aware of the inner logic that had carried them to their mood of peaceful departure.

Such appears to be the inner existential logic of the liturgy: gathering, communicating, communion. Such is the external movement of the liturgy, too, which can be acted out physically where architectural circumstances permit, as in the Philadelphia Cathedral: moving from font to ambo to table. Every gesture in that movement has its own essential importance. But there is, experience teaches, a progression of spiritual intensity, each step along the way. The host is her gracious self, fully reaching out to you when she greets you at the door, likewise when she incorporates you into the conversation in the living room. But you see her "at her best," so you may think at the time—you may even imagine that her countenance is radiant in the candlelight—when she is shepherding the fellowship at the table and tending to the needs of all, especially making sure that all have enough to eat and that they are satisfied. And you are therefore all the more grateful. The meal is surely the culmination of the evening, even though in its own way the living room conversations had "been enough." So the Eucharist is the culmination of the liturgy.

This inner existential logic of the liturgy—gathering, communicating, and communion—may also bring with it an experiential differentiation, which the analogy of the dinner party does not directly illuminate, particularly regarding the theme of thanksgiving. Consider this question. If the Eucharist, as the word itself suggests, means "thanksgiving," how, if at all, is that ritual moment to be distinguished from the thanksgiving or the gratitude embodied in the Offertory, as we have just considered it? It may be that this is finally an unanswerable question, and that, in this respect, as in many others regarding the liturgy, we are encountering what might be called a conceptual embarrassment of riches. The liturgy could be thought of in this respect as a kind of horizontal spiral, with thanksgiving being a recurring motif at different points in the unfolding ritual experience. But it does seem possible to identify a difference of accent between the thanksgiving of the Offertory and the thanksgiving of the Eucharist, a review of which might deepen our understanding of both.

Jonathan Edwards once asked the question, Do we praise God because of what God has done for us or because of who God is in God's own glorious being? Behind Edwards's question, surely, was the theology that came to expression in the Westminister Confession, when that statement of faith asked about humanity's chief end, and then responded: to glorify God and to enjoy God forever. In Edwards's view, both reasons for praising God had their own validity. But I do not want to respond to Edwards's question here nor discuss its theological lineage. Rather, I want to observe that the question does suggest a parallel distinction that appears to be helpful when we are considering the thanksgiving of the Offertory and the thanksgiving of the Eucharist, proper.

Is the following perhaps the case? The chief existential weight of thanksgiving in the Offertory rests in the interiority of the believing soul and the believing assembly. In response to the proclamation of the gospel, I give thanks because of what God has done for me (*pro me*). We give thanks because of what God has done for us (*pro nobis*). We give thanks by giving up any righteous claim of our own or any possession that we thought was ours. We give thanks to God for the forgiveness of sins and the life and the salvation that God has given us in Christ, as that was made real for us in the proclamation of the Word.

In the Eucharist, however, there appears to be a change of focus. The thanksgiving in the Offertory and the Eucharist, proper, appears to be elliptical, with two foci. The direction of the thanksgiving in the Eucharist thus seems to be externalized: the focus shifts from ourselves to glorifying God and enjoying God forever. I give thanks, we give thanks, because of who God is (*pro Deum*). In other words, rather than giving up what we thought we had achieved or what we had come to own, in response to God's justifying grace, we give to God what is rightfully and fittingly God's, as we humans would have given "from the beginning," had there been no fall into sin and disgrace and hence no need for God's justifying grace. This moment of thanksgiving is the feast of God. In the Eucharist, we give thanks to God for God's glory, which is God's love, which has prompted God to create, redeem, and consummate the whole world, a universal story that we narrate in the Eucharist with the charged words of praise, and that we experientially enjoy, by our faith, with all the saints on earth and all the saints in heaven, and indeed, rapt in mystery, with the whole creation.

If we choose to entertain such exploratory thoughts, however, concerning the relationship between the thanksgiving of the Offertory and the thanksgiving of the Eucharist, proper, we should do so with caution, with the conscious awareness that such a differentiation, if it is indeed illuminating, as is surely a matter of accent, as I have said. The two expressions of thanksgiving are indeed elliptical. They dwell, as it were, within each other, even as they so appear also to complement each other.

The Invitational Dialogue Revised

The Eucharist typically begins with an invitational dialogue between the celebrant and the people.[4] It appears that the form of this dialogue, and even its wording, has taken on a kind of similarity in the rites of a number of Christian communions during the last half-century, if not before. This is probably due to the influence of the movement for liturgical renewal that has flourished ecumenically over this period.[5] Anecdotal evidence suggests, in any case, that the words of the invitational dialog have had an amazing kind of staying power in the communions that have employed them, much more so, it appears, than the wording of the much more substantial eucharistic prayer that follows in most of these liturgies. It further appears that what can be called the "consensus version" of the dialogue has *not* been subjected, in itself, to extensive theological scrutiny, at least not the kind devoted to the prayer that follows the dialogue in its originating document, the "Canon of Hippolytus" (ca. 215). From the perspective of this study, this is a matter of some concern.

Here is the text of the dialogue in its originating, early-third-century form:

Bishop:	The Lord be with you.
People:	And with your spirit.
Bishop:	Lift up your hearts.
People:	We have them with the Lord.
Bishop:	Let us give thanks unto the Lord.
People:	It is meet and right.[6]

Then, in the Canon of Hippolytus, follow words of thanksgiving that focus on the gift of Jesus Christ, his atoning death, his institution of the supper, and an invocation of the Holy Spirit, which words have been a major object of scholarly attention.

Why, then, are the words of the invitational dialogue itself important, as I believe they are? Why are these words of theological interest? Because these words, in fact, if not necessarily in historic intent, function to introduce and therefore in some sense to "frame" the rich and complex eucharistic expressions that immediately follow. The invitational dialogue from the Canon of Hippolytus, especially as it has been translated into some, if not all, current liturgies, is also beautiful, resonant, and powerful in its own way, which gives it all the more claim on the minds and hearts of the assemblies that employ it.

I am particularly concerned with one part of the dialogue, called in Latin the *Sursum Corda*, as it appears in words like these in a number of contemporary translations:

| *Celebrant:* | Lift up your hearts. |
| *People:* | We lift them up to the Lord. |

My concern here is not about what these words once meant but what they have come to mean, at least by implication, since the gothic era. I have already alluded to the fact that these words take on expansive meanings in a gothic setting, with its accent on the theology of ascent.[7] It appears, moreover, that at least in some expressions of the Reformed tradition, these words have been self-consciously associated with the ascension of the risen Christ to the right hand of the Father. Thus, according to Ronald P. Byars, this is "the reformed *Sursum Corda*" of Martin Bucer, shaped as an exhortation, rather than as a dialogue: "Therefore lift your hearts on high, seeking the heavenly things in heaven, where Jesus Christ is sitting at the right hand of the Father."[8]

The effect of the constant repetition of such words, prominently placed at the beginning of some of the most solemn and sacred moments of the liturgy, can only be this: the tendency to frame the whole eucharistic celebration in terms of the gothic vision of ascent and to undercut countervailing themes of divine descent.

This is a matter of nuance, to be sure. But it is a critically important nuance. Consider, for example, how Romano Guardini contrasts the image of the historical Christ as we see this Christ portrayed in the Gospels with the vision of the heavenly Christ disclosed, Guardini suggests, in the liturgy. Guardini argues that that Gospel image is not abrogated by the heavenly liturgical vision in the liturgy. Rather, the first is taken up into the second. Still, for Guardini, the second, the celebration of the eternal Christ above space and time, is clearly the most important liturgical reality:

He is the God-Man, the Word that was made flesh. The human element, or—involuntarily the theological expression rises to the lips—the human nature certainly remains intact, for the battle against Eutyches was not fought in vain; he is truly and wholly human, with a body and soul which have actually lived. But they are now utterly transformed by the Godhead, rapt into the light of eternity, and remote from time and space. He is the Lord, "sitting at the right hand of the Father," the mystic Christ living on in his church.[9]

This is the Christ, I am claiming, who is already announced in the traditional words of the invitational dialogue: "Lift up your hearts"—"We lift them up to the Lord." This is the Christ who reigns above, far transcending time and space.

The theology of descent transvalues this set of beliefs. The theology of descent focuses on the Christ who is immersed in time and space, who is in, with, and under the sacramental actions of the Eucharist. This sacrament, after all, is the feast of Christ, who is the host at this meal, the Christ, who is immediately present, not a Christ who is somewhere else, high and lifted up. As the WCC's' Faith and Order Paper, *Baptism, Eucharist and Ministry*, states so emphatically, words that I have already cited:

> In the celebration of the Eucharist, Christ gathers, teaches, and nourishes the church. It is Christ who invites to the meal and who presides at it. He is the shepherd who leads the people of God, the prophet who announces the Word of God, the priest who celebrates the mystery of God.[10]

We have to do in this feast, in a word, with the present Christ, not with some absent Christ, sitting at the right hand of God in heaven.[11] Hence, I believe, the time has come, and is perhaps long overdue, to revise these words in the invitational dialogue.

I am aware that this proposal will in all likelihood not be greeted with enthusiasm by many liturgists and that it might well be resisted, with considerable animus, at the grass roots. The words of the invitational dialog in our time enjoy a kind of untouchable status, akin to the status once enjoyed by the "traditional" translation of the Lord's Prayer. But given the fact that in a number of communions many versions of the eucharistic prayer are in use, including a variety of translations of the Lord's Prayer, why should the words of the invitational dialogue be totally immune to revision? What makes them, compared to everything else, so sacrosanct, especially in view of the fact that, in impact, they appear to be doing more liturgical harm than good? For this reason, it makes good if not perfect liturgical sense, to the end of incorporating the theology of divine descent into the liturgy as much as possible at key moments, to change some of the words of the invitational dialogue from the form that is most widely used in our time. Consider this alternative:

| *Officiant*: | Open your hearts. |
| *People*: | We open them to the Lord.[12] |

This rendering of the strategically placed invitational dialogue would announce the thoroughgoing transvaluation of values that the theology of descent requires, over against the spirituality and the theological assumptions of the ambiguous gothic vision.

To be sure, this kind of liturgical transformation would have to be fostered by pastoral leaders who are self-consciously ready to stand the gothic vision on its head, as it were, and who are ready, likewise, to bear the brunt of the questions and perhaps the scorn that might well be directed at them for making that kind of simple change in a ritual form of considerable antiquity and therefore authority. But that could be *a historic teaching moment.* It would probably be a moment not unlike the time when, in the twentieth century, for reasons of accenting the theology of people of God presently gathered, over against the theology of communion of the individual soul with God above, officiants began to stand behind a freestanding altar facing the people, rather than orienting themselves with their backs to the congregation, facing the high altar at the east wall.

The Eucharistic Prayer Affirmed in Its Trinitarian Fullness

There is an emerging ecumenical consensus, stemming from the movement for liturgical renewal of the second half of the last century, that reflection about the eucharistic prayer in its trinitarian fullness is the most appropriate way to begin to explore and to explicate the meanings of the Eucharist.[13] Apart from that consensus, however, and for a variety of reasons, local liturgical leaders across the ecumenical spectrum often have approached the theology of the Eucharist more in terms of functional questions. They have discussed, for example, "what makes a Eucharist a Eucharist"—what are, as it were, the "bare essentials." What actions of the Eucharist are indispensable? What makes this simple meal the sacrament that it is? This kind of thinking has been fostered "on the ground" in our time by numerous pastors who have found themselves pressured to conclude one liturgy in time for the next one to begin. Some pastors, particularly in middle-class Protestant settings, where "time is money" and "wasting time" is a kind of deadly sin, have also felt pressured to keep the liturgy "under an hour" (for reasons unknown, that once much-discussed

"Protestant hour" is still sacrosanct). What can be left out, busy and pressured pastors have naturally asked themselves, without compromising the sacrament?

As a result, practitioners have tended to focus on the "moment of consecration," when the bread and the wine become, for faith, the true body and blood of Christ, as the central meaning of the Eucharist. The "words of institution" are deemed to be, in one manner or another, what is truly essential, since their proclamation is taken as a signal that the consecration of the sacramental elements is happening. In the Eucharist, so this way of thinking proceeds, everything focuses on the Word spoken over the elements, on their transformation, and on the sharing of those elements with the people.

These trends are not new, particularly in the Western church. As Ronald Byars has pointed out, this kind of focus on the words of institution as the moment of consecrating the elements is clearly a medieval, Western development. Before that, "the common belief had been that the eucharistic prayer as a whole effected consecration." A series of papal decrees in the fourteenth and fifteenth centuries solidified this practice. The reformers in the sixteenth century were heirs of these developments. It was easy for them, then, as Byars points out, to deemphasize the full eucharistic prayer, in favor of the words of institution, especially since that larger prayer had become so steeped with the theology of sacrifice.[14]

Thus, Luther could remark that in Christ's words of institution "lies the whole Mass, its nature, work, profit, and benefit."[15] Such strictures were surely necessary, theologically, in Luther's time, when priests regularly *whispered*—they did not *proclaim*—the words of institution; and those words, in turn, more generally were part of a larger ritual of sacrifice. In the Mass against which Luther was reacting, the officiating priest was believed to be *offering Christ*, in the "bloodless sacrifice" of the altar, in order to obtain benefits for the faithful, or certain members of the faithful.

But when Luther says of the words of institution "herein lies *the whole Mass*," his statement surely should be read as invoking the words of institution as a theological *criterion*, not as the sole liturgical *content* of the Mass. According to that criterion, whatever announces and embodies the Gospel of forgiveness of sins, life, and salvation is liturgically acceptable and indeed laudatory and whatever detracts from that gospel must be excised. In practice, however, while never wavering about the gospel criterion for the Mass, Luther was quite flexible about the contents of the Mass.[16] In addition to the words of institution, preaching and giving thanks and praying and singing in a variety of expressions were building blocks of the Mass that Luther took for granted, and indeed affirmed, as long as they "measured up" to the theological criterion represented by the words of institution.

This point is further strengthened, when it is compared with another, parallel, observation about Luther's thought. When Luther affirmed that the doctrine of justification by faith alone is "the article by which the church stands or falls" (*articulus stantis et candentis ecclesiae*), that affirmation should be read as defining a theological *criterion*, not as circumscribing the full theological *content* of the church's faith. In order to give expression to the latter, from Luther's point of view, clearly, one would have to make recourse the Nicene inheritance of the church (as Luther did in his explanation of the Apostles Creed in his Small Catechism, for example) to the themes of Trinity, Christology, pneumatology, soteriology, ecclesiology, and so forth, all measured, to be sure, by the theological criterion of justification by faith alone. So, for Luther, as justification by faith alone functions as a criterion for all the other elements of the faith of the church, not as the chief content of that faith, so the words of institution function as a theological criterion for the rest of the Mass, but not as the chief content of Mass.

Without for a moment wishing to call into question the seriousness or the integrity of those who today understand the Eucharist primarily in terms of the words of institution, it is theologically necessary nevertheless to envision a much broader eucharistic horizon of meaning for our time, if the liturgy is to give expression to the fullness of the biblical witness and be renewed accordingly. As Robert Jenson and others have convincingly argued, to begin with, when Jesus said "do this" with reference to the institution of the Eucharist, Jesus meant what he said, which was: *to give thanks*. "The verbal prayer and praise are not merely the preparation and explanation of holy substances," Jenson states forthrightly: "They are an act of their own, of which all the rest of the supper is—as mandated action—just the embodiment."[17]

Regrettably, a number of congregations have opted, in contrast, merely to invoke the words of institution, as the essence of the eucharistic prayer or, what amounts to the same thing, to employ eucharistic prayers that are skeleton-like structures, with the words of institution remaining, clearly, the most important part of what remains. However much that kind of liturgical paring may have been motivated by a commitment to focus on the essentials in the name of evangelical integrity, it has also been sustained, in all likelihood, in modern American communions by the drive to "save time"—because "time is money"—that has dominated bourgeois Christianity in the West. On the contrary, our situation requires something countercultural, and much more biblical: taking the time to give thanks, as Jesus commanded us to do.

A comprehensive eucharistic prayer, given a place of prominence in numerous ecumenical liturgies in our time, is therefore an appropriate liturgical matrix for the Eucharist. It is also urgently needed, if we are to respond substantively to the challenge of ritualizing nature: since, as a prayer of praise for the mighty acts of God, as it has come to be understood generally in our era, the eucharistic prayer as a matter of course includes a number of vivid and biblically inspired creational and justice themes, often with a biblically driven eschatological frame of reference as well. Those themes and that frame of reference are critically important for renewal of the liturgy today, since the eucharistic prayer frames the Eucharist itself and that rite, in turn, is the culminating completion of the whole liturgy, which, overall, is the church's mode of identity formation. Much, indeed, hinges on the use of the eucharistic prayer in its trinitarian fullness.

Like the celebratory baptismal prayer we have already considered, the full eucharistic prayer is in essence a narration of the mighty acts of God, beginning with creation, focusing on redemption—where "the words of institution" have their fitting and indispensable place—and coming to rest in the vision of the consummation of all things that is yet to come. For those who have ears to hear, indeed, this universalizing narrative is undergirded by the very words of institution themselves, particularly by the widely discussed expression, "Do this, in remembrance [*anamnesis*] of me." That expression—*anamnesis*—can be read as comprehending the whole promissory history of God with the creation.[18] In this sense, historically speaking, the words of institution themselves require a full eucharistic prayer, if their remembrance theme is to be given its full meaning.

Here is an example of some of the contours and contents of such comprehensive ritual addresses to God. The eucharistic prayer in the *Lutheran Book of Worship* begins its universalizing narrative: "Holy God, mighty Lord, gracious Father: Endless is your mercy and eternal is your reign. You have filled all creation with light and life; heaven and earth are full of your glory." Eucharistic Prayer C in the *Book of Common Prayer* proclaims similar themes yet with a more contemporary sensibility: "At your command all things came to be: the vast expanse of interstellar space, galaxies, suns, the planets in their courses, and this fragile earth, our island home."[19] Eucharistic Prayer VII of the more recent *Evangelical Lutheran Worship* book highlights the creative works of God this way: "You formed the earth from chaos; you encircled the globe with air; you created fire for warmth and light; you nourish the lands with water."[20] Such testimony recapitulates the witness of Genesis 1, which is further adumbrated in Psalm 104 and brought to christological completion in Colossians 1:15ff. and Revelation 21: that the God of this holy meal is the One who, from the very beginning, had a purpose for all things, not just humankind, and that this God is indeed in, with, and under all things, and will one day bring all things to fulfillment in the day of the new Jerusalem and the new heavens and the new earth, when God will be all in all.

Then typically follows the narration of the history of salvation, beginning, for example, as does the *Lutheran Book of Worship*, with Abraham and coming to fulfillment "at this the end of all the ages," in the Son sent by the Father, who proclaimed the kingdom of God and instituted his holy meal. This Son is further identified, eschatologically, as the One who will come in power "to share with us the great and promised feast," when he comes again "as victorious Lord of all." *Evangelical Lutheran Worship* is likewise capacious: "With this bread and cup we remember your Son, the first-born of your creation. We remember his life lived for others, and his death and resurrection, which renews the face of the earth. We await his coming, when, with the world made perfect through your wisdom, all our sins and sorrows will be no more."[21] These liturgical meanings reflect the testimony of the book of Revelation, that the Lord who is host at this banquet is the very Lord who, as lord of lords and king of kings, will come again to judge the world in righteousness and will inaugurate the great and eternal cosmic day of *shalom*, when God will finally be all in all. The Lord who is host at this eucharistic feast is the Lord of all, then, the *pantokrater*, in whom, and by whom all things consist, now and forever.

The Real Presence of Christ Transfigured, Cosmically

Seen from this angle of vision, traditional reflection about the real presence of Christ in the sacramental elements can both be reaffirmed and transfigured, cosmically. Of course, according to the Catholic faith, the crucified and risen Lord is *truly and really present*, in, with, and under the eucharistic elements.[22] But that is not all, by any means.

At this point we can learn from some of the early testimonies of Huldrich Zwingli. In rejecting what Zwingli then had received as the normative Catholic doctrine of transubstantiation of the eucharistic elements, Zwingli said, in effect: no, it is not the elements, it is *the people gathered who are transubstantiated into the body of Christ*.[23] While holding to the witness of the church catholic about the real presence of Christ in the eucharistic elements, it is certainly possible and indeed, in a certain sense, mandatory, biblically speaking, also to learn from Zwingli in this respect: that the crucified and risen Christ is truly present, embodied, in the company of the faithful who gather around the eucharistic table in order to receive the bread and wine that they have already offered, now as the true and real body and blood of Jesus Christ. Paul's theology of the church as the veritable and visible body of Christ mandates that we at least say this much about the real presence of Christ in the people of Christ, so that we might fittingly "discern the body" (cf. 1 Cor. 11:29).[24]

With eyes of faith thus illuminated, one can further see the figure of the crucified and risen Christ in, with, and under *the liturgical actions of the priestly celebrant* in particular, the one who is called by God to offer the eucharistic prayer and to administer the bread and the wine, in the name of Christ, to the faithful gathered around the table.[25]

Charged by this vision of the fullness of the cosmic Christ, really present in bread and wine, distributed to all, and really present in people singing and praying and in priestly ministrations, all in the power of the Holy Spirit, it is then possible to envision, in faith and in hope, a kind of pervasively overflowing revelation of the glory of the ubiquitous Christ: beginning with the sacramental elements at the center of ever-expanding concentric circles of divine energy. Like ripples in a smooth pond, driven by a single, centric entrance of a new reality into the whole interrelated universal system, the works of the cosmic Christ in his fullness can come into mystic view for the faithful, by the inspiration of the Spirit, as waves of divine self-disclosure flow from the elements to the people, then encompass the whole house or the cathedral where the people have gathered, and flow, still more, ever expanding, to the whole earth and thence to the entire cosmos. Thus, the faithful participants in this eucharistic feast in some small measure experience the great cosmic banquet that is yet to come, when God will indeed be all in all.

We meet here, to be sure, what Ernst Käsemann referred to as the "eschatological reservation" of theological and liturgical language.[26] In the sacraments of the church, believers encounter the visible Word, the risen and ascended Lord, who is really there for them, granting them "the forgiveness of sins, life, and salvation." But that kind of personal communion is not yet granted them beyond this ecclesial milieu, this side of the eschaton, anywhere else in the whole creation. God and his Christ, as Luther repeatedly insists, are only available to believers where God chooses to disclose himself and his Son, in Word and Sacrament, by the power of the Holy Spirit. This is the milieu, and the only milieu, where Christ is known personally and salvifically (*pro me*). This is the milieu of communion with Christ in an I-Thou relationship.

But once we encounter him here—and this accent of the New Testament witness Luther tended to underplay, as I have suggested—we know him not just as the giver of the forgiveness of sins, life, and salvation for us but also according to the witness of Colossians, as the Lord of all things. In the eucharistic experience, the incarnate Lord reveals himself to us as the *pantokrater*—or in Teihardian language, as the omega point—of the whole creation. So, beyond the ecclesial milieu, still now in the power of the Holy Spirit, believers may indeed venture to contemplate the magnificent visible works of the invisible, risen, and ascended Lord, in, with, and under the whole universe and so find themselves, thereby, lost in wonder, love, and praise, as they sing simple but visionary words like these:

O Lord my God, when I in awesome wonder
Consider all the works thy hand hath made,
I see the stars, I hear the mighty thunder,
Thy power throughout the universe displayed;
Then sings my soul, my Savior God to thee:
How great thou art! How great thou art![27]

In the near and vast reaches of the cosmos, believers thus may contemplate the majestic works of the "Beautiful Savior, [the] king of creation" (anon.), although they do not commune with him yet in these regions. For all his reticence about such things, Luther as commentator on Scripture gave testimony to this revelatory vision of the workings of the cosmic

Christ, in his own earthy terms, in his *Commentary on the Gospel of John*, words I have already cited: "Now if I believe in God's Son and bear in mind that he became man, all creatures will appear a hundred times more beautiful to me than before. Then I will properly appreciate the sun, the moon, the stars, trees, apples, and pears, as I reflect that he is Lord over all and the center of things."[28]

This can be the vision: the bread and the wine on the table are, for those eucharistic moments, positioned *at the center of the cosmos*, and the revelation of the divine energies of the crucified and risen cosmic Christ, in whom all things consist, radiates from that center to reach out to embrace peoples of every nation, male and female, Jew and Greek, slave and free, and indeed to every dimension of the earth and the cosmos beyond as a universal, multibillioned, galactic whole. If the faithful happen to be worshiping in a great cathedral, moreover, as I have already suggested, it can be for them as if the walls and windows and coverings of that magnificent structure were invisible. They can see with the eyes of faith, inspired by the Spirit, the presence of the Christ with whom they are communing "fill[ing] all things" (Eph. 4:10).

Is there perchance, at this point, a distant but suggestively analogous consonance with some of the images bequeathed to us by contemporary cosmological physics?[29] If I can imagine an originating creative moment of all things, when the totality of universal matter was no larger than a small ball that I could hold in my hand, just prior to some universal explosion (the much-discussed "big bang"), is it not also possible to imagine, similarly, a redemptive moment of all things, wrought first in the particularity of the Word made flesh, and then re-presented and extended around the planet, in the power of the Holy Spirit, whenever priestly hands take bread and lift up the cup, in the midst of the assembly of Christ, according to the same cosmic Word of God?

Further explorations along this line might then disclose that what was once called by theologians like Emil Brunner "the scandal of particularity" is in fact no scandal at all. Rather, we might want to conclude that *that* is the characteristic *modus operandi* of the cosmic Word, both in creation and redemption. Is it not the case that the gospel truth is always in the particulars? With such thoughts before us, we might then choose to say: the hands that hold bread and cup are the hands that hold the center of the universe, as that center now is moving through time-space, from the Alpha of the universe to its Omega. William Blake's words could then be taken with a new seriousness, in a way that he more than likely never intended them to be read, in *Auguries of Innocence*: "Hold infinity in the palm of your hand . . ."

The Eucharist Reclaimed in Its Material Setting

As we then witness this vision of the cosmic Christ thus embodied in the sacramental praxis of the church and thus revelatory of the works of that selfsame Christ hidden in, with, and under the whole creation, we may take it for granted that the material setting of the Eucharist will enhance rather than inhibit this kind of liturgical celebration, both theologically and esthetically. We have already had occasion to observe how important the right kind of architectural setting is for the celebration of baptism in accord with the cosmic Word. This is all the more the case for that sacrament which is the culminating center of the church's sacramental ministries. The cosmic Eucharist wants to be at home in its material setting.

First, an observation that shows that the exception sometimes does indeed prove the rule, an account of a charged experience of my own. In 1965 I visited a simple but elegant Orthodox pilgrimage chapel, high on a mountain along the Croatian coast, overlooking the Adriatic Sea. Surrounded by towering, rugged peaks on the inland side, and overlooking what on a clear day was the pristine blue of the Adriatic to the west, that chapel, reachable only by a long and winding footpath, announced to me that the liturgy is the center of the world. Strikingly, a massive stone table had been constructed in front of the chapel, not far from a precipitous cliff. There, I was told, the people from the village miles below gather in the darkness on their Easter morning, with only the light of candles to help them find their way to that place, for their Eucharist that night, celebrated around that outside table, awaiting the rising sun and the time to chant of the rising Son, "Christ is risen! He is risen indeed!" The very thought of that kind of celebration in that kind of setting overwhelmed me.

Could the claims and the joys of the Easter gospel be celebrated in as fitting a material setting anywhere else? Probably—yes. Vincent Van Gogh showed us, in the bright glories of his widely celebrated *Starry Night*, the very kind of vision that so spoke to me as I contemplated that pilgrimage chapel. But Van Gogh also began his creative work with dark and grim paintings, not nearly so famous but glorious in their own way, such as *The*

Potato Eaters. That was a thought that escaped me as I stood transfixed in front of that pilgrimage chapel, imagining that the Easter liturgy that was celebrated there was inscribed suggestively and fittingly in its material setting, like few others. But, I now realize, such experiences need to be set in a larger biblical context.

For the Word was made flesh in the womb of a peasant woman, who gave birth in a stable—and *that* was celebrated beautifully, we may imagine as we read the Lukan narrative, by the angelic chorus. So liturgies celebrated in drab, abandoned warehouses, like the one I visited in Soweto in 1985, then the beleaguered apartheid "sister" black township next to the prosperous white city of Johannesburg, have their own beauty. In that Soweto assembly, a large and brilliantly colored image of the Virgin Mary, mother of all the faithful and especially those of low estate, transformed that dusty—and perhaps polluted—space with the radiance of the gospel promise. The congregants themselves were dressed in their brightly colored "Sunday best," right in the midst of some of the most virulent ugliness of our sinful human condition. The hymns of that congregation transfigured that drab space even more. Did the broken windows of that warehouse also reclaim the glorious heritage of the stained-glass windows of the gothic cathedrals? Perhaps. That assembly meeting place had its own beauty, precisely in that setting, not unlike Van Gogh's *Potato Eaters.* I do not mean to romanticize poverty and oppression; but I do mean to celebrate the Lord who became poor and powerless, so that all might become rich and powerful in conformity to him. That warehouse Eucharist was, for me, effulgent with the beauty of holiness. Would anyone who had been caught up in that warehouse celebration deny that that was a foretaste of the glories of eschatological feast to come?

Could the image of such powerful eucharistic settings—the Adriatic pilgrimage chapel, on the one hand, and the Soweto warehouse, on the other—then inform every other eucharistic celebration? Why not? This, of course, will require a resilient theological imagination, a gifted aesthetic creativity, and a stubborn commitment to marshal financial resources to undergird that imagination and that creativity. But that surely seems possible, assuming the inspiration of the Spirit given to the church. Great liturgical music that lifts up the cosmic universality and the human promise of the Eucharist is readily available, even in the smallest of parish settings. Great liturgical iconography and architecture that serve and elaborate the cosmic universality of the Eucharist and its human promise are often more difficult to put in place, for a variety of typically pragmatic reasons. But the *bon mot* of many a church architect, that good architecture is as cheap as bad architecture, probably needs constant repetition in the hearing of most assembly leaders.

It is a sad irony that the accent on the liturgical center as the home for the people of God that so creatively gained ecumenical prominence during the last century has not always helped, in this regard. That entirely appropriate theological theme has, regrettably, sometimes functioned to cover a multitude of architectural and iconographical sins. It has sometimes permitted financial pressures to rule the day, with the result being liturgical centers that are bereft of what might be called any significant "architectural mystery" and bereft likewise of any iconography that commands worshipers' hearts and minds. One Roman Catholic pastor and theologian, Robert Barron, has called this the "beigification" of worship spaces. He has appropriately lamented "the almost total absence of saints, angels, nature, and the cosmos in our churches."[30]

But this should be the twofold goal. First, an assembly should live in a church house or in a cathedral that attests, wherever possible and however appropriate, the multicultural dimensions and the social diversity of the human family and the multidimensional realities of the universe—cosmic nature, wild nature, cultivated nature, and fabricated nature—and that does not mask those rich diversities by artificial or so-called supernatural esthetic elaborations. Second, an assembly should live in a church house or in a cathedral that, in one way or another, tells the whole gospel truth, that witnesses to the grand story of the faith and thus mirrors the gospel preaching that tells the whole "old, old, story" with narrative richness and attention to the particularities of the experiences of the faithful throughout the ages.

Artists who serve the church should therefore be encouraged to find ways to give testimony to the terrors and the glories of our multigalactic universe, as well as to the desecrations and the beauties of the good earth, nearer at hand. Artists who serve the church should also be encouraged not just to create promissory worlds like that of *Starry Night* but also cruciform worlds like that of *The Potato Eaters*. Assemblies should be challenged, too, to find the financial resources, wherever possible, to allow sculptors to testify to the stories of the saints, written both in suffering and in triumph. Models for such works abound. Powerful statues of St. Francis, for example, exist in remarkable numbers in our time, belying the assumption of some liturgists that the saint from Assisi can only be a captive of religious sentimentality or romantic escapism. Icons of urban elegance, moreover, perchance a large polished brass crucifix in the simple but transfixing style of a Brancusi, should also be given liturgical prominence wherever possible, as an affirmation of the renewal of all things through the mission of the cosmic Christ, a renewal that will include the world of fabricated nature as well as cultivated, wild, and cosmic nature. The widespread introduction of the freestanding central table as the focal point of eucharistic celebration in the twentieth century has, in this respect, done much to accent the presence of God with God's people, as distinct from the high altar against the east wall, removed from the people, which suggested that the way of salvation is the way of ascent. Hence, that liturgical table practice should not only be preserved but fittingly accented whenever that is possible.

The Eucharistic Sending Extended

Liturgical leaders in our time have struggled to make something large out of the small versicle that often—perfunctorily—ends the whole liturgy, typically called "the dismissal." I think we are best advised to call this versicle "the sending," rather than "the dismissal," because of the dismal connotations of the latter term, suggesting perhaps the end of a Latin class or a military drill. And "sending" is, in fact, the underlying theological intentionality of this versicle, as simple words like these indicate:[31]

Officiant:	Go in peace to serve the Lord!
People:	Thanks be to God!

Most liturgical leaders have been rightly convinced that the worship life of the church should not only afford and indeed accent the experience of God-with-us in the liturgy itself but should also overflow beyond the walls of the house or the cathedral space into God's world.[32] In this sense, the liturgy never ends, or it should not.

For the faithful, the liturgy can be the canopy of meaning that unites the so-called sacred sphere with the so-called secular sphere of human experience, so that the sacrality of all creatures and of human history in particular may be disclosed. There is good reason to think that this is the kind of theological meaning Paul was attempting to convey in Romans 12:1, when he urged members of the Roman assembly: "I appeal to you therefore, bothers and sister, by the mercies of God, to present your bodies as a living sacrifice, holy and acceptable to God, which is your spiritual worship." Likewise, in the following verse when he appealed to them not to be "conformed to this world."[33] At this point in his letter, Paul apparently wanted the theological center that he had been highlighting in the first eleven chapters of his letter—summarized by his phrase, "by the mercies of God"—to be expanded and extended to the circumference of the whole world of human experience.[34] With the sending, in other words, *the liturgy should continue in a different kind of public setting,* as the mode of identity formation of the assembly. Most liturgical leaders instinctively understand this, although some appear to be hesitant about how to guide their assemblies in this respect, at least in part for some theological reasons. I think I know what those theological concerns are.

Whereas ours is an era of a profusion of religiosities in public, sometimes with scandalous effects, as in the crusade mentality of some fundamentalist Christians and some fundamentalist Muslims and some fundamentalist Hindus, Christian leaders attuned to the gospel of peace that they encounter in the life and teaching of Jesus, sometimes shy away from—even are horrified by the thought of—*public praxis of any kind* on the part of any Christian assembly or assembly of assemblies. Some find support for this kind of hesitance in the theology of the Christian martyr and theologian Dietrich Bonhoeffer. In his prison writings, Bonhoeffer advanced the thought that ours is the time for Christians to practice "the discipline of the secret" (*disciplina arcana*).[35] When Christians worship and pray "in secret," Bonhoeffer believed, the faith they profess will be protected from profanation in the public world—a strategy that appears to be needed all the more in our time, which is satiated, even glutted, with many religiosities of questionable public value. Bonhoeffer also envisioned that that discipline of the secret—the liturgy, the life of prayer, the study of the Bible, the commitment to bear the cost of discipleship—could and would transform Christians in order to launch them anonymously, as it were, into responsible action in the world. This was the sobering course that his own life had taken and was to take, as he participated in the plot to kill Hitler and its failed aftermath, when he was executed in prison. There is no reason to deny that this view of the life of the assembly, depicted in terms of the discipline of the secret, should be taken with full seriousness.

The problems the world confronts today may well be exacerbated by too much religion rather than too little.

On the other hand, we should not take Bonhoeffer's teaching as a kind of ironclad law or rigid ideology either. It all depends on a reading of the signs of the times, as Bonhoeffer himself recognized. While in prison, indeed, in a communication reflecting on the baptism of his godchild, Bonhoeffer envisioned the possibility of a coming era when a new kind of powerful public witness by the church could emerge, born out of the "prayer and action" of the church's discipline of the secret. "Our church," Bonhoeffer wrote in 1944, "which has been fighting in these years only for its self-preservation, as though that were an end in itself, is incapable of taking the Word of reconciliation and redemption to mankind [sic] and the world." But a day will come, he said, when the church will be once more "called so to utter the Word of God that the world will be changed and renewed by it." This Word will proclaim God's peace with all and God's coming kingdom publicly in a way that will claim people "of the world" by its power.[36] I venture to affirm that this day has arrived in our time, but that it is calling forth a witness by the church which is *not* a new *word* that the church can proclaim, as such, in public, but a new kind of *action* that the church can undertake in public.

Anecdotal evidence suggests, however, that, even when the liturgical shepherds do propose new kinds of public enactments by the assembly, the sheep are not always eager to do the bidding of their shepherds (in this respect as in some others). The carryover from the liturgy to life, as the shepherds often like to think of this matter, typically seems to end abruptly when the people of faith dash off to their next Sunday appointments, once the words of the sending have been uttered. Whether the people are merely heading "back to business as usual," having been energized anew with the "refueling" of the liturgy, as they sometimes think of the matter—with a theological conceptuality that owes more to the spirit of capitalism than the spirit of Jesus—is a question that is not always easy to answer. The discipline of the secret thereby, in this respect, does not in fact produce the fruits that Bonhoeffer had hoped that it would.

Obviously the sending is a key transition in the life of the people of God, and it requires careful and imaginative teaching and preaching, if the people are to think of their weekday callings as extensions of the meanings and the commitments of their Sunday assemblies. But probably education (*catechesis*) is not enough. This may well be an instance where more ritualization is required rather than less. The public life of the assembly itself, as a body, can and probably should be offered, again in Paul's terms in Romans 12:1, as a living sacrifice, beyond the time of the Sunday gathering, at any appropriate time of the week. The sending can be ritualized immediately following the conclusion of the liturgy or any time thereafter.

I have in mind an ancient tradition, whose practice is still in evidence here and there in the ecumenical church but which could well take on much more significance, if it were claimed anew in these times by many assemblies around the world, especially in America, where the tendency is to keep everything religious privatized. Picture the members of the assembly flowing forth from the liturgical center on Sunday but not dispersing—rather *processing*. Obviously, liturgical processions in and around the so-called secular world neither can nor should be a fulltime calling, a kind of perpetual church parade. But some processions might work wonders in the lives of the faithful and even in the hearts and minds of some onlookers. This is a glimpse at the historic precedent, as Aidan Kavanagh described it:

> As the cities [in the Roman Empire] became more thoroughly Christian by the latter half of the fourth century, public processions from one worship site to another increased in frequency. In the tenth-century Typikon of Hagia Sophia in Constantinople, there are still at that late date sixty-eight processions listed during the course of the year (an average of one every five days), and indications are that this number was fewer than in earlier centuries. These processions, moreover, were not separate events but an integral part of the whole urban pattern of worship, so much so that their execution and contents help to structure [entrance rites] of both Byzantine and Roman Eucharists.[37]

It does not take too much imagination to think of the pilgrimage of the villagers, carrying candles, to that Aegean chapel on the mountain for their Easter celebration in these very processional terms. In the same spirit, an ecumenical community of congregations in Hartford, Connecticut, has for some years sponsored a public procession, led by a crucifer, through the streets of that largely impoverished city on Good Friday, as testimony to the presence of the suffering Christ in the neighborhoods where the poor live and as a reminder to the powerful that another Lord has laid claim to that city, over against the powers of Mammon. With similar inspiration, a single Lutheran congregation has found a way to walk the boundaries of power, in the heartland of capitalism. St. Peter's Church begins its Easter Vigil with a candlelight procession around one of the busiest blocks in central Manhattan, with the entire congregation on foot, led by vested clergy, with crucifer and candle bearers. As this procession plows its way, as it were, through the urbane crowds that pack the sidewalks at that time of night in midtown, that "assembly on the way" sings great Easter hymns of the tradition, led by a cantor who carries an electric megaphone (!!). The procession stops at each corner of the block, where there are readings, responsory psalms, and prayers for the city, on its way back to its sanctuary in the Citigroup Building. Other churches in other settings have organized similar public processions, some reclaiming largely forgotten traditional practices. Rural churches have sponsored processions to bless the fields. Coastal churches have sponsored processions to bless the fishing boats. Even something as simple as a Palm Sunday procession from the church grounds into the sanctuary, prior to the liturgy that day, can be steps in the right direction.

Perhaps the most renowned of contemporary church processions is *an inversion*. In this case the people do not process out into or around the world. Rather, the world processes into the space of the gathered assembly. And this inverted procession is perhaps all the more meaningful, for that reason. It is particularly noteworthy in the context of the unfolding discussion of this book—predicated as it has been, on a critique of the gothic vision—because this inverted procession takes place *inside the largest gothic cathedral in the world*, the Episcopal Cathedral of St. John the Divine, in upper Manhattan.

The occasion is the annual feast day of St. Francis, on October 4. The liturgy includes a blessing of the animals, in keeping with the spirit of St. Francis. For several hours, more than four thousand men, women, and children, and many of their companion animals, enter into a liturgical celebration, which is perhaps unequaled in its ritual magnitude in the whole global church. At the ending of the two-hour celebration, the great bronze doors of the cathedral swing open. A procession of larger, less domesticated animals, with their caretakers, moves silently down the center aisle, perhaps a camel, two llamas, a ram, a full-grown bull, a man carrying a boa constrictor, and a woman holding a large blue-gold macaw. When this procession is gathered before the main altar, the bishop prays, using words like these: "We give you thanks, most gracious God, for the beauty of earth and sky and sea . . . , for the songs of birds and the loveliness of flowers, and for the wonder of your animal kingdom. We praise you for these good gifts and pray that we may safeguard them for posterity. . . . Amen."

Obviously, the Cathedral of St. John the Divine may be uniquely equipped to sponsor that kind of liturgical celebration, with its inverted procession, accompanied by music offered by groups such as the Paul Winter Consort. The congregation of St. John Next-Door has neither the space nor the financial resources even to contemplate such an event. But the congregation of St. John Next-Door does have the imagination, by the inspiration of the Spirit, to sponsor analogous processions, whether outgoing or inflowing, in its own setting. Likewise, for assemblies that would be inspired to learn from the other processions I have instanced, in Hartford and downtown Manhattan, and in rural and in coastal settings.

But these are the most critical questions, in this connection. Do the faithful who participate in the outgoing processions learn more fully by virtue of their public witness that Jesus Christ goes before them into the world everyday, that in fact he is in, with, and under the world of the poor and the powerful every day, that in truth he knows how to minister, without ceasing, to those who grieve when they remember 9/11, that he knows how to cast out the money changers from the stock exchange on any day? Do the faithful in those outgoing processions see more clearly that as they themselves are thus offering their bodies as a living sacrifice to God they can be transformed, by the renewing of their minds (cf. Rom. 12:2)? And do the faithful who participate in inverted processions like the Feast of St. Francis at the Cathedral of St. John the Divine learn more fully by virtue of this kind of internalized, yet profoundly public witness that Jesus Christ is with all the animals of the world, as their Creator, Sustainer, Redeemer, and Consummator, and that therefore the Good Shepherd of God is sent not only to the human family, but to all creatures?[38]

To foster such public, ritualized assembly processions, whether outgoing or inverted, the preachers and teachers of the church will have to deal with the issue of "taking time." Processions on any day take time. Processions tend to incorporate the spontaneous, and therefore they tend to take more time than the time allotted. Time-conscious—not to say time-obsessed—middle-class Americans do not easily tolerate such uncertainties. They tend to be horrified by the prospect of "wasting time."

But the whole point of the liturgy is to enter into the time of God, and to leave behind the sometimes tyrannical time of this world (signaled by the two New Testament Greek words for time, *kairos* and *chronos*). Hence that "crisis [*krisis*] of time [*chronos*]" in the minds and hearts of the faithful that preachers and teachers of the church will surely have to confront (here drawing on another Greek word, *krisis*, this one meaning "judgment") in itself will be well worth inciting, since the identity-forming ritual process of the liturgy is, in significant measure, whether in the sanctuary or on the streets, a conversion process, befitting the liturgy's function as formative of a counterculture, which is not supposed to be conformed to this age.

Such timely public processions of the faithful, announcing the promised divine world of peace and justice, as they move from one setting to another, will as a matter of course be accompanied at other times by a corporate public advocacy for peace and justice, by the assembly or by communions of assemblies, whether in a neighborhood, a bioregion, a nation, or the whole inhabited world. The assembly, or an assembly of assemblies, which is a counterculture that lives by the eschatological vision of the peaceable kingdom, will as a matter of course be a public voice for the voiceless in the times and spaces between every liturgical celebration. The assembly, or an assembly of assemblies, will as a matter of course "speak the truth to power." This could be something as dramatic as a march on Washington in behalf of the poor of the earth and the downtrodden plants and animals of the earth, in this time of global warming, or as pedestrian as a church statement issued in behalf of ecojustice, used, in turn, by church advocates to promote prophetic kinds of ecojustice legislation and to reject others.[39]

Nature Ritualized

Such are some of the textures and the contours of the assembly's liturgical practices, when they have been renewed according to the canons of the theology of descent. Whether in baptism or Word and Offertory or Eucharist, the liturgy renewed in this way becomes that "sacred canopy" of hope and peace, or it can, which gives meaning to everything else, not just to human history nor just to the individual human soul, but to all things (*ta panta* in the Greek New Testament). The renewed liturgy is, if I may, *pantalogical*. Its theological and spiritual reach is cosmic. The gospel it proclaims and embodies is not just the forgiveness of sins, although that is a critically important part of the whole gospel truth. The gospel it proclaims and embodies is "Jesus is risen!" And that good news comprehends the Alpha and Omega of the whole creation and the whole of human history, as well as the Alpha and Omega of my own soul and the Alpha and Omega of my own assembly and "all the assemblies of the nations" (Rom. 16:4).

The letter to the Ephesians takes this kind of ritualized cosmic experience for granted. It assumes that God the Father is the One who is "above all and through all and in all" (4:6) and that the Son of this cosmic Father is the One in whom "all things [*ta panta*]," things on heaven and things on earth, are gathered up (1:10). It tells us that this Son has "ascended far above all the heavens, so that he might fill all things [*ta panta*]" (4:10). It further assumes that this cosmic ministry of God the Father and the Son is magnified and celebrated by the strangers and sojourners who are called together in peace (2:17) from every nation (2:19) and who are, at once, inspired by the Spirit of the same God, in one exuberant moment of thanksgiving, a text which I have cited before: "Be filled with the Spirit, as you sing psalms and hymns and spiritual songs among yourselves, singing and making melody to the Lord in your hearts, giving thanks to God the Father at all times and for everything in the name of our Lord Jesus Christ" (5:18-20).

With this kind of biblical vision before us, appropriately interpreted, we can move beyond the milieu of the gothic vision of human ascent and recapture the insights of the theology of divine descent, in its fullness, for the sake of an ecstatic liturgical experience in the body of Christ and a robust and caring encounter with all our brothers and sisters in the whole creation, especially for the sake of our encounter with the otherwise invisible poor and with the otherwise voiceless creatures of nature. With such a renewed liturgy shaping the life of Christian assemblies in these times of global crisis, members of those assemblies will be inspired, I believe, to proclaim and to embody the vision of *shalom* for the sake of the whole creation with new confidence, enthusiasm, and power.

9

The Habits of Awe and Serving: Our Walk with Nature Ritualized

The liturgy does not end. We have seen that already in our explorations of the "sending" of the liturgy. In many and diverse ways, Christian assemblies ritualize nature publicly by their liturgical practices and by their accompanying advocacy initiatives. But this public witness cannot stand alone. It must be undergirded by a myriad of practices by individual members of the body of Christ, each practice serving as a kind of leaven for the general public witness of the church. Call these practices *habits of faith*. So we will conclude our explorations by identifying those places where the ritualizing of nature by the liturgy shapes the believer's habits of faith.[1]

This is the sharpest way to put the question before us in these last two chapters. *How is the individual believer's walk with nature to be ritualized?* This question brings our explorations in this book full circle, back to the Thoreauvian invitation with which I began, telling about my own walk with nature and bidding the reader to come with me. I will propose the following responses to the question. The renewed liturgy, I will suggest, as the church's mode of identity formation, inculcates *three habits of faith, three ways of walking with nature*:

- *First*, as the believer praises the God of cosmic grace in the liturgy, he or she learns to *stand in awe of nature*, habitually.

- *Second*, as the believer is claimed by the love of Christ in the liturgy, he or she learns how to *serve nature*, habitually.

- *Third*, as the believer is shaped by the community-building hospitality of Christ liturgically, he or she learns how to *build human community partnering with nature*, habitually.

I will discuss the first two of these habits of faith in this chapter and the third in the final chapter.

In exploring these habits, I will proceed as follows. *First*, I will identify fundamental, shaping moments of the liturgy that particularly inculcate these habits. *Second*, I will show how each of these habits itself is undergirded, particularly and concretely, by the witness of the church's Scriptures. In this way, readers should be able to see how powerfully the witness of the church's liturgy and the church's Scriptures reinforce each other and how, by the power of the Spirit, the liturgy and the Scriptures together can transform and energize the lives of individual believers, to the end that nature is ritualized one believer at a time.

This discussion of these three habits of faith *could* then set the stage for further explorations in both Christian spirituality and Christian ethics— explorations that might take the form of connecting with and undergirding works already written by others. But a full discussion of a Christian spirituality of nature and a Christian ethics of nature is beyond the scope of this book. Think of the discussion that immediately follows, therefore, as offering possible mediating insights on the way to a renewed or strengthened Christian spirituality of nature and possible mediating axioms on the way to a renewed or strengthened Christian ethics of nature.[2]

In what follows, moreover, I will not discuss at length the great variety of extra-liturgical initiatives that assemblies and especially their leaders will likely need to establish in order to give legs to these habits of faith. I do want to note, however, that the habits of faith that a renewed liturgy inculcates can readily be rooted even more deeply in the lives of individual believers by reinvigorating a range of familiar congregational educational and spiritual growth ministries that are in all likelihood already in place. Consider these possibilities:

- A prayer group also becomes a mutual accountability group regarding individual members' habits of consumption.

- A social-service group takes on the challenge of addressing the concentration of toxic pollutants from a nearby garbage dump in a poor neighborhood.

- Two church youth groups, one suburban, one inner city, plan a wilderness retreat, with expert theological and ecological guides.

- A women's group takes on the project of congregation-wide educational and lifestyle initiatives under the rubric of "voluntary simplicity," focusing on Christmas consumption.

- A men's group takes on the project of an environmental audit for the church "plant," with the goal of radically reducing the congregation's energy (carbon) footprint.

- In response to a series of Bible studies, an adult Sunday school class rallies members of the congregation to join a regional "march" to the state capitol, in behalf of climate-change legislation.

- An annual congregational meeting votes to make one Sunday a month a "Ride the Bus Sunday," with as many members as possible leaving their cars at home.

- A fellowship committee votes to purchase only fair-trade coffee for church gatherings and to recycle all papers and bottles used in such activities.

- A property committee in a midwestern church votes to restore its considerable grounds to their original prairie status and to install solar panels on the roof.

- A yearly retreat for the entire congregation is devoted to the theme "The Bible and the Earth."

- The congregation's vestry, board of deacons, or governing council votes for the congregation to be a member of a regionwide "Green Congregation Project" that offers mutual support, guidance, resources, and public-advocacy opportunities for member churches.

- The then-emerging Green Congregation Committee joins with other partners of the coalition to sponsor a Community-Supported Agriculture project for all the congregations involved.

Indeed, this is probably a case where putting new wine into old wineskins *will* work. There is no dearth of such opportunities available to most

American assemblies. The denominational and ecumenical resources at hand for such initiatives are considerable, too. Most denominations and ecumenical bodies have excellent leaders upon whom to call, as well. The problem, however, as I have observed these things for more than four decades, has not generally been identifying the resources but finding the congregational imagination and will to adopt and to adapt the resources that are readily available.

Where there is a will, there is a way—that is surely true in this context. That is why developing the habits of faith I am about to discuss is so important. And this is what the renewed liturgy can, by the grace of God, make happen.

Standing in Awe of Nature

At the heart of most eucharistic prayers in a variety of liturgies, at least from the fourth century on, are words like these, commonly used today in English language rites, called the "Sanctus" (Latin for "holy"):[3]

Holy, holy, holy Lord, God of pow'r and might:
Heaven and earth are full of your glory. Hosanna.
Hosanna in the highest.
Blessed is he who comes in the name of the Lord.
Hosanna in the highest.[4]

These words, properly interpreted against the background of the biblical texts that inspired them, tell us much of what we need to know about how the liturgy can and hopefully will shape the lives of individual believers and their relationships with nature. They give witness, on the one hand, to the universality of God's purposes and, on the other hand, to the world-historical realization of those purposes, through the One who comes in the name of the Lord. They also testify to what I have earlier called the sacrality of nature, nature's openness to the glorious presence of the omnipresent Christ. As the believer so praises God, we shall see, he or she can only stand in awe of nature, where God's glory is so dramatically displayed and which will one day be consummated in divine glory, with all the children of God, when the mission of the One who comes in the name of the Lord is finally concluded, when God will be all in all (1 Cor. 15:28).

Roman Catholic theologian Elizabeth Johnson has elegantly summed up the meaning of the biblical texts concerning glory, which inform the Sanctus, this way:

> . . . the glory of God is a luminous metaphor for the elusive nearness of the transcendent God glimpsed in and through the wondrous processes of nature, the history of freedom, and communities where justice and peace prevail. Using the term "glory of God" signifies that the incomprehensible holy mystery of God indwells the natural and human world as source, sustaining power, and goal of the universe, enlivening and loving it into liberating communion.[5]

So Isaiah, in the ancient Temple, had a vision of the holy God, which left both the prophet and the people convicted as unholy, as unworthy to stand in the presence of God. That vision also revealed to the prophet the universal God of the whole creation: "Holy, holy, holy is the LORD of hosts; the whole earth is full of his glory" (Isa. 6:3). Isaiah was in the Temple, presumably in the midst of its great rituals, yet the walls of the Temple for him were spiritually transparent to the whole creation.[6] The glory of God disclosed in the Temple, for the faith of Isaiah, and the glory of God revealed in the whole earth went hand in hand (later, church tradition, as reflected in the Sanctus, added the expression "the heavens" alongside "the earth," as reflecting God's glory). John Calvin picked up this theme with a figure of his own. The world of nature, he believed, is the theater of God's glory.[7]

A similar kind of polarity between the Temple of Jerusalem and what might be called the larger temple of nature appears, strikingly, in the poem of Psalms 42 and 43, as William P. Brown argued convincingly in a 2006 lecture.[8] The psalmist laments: "My tears have been my food day and night" (42:3). And to find a way through his tears, he remembers "passing into" the abode of the Holy One, the Temple, in the midst of a joyful, boisterous crowd, "the throng . . . in procession . . . with glad shouts and songs of thanksgiving, a multitude keeping festival" (42:4). In virtual parallel, the psalmist also remembers being at Mt. Hermon, "almost a paradisiacal scene," said Brown, a nine-thousand-foot, snow-covered mountain, with many streams cascading from its heights and slopes, which waters are the source of the Jordan River. Surrounded by this natural magnificence—as if he were in a different kind of temple—the psalmist hears what for him is nature's loud praise of God, akin to the people's boisterous praise of God in the temple, and the psalmist is likewise consoled: "Deep calls to deep at the noise of your cascades" (42:7).[9] Both of these "temples," for the psalmist, are expressions of the mercy or the steadfast love or the grace (*hesed*) of God (42:8). Like Isaiah in the Temple, seeing the whole earth full of the glory of God, the psalmist, imagining himself processing into the Temple surrounded by the praises of God and claimed by God's grace, thinks of himself likewise at the foot of that great mountain in the wilderness, similarly surrounded by the praises of God and likewise claimed by God's grace.[10]

Seeing this polarity between the two "temples," the liturgical center of ancient Israel, on the one hand, and the magnificence of the whole creation, on the other, will not surprise those who have followed recent field-changing studies of Old Testament theology. This theology now appears, convincingly, to be first and foremost a theology of God and the whole creation rather than merely a theology of God and human history (the latter view reigned supreme during the middle years of the last century; it still has its defenders).[11] This is already signaled, paradigmatically, by the creation narrative of Genesis 1, which envisions God as having a universal history of seven "days" with the whole creation, which, taken as a whole, God sees as "very good" (Gen. 1:31). The same kind of cosmic theological vision is adumbrated much more poetically in Psalm 104, which is, in effect, a commentary on the traditions that come to expression in the Genesis 1 narrative.[12] We will review both Psalm 104 and Genesis 1 in the next chapter.

Nature's Life of Its Own with God

Some Old Testament traditions take these creation themes a remarkable step further. They lead the believer out beyond the world of the Jerusalem Temple, as it were, and out beyond the urban world where that Temple has its setting and, further, out beyond that urban world's immediate cultivated environs—into the wilderness, where memories of the Temple and its civic and agricultural environment are quiescent. There believers are shown what I called many years ago "nature's life of its own with God."[13] The Scriptures abound with this kind of testimony.

Thus, Psalm 29 attests nature's life of its own with God as it celebrates the cacophonic thunder of God in the mountains, where lightning splits cedars of Lebanon. Psalm 148, in the same spirit, calls upon sea monsters and all deeps, fire and hail, snow and forest, stormy wind fulfilling God's command, mountains and all hills, fruit trees and all cedars, wild animals and all cattle, creeping things and flying birds, to praise the Lord from the earth. All the more so, the seer of the book of Job invites readers to contemplate the great and wild beasts of nature, and suggests that God has purposes with them of God's own and that God graciously hears and responds to their cries.[14] Similar motifs appear strikingly in Genesis 1 and Psalm 104.

Drawing out meanings from such texts in terms of twenty-first-century cosmology, we can say that God has a history of God's own with all the billions of galaxies and the black holes and the dark matter and the cosmic expansion of our universe, as well as with the ichthyosauruses and dinosaurs and great white sharks and the huge squid of the depths on Planet Earth. While we surely cannot grasp everything that this history means for God from where we stand, for we are as grasshoppers, as Isaiah says (Isa. 40:22), we can and do affirm that relationship between God and all the creatures of nature and God's bonding with all those creatures. God engages Godself personally with the creatures of nature. God calls the stars by name, for example, much as a traditional shepherd would sometimes call his or her sheep by name, making sure that none had been lost: "He . . . brings out their host and numbers them, calling them all by name; because he is great in strength, mighty in power, not one is missing" (Isa. 40:26). In a like manner, the psalmist vividly celebrates Yahweh's glorious relationship with the mythical monster of the deeps, the Leviathan, saying that God has created that incomprehensible creature "to rejoice in it" or "to play with it" (Ps. 104:26). So it comes as no surprise to notice, then, that in the flood story, once the chaos of the waters has subsided, God is depicted as making a covenant "with all flesh," not just with humans (Gen. 9:12). For the God whom we know in the Scriptures is, of course, the God of the whole creation.

It is clear from all this that the God attested in the Sanctus and described more fully in the texts that the Sanctus presupposes is a God who wants all creatures to flourish and a God who wants to bond with all creatures, not just with humans. This God communicates the divine glory to the whole earth, and to the heavens as well. Why? This is a question that must be addressed here, although it cannot be argued at length, since the reigning assumptions of much modern Christian thought run at cross-purposes with the vision of God taken for granted by the texts that the Sanctus presupposes.

The great majority of modern Christian theologians confidently answered the question why God communicated the divine glory to the whole creation in the following manner.[15] They thought of nature as a kind of stage that God posits, in order for God to carry out God's primary purposes with humanity. Thus, Karl Barth thought of creation richly but always as subordinated to God's primary purpose (rooted eternally in God's electing grace) of communicating salvation to humankind. Emil Brunner was almost flippant about the matter. Nature, he said, is the scenery and the stage God created in order to enter into a history with humankind. Clearly, such views are thoroughly anthropocentric and do not offer any satisfactory way of giving expression to the biblical under-standing of nature's life of its own with God, of God's special bonding with the creatures of nature, no less than human creatures. But it is no longer necessary for the church to be beholden theologically to this kind of anthropocentrism.

A different approach is thinkable, if we begin with a more generous reading of trinitarian theology than was characteristic of figures like Barth and Brunner. If we invoke traditional teachings about the Trinity, as they are presupposed by the liturgy throughout the ages, we can envision the one eternal God, the Father and the Son bonded together by love, which love is the Holy Spirit. Then we can imagine the same eternal God, Father, Son, and Holy Spirit, resolving to communicate Godself in love, to give of Godself in love, to a cosmic other, so that this cosmic other might flour-ish and so that God might bond Godself in love, in a history with that cosmic other. In the language of Jonathan Edwards, "it is fitting" for a God who is eternal and infinite self-giving to give of Godself to a near-infinite other and to engage in a history with that other. We will encounter a vivid expression of the meaning of this kind of divine bonding presently when we review the creation-narrative of Genesis 1 and have occasion to notice how God is depicted as entering into a partnership with the creatures of nature, as well as the human creature, during the deliberate, six-day sequence of God's originating creativity.

But why the diversity of the creatures? They are paraded before our eyes, as it were, in the Noah story, the clean and the unclean, the wild and the domesticated. Modern science has told us much more about crea-turely diversity on the earth alone, not to speak of the cosmos at large.

If God has resolved to communicate Godself in love to a cosmic other, why that enormous parade? Thomas Aquinas once pondered this kind of question, and he gave a complex metaphysical answer, which actually can be expressed quite simply. If an infinite God is to communicate Godself to a finite other as fully as possible, Thomas said, that finite other would fittingly be a world of nearly infinite but still finite diversity.[16]

Thomas is saying something like this. Imagine the God of infinite glory wanting to mirror that glory in a finite other. Fittingly, God's incomprehensible *power* would best be mirrored in billions of galaxies, let us say, rather than in the lilies of the field, although they would certainly have their appropriate share in the divine glory. Likewise, the vitalities of the divine *life* might best be mirrored in the lives of the great sea and land creatures, imagined by Job. And God's *personal center* and the intimacies of the shared love between the Father and the Son might well best be mirrored in the human creature and in human relationships like marriage and table fellowship, in particular. Hence, this universe of galaxies, ichthyosauruses, and humans.[17]

This is not the place to argue such thoughts at any length. But it is necessary to have them in mind, as possible and indeed helpful thoughts about God and God's purposes with the creation, since otherwise there could be a kind of theological vacuum in readers' minds, in this respect, and that vacuum could easily be filled, unconsciously if not consciously, by the kind of anthropocentric thinking about these matters that much modern theology has taken for granted.

Nature and the One Who Comes in the Name of the Lord

What thus can be heard in the first lines of the Sanctus, when voiced on the basis of its Old Testament heritage, that the God of glory communicates that glory in love to the whole creation in appropriately diverse ways, is then reaffirmed *and* particularized, in the lines that follow in the Sanctus:

> Hosanna in the highest.
> Blessed is he who comes in the name of the Lord.
> Hosanna in the highest.

"Hosanna," from Psalm 118:25, was used in the time of Jesus to give expression to messianic expectation, to salute the One who was called to restore the fortunes of Israel and to inaugurate the days of the new creation. "Blessed is he who comes in the name of the Lord" then interprets and expands similar messianic meanings, with reference to Jesus' celebrated entrance into the Holy City, Mount Zion, Jerusalem (see, for example, Matt. 21:9). Here the redemption of Jerusalem is understood, in keeping with expectations expressed in texts like Isaiah 25:6-10, as the center of a new creation of all things, a theme that finds its most explicit witness in Revelation 21, where we see the New Jerusalem coming down out of heaven from God and being established in the midst of a new heavens and a new earth. Paul gives voice to similar themes in Romans 8: to the whole creation groaning in travail, awaiting its own salvation, through the work of Christ, pending the redemption of the children of God, by the same Christ.

Paul Tillich once spoke memorably about the being and work of Christ in this respect as "the concrete universal." This abstract-sounding, but in fact deeply existential, language might be helpful for some to ponder in order to grasp more deeply the significance of the liturgical testimony here to "the One who comes." For Tillich, "In so far as [Christ] is absolutely concrete, the relation to him can be a completely existential concern. In so far as he is absolutely universal, the relation to him includes potentially all possible relations and can, therefore, be unconditional and infinite." Tillich also insisted that that vision of the universality of Christ was not born of philosophical speculation, but was "a matter of life and death for the early church" as it proclaimed the victory of Christ over death and the demonic.[18] To speak here, then, of the universal God of the whole creation is at the same time to speak, in the same kind of language, of the concrete God of the whole creation, in the person of the One who comes.

That is the all-inclusive scope and the concrete focus of the witness of the Sanctus. In modern theological language, it points us to the Wholly Other and the Wholly Near God, who is at once the Wholly Universal and the Wholly Concrete God. Consider Karl Barth, the great Reformed theologian of the last century, who first gained notoriety in the 1920s for his "Theology of Crisis" that accented and indeed celebrated the God whom he called the "Wholly Other."[19] While there were historically justified reasons for this approach to God in that era, that vision of God can no longer be considered to be a fully valid interpretation of the witness of the Scriptures, particularly in light of our purpose here to give a new hearing to the theology of descent. "Wholly Other," taken by itself, sounds too much like a proclamation of the theology of ascent. In this respect, we will be better instructed to speak of God, drawing on Luther's paradoxical theology, as both "Wholly Other" and "Wholly Near."

Barth himself moved in this direction in his mature thought, christologically and anthropologically, when he talked about "the humanity of God." But even to say this much is not to say enough, from the perspective of the Sanctus, interpreted along the lines of its biblical intentionality. For the Scriptures, and for the texts that inform the Sanctus in particular, the God who is attested is not only the God who is Wholly Other and Wholly Near. This God is also the God who is Wholly Universal and Wholly Concrete, encompassing and enlivening and loving all things, pantalogically. Barth also attempted to make this claim his own, by his emphasis on what in Tillichian terms is the Wholly Concrete God, but Barth did so in a way that finally subordinated the world of nature to human history anthropocentrically and to that degree denigrated nature, probably without intending to do so.[20] Hence the emphasis here on the Wholly Universal God, as well as the Wholly Concrete God, in creedal terms, "God the Father Almighty," as well as "God the Son."

What is thus announced in the Sanctus about the Wholly Universal and the Wholly Concrete God is then recapitulated in the remainder of the eucharistic prayer, which, as we have seen, in its most expressive forms, celebrates the works of God in the whole creation and the works of the One who is to come, the Messiah, who consummates the universal history of God with all things.

The Believer: Standing in Awestruck Wonder

In all this—summarized in the Sanctus—the believer steps back and praises God for this universal history, consummated in Christ. As the eucharistic prayer unfolds, it is not until the words of institution that the believer emerges explicitly into the picture: "This is my body, given for you." But in the context of that prayer, even the words of institution, which so deeply claim the believer, are words of thanksgiving and praise that proclaim what *Jesus* did on the night in which he was betrayed. It is only with the words of administration—such as, "the body of Christ, given for you" and "the blood of Christ, shed for you"—that that universal praise comes to rest, with explicit reference to personal meanings for the believer himself or herself.

The Sanctus and the ensuing eucharistic prayer are profoundly theo-centric (more specifically, trinitarian) and christocentric, not primarily anthropocentric, surely not egocentric. They give testimony to the cosmic purposes and providence of the Wholly Universal and Wholly Concrete God. And of course, in this respect, the Sanctus and the eucharistic prayer itself by no means stand alone in the liturgy. The same theocentric and christocentric themes are announced virtually everywhere in the liturgy, in hymns and Scripture readings and proclamation and prayers and creeds. The whole liturgy is, in this respect, one single great song of praise for the cosmic grace of the Wholly Universal and Wholly Concrete God.

This framework of praise of the God of the whole creation means, in turn, that nature has its own place, its own right, its own history, in the universal history of God, alongside of God's history with humankind. This theocentric and christocentric symphony of praise is testimony to nature's own life with God, independent of the blessings that nature also showers upon humans, by the grace of God. We can talk about nature in this respect as an Ens—that is, an "other" in its own right, validated by God, calling for respect in itself, not open, as such, to human intervention of any kind, surely not human dominion of any kind. Human dominion over nature is of course attested in the Old Testament, but it is by no means the only kind of relationship with nature to which the human creature is called. There is also "serving," which I will discuss next, in addition to what may best here be called awestruck wonder.

The American philosopher Norman O. Brown once stated: "Doing nothing is the supreme action." Whatever Brown may have intended to suggest by those words, they help to tell a liturgical truth. In relationship with nature, as with God in the first place, the first and definitive act by the believer is to do *nothing*—other than to praise God. The first and definitive act in the life of the liturgically molded believer is to step back and to contemplate all the wonders of God's gracious acts, as Creator, Savior, and Consummator, more particularly, in our view here, wonders that are given in the world of nature, by grace alone—and to be grateful.

This, importantly, is not to romanticize nature. This is a particularly important point for American Christians to grasp, since American culture, at least since the time of writers like Thoreau and John Muir, has been shaped by a romantic, even sentimentalizing, sense for nature.[21] This has run the gamut from the gigantic, idyllic canvases produced by the Hudson River School to the saccharine images of Hallmark greeting cards, from the heroic stories of Kit Carson in the wilderness to the touching narratives of the likes of Bambi.

The Bible, in contrast, sees nature as it is, in terms of its own evolutionary history with God, with its dark depths as well as its bright heights. It shows us the terrible Leviathans and bids us to listen to the cacophonous thunder, to see the cedars of Lebanon being split by lightning and to hear the lions roaring for their prey in the night—all themes from the Psalms. An I-Ens relationship, as I have indicated earlier, can and often does comprehend an encounter with the sublime, even the repulsive, no less than the beautiful or the alluring. But whether sublime or beautiful, repulsive or alluring, the Ens stands in its own right before God and with God. We humans do not, in any theological sense, "own" nature or any creature of nature, whether bright and beautiful or dark and sinister. Nature is not our scenery, nor our storehouse of resources. The earth is the Lord's and the fullness thereof (Ps. 24:1), not ours. Our most fundamental, God-given relationship with nature can only be awestruck wonder and then praise to God, the Creator, Savior, and Consummator of all things.

That is the way I felt one summer day in the Swiss Alps a few years ago, when dark clouds suddenly cleared and the afternoon sun seemed the create the world anew, as my wife and I were hiking down from the chilling and fog-bound terrain at the base of the Eiger, Moench, and Jungfrau mountains, whose peaks had just come into view. As the clouds parted, we discovered that we were descending on one side of a lush green valley. More than a mile across that valley, to our left, we saw the face of towering cliffs, from which poured stream after stream, cascading hundreds and hundreds of feet down to the depths of the valley below, with sounds of occasional ice-falls of the breaking glaciers above thundering in the distance.

At that moment, it was time for us to step back and to do nothing, except to share our amazement in silence and to praise God in our hearts for all that magnificence. As the psalmist did, when he stood in a similar place below the great heights of snow-covered Mt. Hermon, and contemplated the many roaring streams cascading hundreds of feet down to streams that fed the beginnings of the Jordan River: "Deep calls to deep at the noise of your cascades; all your breakers and your billows sweep over me. By day Yahweh commands his grace [hesed], and by night his song is with me, praise to the God of my life" (Ps. 42:7-8).[22] This is the primordial beginning of the Christian's walk with nature, to stand back in awe and wonder and to do nothing—except to praise the cosmic grace of God. The Christian's walk with nature that is shaped by the renewed liturgy begins with no steps.

The Believer: Contemplating the Glory of Christ

And more. Inspired by the Spirit, the believer who stands still in awestruck wonder before nature can know that he or she is contemplating the glories of the resurrected and ascended Christ in all things. We have already considered this theme—the ubiquity of Christ—at some length. Instructed by the witness of Luther and indeed extending it further, we can now see how the believer, whose life is shaped by the liturgy, may encounter this Christ as the believer engages the world of nature. Now it is time to explore the contours of that encounter more concretely.

To this end, we Christians in the West will benefit from some spiritual instruction from our brothers and sisters in the Orthodox churches of the East. In the West, surely since the time of St. Francis in the thirteenth century, if not before, the Christian imagination has been affixed intensely on the image of Jesus Christ as "the man of sorrows." This imagery was engraved in the Western Christian soul by the immensely influential spirituality of Francis, particularly by his own identification with the suffering human, Jesus. It was further sealed in the Christian mind and heart by the image of Francis's stigmatization, his being marked with the wounds of Christ. Christian art in the West has, accordingly, been preoccupied with, even reveled in, the rich symbolism of the human figure of Jesus on the cross. Theologically this spiritual and esthetic thematizing was given classic expression by St. Anselm, who, as his study of 1098, *Why the God/Man? (Cur Deus Homo?)*, showed, was preoccupied with the image of Christ the Victim (*Christus Victim*).

In contrast, the theology of the Christian East, at least since the time of Irenaeus in the second century, has been preoccupied with the risen and exalted Jesus, Christ the Victor (*Christus Victor*). This, as is well known, is reflected in the iconography of the Eastern churches, especially in the great domes of Eastern basilicas, where typically the commanding image of Christ the ruler of all things (*Pantocrator*) towers over and spiritually charges the central space where the liturgical action unfolds. Can we Western Christians live our way into the theological and esthetic world of that kind of iconography, not abandoning the *Christus Victim* imagery, surely but claiming the *Christus Victor* imagery in a new way, if not for the first time? Western travelers have flocked to places like Ravenna for centuries, in order to marvel at the aesthetic riches of the Byzantine mosaics in churches like the Basilica of San Vitale. Can we contemplate the great dome in that basilica, where at the center the image of the Lamb Triumphant, held aloft by angels, defines that whole starry, blue curving space, and then adore the cosmic Lord who is there proclaimed?

Strikingly, Joseph Sittler, the leading Western proponent of cosmic Christology in our era, lived into precisely that kind of experience, as he himself once recounted. It was for him a kind of conversion experience. In the context of a discussion of Christ as *Pantocrator*, Sittler tells this story:

> In the Cathedral of the Holy Trinity at Zagorsk, Russia, during the Feast of the Dormition, standing for hours amidst the prayers of the faithful before the iconostasis [the screen that separates the sanctuary from the nave, covered with icons, hence its name] with its Anton Rubleff icons—literal presences of the "mighty cloud of witnesses"—I came to understand a mode of Christ's reality that shattered assumptions about Western christological comprehensiveness and beckoned toward partly forgotten dimensions of Catholic christology.[23]

Like Sittler, when I was a young theological student in 1965, I myself was led to make what were for me astounding spiritual discoveries during some travels in the conglomerate nation that was then still known as Yugoslavia, where I had gone to visit several of the hundreds of centuries-old Orthodox monasteries and churches that so enhance that region in the Balkans. In Kosovo, in particular, I was overwhelmed not only by the variegated iconography of many kinds in monasteries like those at Pec and Decani but above all by the great images of the cosmic Christ inscribed in the sanctuary domes and elsewhere, images to which I have already referred. Like Sittler in Russia, I began to see testimonies to the cosmic Lordship of Christ that I had never seen with my own eyes before. I commend that kind of imaginative journey to my readers. Think yet again of Jesus—imagine Jesus—not only as the man of sorrows, but also as the cosmic Lamb Triumphant, risen and ascended, and thereby in, with, and under all things.

Behind that iconographical testimony in those Orthodox churches is the faith of the New Testament itself, which that testimony helps to illuminate. The witness of the letter to the Colossians is particularly suggestive at this point, as Joseph Sittler proclaimed to the whole ecumenical church in 1961. It celebrates Jesus Christ as "the image of the invisible God, the firstborn of all creation" (Col. 1:15). We encounter similar claims concerning Christ in the letter to the Hebrews: "He is the reflection of God's glory and the exact imprint of God's very being, and he sustains all things by his powerful word" (Heb. 1:3). This witness to Christ as "the image" has fascinated Christian theologians and mystics throughout the ages. What I can affirm here in short compass, compared to that long tradition of reflection and contemplation, can at best only be written in minuscule. But hopefully these observations will nevertheless draw out some of the meanings of the originating biblical texts.

If we begin with the prophet Isaiah's vision of the glory of God in the Temple, which glory Isaiah also contemplates filling the whole earth, we have a way of envisioning some of the meanings that appear to have been given with the texts from Colossians and Hebrews. When we contemplate the glory of God reflected in the world of nature, as the psalmist encountered it at Mt. Hermon and as my wife and I did likewise in the Swiss Alps, we can know that that which reflects that glory back to us, as if it were a mirror, is the image of God, the cosmic Christ, who is in, with, and under all things. Those mountains are, in that sense, icons of Christ.

Instructed by Luther, likewise, we also are free to contemplate the glory of God reflected in that image not only macroscopically but also—in the root meaning of the word—microscopically. Yes, inspired by the Spirit, we can surely see all the glory of God reflected back to us from those mountains, through the ubiquitous Christ. Likewise, from the starry skies at night in all their beauty and unfathomableness, as the psalmist says: "The heavens are telling the glory of God" (Ps. 19:1). But just as much, if we are also inspired by the Spirit, we can contemplate all the glory of God reflected back to us in a single lily. This, in keeping with the invitation of Jesus, to behold the lilies of the field (as Sittler instructed us to translate this text), for Solomon in all his glory was not arrayed as one of these (Matt. 6:28–29). Can we imagine the fullness of God's glory, reflected to us by the risen and ascended Christ, who is in, with, and under that flower? Luther could entertain thoughts like that—he once observed that one will die of wonder, if one truly understands a grain of wheat—because he could imagine space first and foremost in terms of God's space, rather than our mundane, three-dimensional space. The young Paul Tillich may have been giving voice to the same kind of experience once, when, as he was visiting a steel plant, he was shown flowing molten steel and stood there in charged silence and contemplated that glowing, fiery mass, he said to himself: "That is God."[24]

As my wife and I stood that day in the Swiss Alps in rapt attention before the towering cliffs and the plummeting cascades of the waters, hearing the thunderous ice-falls, we decided to sit down on the grass, and have a repast of some crusts of bread, a few sausages, and a small flask of wine. As I opened my pack to find the food, I noticed delicate white flowers all around us in the grass. Were these the edelweiss blossoms that I had learned to sing about as a child? I held her hand as we prayed together, as is our wont, the table grace my parents taught me—"Come Lord Jesus, be thou our guest. And let these gifts to us be blessed." Holding the hand that had held mine for more than forty years, with that sacral vista before us and those sacral blossoms in the grass around us, those were the only words I could find to express my overwhelming gratitude to God, for so disclosing Godself to us, through Jesus Christ, our Lord.

Serving Nature

To stand in awestruck wonder before the creatures of nature, contemplating God's mysterious yet glorious history with the whole world of nature, beyond the environs of human history, is where the story of the individual believer's liturgically shaped walk with nature may appropriately begin. But that encounter with the sacrality of nature surely is not the whole story.

Nature and Human Fallenness

Things did not work out as they should have. That is the often explicitly stated assumption of the whole Bible and of the liturgy in particular. However it is expressed in the Scriptures, whether discursively, as by Paul in his letter to the Romans when he states that "all, both Jews and Greeks, are under the power of sin" (Rom. 3:9); or narratively, as by the Yahwist in his creation-and-fall story in Genesis 2–3, the Scriptures presuppose that humans have "fallen" and that, with that fall, something has gone radically wrong with the whole of human history—although *not* with the whole of nature (a thought I will return to). The Old Testament depicts the human universality of that radical wrong in narratives like the Tower of Babel and the flood stories.

By the time of the early church, biblical witnesses also took it for granted that other mysterious "powers" of Death and evil had become implicated in the fallen condition of human history as well. Whether these biblical witnesses believed, in addition, that the world of nature, in its own life with God, had fallen, is another question. Notwithstanding the fact that a number of theological interpreters of the Bible, beginning with Origen in the second century, have taken it for granted that the world of nature has fallen, along with humanity, the biblical evidence points in the opposite direction. For the Bible, there has been no "cosmic fall."[25] While the whole of nature has *not* fallen, *the human relationship with nature has fallen*. Of that there need be little doubt, whether we read the Scriptures or review accounts of human history in recent centuries. By our own time, few would deny that humans have become the archenemy of the world of nature. We can read the Scriptures, indeed, as giving us grounds for precisely such a claim, whether it be in the story in Genesis 3 of God cursing the earth because of human sin or Paul's vision in Romans 8 of the whole creation groaning in travail, waiting innocently for its liberation, pending the prior liberation of the sinful children of God.

This "reality check" casts a kind of dark veil over the vision of the believer's habit of faith that we have thus far identified. How was it possible, for example, for my wife and me to stand awestruck before the wonders of God in the Swiss Alps, while at the same time in other parts of the globe an insane war was raging in Iraq and a despicable genocide was beginning to unfold in Darfur? Did it not matter to us, likewise, that those great glaciers of the Alps, which so thunderously proclaimed to us the glory of God when mammoth ice-falls from them plummeted into the depths of the valley below, were under attack by forces of climate change, forces that themselves were also poised to wreak even greater havoc in the already impoverished world of the coastal peoples of Bangladesh? Was our encounter with the Alps mere tunnel-visioned, escapist romanticism?

Sinful creature that I am, who am I to say that it was not? I do not believe that it was. But, be that as it may, I know that I must tell the whole truth here, as everywhere else, of course. And that is what I propose to try to do.

The One Who Comes in the Name of the Lord—to Die

Building on the witness of the Scriptures, the liturgy announces through-out that the One who comes in the name of the Lord is the One who comes to die on the cross in order to save the children of Adam and Eve from their sins. The liturgy is, in fact, a cruciform ritual.

The liturgy presupposes, to begin with, the stance of Isaiah in the Temple, on the part of the entire assembly: "Woe is me! I am lost, for I am a man of unclean lips, and I live among a people of unclean lips; yet my eyes have seen the King, the LORD of hosts" (Isa. 6:5). This awareness of individual and corporate sinfulness permeates the liturgy, from beginning to ending, and comes to expression in acts of confession, hymnody, proclamation, and in the eucharistic rite itself, with prayers like this one: "Lord, I am not worthy to come into your house." Liturgical proclamation, in particular, regularly tells and illustrates the horrendous story of human evil, both individually and globally, and therewith convicts the people of their complicity.

All this is heightened and further disclosed by liturgical testimony, at every juncture, to the One who comes in the name of the Lord to die so that all may live. Perhaps the apex of this testimony is the hymn *Agnus Dei* ("Lamb of God"), which has been a freestanding part of the liturgy at least since 700 C.E. In our day, it is often sung at the time of the administration of the bread and the cup during the Eucharist, in words like these:

> Lamb of God, you take away the sin of the world; have mercy on us.
> Lamb of God, you take away the sin of the world, have mercy on us.
> Lamb of God, you take away the sin of the world, grant us peace.[26]

The mention of "peace" in the *Agnus Dei* is surely no historical accident. For that is how the death of the Messiah was envisioned from the very beginning.[27] In terms of the Suffering Servant announced by Second Isaiah, the Messiah was seen from the first by early Christian assemblies, as the One who comes to die in order to make peace. He was the One, according to Luke, whose coming would bring peace to all the people (Luke 2:14). He was the One, indeed, who, by his death, according to the Pauline author of Colossians, would bring peace to all things, to the entire cosmos (Col. 1:20). Testimony from the book of Revelation, with its powerful imagery of the crucified and exalted Lamb of God at the right hand of God, the Alpha and the Omega of all things, points in the same direction (Rev. 1:4-9).

So the liturgy, implicitly and explicitly, proclaims that there is a gracious divine remedy—and more—to human fallenness and its effects. For Paul and other New Testament witnesses, as Jürgen Moltmann and others have argued, the coming of the Messiah was not only a remedy for human sin but also a new act of divine creation, especially by the resurrection of the Messiah. And that new act, presupposing the restoration of human history to its originally intended role in the history of God with all things through the death of Christ, *also* inaugurated, by anticipation—proleptically—the new age of the coming peaceable kingdom of the end times.[28]

Even if we had much more space to consider this theme, however, we would still, in the end, not be able to reach beyond the mystery of the cross and resurrection. This is why, throughout the ages, the church has found it most advantageous to announce this great and mysterious truth of remedy for sin and new life in Christ liturgically by a progression of seasonal celebrations, from Lent and Good Friday as its culmination, through the Easter Vigil, to the great celebration of Easter Day itself.

The Servant Lord and the Cosmos

And the mystery of the Servant Lord who came to die and who rose again is even larger. It has a cosmic reach, which we will of course want to notice, if not extensively describe, given the focus of our explorations in this book.[29] Paul announces this cosmic reach in citing the great christological hymn known to the early Christian assembly in Philippi, giving glory to Christ:

> who, though he was in the form of God . . . humbled himself and became obedient to the point of death—even death on a cross. Therefore God also highly exalted him and gave him the name that is above every name, so that at the name of Jesus every knee should bend, in heaven and on earth and under the earth. . . . (Phil. 2:6-10)

The Pauline author of Colossians sees the vocation of the servant Christ similarly in cosmic terms, again quoting an early Christian hymn: ". . . through him God was pleased to reconcile to himself all things, whether on earth or in heaven, by making peace through the blood of his cross" (Col. 1:20).

Drawing on insights from the theology of descent, it is possible to envision in what way the Servant Christ is the Lord of all, in, with, and under all things, as well as being the Lord of those gathered in the assembly who confess his name. We have already considered the cosmic vocation of Christ in our explorations of the theme of Christ the image of God, who reflects back from nature, for those who are given eyes to see, the glory of God in all things. Here we can extend those thoughts in terms of another biblical image, Christ as the good shepherd.

"I am the good shepherd," Jesus says in the Gospel of John; "the good shepherd lays down his life for the sheep" (John 10:14, 15). This is one of several noteworthy "I am" statements in Fourth Gospel. It is generally agreed that such claims, in addition to all their specific meanings in their particular contexts, hearken back to the name of the Creator and Redeemer God in the book of Exodus (Exod. 3:14), usually translated, "I AM WHO I AM." These sayings also give expression to the Gospel of John's "*Logos* theology" (or "Word theology") announced in its very first chapter. That *Logos* theology was anchored in the confession of the *Logos*-made flesh, and that made John's theology in this respect unique in its own philosophical and theological environment. Yet the accent on the incarnation of the *Logos* was only one of the meanings John meant to convey, as Russell Bradner Norris Jr. explains:

> Johannine use of the term *logos* emerges from deep theological reflection on the life of Jesus as the central revelation of God. The Evangelist speaks not of some philosophical abstraction, but of the *logos* incarnate in human form, who is the *logos* for precisely that reason. At the same time, John emphasizes more strongly than other New Testament writers the cosmic dimensions of the Word, and specifically the participation of the pre-existent Christ in the creation of the world. It is significant that the Gospel of John begins with the same words found in the first book of the Hebrew scriptures. . . . The evangelist offers a new Genesis account, a new creation story, one centered in the life, death, and resurrection of Jesus Christ, the incarnate *logos* of God.[30]

The "I am" statements throughout the Gospel of John further attest that kind of cosmic meaning that John wants us to attach to Jesus, the *Logos* made flesh.[31] Seen in this setting, it is possible to claim Jesus' good shepherd pronouncement as a paradigmatic text for our purposes here.[32]

I am the good shepherd, says Jesus. Is it not possible to imagine Jesus Christ as the *cosmic* good shepherd? Is it not possible to imagine him gathering all things, calling all things into being in relationship to each other, as a shepherd gathers the flock? Is it not also possible to imagine the cosmic shepherd in some sense stepping back, even resting, in accord with the vision of Genesis 1, so that every creaturely domain might be on its own and in relationship with all others, as a shepherd on occasion will rest, contemplating his or her flock and taking joy in the growth and uniqueness of individual sheep or, on some occasions, patiently enduring what they are, on their own, making of themselves?[33] Is it not possible, as well, to imagine the cosmic shepherd as bearing with all creatures, suffering especially with those creatures who experience pain, even singling out some creaturely domains or even individuals for special care and attention, as a good shepherd does, when he or she leaves the flock behind and seeks out the sheep which is lost?[34] Is it not possible, finally, to imagine the cosmic shepherd as leading the whole cosmic flock one day, through and beyond the valley of the shadows of cosmic entropy, to a new and eternal pasture, where the lamb will lie down with the lion and where, finally, the cosmic shepherd will bring his gloriously variegated galactic flock into the presence of the Giver of every good and perfect gift, in the power of the Spirit,[35] in eternal peace, so that this God may then be all in all?

The Servant Lord and the Believer Who Serves Nature

The theme of the Servant Lord who came to die, since "God so loved the world" (John 3:16), is, without a doubt, essential for the liturgy. The liturgy, as I have said, is a cruciform rite. Since the liturgy itself is so formed, therefore, and since the liturgy more generally is the mode of identity formation of the church, we now are ready to inquire how the liturgy shapes the believer's habit of faith in this respect.

The answer will be no surprise to anyone who knows anything about the liturgy or the biblical traditions that inform the liturgy. Paul announced it memorably in the text we have just reviewed, his letter to the Philippians, as the lead theme in the hymn he quoted: "Let the same mind be in you that was in Christ Jesus, who, though he was in the form of God . . . , emptied himself, taking the form of a slave . . . and became obedient to the point of death—even death on a cross. Therefore God also highly exalted him and gave him the name that is above every name . . ." (Phil. 2:5-9).

How is the individual believer, then, shaped by the cruciform liturgy, to have the same mind as the crucified and exalted Christ? More particularly, how is the individual believer to be a servant of the Servant in his or her relationship with nature? And how is the individual believer to do this, in a world that is not yet fully redeemed, that is still very much in the grips of human fallenness and the principalities and powers of Death and destruction?

A servant of nature? This very construct has to be addressed at the outset, since to modern ears and indeed to many modern Christian ears in particular, it may well sound counterintuitive. Everyone, critics of Christianity and believers alike, knows that Christians have been taught throughout the ages that humans have been given *dominion* over nature. What has become of that teaching? We will have occasion to discuss the meanings of human dominion over nature presently. Here it is sufficient to observe that human dominion over nature in a sinful world is perhaps the single most important *problem* that must be addressed in these times of global crisis. First, however, I need to identify another theme that could come as a surprise to many moderns, Christians and others alike.

The liturgy instills the habit of serving nature in the believer, just as it instills the habit of standing still, in awestruck contemplation of nature. Call this theme of serving nature a friendly amendment to the idea of servanthood that has been cherished in major Christian traditions throughout the ages. For many, it will indeed be surprisingly new. But it is given with the treasury of testimony, biblical and liturgical, that is the church's heritage today. It has surfaced at various points in Christian practices throughout the ages, above all in the towering figure of the humble, down-to-earth St. Francis. His life was profoundly shaped by the liturgy; following his conversion, Francis attended Mass daily. Francis learned his love of otherkind, of the worms, the wolves, and the birds, from the self-giving figure of Christ on the cross, whom he encountered in the Eucharist. Francis also celebrated this love of nature, as we have seen, in one great, climactic witness of his life and ministry: his creation of the Christmas Creche Mass, in the dark woods, in front of a cave, with domestic animals gathered for the occasion. Francis was a servant of nature perhaps *par excellence*.

There are biblical roots for these kinds of practices, which, ironically enough, are as thoroughly attested as the dominion traditions in the Bible but rarely recalled in public discussions of the matter, if known at all. We will return to our explorations of the theme of the believer as a servant of nature after we have taken the time to review the theme of serving nature in Genesis 2.

The Human Servant of Nature according to Genesis 2

Above all, at this point, we can turn to the testimony of the author in Genesis 2, generally called "the Yahwist." In its historic setting, the narrative of Genesis 2 is thoroughly influenced by its agrarian setting. As Theodore Hiebert has emphasized, for the writer of Genesis 2, "arable land is the primary datum in his theology of divine blessing and curse." In response to human sinfulness, the divine curse diminishes the land's productivity, until the curse is lifted. God's blessing of Abraham is chiefly the gift of arable land. Also for the Yahwist, the three great harvest festivals of Israel shape the cultic calendar, and the primary cultic activity of these festivals is the presentation to God of the first fruits of the land and the flock.[36]

So it comes as no surprise then to hear in the Yahwist's creation story that Adam is made from the earth—*adamah*. This is an observation that is frequently made, but Hiebert instructively wants to underline the concrete meaning of that Hebrew word. Adam, it turns out, is not just created from the earth; he is created from the "arable soil." Such is the first human's agrarian identity, according to the Yahwist. "It is the claim that humanity's archetypal agricultural vocation is implanted within humans by the very stuff out of which they are made, the arable soil itself," Hiebert observes. "Humans, made from farmland, are destined to farm it in life and to return to it in death" (Gen. 3:19, 23).[37]

For the Yahwist, it is almost as if God himself were the premiere gardener. After forming the human creature from the arable soil, Yahweh himself "planted a garden in Eden," where he placed the human creature. Then "out of the ground the Lord God made to grow every tree that is pleasant to the sight and good for food" (Gen. 2:8-9). Yahweh also, in due course, brings forth animals to be part of this landscape (Gen. 2:19). The strong implication seems to be that Yahweh himself is involved in the care and the protection of this garden, setting the stage for the human creature to do likewise.[38]

Further, for the Yahwist, *the land* is a character in its own right in this theological drama. The land has its own integrity, in this sense, its own essential place in the greater scheme of things. It is not just a platform to support human life. The reason why the human is created, to begin with, is that there was no one to serve the land (Gen. 2:5). So we see Yahweh forming the human being from the arable soil—a theme that is missing from the narrative of Genesis 1, where the humans are created, as it were, directly—and then taking the human and placing him in the Garden of Eden in order to serve (*abad*) the land and protect (*samar*) it.

The most familiar English translations of these words—"to till and to keep"—are profoundly misleading. The Hebrew tells a much different story. The first term has the same Hebrew root as the word used by Second Isaiah to refer to "the *servant* of the Lord." The second term has the same Hebrew root as the word used in the Aaronic blessing: "May the Lord bless you and *keep* you." With only the received translation before them, general readers of this text might well understand it as a kind of agribusiness manifesto: to develop the productivity of the land and keep the profits. They would have no reason to think that the words refer in fact to identifying and responding to needs of the land itself and protecting the land from abuse or destruction.

The image we have here is something like this: the experienced family farmer communing with the land—not too strong an expositional phrase in this context—down on his or her knees, gently transplanting a seedling, carefully finding a source of water for the plant, and then assessing ways to protect the plant from predators. Or we see the same farmer, thoughtfully and contemplatively pruning a fruit tree, so that it can blossom to its fullest, and then fertilizing it with carefully gathered manure. Yet again, to cite a nonagricultural example, we can well imagine suburbanites living in the northeastern United States, replacing their omnipresent lawns with meadow grasses and their Norway maples with less invasive species for the sake of enhancing the biodiversity of the entire northeastern forest system.[39] Here we can see coming into view the service of nature that the Yahwist champions.

The Yahwist depicts the human's relationship to the animals, in much the same manner, in terms of tangible solidarity rather than intervention, certainly not any kind of domination. To begin with, both the human and the animals are made from the same arable soil (Gen. 2:7, 19). Further, there is no apparent theological reason, as there was for Genesis 1, sharply to define the differentiation between the two families of creatures, no "image of God" construct for the human in the Yahwist's view. Instead, the Yahwist is apparently quite comfortable with the thought that God makes both the human and the animal a "living soul" (*nephesh hayya*)

(Gen. 2:7, 19). One can recall here that in traditional agricultural societies humans and domesticated animals lived in very close proximity indeed, often occupying the same quarters. That kind of familial closeness is taken for granted by the Yahwist.

The account of Adam naming the animals reflects the same Yahwistic assumptions, although the text has often been interpreted otherwise.[40] Many commentaries in the last century routinely voiced the judgment, often drawing on examples from the history of religions, that naming is an act of power and that therefore Adam's naming of the animals was to be interpreted in terms of dominance.[41] The text, however, seen in its biblical context, actually tells a radically different story. In a certain sense, God is depicted as withdrawing, for this moment, from the scene, when God brings the animals to Adam to see what the human might name them (Gen. 2:19). But this can be read as a thoughtful withdrawal to encourage creaturely bonding, rather than as some disinterested deistic withdrawal whose purpose would be to hand over power to the human. The naming itself, moreover, can be understood as an act of affection on the part of the human, akin to the notion that Yahweh gives Israel, his beloved, a name (for example, Isa. 56:5) or when Adam, rejoicing, gives the woman who is to be his strong, personal partner, a name (Gen. 2:23). Comradeship on the part of Adam with the animals seems to be implied here in this naming scene, perhaps even with nuances of friendship and self-giving.[42] All this indicates that, for the Yahwist, God plants the garden and then places the humans in it as a blessing for the humans *and* as a calling, to serve and to protect the most fundamental stuff of the garden, the arable soil.

The Yahwist leaves us in little doubt, however, that the human is distinct from the animals and destined for personal communion with God and other humans in a way that animals are not. Adam finds no one with whom to commune among the animals. Adam only finds such a partner in the woman—exuberantly—who is fashioned by Yahweh not from the arable land directly, as Adam and the animals were, but from Adam's own flesh. The idea of intense personal intimacy that is here suggested is sealed by the notion that the two are to be "one flesh" (Gen. 2:24). The idea of the humans' intimacy with Yahweh is sealed, in a like manner, by the story of Yahweh conversing with them (for instance, Gen. 2:16), as he does not do with the animals.

All this transpires in a setting of extraordinary natural fecundity, indeed in a garden of "delights," which is what "Eden" means. While

Adam and then Eve are placed in that garden to serve it and to protect it, there is no sense that that kind of daily work was in any sense to be burdensome for them—that kind of experience awaited them "after the fall." The garden was a place of delights where they communed intimately with their Creator, who, we are told, walked with them, where they found bountiful and beautiful blessings in the creatures all around them, and where they lived at peace, in a certain kind of fellowship with all the animals. Although the Yahwist did not use these exact words to describe this primal scene, he very well could have depicted God at this point in his story, as the Genesis 1 writer did in his own terms, seeing that all things were "very good."

The Believer Serving Nature in a Sinful World

The narrative of Genesis 2, however, and its account of the divine intention for the human being to serve nature, cannot be allowed to stand by itself, any more than the biblical witness to standing in awe before the glories of nature in all the earth and beyond can be allowed to stand by itself. If the believer were to hold firmly to the witness of Genesis 2 alone, the result would in all likelihood be some kind of agricultural romanticism, disconnected from the realities of our globalizing world in crisis. The motif of serving nature must therefore be seen in its setting in the whole biblical narrative.[43] Which means, first and foremost, from the perspective of a liturgically formed faith, that the theme of serving nature in Genesis 2 must be coordinated with texts like the hymn celebrating the Servant of God in Philippians 2. The believer who is habitually committed to serving nature must have the same mind that was in Christ Jesus (Phil. 2:5).

We have already seen some of the implications of having the mind of Christ Jesus in the writings of Paul. The apostle worked to establish countercultural communities in the name of Christ, communities in which the ideology of domination of Roman society of the time was radically challenged, communities in which male and female, rich and poor, Jew and Greek were understood to be one—equals—in Christ Jesus. Whether Christians today in America have the spiritual wherewithal and the hands-on theological resources to walk that walk of Pauline equality with the whole earth is a real question. If we are to translate the indicative of Genesis 2—you are created to serve and protect nature—into an imperative for individual Christian countercultural discipleship in our sinful world, what would that look like?

American Christians face a special challenge at this point, in view of the affluence of many of us, certainly by most global standards. Mindful of the teaching of Jesus about the difficulty of the rich entering into the kingdom of God, something as easy as a camel going through the eye of a needle (Matt. 19:24), it will be prudent for us to follow the directions of the old railroad-crossing signs: *stop*, *look*, and *listen*. Simply plunging forward, as it were, to serve nature may be more self-serving than serving. So we must stop and look at who we are, to begin with.

Here the example of St. Francis can be instructive. While Francis's commitment to serve nature, to which I have already alluded, is compelling for many American Christians, the inner side of that Franciscan commitment is rarely discussed in American church circles. Francis's love of nature was intimately related to his commitment to voluntary poverty.[44] It may be tiresome for American Christians to hear this fact again and again, but it remains true and noteworthy. With some 6 percent of the world's population, Americans consume more than 50 percent of the world's resources. It all comes to a head for many American Christians when they celebrate the birth of the Lord born in a stable, who was to have no place to lay his head, by consummating a glut of consumerism. Few Christians that I know are happy with this situation. But few, myself included, have been able to address it effectively over any length of time. We may "talk the talk," but we find it difficult to "walk the walk." But how can we serve nature with integrity, if we continue to depend so thoroughly on a way of life that often exploits nature so mindlessly?

There is a way to begin to address this impasse. It is variously called the way of "creation-loving asceticism" or "voluntary frugality."[45] This appears to be one way to begin to honor the full testament of St. Francis. At this point, however, pursuing such explorations in this book would take us beyond the domains of liturgical theology into the milieu of the theology of spirituality. But it is necessary for us to go at least this far, for the sake of our integrity, with the resolve to go further in another setting. Many resources are available to help American Christians to pursue the way of voluntary frugality, especially centering on patterns of celebrating Christmas.[46] Likewise for resources that interpret what a new asceticism might mean for American Christians.[47] But resources will not be enough, given the tenacity of the socioeconomic forces arrayed against every individual believer.

I will presently find occasion to refer to the liturgical assembly as a "community of moral deliberation." It should be more than that. It should also be "a community of mutual accountability." By this I mean something quite different from a community of moral enforcement, where a powerful few together perhaps with clerical leadership impose their will and their scarlet letters on others. I have for many years believed that American assemblies could learn a great deal from Alcoholics Anonymous in this respect. Imagine at least one small group of people in one liturgical assembly that would form itself as a kind of Consumers Anonymous, who would hear simple or even complex challenges from individual members, and then offer support and consultation, beginning perhaps with the challenge of deconsumerizing members' family Christmas celebrations. Every impulse to serve nature that is shaped by the countercultural liturgy must surely begin by taking that consumerism into account, in some manner, by stopping us in our tracks and inviting us to look at ourselves. It will also be prudent for us to listen.

Following a principle we have already examined, the preferential option for the poor, members of the assembly can resolve to listen to the voice of the voiceless. The whole creation is groaning in travail, and Christians shaped by the renewed liturgy will have ears to hear that groaning. That will not be easy for most American Christians, since so many in our society have been trained, in a variety of ways, to be deaf to that groaning. For this reason, in humble recognition of our sinful deafness, we will probably be best advised to sit at the feet of those who *can* hear, in some manner. Some assemblies are already in an advantageous place to do this, ministering as they do to the poor and the oppressed of the human species. Other assemblies, which are at a further remove from the world of poverty, should probably seek to partner with those assemblies that live and minister in the midst of the voiceless.

Hearing the voice of the voiceless creatures of nature beyond the human community may be an even greater challenge. But there is a way. Native peoples will sometimes—when genuine eagerness to learn is in evidence, not merely theme-park voyeurism—graciously consent to walk and talk with those who are more or less oblivious to the greater world of nature. Many of the staff members of Christian outdoor ministries (commonly called church camps) are also well equipped to introduce those who have no experience of nature beyond the weather or "scenic" trips to national parks, to encounter evolutionary and wild nature in its own right and to show them how "to live lightly off the land," both in gathered communities and apart from them. Most Christian communions in the United States also have offices of rural ministry; members of their staffs, especially specialists in support for the family farm, can also serve as conversation partners. Advocates of animal rights are almost always willing to engage others who also are committed to serve animals, if those hearers are also willing to undergo the discomforting experience of really seeing the pain and the suffering that our society thoughtlessly inflicts on many animals, in medical research, agribusiness, and habitat destruction. Professional ecologists are usually delighted to talk with people eager to learn about their bioregions and the complexities and fragilities of those bioregions.

How Can the Believer Serve Nature?

Once members of the assembly have stopped to look at themselves and their way of life, to take an accounting, and the process of listening to the voice of the voiceless has commenced, what then? What does it mean, in practice, for the accountable, informed believer to serve nature?

All this is fraught with complexities and imponderables. In a sinful world, where humans are making unprecedented demands on the biosphere, it is by no means self-evident what serving nature should mean in any given set of circumstances for Christians. The fundamental idea is to serve nature for itself, not for anything nature can do for us. But in practice, determining how to serve any single creature or any set of creatures of nature, not to speak of whole ecosystems, is often exceedingly difficult. Balancing just human needs, moreover, with the needs of otherkind may sometimes seem next to impossible. Should a state oversee the construction of a dam, for example, which would destroy a precious ecosystem, yet which would provide electricity for all the residents in an impoverished city? Such challenges must be faced even by those who are committed to the most equitable and the most earth-friendly kinds of sustainable development.

We all will therefore need help at this point from ethicists, who are equipped to measure and balance the great variety of moral claims that we are confronting in this kind of context. This is also why it is helpful to think of the liturgical assembly not only as community of mutual accountability, as I have said, but also as a "community of moral deliberation."[48] Participating in such a community, members of the assembly can hone their listening skills to the voices of the voiceless, in conversation with one another and in conversation with those who speak from a variety of other perspectives, representatives of impoverished neighborhoods or regions, native peoples, staff from Christian outdoor ministries, advocates for animals, spokespersons from the world of family farms, professional ecologists, as well as with ecological theologians, political scientists, economists, artists, and poets, among others.

By way of offering some grist for the mill of further ethical reflection, the kind that a local assembly might choose to mull through, I make the following suggestions. *First*, as servants of the Servant Lord, Christians will be advocates—joining hopefully with many others of goodwill—for the preservation of wilderness areas, for their own sake. Yes, it is probably right to say that the remaining wilderness areas of the Amazon basin are the lungs of our planet and that therefore the preservation of those wonderfully complex and beautiful regions is in the best interest of the human species. But in addition to such prudential considerations, Christians will be advocates for the preservation of those regions for their own sake, because the Creator wants a world with such ecological riches in it. Christians will likewise be advocates for the preservation of species, again, not only because, let us say, plant species might hold within their biological structure resources from which new kinds of medicine for humans might be developed, but also because, in the eyes of God, those species have a right to exist and to flourish.

Second, Christians will also serve nature by being advocates for the health and well-being of their animal kin—again, joining hopefully with many others of goodwill in the process.[49] Created on the same day with the animals, according to Genesis 1, and created to bond with animals by naming them, according to Genesis 2, humans rightly should live in a kinship relationship with animals. An argument can be made, in this respect, that the benefit of the doubt should be given to those Christians, who, inspired by the vision of eschatological peace and by images of the lamb lying down with the lion, will choose to become vegetarians. The eschatological imperative would seem to require that Christians should serve animals by not killing them for food. On the other hand, the Scriptures themselves tell us that the Lord permits, in this sinful world, a certain compromise on this matter, according to the command given to Noah (Gen. 9:1-4) and, in keeping with the vision of Peter, to be permitted to eat both the clean and the unclean (Acts 10:9-16). In any case, Christians will surely be in the vanguard of those who advocate for animal rights and who constantly seek to reduce, if not totally to eliminate, all human-inflicted animal suffering.

On the other hand, moral guidelines such as wilderness preservation and animal protection should not be absolutized either. This is why the contribution of ethicists and the moral deliberation of assemblies are almost always required to help individual believers in their decision making. The construction and sustenance of human communities requires intervention in natural systems, and historically that has as a matter of course meant disruption of wilderness areas, in order to create farmland and courses for roads, for example. Likewise, human communities must be protected from destructive invasion by certain animal species, mosquitoes, for example, or rats. Rats may have rights, I have more than once observed over the years, but they do not have the right to crawl into the cribs of our babies at night. Such thoughts should indicate, minimally, how critically important the work of Christian ethicists is and also why liturgical assemblies must also be communities of moral deliberation. Serving nature is not a self-evident mandate for Christians, by any means.

As the example of the mosquitoes and the rats indicates, moreover, serving nature, in a certain sense, begins with the protection of humans, within their own created niche. Never mind the ravages of genocidal and suicidal wars in our time. Those disruptions and destructions of human communities around the world and their environmental side effects will as a matter of course command the minds and hearts of Christians, always. Rather, I have in mind here the more silent scourges that destroy countless millions of human bodies, many before they ever have had the time and space to grow into maturity. The global HIV/AIDS epidemic. Human hunger and starvation around the world. Devastating diseases like malaria. When we truly hear the whole creation groaning in travail, we will understand that unimaginable numbers of those voices are emerging from emaciated, brutalized, but still living *human* bodies. Whatever else the biblical mandate to serve nature may comprehend, it surely means reaching out to those groaning human selves, with medicine and food and, above all, resources to empower them to claim the divine promise to all humans for justice and an abundant life on this good earth.

When confronted with issues of such magnitude, moreover, believers will as a matter of course seek out other civic, religious, and cultural partners, to marshal aid and to bring pressure to bear on the powers that be.

This kind of coalition building may, in the end, hold the most promise for developing meaningful global responses to such problems.

Beyond that kind of strategic initiative, also, individual believers will want to seek out ways to serve nature indirectly. One could financially support church global relief agencies. One could financially support a public advocacy group of foresters, whose purpose is to protect old growth forests like the Tongass in Alaska from senseless exploitation. Another could contribute to the support of groups working to protect endangered species or to groups seeking to protect seal pups from slaughter in the Arctic or to groups seeking to protect domesticated animals from unnecessary suffering. These are obviously but a very few examples of the kind of support that Christians seeking to serve nature for its own sake could offer.

There is a *bonus* for believers in all this, given the logic of the cruciform liturgy. It is signaled by the saying from the Sermon on the Mountain, in the resonant language of the King James translation: "Seek ye first the Kingdom of God, and all these things will be added unto you" (Matt. 6:33). What does that mean? Many things, surely. But at least this much. Self-sacrifice in the name of Jesus is a blessing: "Those who lose their life for my sake will find it" (Matt. 10:39). That is surely the way that the Jesus of the Synoptic Gospels invites his followers to seek the kingdom of God. What is this blessing, then, that believers will find by taking up their cross to serve nature for the sake of Jesus?

This much is suggested by Jesus' parable of the shepherd separating the sheep from the goats in the last times (Matt. 21:31-45). The blessed are those who have served the lost and the forgotten ones, the hungry, the strangers, the naked, the sick, the imprisoned. And each of these, according to the parable, is *Jesus himself*, as he says of one of these: "I was hungry and you gave me food." This, then, is the bonus that believers receive when they serve nature, not as a reward but as a gift of grace, the knowledge that they are serving Jesus himself, then and there.

We are able to think such thoughts quite concretely here, since we have seen that it is possible to envision Jesus, as the cosmic Christ, in, with, and under all things, shepherding all things. This means, for example, that Jesus Christ is the Lord of the Tongass, that he is caring, in ways appropriate to each creature, for the gigantic five-hundred-year-old spruce trees and for the magnificent grizzlies who go forth to fish for salmon and for the salmon themselves as beautiful creatures who have every right to flourish as a species. So when believers pay a price—perhaps sacrificing their standing in the community, perhaps taking on financial burdens of their own, perhaps even, in some timely circumstance, endangering their own lives—to seek "to serve and to protect" the creatures of the Tongass, they can know that they are serving the same Lord, there and then, who has already made himself known to them in the breaking of the bread.

10

The Habit of Partnering:
Our Walk with Nature Ritualized

Sometimes it is necessary to state the obvious in order to clarify the subtleties. This is one of those instances. I will state that which is obvious in a moment.

Why this approach? We are now about to engage a theme that is perhaps the most controversial of the three we are exploring in the foregoing chapter and in this one, a theme that is usually identified as "human dominion over nature." I will speak of it as such, for now, since that is how most readers will recognize it. But I serve notice here of my intention, in a baptismal spirit, to give it a new name in order to signal a new understanding, *partnering with nature*, rather than dominion over nature.[1] This is the third habit, the third way of walking with nature, which liturgical formation of the faithful makes possible, along with standing in awe of nature and serving nature.

These are the words from Genesis 1:28 that have defined this theme for the scholarly and the public mind: "God blessed [the human creatures], and God said to them, 'Be fruitful and multiply, and fill the earth and subdue it; and have dominion over the fish of the sea and over the birds of the air and over every living thing that moves upon the earth.'" And this is the question that inevitably arises in scholarly and other public discussions of this matter: Can we humans live—literally survive—on earth today if we perpetuate that way of thinking about our relationship with nature and then turn it into social and economic policy as we have been doing with ever-increasing determination during the modern era?

Without for a moment wanting to deny the legitimacy of this question, I ask the reader to catch his or her breath, step back, and be ready to think these things through, before jumping to any conclusions, as countless critics of Christianity and of biblical traditions in our time have regularly done.

Two additional preliminary observations are appropriate here. First, as I have already shown, the Scriptures know two other major ways of relating to nature, as we have seen, standing in awestruck wonder before nature and serving nature. Why is it that virtually all, believers and critics alike, are so concerned with, not to say totally consumed by, issues pertaining to the Genesis 1:28 text and generally are ignorant about or uninterested in other, quite different texts? I do not propose to answer this question here, but it is good to keep it in mind as we proceed, for the sake of doing justice to the Scriptures if for no other reason.

My second preliminary observation is this. Genesis 1:28 and similar texts must be read in their own historical contexts, in order to assess their meanings. Could it be possible, indeed, that many biblical interpreters in the modern era have not done that? Could it be that modern interpreters may have read the dominion theology of Genesis more as a pretext for undergirding the modern industrial project, rather than in the context of its own ancient sociocultural setting? Some readers may be surprised to learn, as a matter of fact, how strange Genesis 1 sounds to modern and postmodern ears when read in its own context. And they may be all the more surprised to learn that, freshly interpreted, how that text has much to say to us, specifically in terms of the concerns of this book.

Building Human Community Partnering with Nature

This is the obvious I propose to state, a liturgical fact. Whatever else it has been, and whatever else it is today, the liturgy is essentially a *gathering of humans*. "In the beginning," I have argued, "was the assembly"—of *humans*, of course. Further, in confessional terms, the liturgical assembly is gathered and hosted by the invisible God who has become *human*, in Jesus Christ. This is the way the premiere ecumenical statement of our time, *Baptism, Eucharist, and Ministry*, describes this gathering and this hosting by the resurrected and ascended Christ, in words that I have already quoted more than once: "In the celebration of the Eucharist,

Christ gathers, teaches, and nourishes the church. It is Christ who invites to the meal and who presides at it. He is the shepherd who leads the people of God, the prophet who announces the Word of God, the priest who celebrates the mystery of God." Strikingly, this ecumenical statement goes on to link the presence of Christ, in particular, with the presence of the presiding priest at the Eucharist.[2] The whole liturgy is a matter of *human* interaction *coram deo* ("before God").

To underscore this obvious point still further, consider this unremarkable fact. When St. Francis called together all sorts of people in the thirteenth century, hermits, clergy, laborers, peasants, nobility, and others, to celebrate the Christ Creche Mass outdoors, in a woods at night, in front of a dark cave, and when he gathered a variety of domestic animals to be present, too, we have no reason to think that the bread and the wine of that Eucharist were also fed to the animals. The presiding of Christ in the Eucharist and the communion with Christ in the Eucharist were then— and are now—for humans only.

This obvious anthropocentrism of the Eucharist is surely something to be celebrated, insofar as it points to a unique, personal kind of gracious communion that obtains between Christ and humans and among humans who are in communion with Christ. This, at least from the perspective of faith, is really good news! Christ has chosen to give himself, in gracious personal communion *to us*! But it is also bad news. We humans were in need of such a physician. We needed healing. We could do nothing in our fallen state to redeem ourselves and to live the kind of life the Creator had intended us to live. Now it was not only human sin that prompted such a great redemption. But surely the divine purpose of that redemption, above all the death of the Messiah, the Son of God on the cross, was intended to provide a remedy for our sin, among other things, so as to restore us, in faith, to God's originally intended place for us in God's good creation.[3]

The liturgy as a ritual for humans, therefore, is a ritual that is intended to make it possible for humans to be restored to their rightful standing before God, the God before whom no sinner can stand, as Isaiah once discovered in the Temple. And that rightful standing allows those humans who have been thus restored to see the world, and live in it, with new eyes: to see the whole world as charged with the glory of God and to stand ready to serve that world in appropriate ways, as we have already had occasion to discover. For participants in the liturgy that new seeing of the glory of God also has a further meaning, as we have also seen: redeemed in Christ,

Christians now can see Christ as the image of God, in, with, and under the whole creation, as the One who reflects back God's glory to them and also as the one whom they serve when they serve nature.

But I must be more specific, lest we pass by the cornerstone of this community building process too quickly and thereby not fully appreciate its richness and its complexity. The liturgy is a ritual for building *embodied* human community.

Building Embodied Human Community

I once had a long conversation with a sociologist from India, mostly about his experiences in the United States. For a while we talked about a topic that has in subsequent years been widely discussed in the popular press in the United States—personal space. He told me how carefully he had learned to avoid standing too close to Americans with whom he was conversing. We talked about why Americans appeared to be so defensive about their personal space. Did it have something to do with the historic American pursuit of its "manifest destiny" in "the wide open spaces" of the western frontier? Surely it is tied in with American "rugged individualism," we agreed. The Indian world where he grew up, he observed, was radically different. "You cannot imagine what it's like just to walk along the streets of Calcutta, with *all* the people," he said. "I cannot help it;" he concluded, "I love the smell of human flesh."

I could say the same about my own experience with the liturgy, but I will not, since I am speaking with American readers, most of whom, I imagine, are not comfortable with those kinds of sensibilities. Let me say this, then: one of the reasons why the liturgy has claimed me, body, mind, and soul, for as long as I can remember is—I love the proximity of human flesh. This thought, it turns out, idiosyncratic as it may sound, takes us to the heart of the liturgy and provides an angle of vision for us to see something of the third habit of faith that the liturgy inculcates in believers as far as their relationship with nature is concerned: *building human community in partnership with nature*. To this end, I want to begin by exploring the meaning of human community in the liturgy, attending first to the human body, then to the human voice. The human body, after all, and with it the human voice, are very much a part of nature. Theologically speaking, we do not rightly relate ourselves to nature, if we do not rightly relate ourselves to our own bodies and to the bodies of other humans.

Sometimes neglected in discussions about the liturgy, both at the highest scholarly levels and in the pews at St. John's Next Door, is this. Whatever else it was in the early church, whatever else it may be in our liturgical churches today, on any Sunday, in addition to everything else, the liturgy has always been and is now a gathering of human bodies. Sometimes, as in the passing the peace or when worshipers crowd the center aisle on their way to the table or feel the priest's hand as they receive the bread in their hands, the liturgy means tangible, physical touching of bodies. Not to speak of actual embraces, which on occasion spontaneously do occur during the liturgy, perhaps most movingly during the passing of the peace or in the midst of quiet conversations between believers, who may touch each other as they console one another or rejoice with one another, after the liturgy has concluded. Luther, interestingly enough, as I have already observed, thought of such tangible conversations—he called this the mutual consolation of the brothers and sisters—as embodiments of the real presence of Christ, no less embodiments, in Luther's view, than the proclaimed Word or the bread and wine offered to believers during the Eucharist.

Paul must have had such enfleshed liturgical experiences in mind, unconsciously if not consciously, when he urged the early Christian assembly at Rome to present their bodies as a living sacrifice to God (Rom. 12:1) and when he also urged believers to "Greet one another with a holy kiss" (Rom. 16:16). This kissing was apparently associated in those assemblies with the passing of the Spirit from one believer to another.[4] Strikingly, too, the Pauline author of Ephesians seizes on the image of the body to describe the life of the assembly as a whole, as the body of Christ, with the further figurative associations of the body as a temple: "In [Christ] the whole structure is joined together and grows into a holy temple in the Lord; in whom you also are built together in the Spirit into a dwelling place for God" (Eph. 2:21, 22). In a like manner, Ephesians announces that the goal of the church's life is "building up the body of Christ . . . , from whom the whole body, joined and knit together by every ligament with which it is equipped, as each part is working properly, promotes the body's growth in building itself up in love" (Eph. 4:12, 15, 16).

Such images of bodily proximity and of parts of the body working together must have come readily to Christian minds and hearts in the first century, because their assemblies were "meal-keeping assemblies," and bodily proximity, bodily interaction, and, dare I say, bodily enjoyment were—and are—of the essence of most communal meals. Theologically, this thought makes sense, too, since a central teaching of the ecumenical church today is that the risen and ascended Christ *presides* at the Eucharist, as host at the table, and likewise throughout the whole liturgy and that, in some manner, the presiding officer of the assembly particularly embodies the presidency of Christ. This kind of affirmation of Christ's presiding presence in the liturgy can be heard all the more vividly when we listen to it in the context of the theology of descent and of that theology's image of the risen and ascended Christ's presence in, with, and under all things, particularly in those places where Christ discloses himself to his people by his Word.

This thought then leads us to identify yet another critical quality of the Eucharist as a meal fellowship that presupposes bodily proximity. Not only does the Eucharist presuppose that proximity around the table and the presence of the One who presides, in, with, and under the actions of the table fellowship. It presupposes, too, that the One who presides also communes with all who come to the table and that all who commune with him also commune with each another, all this effected by the communication of the Word of Christ. The table fellowship of the Eucharist is in this sense a paradigmatic instance of I-Thou relationships, of embodied persons communicating intimately with each other through speech. Accordingly, I, for one, as I participate in the Eucharist, not only love the proximity of human flesh, I also love to hear the sound of the human voice. Both flesh and voice are of the essence of I-Thou relationships, as we have already seen.

In the liturgy, voice is the physical medium that communicates the proclamation to the people; and voice is the physical medium by which, in some liturgical churches like my own in Roxbury, the people respond to the proclamation. Voice is also the physical medium that, in proclamation, can call forth other bodily responses, too, such as nodding of heads or smiles or frowns or clapping of hands. All the more so, voice is the physical medium that can become song in the liturgy, and thereby work to bind the people together as one body, whether in lament or in exultation. Touching the bodies of the faithful, voice in the liturgy thereby builds up the body of Christ. When assemblies are so graced, this touching is a sign of heaven on earth, a revelation of what, in some respects, the life of the faithful will be like when the eschaton arrives, when God will be all in all.

If, then, the liturgy thus functions to build up embodied human community, if the liturgy is anthropocentric in that sense, how are we to understand the habit of relating to nature that the liturgy fosters in its participants in this respect? This question brings us back to the theme that I identified at the beginning of this chapter, what has commonly been called "human dominion over nature," which is an anthropocentric theological theme *par excellence*.

The Two Kinds of "Human Dominion over Nature"

By stating that the liturgy is, in significant ways, anthropocentric, since it is a rite for humans, I have stated what I have taken to be the obvious. Just as obvious, in my view (although far less so in many discussions both by scholars and by the general public), is this: theologically speaking, there are *two kinds of human dominion over nature*, sinful human dominion and redeemed human dominion. The first needs little description here. It is written in the history of our times. We have encountered it vividly in our engagement with the scope of the ecojustice crisis that now has the planet in its deadly grips.

But historic sinful human dominion over nature has not been all bad, by any means. Theologically, this is usually—and rightfully—identified as being a sign of the grace of God. Notwithstanding human sinfulness, so this teaching plausibly explains, God continues to work graciously everywhere. God sends rain on the righteous and the unrighteous (Matt. 5:45). God graciously works everywhere to restrain sin and to bless every creature, in some measure, by the goodness of God's creative presence. So we can also be grateful that sinful human dominion over nature often does bring forth good fruits, too, like housing to protect us from the elements, technologies to increase food production, resources to support the human scientific quest, arts to beautify the human experience, and the gifts of modern medicine. Nevertheless, notwithstanding the constant divine working to conserve the good creation and to bless all creatures by that working, human sin together with the principalities and powers of Death still rides roughshod over human history. An argument can be made that that sinful abuse of nature in our time has reached unprecedented proportions. So it is understandable that the sinful abuse of human dominion and the destruction which has resulted from that abuse is most on our minds in these times.

But that is not the only kind of human dominion, as I have stated this obvious truth, although not regarded as such by many. Our challenge here, then, is to identify what the second—the redeemed—kind of human dominion actually is. This kind of dominion, in practice, is *a new kind of human partnering with nature* in our sinful world. We will want to take a careful reading of it here, as we now leave behind the received terminology of human dominion over nature, and opt for what is biblically speaking a much more adequate terminology, partnership with nature. The reasons for this terminological change should be apparent as we explore the classic text for this subject, Genesis 1.

We will also see, as we embark on this exegetical study, that the partnering in question is twofold, first of all God's partnering with nature, and, second, human partnering with nature, the latter in imitation of the divine partnering. Another way of making the same point is this: we will discover that the theocentric witness of Genesis 1 is both cosmocentric and anthropocentric. This text is most fundamentally about God and God's creative purposes, yet it is also about the world of nature and humanity. It is not just about God and humanity. And it surely is not solely focused on the human creature alone.

The Cosmic Vision of Genesis 1

Sometimes biblical interpreters assume that the Scriptures always say "either/or." Either God created the world by God's own agency, for example, or God worked with preexistent materials. The Christian tradition has affirmed throughout the ages that the Scriptures are to be read, notwithstanding other kinds of indicators in the Genesis text itself, as teaching that God created the world out of nothing (*ex nihilo*), by God's own agency alone, not with the help of any preexisting materials. I do not want to discuss this theme here. I identify it only as a case where one of two answers *is* the correct one, in terms of normative Christian teaching. But sometimes it is best to read the Scriptures as saying "both/and." Genesis 1, I am convinced after many years of attending to this text, in conversation with a whole household of biblical interpreters, is a text that requires us to read it in terms of "both/and" if we are to understand it properly.

So I propose these two themes as necessary tools to open up the meanings of Genesis 1, for the purpose of our explorations here. *First: God seeks to partner with nature and human community in order to bring that whole creation to fulfillment.* This theme gives expression to biblical meanings that we have already encountered, in some measure, in our explorations of what it means, from the perspective of Isaiah's vision in the Temple and the psalmist's encounter with Mt. Hermon, for humans to stand in awestruck wonder of nature. It also gives expression to the biblical theme of servanthood that we have already reviewed, of God serving nature and humans serving nature. *Second: God seeks to build human community partnering with nature in order to bring that human community to fulfillment.*

Call these two themes *the cosmocentric and the anthropocentric readings of Genesis 1.* Both readings, I believe, are correct, and both readings are necessary, if we are to hear the meanings of the text as fully as we can. Once we have explored these two ways of interpreting this classical text, we can then turn to a particular reading of the famous—or infamous— "dominion" text of Genesis 1:28 itself.

An entry point for reading Genesis 1 cosmocentrically is a closely related text, Psalm 104, which most scholarly interpreters think of as a poetic commentary on the traditions brought together, more didactically in Genesis 1. The text of Genesis 1, in some form, and Psalm 104 may well have served originally as librettos for a festival in the Jerusalem Temple.[5] This long and gracious poem is a kind of painting of a great and beautiful cosmos, full of enormous diversity, all of which is cared for by God and indeed a source of joy for God, a beautiful world in the midst of which is to be found a niche that God has established for the human community.[6] The psalm celebrates the majesty of God, clothed in light, and the vast earth-world that God has built, stretching out the heavens like a tent above and putting its foundations in place, undergirding it all, beneath the primeval waters (vv. 1-7). The waters, no longer chaotic, rise up to the mountains and run down to the valleys to the places God has appointed for them (vv. 8-9). God makes springs to gush forth in the valleys, which give drink to every wild animal. By the streams, the birds of the air have their homes in the trees that God waters. From above, God waters the mountains and "the earth is satisfied with the fruit of [God's] work" (vv. 9-13). God causes grass to grow to feed the cattle and plants for people to use, even wine to gladden the human heart (vv. 14-15).

Then there is the whole world of nature that has its own life with God, apart from human settlements and human needs: the cedars of Lebanon that God plants; the high mountains that God provides for the wild goats; the night, when all the animals of the forest come creeping out, the young lions roaring for their prey, "seeking their food from God"; even the sea, great and wide with innumerable creeping things, including the monstrous Leviathan, which God formed to play with it (or rejoice in it) (vv. 16-26). All these things look to God for life and death, and God rejoices in all these works (vv. 27-31). Humans come into this cosmic picture only in two places: one, in the midst of this vast diversity in their own small niche, although not without their own joys, like wine and bread (v. 15); and at the end, with reference, presumably, to their roles as spoilers of God's creative intentions and works, as sinners who should be "consumed from the earth" (v. 35).

Genesis 1, composed by "the Priestly writers," as they are usually called, presupposes the same kind of cosmocentric vision.[7] The very first verse of this narrative speaks the most important word—*God*. However the first verse of Genesis 1 is translated—and this is much discussed—the whole point of this crucial text is *the God who creates*. More particularly, in view of the immediate story that is to follow in Genesis 1 and later testimonies in the Priestly narrative, such as the covenant of promise that God makes with all creatures in the Noah story, this text concerns the God who creates in order to give of Godself so that a whole range of creatures might have being and life, and have it abundantly, in a history with God, who (once the covenant with Noah and all flesh has been established, according to the Priestly writers) will be faithful to the divine promises, come what may. And this self-giving of God, according to the Priestly writers, is always understood not as some impersonal force, however serendipitous that force might be envisioned to be, but as an amazing and mysterious *personal* giving, a personal sharing, a partnering in that sense, as is indicated in Genesis 1 by the repeated witness to God *speaking*. A "force" does not speak.

If the whole point of the story in Genesis 1 focuses on God, it then is dramatically apparent right from the start that this is a God who indeed wants to have a history with a world of many creatures. Why? We have already encountered the thought experiment of Thomas Aquinas, who affirmed that for an infinite God to create a finite world in order to mirror the divine glory, that world would be filled with a nearly infinite gradation of diversity. Nothing like that thought experiment is in evidence here. Rather, we encounter a kind of descriptive celebration of God's bringing into being and caring for a marvelous range of creatures, a vision very much like that we encountered in Psalm 104. Think of this text even as liturgical. The origins of Genesis 1, as we have seen, may be in rituals known in the Temple. Nowhere is this more in evidence than in the ritualistic repetition of the phrase, "and God saw that it was good." If this text is far away from Thomas's thought experiment (although this is not to suggest that Thomas's ideas of diversity are without biblical warrant), it is even further away from the modern Christian idea that nature is a stage created for God's history with humanity. On the contrary, for the Priestly writers, each day of God's creative activity has its own integrity and its own meaning in the greater scheme of things.[8] Hence the repeated expression, "And God saw that it was good."

Which is to say, for Genesis 1, God chooses to engage Godself and to share the divine life with all these creaturely domains, in their own right. Yes, humans are created to "rule" over the earth (1:28) but, likewise, in the same language, the sun and the moon are made to "rule" over the day and the night (1:16-18). We see here a vision of a beautiful, interrelated whole of many different creatures, all of which are created by God to have a history with the divine: which is, in so many words, the whole point of the whole project. When God finally comes to the point of creating the human creature, be it noted, God does not rejoice over just the emergence of the *human* creature, as if that were the whole point of his creativity (as some later Christian interpreters, like Ambrose, imagined): God saw "*everything* that he had made, and indeed, it was very good" (1:31). The whole point of God's creativity is the prospering of the whole in all its diversity.

Likewise, in keeping with the motif of the goodness of every creature, God does not rush through, as it were, the first five days. God does not instrumentalize or "thingify" what some might think of as the "lesser creatures," in order to enter into personal communion with the human creature, although, as we shall see, that special kind of relationship between God and the human creature is taken for granted by the Priestly writers. On the contrary, God enters into a kind of *partnership* with all creatures. God respects all creatures, works with them, takes time with them, befitting their own created potential, in order to enhance and realize the integrity of the whole. God blesses *the fish and the birds* and calls them to participate in his creative project: to multiply and fill the earth (1:20-22). *The waters*, even more dramatically, in view of the connotations of chaos they had in cultures of the time, collaborate with the Creator, by divine invitation: "Let the waters bring forth swarms of living creatures . . ." (1:20). In a like manner, God calls upon *the earth* to "bring forth living creatures of every kind" (1:24). *Humans* are mandated by God, in the same way, to be participants in the divine creativity by being fruitful and multiplying—and also, again, as we shall see, by ruling and subduing the earth (Gen. 1:28). All creatures are, in this sense—some explicitly, others by implication—*partners* with God's creativity, not mere objects of God's creative will posited for the sake of God's relationship with humans.

Further, God is depicted as creating both humans and the animals, the wild and the domesticated, on the same day (Gen. 1:24ff.), thus suggesting a certain kind of solidarity between the two kinds of creatures. This suggestion is underlined by the strong implication of the solidarity of non-violence: humans and animals are created to be at peace with each other, and not to prey on each other or on one another (Gen. 1:29-30). This is also a critical ingredient of the goodness of God's creative project that the Priestly writers envisioned at this point in their narrative (later, in the aftermath of the Noah narrative, a different, qualified answer is given). In that sense, God depends on the humans *and* the animals, right from the start, to establish his creative purposes by eschewing violence.

Such is what I take to be a compelling cosmocentric reading of Genesis 1, which I have summarized this way: God seeks to partner with nature and human community in order to bring that whole world to fulfillment. But this text can also be read, legitimately, from a different angle of vision, anthropocentrically, which I have summarized in these words: God seeks to build human community in partnership with nature in order to bring that human community to fulfillment. For the Priestly writers, there is no doubt that God established a special vocation for humans, in the midst of the vast and diverse goodness of the whole creation.

The Anthropocentric Vision of Genesis 1

According to Genesis 1, humans alone are created according to the image of God; the animals are not created according to that image (Gen. 1:27). This surely suggests a special relationship between God and humans, of a kind that does not exist between God and the other animals.[9] This is already signaled by the fact, noted by William Brown, that the creation of the humans is introduced as a unique product of divine intervention: whereas the land-based creatures are products of the land (Gen. 1:24), human beings are not. "The opening command," Brown observes, "is 'Let us make human beings in our image,' not 'Let the earth bring forth human beings.' Unlike the Yahwist's story of human origins, with the vision of Adam coming from *adamah*, the Priestly writer makes clear that the land is not the source of human identity but only humankind's natural habitat."[10] The relationship between God and the human creatures is also understood to be reciprocally personal: here for the first time in the story of God's creative acts, God speaks in the first person (Gen. 1:26). Here the divine "I" calls the human "thou" not just into being and becoming in partnership with God, but into communion with one another, into the intimacy of personal communication.[11]

In this respect, the Genesis writers—they were, after all, Priestly—must surely have presupposed that the divine-human relationship is one of self-conscious praise on the part of humans. The thought of the coming Sabbath on the seventh day, as the appointed setting for the humans to glorify the Creator for all God's good works, was undoubtedly not far from the Priestly writers' minds, as they shaped the construct of humans created according to the image of God. From this Priestly perspective, in other words, the relationship between God and the human creatures has a particular purpose, in a way that God's relationship with the other animals does not.[12] The Creator brings the human beings into existence, so that they may in some sense "image forth" God's purposes—or imitate God's actions—on the earth both by working to establish human community—by "making history," as Jürgen Moltmann likes to say—and by self-consciously worshiping the Creator.

For sure, the Priestly writers take it for granted that *God* alone is the Creator, as indicated by the oft-observed fact that the word for creating (*bara*) is used only for the creative activity of *God*, here in Genesis 1 and throughout the Old Testament. Clearly this project of cosmic creation is intended to be viewed as beginning and ending, and as sustained, by the creative power and wisdom and self-giving of the God of glory. It is radically theocentric in that sense. The Creator is the Creator, and the creation is the creation. For this reason, the Creator is to be glorified, as the psalmists often say, and as the Priestly writers surely believed, not the creation or any other suprahuman powers that might be thought to contend with God.[13] In no sense is the creation itself divine. At the same time, by God's gracious engagement with, respect for, and, in the human instance, communion with, God's variegated creatures, they surely are intended to be viewed as having their own integrity and, in various ways, their own spontaneity and so their own goodness in God's eyes—and hence have their being and becoming as God's partners, each creature in its own way.[14]

So the radically theocentric project envisioned by the Priestly writers is also, in this sense, thoroughly cosmocentric and thoroughly anthropocentric. More precisely, it is profoundly *relational*—even ecological, to borrow a term from a different world of discourse—rather than exhibiting a kind of hierarchical, regal-command character. For the Priestly writers, God is profoundly *with* all creatures, related to them and interacting with them as they respond to God's creative initiatives. Terence Fretheim's summary of the Old Testament's view of God's creative presence with creation surely reflects, overall if not in every nuance, the witness of the Priestly writers in Genesis 1 in particular:

> God is graciously present, in, with, and under all the particulars of his creation, with which God is in a relationship of reciprocity. The immanent and transcendent God of Israel is immersed in the space and time of this world; this God is available to all, is effective along with them at every occasion, and moves with them into an uncertain future. Such a perspective reveals a divine vulnerability, as God takes on all the risks that authentic relatedness entails.[15]

This is the God whom the human creature is called to image forth.

In this sense, the theology of the Priestly writers in Genesis 1 is countercultural: it stands opposed, implicitly if not explicitly, to some of the most fundamental cultural imagery of the writers' own sociopolitical milieu. It has often been observed that the Priestly accounts of the creation were given their literary shape—although they contain materials from much earlier times and may have received their final editing much later—in the setting of the exile, that is, in the context of Babylonian rule. And that society was a hierarchical, command society, without a doubt. For the Babylonians, the word of the monarch was law, absolutely, and that word dominated both people and nature at will, as it was implemented by the monarch's subordinates, who could readily be executed if they did otherwise.[16] Soberingly, historic Israel from the era of David and Solomon at least into the exile often took that kind of command royal ideology for granted and, with it, images of God as the chief monarch of the cosmos.[17] However, while the Priestly writers readily, even enthusiastically, claim the vision of God speaking with power, an image akin to the speech of historical monarchs, their relational, ecological assumptions contradict the ideology of kingship.[18]

Walter Brueggemann has suggested instructively that an inner theological dynamic in operating here. The vision of God presupposed by the Priestly writers is very much like the vision of God presupposed by the prophet Ezekiel (chap. 34), who wrote in the same kind of sociopolitical context. For Ezekiel, God is the "shepherd King" who himself cares for God's flock.[19] God is not the absolute monarch, whose word dominates God's whole realm. Further, an anti-monarchical polemic seems to emerge here in this priestly setting, almost in so many words, and is taken for granted by the Priestly writers, in any case: insofar as *humans*, in particular, are said to be created according to the "image of God" (Gen. 1:27). In the ancient Near East, typically, only *kings* were thought of as bearing the image of a god or gods.[20] Thus, the monarchical imagery in Genesis 1 is evident, even essential, for the Priestly writers in light of their faith in the power of the God of wisdom and mercy who creates by speaking. At the same time, that imagery is thoroughly qualified by other theological assumptions, which keep this text well within the overall Old Testament and, indeed, the general biblical view of God as the God of self-giving love, a faith rooted in experience of the earliest of Israelite communities.[21]

It is in this exegetical context that the much-discussed theme of human dominion over the earth, announced by the Priestly writers in Genesis 1:28, should be heard. The words themselves seem to tell a harsh story, as has often been noted. Dominion or "rule" (*rada*) generally means "exercise authority over," and "subdue" (*kabash*) literally means "tread upon." At the level of word study alone that would seem to imply—taken together with the idea that the human creature is to image-forth what could be thought of as the supposed absoluteness of a divine monarchial rule—that God creates the human creature to dominate, even exploit the earth, as monarchs in the ancient Near East routinely did. But that kind of interpretation of Genesis 1:28, as it stands, while sounding plausible, in fact appears to be more a matter of reading meanings into the text, rather than reading what the text itself says, once it is compared to much more plausible interpretations.

To begin with, the sociopolitical setting of the Priestly writers in Babylon merits some attention. This was no simple agrarian society. An urban society for the most part, it was both hierarchical and highly organized. This kind of society as a matter of course presupposed massive human interventions in the earth, above all through irrigation projects, in order to sustain its economy. In this socio-ecological setting, if there was going to be urban life of any scope, in contrast with simple agrarian life of small communities in regions like the hill country of Palestine, such large-scale interventions in nature were a *sine qua non* of social existence. One would expect economic realities such as those to be reflected in biblical texts that were shaped in such a sociopolitical world.[22] And indeed they are—and even, in one sense, are celebrated—in contrast to the simple, agrarian assumptions of the Yahwist in Genesis 2. Such human intervention in the earth is for the Priestly writer *theologically* noble, since it represents carrying out the particular partnership with God that is part of God's creative purposes: it makes the land "fillable" with human life, as Brown suggests. Anyone who has ever had any hands-on experience with the establishment of human community in some "untouched" natural setting will surely not find this point difficult to comprehend—for example, laying foundations or drilling for water or clearing fields. Such projects can be highly disruptive of natural systems.

"Nevertheless," Brown observes pointedly, "such a commission does not require exploiting the earth's resources, as the specific language of subduing might suggest. The priestly author gives clear contextual clues that clarify and qualify this dominion over the earth."[23] Brown suggests, for example, that the hoarding of resources by humans is implicitly forbidden, since the vegetation given by God for food is also given to the animals. More substantively, Brown explains: "As God is no divine warrior who slays the forces of chaos to construct a viable domain for life, so human beings are not ruthless tyrants, wreaking violence upon the land that is their home. By dint of command rather than brute force, the elements of creation are enlisted to fulfill the Deity's creative purposes."[24]

In order to underline this point, Brown instructively points to a later figure in the unfolding Priestly narrative, beyond Genesis 1: Noah. Brown observes that Noah "models primordial stewardship"[25] (I would prefer to speak here in terms of "partnership") by sustaining all of life in its representative forms. His "subduing" of the earth entails bringing together the animals of the earth into his zoological reserve, a floating speck of land, as it were. By fulfilling humankind's role as royal steward over creation (1:28), Noah is a beacon of righteousness in an ocean of anarchy. Noah exercises human dominion over creation by preserving the integrity and diversity of life.[26]

Strikingly, a point not noted by Brown but very much in support of his claims here, Noah takes *both* the clean and the unclean animals with him on to the ark! Had his assignment been to "make this a better world," he surely might have seized upon this opportunity to leave the unclean behind—or the mosquitoes, for that matter. But, on the contrary, Noah's vocation is to serve as a partner with God in behalf of the world that *God* created, with all its diversity, not first and foremost to improve the lot of humans on this earth. Human intervention in nature is thus envisioned by the Priestly writers as within *limits*, both theocentric and cosmocentric. It could be called *a limited partnership*. One could say, in this sense, that God expects humans to establish their own unique communities, yet not with wanton destruction, but always in cooperation with and respect for all the other divinely mandated domains of creation, each of which has its own intrinsic value, since it is valued itself by God: each creaturely domain is created with its own goodness in the eyes of God. Hence, the divine command to Noah to take all the animals with him on the ark. Hence, the divine covenant with "all flesh."

With this theocentric definition of human partnering with nature it is also possible to detect nuances that the human creature is fashioned by God to imitate the deliberate and wise ways the Creator works with nature: *by building*. Commentators have often noted that there is an architectural character to the works of the Creator attested by Genesis 1 (a theme that appears explicitly in Job). The Creator has a plan for building the creation, the Creator follows that plan, with the cooperation of some of the creatures. Finally, having accomplished the plan, the Creator pauses, as it were, and takes delight in the beauty of the resultant world. The Creator sees that the whole structure is "very good." Does it not make sense, then, to imagine that the Priestly writers were thinking of the human creature imaging forth such a Creator by engaging the world that God has made, in the same manner, deliberately, with wisdom, cooperatively?[27]

This, then, is the consummately beautiful mosaic of God's creativity at the very beginning of all things, according to the Priestly writers.[28] This is why, all things, taken as a beautiful whole, each creature or creaturely domain with its own purpose in the greater scheme of things, all working together in majestic harmony, are seen by God, in the priestly vision, as "very good" (Gen. 1:31).[29]

And this is how the cosmocentric and anthropocentric readings of Genesis 1 are, in a sense, mirror images of each other. For this is what a reading of Genesis 1 shows us. It is a question of both/and. It is true to say that this narrative is about God seeking to partner with nature and human community, in order to bring that whole world to fulfillment and also about God seeking to build human community in partnership with nature in order to bring that human community to fulfillment. In Genesis 1, the second theme is woven seamlessly into the first.[30]

Still, hearing the voice of Genesis 1, even when read together with Genesis 2, striking and edifying as both witnesses are, is not enough, biblically speaking. Something central for the biblical understanding of the divine purposes with the creation is missing. I can see it when I look out my window—the city.

Rebuilding the Human City Partnering with Nature

The end is not like the beginning. This thought has not escaped numerous biblical interpreters. The Scriptures begin with the narrative of a world with a *garden*, in Genesis 2, and end with the narrative of a new world with a new *city*, in Revelation 21. The Scriptures also begin, in Genesis 1, with the narrative of the birth of human community, in the midst of a vast and variegated and beautiful divinely created world, but with a picture of the human community that, on the surface anyway, seems to have little relationship to any human city whatsoever, whether in its promisory expressions—above all, Jerusalem—or in its threatening expressions in the era when the Priestly writers did their work—above all, Babylon.

Left with the witness of these two pivotal chapters of Genesis, then, we could be left only with a vision of what would presumably be a small agrarian community (Genesis 2) or an even smaller human community, marriage (Genesis 1), which the Priestly writers apparently understood was intended to be the original (and only?) form of human community that was created by God to fill the niche which God had allotted for humans in all the earth. True, the Priestly writers were at home with the thought of the earth being populated with large "families" or even with "nations," in the limited sense that that term can be used regarding ancient Near Eastern culture. And they obviously knew about cities, since they did their work, in all likelihood, in exile in Babylon, perhaps the premiere "urban" culture of their time. But "male and female he created them," says Genesis 1. Male and female are in that explicit sense the image bearers of God. *What becomes, then, of the city?* Is it only to be regarded as an expression of human sinfulness "outside the garden" or as a sinful human institution that obstructs the divinely intended, peaceful expansion of male and female throughout the earth?

Much the same kind of question could be asked about those biblical motifs that we encountered earlier under the rubric of awestruck wonder before nature. The prophet Isaiah, after all, was in the Temple when he was claimed by the vision of the whole earth being full of the glory of God. The holy city, Jerusalem, apparently was not consciously on his mind at that time. And the psalmist, who found consolation both in the Temple and at the foothills of Mt. Hermon in the wilderness, seems to betray little awareness of any city, including Jerusalem, as he celebrates the mercy of God (in Psalms 42 and 43). All the more vividly, the great creation poem, Psalm 104, takes the hearer through virtually every height and depth and every niche of the creation, without once even hinting at the existence of a city anywhere.

Should that be our definitive reading of the Scriptures in this respect? Should the thought of the human city therefore be left at the margins of our explorations of the ritualizing of nature, either on the grounds that it is not of much interest in the Scriptures or in the liturgy (so it would seem, on the basis of the texts that have claimed most of our attention thus far) or that, if anything, the city will be of interest to us mainly as a sign of human sinfulness? Call the latter the sign of Babylon, the ominous city of biblical imagination, from the exile to the book of Revelation. Such thoughts have found expression in the writings of a variety of Christian interpreters throughout the ages, most notably perhaps during the last century in the writings of the influential French sociologist and theologian Jacques Ellul. T. J. Gorringe describes Ellul's viewpoint this way: "Cities represent the hubristic attempt to build an ideal place for human development, equilibrium, and virtue, the attempt to construct what God wants to construct, and to put humankind in the centre, in God's place."[31]

This tradition of Christian anti-urbanism, however, must be rejected out of hand. Of course human fallenness shapes urban life as we know it, as that fallenness also shapes human encounters with the glories of God mirrored in the creation and with human efforts to serve nature. But this anti-urbanism is neither biblically founded, as we shall see, nor is it tolerable any longer—if it ever was. The latter point is perhaps self-authenticating for anyone who reads the newspapers in our era. By the turn of this century, the human species had entered a global era of urbanization on a massive, indeed unprecedented, scale.[32] It is impossible to talk about nature today with any political traction—surely not to talk about standing in wonder before nature or serving nature—without confronting this huge social trend.[33]

There are no "pure" wilderness areas anymore, if there have been since the beginnings of human dispersal around the globe. That truth was apparent to me, as I indicated earlier, when I contemplated the awesome glaciers of the Swiss Alps and realized at once that they were being destroyed by a changing climate that in turn was largely induced by humans all over the globe. Nor is there any "pure" human relationship with the arable soil anymore, of the kind envisioned by the Yahwist in Genesis 2—and then denied by the same writer in Genesis 3, of course, under the rubric of the divine curse of the soil, because of human sinfulness. And obviously the vision of the Priestly writers in Genesis 1 of humans, created according to the divine image, peacefully spreading throughout the earth, as male and female, to fill the niche allotted to them by the Creator, was controverted by the narratives of the Tower of Babel and the flood that those writers took for granted. It will be recalled, too, that the Priestly writers incorporated the account of "the fall" in Genesis 3 into their master narrative for a reason. They, too, knew that the earth had been cursed, because of human sinfulness.

The first reason to reject Christian anti-urbanism, wherever it appears, is thus because of the importance of the sin-stricken city in our globalizing world. The sociologist Kenneth Boulding once observed, in response to someone who had talked about throwing garbage away: "there is no 'away.'" In a like manner, for us, in this era, there is no nonurban world. "Urbanity is destiny" for the human species today and for the foreseeable future, for better or for worse. In our times, Christians like everyone else—"green Christians" all the more so—have to come to terms with this enormous socioeconomic trend.

But this is only half the story. There is no such thing anymore that is just the city. Urban life in our era is inextricably bound up with the whole biosphere. "Globalization," as Larry Rasmussen has said, "is about the socio-communal, biophysical, and even geoplanetary simultaneously in an upending of nature and culture together." This means, Rasmussen concludes, that "any church urban mission now that is not about the sociocommunal, biophysical, and geoplanetary together is truncated, blinded by its own anthropocentrism, and ignorant of its actual historical legacy." Which is to say of today's world: not only must we say "urbanity is destiny," we must also affirm that "ecology is destiny." Even the legitimate and passionate concerns on the part of some Christians in behalf of the city in the last century, over against the traditional expressions of Christian anti-urbanism, if they are now to be carried over into our infinitely interconnected global society, will function, ironically, as a kind of anti-urbanism. Christians like everyone else —those committed to urban ministry all the more so—must come to terms with this momentous global interconnectedness.

The second reason to reject Christian anti-urbanism, wherever it appears, is because it is, finally, not biblical. Once we encounter this exegetical truth, moreover—at least for those like myself who take the Scriptures to be the chief norm for theological reflection—this second reason will become in fact of first importance. Then the question will be: Do we Christians preach and teach what we know, and do we then practice what we preach and teach?

To this end, I hope the reader will give me some terminological latitude. Insofar as the Scriptures are anthropocentric (as well as cosmocentric), I believe, and we have just encountered this biblical anthropocentrism (and cosmocentrism) in our engagement with the narrative of Genesis 1, the Scriptures are also centered on the city. They are "urbacentric." The master narrative of the Scriptures, after all, *does* flow from the Garden of Eden to the New Jerusalem, situated in the midst of a new heavens and a new earth. But it is not only those "bookends" of the narrative that should instruct us. The flow of testimony throughout the narrative from Alpha to Omega gives the same witness. We have already encountered a pivotal case in point, right at the center of the master narrative, in our explorations of the meanings of the Sanctus.

"Blessed is he who comes in the name of the Lord"—we have already seen that this text in the New Testament points us to Jesus as an eschatological figure who comes to inaugurate the beginning of the end times. Now I want to underline this crucial fact, which I passed by earlier. Jesus inaugurates the beginning of the ending of all things *by entering into Jerusalem*. Jesus hereby reclaims Jerusalem as the city of God, the city that is to be redeemed, as the center of the promised coming of the new heavens and the new earth, a theme picked up by the seer of the book of Revelation, as we have also seen. In this sense biblical testimony is not just anthropocentric (as well as being cosmocentric). Right in the middle, in its heart, it is urbacentric.

This thought can now help us to reconnect with the witness of Isaiah in the Temple, of his and the people's sinfulness, in face of the holy God, whose glory fills the earth. The same prophet could also say, much more particularly, of the "faithful city" of Jerusalem, that it had become a whore, full of murderers and rebellious princes who love bribes, and who do not defend the widow or the orphan (Isa. 1:21-22). Over against this ugly, sinful urbanism, the prophet then proclaims a new vision of the beautifully redeemed city of God:

> In the days to come the mountain of the LORD's house shall be established as the highest of the mountains, and shall be raised above the hills; all the nations shall stream to it. Many peoples shall come and say, "Come, let us go up to the mountain of the LORD, to the house of the God of Jacob, that he may teaches us his ways and that we may walk in his paths," For out of Zion shall go forth . . . the word of the LORD. . . . He shall judge between the nations, and shall arbitrate for many peoples; they shall beat their swords into plowshares, and their spears into pruning hooks; nation shall not lift up sword against nation, neither shall they learn war any more. (Isa. 2:2-4)

What then becomes of this urbacentric, prophetic vision of peace, a vision that presumably also shaped the mind and heart of Jesus as he entered Jerusalem, when the people cried "Blessed is he who comes in the name of the Lord!"? Christians, who "have this mind" that was in Christ Jesus, as Paul bade the assembly at Philippi to have, will not only stand in awe before nature and stand ready to serve nature, but, inspired by the vision of Jesus entering Jerusalem that is celebrated in the Sanctus, they will dedicate themselves to building human community—above all, in the city—in partnership with nature.

Christians Building Human Community in Partnership with Nature

As sinful creatures, who by the grace of God mediated to them through the liturgy, know themselves as having been restored to God's original intentions for them, Christians will as a matter of course be formed so as to partner with nature, in behalf of human community, particularly in behalf of the human city. In this way, the Christian images forth the kind of partnering that God has already established with nature.

This implies that, in this respect, Christians will judiciously avail themselves of the privilege of *using* nature, relating to nature in an I-It relationship, in behalf of addressing legitimate human needs. But there is a critically important distinction here between using and abusing (which parallels the earlier distinction we noticed between the redeemed and sinful forms of human dominion). And the line that demarcates the two is the line of partnering.

A paradigmatic case would be cultivating a fruit tree and harvesting its fruit, rather than cutting down the fruit tree for firewood. In the first instance, the user partners with the tree. In the second instance, the user becomes an abuser and destroys the tree. That, of course, is only a simple example. Indeed, it would be simplistic if it were taken as some kind of an axiom for Christians and their relationships with trees generally. For, often, cutting down trees is fully legitimate, as it has been throughout the ages, for building human dwellings and for providing fuel for heat and cooking. But the case of the fruit tree is nevertheless illustrative. The Christian's partnership with nature will always be a limited, not an unlimited, partnership.

A related simple case would be the challenge of building a road from one city to another. That road could be built to run roughshod over cultivated and wild nature. Or with the investment of ecologically sensitive human wisdom and ingenuity, and with the human commitment to invest the appropriate financial resources, it could be built to be minimally invasive. But it *will be* invasive. Theologically informed Christians will, as a matter of course, be advocates for that kind of limited partnership with nature.

A more dramatic case is the challenge of responding to climate change today. Christians are sometimes tempted to side with wilderness and agrarian romantics, who in one way or another want to call a halt to, or even cut back, what they perceive to be "the drain" of global, urbanizing civilization on the biosphere. On the contrary, for biblically responsive Christians, the choice will be between what can be called creative global urbanism and destructive global urbanism. The former is structured in partnership with the earth, the latter presupposes domination of the earth. Such Christians thus will be advocates of global policies that are predicated on humans sharing of the common good and "living light" on the good earth, our divinely given commonwealth. This would mean, for example, championing renewable fuels and sustainable agricultural practices that draw on the wisdom of many cultures and equitably bene- fit all. Likewise, this would mean, especially in the United States, an end to uncontrolled suburban sprawl and uncontrolled agribusiness and, all the more so, uncontrolled consumption of the world's goods. Further, this would mean developing new approaches to human dwelling places and neighborhoods and cities themselves, for the sake of just and equitable and sustainable and indeed beautiful homes for all.

To this end, many Americans—Christians who have been shaped by an anti-urban vision, no less than others—will have to experience a renewal of their minds (cf. Rom. 12:2). Biblically speaking, the glass of the city is half full. The time is long overdue to see the city not a bottomless pit of problems, but as a rich well of promise. To illustrate this truth, I quote at length from an essay by two urban advocates, Douglas Foy and Robert Healy, "Cities Are the Answer."[34] They write:

> Many of the world's most difficult environmental challenges can be addressed and solved by cities. This may come as a surprise to those who think of envi- ronmental issues largely in terms of wild places and open spaces. Cities, often congested, dense, and enormous consumers of resources, would not be the place one might first turn for environmental solutions. But in fact, cities are inherently the "greenest" of all places. They are much more efficient in their use of energy, water, and land than suburbs. They provide transportation services in remarkably equitable and democratic fashion. They may be the best of all places for seniors to grow old. Development in cities helps to save natural areas and open space by relieving growth pressures on the countryside. And cities will, without question, be the pivotal players in fashioning solutions to the growing problem of climate change.
>
> New York City, for example, turns out to be the most energy efficient place in America. Yes, it houses 8.2 million citizens, and uses an enormous amount of energy to do so. Its electrical load, more than 12,000 megawatts, is as large as all of Massachusetts. Yet because the buildings are dense and thus more efficiently heated and cooled, and because 85 percent of all trips in Manhattan are on foot, bike, or transit, New York City uses dramatically less energy to serve each of its citizens than does a state like Massachusetts. Indeed, it uses less energy, on a per capita basis, than any other state in America. When one considers that another 750,000 commuters also enter New York every day to work, and use large amounts of energy in their daily business there but don't even count in the

per capital energy calculation, the city's efficiency performance is even more remarkable. . . .

In order to address the challenge of climate change, it is imperative that we make both buildings and transportation vastly more energy efficient. And cities are the place to start. In a way, cities are the Saudi Arabia of energy efficiency, vast mines of potential energy savings that dwarf most of the supply options our country possesses. . . .

The old paradigm of the pollution-filled city as a blight on the landscape, and the leafy-green suburbs with pristine lawns as the ideal, is outdated and does not lead us to a future of energy independence, clean air, and a stable climate. Cities are the best hope to realize our need for a bright, sustainable, and promising future.

This is just to touch on an enormously complex conversation in which biblically responsive Christians will be eager to participate, but I hope that these thoughts give some indication of the scope of the challenge and the extent of the promise, particularly to those who are relative newcomers to these discussions.[35] Biblically responsive Christians will have a passion for a just urban life that grows in partnership with nature.

Another paradigmatic and much more particular example of partnering with nature that is closer to the liturgical matrix of the Christian life is this: building a home for the liturgy that is structured with sustainably produced materials, manufactured by justly compensated workers, and shaped by the canons of "the beauty of holiness" (Ps. 29:2 [KJV][36]). Such criteria can surely be brought to bear on the design and building of new cathedrals today and on the design of smaller church structures in a variety of settings, as well.

The illustrative case of building new homes for the liturgy also suggests an appropriate starting point for all Christian initiatives in behalf of building human community in partnership with nature—beginning at home. This is surely an instance where teaching of Jesus about the vocation of his followers has obvious traction: "You are the light of the world. A city built on a hill cannot be hid. . . . In the same way, let your light shine before others, so that they may see your good works and give glory to your Father in heaven" (Matt. 5:14-16). The Christian liturgical assembly will want to be an exemplary community in every respect, but no less so as it seeks to build human community, intramurally and extramurally, in partnership with nature.

How many recently constructed church buildings, not to speak of church buildings of the past, have been monuments to human arrogance? Some are still being built without regard to their environmental or their human costs (for instance, materials from old-growth forests harvested and manufactured by underpaid third-world workers). It is appropriate to invoke a theme from Dietrich Bonhoeffer, in this respect, "the cost of discipleship." In this era, when political and economic realities still make "green materials" more costly than the market rate for other materials and when, likewise, when the same realities still make materials produced by justly paid labor more costly than others, Christian assemblies that have resolved to construct new buildings for their liturgies will also have to resolve to pay this cost of discipleship, in order to be a light to the world. That these structures will be designed to be beautiful, not just functional, moreover, goes without saying, although that may be an easier financial challenge to address, since beautiful structures typically cost no more than ugly ones. In the end, some Christian assemblies that are seeking new homes for their liturgies, as they face up to such theologically mandatory costs, will be best advised to redeem other spaces rather than build dys-functional new ones. I have already instanced the assembly I once visited in Soweto, South Africa, which was worshiping "in the beauty of holiness" in a reclaimed warehouse.

Beginning at home also must mean instituting a whole host of educa-tional ministries, of the kind I have already instanced in my discussion of what it can mean for a Christian to serve nature. To recall the *bon mot* attributed to Karl Barth, the Christian is the one who carries a Bible in one hand and a newspaper in the other. Beyond the newspaper, I would suggest that, notwithstanding the biblically identified fact that different people have different gifts, the burden of proof is on the shoulders of any American assembly in this era to show why it should not offer study/action groups on the likes of city planning and knowing your bioregion and greening your lifestyle and fair-trading your consumption and practicing sustainable agriculture and understanding climate change and identifying strategies for peacemaking in this atomic era. Why not take up Barth's implicit recommendation, too? Why not begin each of those study groups with an appropriate investigation of the Scriptures? As each assembly is called to be a light to the world in this era of global ecojustice crisis, so is each individual believer. And the assembly and its leadership must take the initiative to "equip the faithful" in this respect, as in all others.

Sometimes Christian assemblies will need to make other visible statements, precisely for the sake of their members' growth in grace, as well as ends in themselves. One such visible statement might be the installation of solar panels on the sanctuary roof. Such a project may not fully repay its cost in the short term; but it would nevertheless be worth the expense, as an example for all the members and for the church's neighborhood more generally.

Installation of a garden on the church grounds could have the same effect. While financially it might well be cheaper for people to continue purchasing vegetables commercially, the example of the garden could be a light to the members and to many others. If the assembly found itself in a city location, more particularly, it would have to begin by having the soil tested for toxic chemicals; but that would be an education in itself. And the joy of members working together on the project, shaped as it naturally would be by studies of Genesis 2 about the biblical garden, could be palpable. Even more, to offer the fruits of the harvest on a given Sunday and then to take those fruits to a shelter to help feed homeless souls could be gratifying for the assembly, if not always a great moment in the life of the people who are homeless.

Such an intramural building up of the body of Christ so that it and its members might be a light to the world, will as a matter of course be matched by a strong extramural witness. Doubtless this will be done, for prudential reasons if for no other, in cooperation with other church, religious, and civic groups. This is all the more appropriate these days because the challenges we are confronting are increasingly regional, national, and global.

In all this, the Christian mind and heart will be driven by a passionate love for the city, in testimony to the coming eschatological redemption of the city, amidst the new heavens and the new earth. How shall this passionate love be pragmatically embodied? Here we come to the limit of these reflections, where they would as a matter of course begin to take the form of ethical reflection. But this much cannot be said too emphatically at this point. American Christian assemblies in our time *will* hear the words of the prophet Jeremiah: "Seek the welfare of the city where I have sent you into exile, and pray to the LORD on its behalf, for in its welfare you will find your welfare" (Jer. 29:7). And they will therefore be passionately committed to building human community in the city in partnership with nature, by collective advocacy and personal engagement.

In this respect, as in all others, of course, Christians will want to be wise as foxes, as well as innocent as doves. They will want to be well grounded not only in contemporary sociological and cultural studies of the city but also in reliable theologies of the city. A good place to begin all of these studies will be by mastering the findings of the ground-breaking work of T. J. Gorringe, *A Theology of the Built Environment: Justice, Empowerment, Redemption.*[37] This pioneering study should be required reading for all American Christian theologians and liturgical leaders, to equip them both to contend with the forces of Christian anti-urbanism which are still very much alive in contemporary American life, and to grasp much more firmly the challenge of building human community in partnership with nature, in this, our globally urbanizing era.

The irony of this situation, however, is staggering. Virtually all of the statements about the global ecojustice crisis adopted by liturgical churches in our time have been well researched and are theologically insightful. Virtually all denominational bodies, too, have leadership in place to help enlist their member assemblies in advocacy efforts in behalf of the voiceless of the earth. Likewise for ecumenical bodies, such as the World Council of Churches and the National Council of Churches: all have produced studies and statements about these issues that are not only substantive and well researched, but which have typically been "ahead of their times," anticipating global discussions that would only emerge later, such as the WCC's longstanding concern to foster a just, peaceful, and sustainable society. The problem, as I have already suggested more than once, is not a lack of vision or insight or expertise at these levels but a lack of support, generally, from the grass roots, particularly from American sources. Funds for such public advocacy have been "drying up" increasingly for many decades.

Which brings me back to the local assembly. Will its members be willing not only to hear but also to take seriously what their own theologians and liturgical leaders who have recovered the urbacentric vision called forth by biblical eschatology are saying? And, in response to that teaching, will those members be willing to bear the cost of discipleship in behalf of this increasingly global, public arena, as well as in its own intramural life?

When members do chose, however, to seek the welfare of the city, the bonus, again, will be magnificent, as it is when they stand in awe before nature and when they serve nature, nothing less than an encounter with the living Christ, whom they know in the liturgy, who himself wept over Jerusalem and who wanted to take Jerusalem under his wings the way a mother hen does for her brood (Matt. 23:37). He is the One whom believers serve when they respond to the needs of the hungry and the refugees and the godforsaken in the cities of our world.

The Habits and the Promise of Awe, Serving, and Partnering

Thus we have seen that the liturgy, rightly renewed, inculcates habits of faith in individuals who participate in the liturgy faithfully, three of which habits focus on the participants' relationship with nature:

1. Given ritual expression especially by the Sanctus, with its celebration of the glory of God filling heaven and earth, the liturgy forms the habit of standing in awe before nature in the walk of the believer with nature.
2. Given ritual expression especially by the *Agnus Dei*, with its proclamation of the Lamb of God who sacrifices himself to take away the sins of the world and to grant peace to the world, the liturgy forms the habit of serving nature in the walk of the believer with nature.
3. Finally, given ritual expression especially by the confessed hospitality of Christ for humans whom he gathers in the Eucharist, the liturgy is thereby the celebration of the One who calls together a new human community in partnership with nature, thus forming the habit of partnering with nature in the walk of the believer with nature, in particular in behalf of the upbuilding of human community in the cities of this world.

In this comprehensive sense, then, when the liturgy is rightly and faithfully celebrated, the liturgy will mold the liturgical assembly, like a potter shaping the clay, according to its biblical calling, to be a city set upon a hill and a light to the nations. That is the promise of the renewed liturgy. That is the promise of ritualizing nature.

Epilogue

"Come and See"

It is time to conclude these explorations. I propose to do this not by looking back over the way we have come. Rather, I propose to end the course we have followed by returning to the Thoreauvian invitation with which I began this book, to come walk with me along the Charles River. But now I want to focus that request, by extending a more particular, Johannine invitation, which has to do with a single point along the way. Let me explain.

When it comes to assessing the state of church life in the United States today, I am of two minds. First, this is what I see on Monday, Wednesday, and Friday: Reports in the last couple of decades tell us that the membership of so-called mainline denominations in the United States, such as the Episcopal, Lutheran, Presbyterian, and Methodist churches, have been declining for some time.[1] In the most recent year for which we have complete information, 2005, even the Southern Baptist Church declined in membership somewhat (1 percent). In that same year the Catholic Church did experience a miniscule growth (less than 1 percent), but that figure masks large losses, which have been compensated for by sizeable increases of immigrant members. The Catholic story is particularly poignant, given the fact that that communion is facing an ominous shortage of priests. On the basis of such reports alone, a number of news stories have raised the question, by implication if not in so many words, whether or not, across the board, churches in America are in serious decline.

To be sure, American churches have not yet reached the point of empty cathedrals confronted by our European brothers and sisters in the faith.

(Although, it bothers me every time I drive to the center of my own urban neighborhood when I have to pass a beautiful turn-of-the-last-century brownstone church edifice that is now being converted into offices, apartments, and boutiques, with a food court. And it bothers me even more when I read stories about Catholic churches being boarded up in metropolitan regions like Boston and New York.) America is still the land of religion, certainly compared to Europe. Witness the astounding membership growth of evangelical megachurches over the past five years—83 percent. Numbers of these huge congregations, and the parachurch ministries that they support, like Focus on the Family, have also been wielding considerable political influence nationally in recent years, not always for the good, in my view. Be that as it may, students of these trends say that in a generation or so, when these growing megachurches and the parachurch ministries they support have become more "established," they themselves will in all likelihood cycle into the same patterns of decline that now afflict most mainline Protestant churches and a growing number of metropolitan Catholic parishes.

Whether declining or growing, however, virtually all American churches and their members seem to be caught up in the larger patterns of American society, the famous (or infamous) American individualism and the narcissism that sometimes goes with it, the rampant consumerism, the participation in global economic systems that privilege the prosperous, and the resultant and inordinate contributions to global warming, global pollution, and the exhaustion of nonrenewable resources around the earth. These are the kind of issues I regularly talk about with colleagues at religion and ecology meetings—to which we have flown over long distances and at which we stay in top-of-the-line hotels and eat foods that have been transported there from all over the world.

Further, there is not a little evidence that what most American Christians most care about, passionately and pervasively and vociferously, are not issues related to our global ecojustice crisis, but something else—sex. Virtually all Christian communions today are being shaken, if not rent asunder, by issues related to sexuality, including gay marriage, abortion, and abuse. Or, in the case of many evangelical churches, a range of denominations is preoccupied with fighting what they consider to be the sexual ways of this world that, in their view, are being imposed upon their members by the larger society (and to which a few of their own most prestigious leaders have succumbed). Is there really sufficient room in

Christian minds and hearts these days for caring about the earth and its downtrodden peoples as well as being so focused, not to say fixated, on sex, important as that issue certainly is?

This situation has left some friends of American Christianity, never mind its critics, shaking their heads in disbelief. Thus, Dieter Hessel, a longstanding church leader in the struggle for global ecojustice, has lamented that "the bulk of clergy and laity who lead local, denominational and ecumenical communities of faith tend to leave the well-being of creation to others called 'environmentalists' [and] have yet to 'get it' with regard to an 'ecological reformation of Christianity' that focuses on the new context of imperiled earth community and responds by reorienting liturgy, theology, ethics, and mission."[2] Such are some of the reasons why the rumor has been making the rounds in the American body politic, in the ranks of friends as well as critics, that the American church today is both declining and irrelevant.

No wonder I am tempted, with many other Christians who are committed to addressing our global ecojustice crisis, to look beyond American shores for signs of hope. We look to Asia and Latin America and Africa, where churches are growing exponentially in numbers and apparently in vitality, even as some of them are being persecuted or threatened with persecution. A case in point would be the already mentioned African Earthkeeping Churches, which are liturgically alive, growing in numbers, committed to addressing the needs of the downtrodden, and at once resolved to care for the earth, most visibly by planting trees in the desecrated regions where its members live. The Spirit, so it seems, is aflame everywhere but in places like the United States. But no sooner do I think such things than I realize that that kind of grass-is-greener-on-the-other-side-of-the-fence thinking may be little more than me finding a way to avoid engaging the challenges of my own world, a realization that only works to deepen my own depression.

On Monday, Wednesday, and Friday, it *can* be depressing for those of us who care deeply about the life and mission of the church and who likewise deeply care about the earth and the downtrodden of the earth. What sometimes locks us into that depression, moreover, is the thought that we, too, like everybody else, are very much part of those trends.

On the other hand, there is Tuesday, Thursday, and Saturday. On those days I see the life of the church in the United States quite differently. Commitments on the part of the churches, in this respect, that are already in place are impressive, as I observed at the outset of these explorations. Most major Christian communions in the United States have already spoken forthrightly and prophetically about the global ecojustice crisis. Church leaders, like the Catholic Bishops of the Pacific Northwest who addressed the needs of the Columbia River and the many peoples in that region, have also issued critically important public ecojustice statements. Ecumenical bodies like the National Council of Churches have done likewise. Most recently, but of major importance, evangelical groups—now including Southern Baptists—have taken up the cause of addressing the issue of global warming.

Most of the major Christian communions in the United States also maintain advocacy offices in Washington, D.C., and in many state capitals, as do various ecumenical bodies. They typically marshal their lobbying efforts in behalf of ecojustice issues in highly effective ways, often working in concert with each other and with other secular advocacy groups. Thus, church advocacy groups arranged for prominent bishops to testify before Congress early on in the public discussion of global warming. All this is surely encouraging.

But, for me, the church news that does not typically make its way into the public arena is even more encouraging. Here I must depend on anecdotal reports and personal experiences. But, for me, this is impressive news nonetheless. I have already mentioned the longstanding ministry of Holden Village in Washington state. Hundreds of similar outdoor ministries of the church around the country are also taking the lead in educating children, youth, and adults about ecojustice issues and the theology of nature. There are likewise scores of Catholic monastic communities that are serving as centers of liturgical and ecological renewal and numerous parachurch groups, like Earth Ministry in Seattle, that are mobilizing church people around the country to respond to the ecojustice crisis. A number of church seminaries have been participating in the "Green Seminary Initiative," which aims to transform not only institutional praxis that affects the biosphere, such as reducing carbon footprints, but also reforming curricula in many departments. In addition, hundreds, perhaps thousands, of Christian congregations have taken steps of their own to shape their educational and advocacy ministries in behalf of earthcare, as well as for the sake of the poor, and have likewise made commitments to reduce their carbon footprints and to institute other kinds of resource conservation. I can report, too, on the basis of personal experience, that Christian students across the country appear to be committed more than ever to addressing ecojustice issues, both locally and in larger arenas.

Could it be that American churches are now approaching what is called a "tipping point" regarding serious commitment to earthcare and to the poor of the earth? That question has crossed my mind with increasing frequency in the last two or three years, as I have given lectures, consulted with church agencies, and engaged colleagues in conversations around the country. Such thoughts preoccupy me Tuesdays, Thursdays, and Saturdays.

But I do not want to leave the reader with this perhaps imponderable question: Which days of my experience with the church, the days of depression or the days of hope, are most attuned to actual trends in American church life today? Either way, I believe, never mind Monday through Saturday. Instead, think first of the first day of the week. On Sundays, thankfully, I am in church, singing my heart out in the liturgy, and that Sunday experience gives me my bearings.

Every Lord's Day, I find hope in the countercultural liturgical assemblies where I worship, whether at home or on the road. The simple liturgy of the church helps me to identify with those who weep and with those who rejoice and, in so doing, makes me ecstatic, in the name of Jesus. And more, I am captivated by the thought that this very liturgy *can* give birth to Christians who know how to stand in awe of nature, serve nature, and build just and sustainable human communities in partnership with nature. I participate in those Sunday liturgies, moreover, in the knowledge that my experience is not unique, by any means. Vital liturgical assemblies are flourishing, here and there, in every corner of America, as well as around the world.

So first things first. "The hope that is in me," to use the language of 1 Peter once again, does not depend first and foremost on the hopeful signs I witness on Tuesdays, Thursdays, and Saturdays. I see and indeed celebrate those signs, and many other like them, because, I believe, I have been formed and gifted to see them—on Sundays. In this sense, "I once . . . was blind, but now I see," thanks to God's amazing grace, in, with, and under the liturgy. The experience of the Sundays, indeed, readies me to deal with the depression of the Mondays, Wednesdays, and Fridays and to foster and to celebrate the signs of hope I see on the Tuesdays, Thursdays, and Saturdays.

Which brings me back to my walks along the Charles River. Those walks are charged with signs of eschatological hope for me, precisely because of that single point along the way, the monastery chapel of the Society of St. John the Evangelist, where my life is regularly claimed by the life of the liturgy. Fragmentary and self-reflective as my own vision undoubtedly is, I know that if I have eyes to see at all, it is because such liturgies have touched me and inspired me. I also know my own vision, idiosyncratic and self-serving as it surely is, is cleansed and clarified and magnified enormously, in the power of the Spirit, as all the faithful join together in their assemblies all over the inhabited world, if only they will be called to open their eyes, once the liturgy has been renewed.

This brings me finally to my Johannine invitation. At the very end, mindful of the importance of the liturgical assembly along the way in my own life, I want to invoke the words of the apostle Philip to the questioning Nathaniel, as reported in the Gospel of John. I enthusiastically invite readers new to the liturgy and also readers who, to one degree or another, are familiar with the liturgy, and, further, anyone who is deeply discouraged by our world or by our churches today, as I sometimes am, to "Come and see" (John 1:46). Never mind thoughts of American and global church megatrends, in the short term. Don't bypass that particular assembly experience available to you right where you're walking today.

Come and see how the liturgy, now an expression of a thriving counterculture, now a simple but ecstatic communal rite, moves those who participate in it faithfully to hear and to respond to the voices of all the voiceless creatures of God's good earth and indeed attunes them to hear the groaning of the whole creation. Come and see how participants in that communal rite exult in the Grace of God, Creator, Redeemer, and Consummator of all things, and celebrate the glory of that God, which fills the heavens and the earth, as they also rejoice in the blessed mission of the One who comes in the name of that same God, the cosmic Lamb of God. Come and see how the liturgy, once it has been renewed, can ritualize nature in hope and peace for every believer.

Appendix

On the Ambiguities of "Stewardship"

For the most part, I have carefully avoided using the term *stewardship* in this book. Throughout, where readers might have expected me to use the term, as well as in other contexts, I have consistently used the word *partnership*, for reasons that I hope readers will understand, once they have finished this book.[1] I have also made every effort I could to interpret the related construct, human dominion over nature, in terms of partnership.

I have avoided employing the term *stewardship*, I want to stress, not because I think that stewardship is not a good idea. I consider the widespread use of the term in American culture today, and in Christian circles in particular, generally to be a gain, certainly compared to ideas formerly employed to justify the mindless exploitation of nature. Stewardship is often the first construct that people who are searching for a less exploitative relationship with nature seize upon. As I have spoken around the country in many settings for decades, I have noted that some will even approach me with the excitement of new converts and tell me how important stewardship has become for them. I am always grateful that they have come that far. But I usually try to find a way to tell them: "Now that you have discovered the meaning of stewardship, I think we can do better."

These are my reservations, pending further detailed study and careful reflection about the matter.[2] The reader may wish to compare what follows with a similar set of reservations expressed by Larry L. Rasmussen in his book *Earth Community Earth Ethics*.[3]

The problem seems to be that the term *stewardship* itself has such a widely established usage in the general culture and, not unrelated to that wider usage, in the life of grassroots Christian congregations, especially in the United States, that *it resists normative theological definition*. Exxon-Mobil, for example, to cite but one of many of such instances that could be noted, regularly uses the language of stewardship in its promotional materials, which seek to explain how that corporation is wisely using and protecting the planet's resources. That ExxonMobil also has been the prime funder of an anti-global-warming propaganda campaign in recent years and that, as a result, has been called by *New York Times* writer Paul Krugman "an enemy of the planet," will perhaps show how elastic the concept of stewardship is in the public domain.[4]

This kind of public-relations material helps to define how the language of stewardship is heard in grassroots Christian communities in the United States and perhaps even in some scholarly circles. True, theologians and biblical scholars and preachers can—and do—point to texts like 1 Corinthians 4:1, "stewards of the mysteries of God" and 1 Peter 4:10, "Like good stewards of the manifold gifts of grace," with the intent to shape the usage of the construct by a theocentric theology of grace, but, as I see it, sociological forces—like the ExxonMobil materials—keep dragging the stewardship theme back to anthropocentric and secular default meanings in general cultural usage.

Popular discussions in church circles then more often than not affirm such tendencies, consciously or unconsciously. I would not want to say for sure that I have never, after more than forty years of active engagement with these matters, read anything *critical* about the idea of stewardship in materials from denominational publishing houses. But that is my recollection. This is sobering, since perceptive thinkers, from Aristotle to Karl Barth, have generally maintained that in order to say yes, one must also say no. To affirm something, one must deny something. Scores of books by theologically trained writers show signs of this yes-only fallacy. Often, it appears, professors at denominational schools are asked by church publishers or denominational stewardship offices to write books on stewardship, and that the professors then dutifully do, usually with enthusiasm, rarely raising questions about whether the stewardship idea has any downside.

This is not to say that there are no public controversies hovering around the theme. But such disputes tend to be about how stewardship should be applied politically, not about the validity of the construct itself. It often comes down to this: whether church members should support "wise use" of the environment for the sake of sustaining the current economic system and perhaps streamlining its functioning (the preference of the theological right) or "wise use" of the environment for the sake of addressing the needs of the poor around the world (the preference of the theological left). In both cases, the assumptions are anthropocentric and managerial in character, and frequently seem to betray little concern for nature in itself. This kind of usage surely does not reflect the mandate of Genesis 2, that we are *to serve and protect* the earth *for its own sake.* The chief concern on both sides is how best to manipulate or exploit nature for the sake of human well-being. "Wise use," of course, is language that corporate interests love to employ. To be sure, no one can rightly contest the conceptuality of "wise use" in the abstract, but, from a theological perspective, it surely must be effectively shaped—and corrected where necessary—by the full range of biblical teachings about nature, not to speak of biblical concerns for social justice.

In this context, one might blame, as it were, the power of some of *Jesus'* parables (!!), which, *popularly interpreted,* tend to be heard as advocating that predominantly managerial, exploitative approach to nature: above all, the parable of the talents in Matthew 25 and the parable of the "unjust steward" in Luke 16. In the former, the man of means hands over the five, the two, and the one talents to his "slaves"—in the default, popular reading, these are the "stewards"—then goes away. This can readily be read—and often is, notwithstanding emphatic instruction to the contrary by official interpreters—as pointing to an absent God who has given riches to his stewards to manage productively on their own, an absent God who has harsh expectations that they will do precisely that. The parable then narrates how the man of means comes back and rejects the one-talent steward who did not invest his money for the sake of growth: "You ought to have invested my money with the bankers, and on my return I would have received what is my own with interest" (Matt. 25:27).

In the popular mind of American churches, this parable then resonates with the parable of the unjust steward in Luke 16. The rich man in this parable, suspecting financial mismanagement on the part of the steward to whom he had delegated the management of his estate, asks the steward "to turn in an account of your stewardship" (16:2). The steward, according to the story, schemes with the tenants, "cooks the books," as we have learned to say, and then is praised by the owner for being so shrewd (16:8)!

With those particular parables of Jesus read in such a fashion, this, then, is often the default meaning of stewardship in the popular mind of the church, baptized, as it were, with the authority of Jesus: *we are called do whatever it takes to manage the absent owner's resources as productively as we can.* (Interestingly, while the RSV translators used the traditional term *steward* in the Lukan parable, the NRSV translators chose, instead, *manager.*)

All this is not unrelated to the fact that in most American congregations the time of the year when stewardship is most extensively discussed is when *the budget* is at issue. Granted, the messages presented by denominationally produced materials and by hard-pressed parish pastors are often shaped by a theocentric theology of grace: that God gives us so much, above all in Jesus Christ, but also in the blessings of creation, that we cannot help but respond by giving of our entire lives to God in gratitude by being good stewards of all the gifts we have been given. In recent years, such materials and related sermons have also been broadened to include observations about "the stewardship of creation" and even some "ecojustice" themes. But, however nuanced the theological materials and presentations might be, the people in the pews get the message: stewardship chiefly has to do with fundraising, that is, with the economy of money, good planning, wise management, productivity, and growth.

In this respect, a 2006 issue of the pastoral journal, *The Living Pulpit* is quite representative.[5] Virtually all the several articles address issues related to money and management, theocentrically and spiritually considered, to be sure, but clearly focused on those issues. This is the default meaning of stewardship, here fostered with genuine theological authority. The one article that does consider the human relationship with nature concludes— in contradistinction to all the other articles—that stewardship means "the shepherdly care of creation."[6] When busy pastors read such journals (they will probably have saved them to revisit for their "stewardship" sermon[s] just prior to their congregations' pledge days), what will be on those pastors' minds? Making the best case for congregants to support the church budget or exploring what "the shepherdly care of creation" might mean?

All this, in my view, is intricately and inseparably related to that cultural phenomenon of the modern Western world that Max Weber called the "spirit of capitalism." Weber showed how some of the most fundamental theological assumptions of Calvinism—themes such as election and vocation—set the stage for the rise of capitalism. Simplified, this was Weber's thesis: that the elect of God consciously or unconsciously sought to demonstrate to themselves or to others that they were indeed among the elect by producing the fruits of righteousness, in particular the fruits of economic success, by being productive and amassing wealth, all in order to glorify God.

Larry Rasmussen has filled in more of the historical details in this respect.[7] He writes:

> It was precisely stewardship ethics that were enunciated by seventeenth-century scientists and theologians in keeping with early commercial and industrial advances, and on the basis of mechanistic science and homocentric philosophy and theology. In the religious versions, God had assigned human caretaking and supervisory tasks. Nature was to be managed responsibly for the benefit of human welfare.[8] Stewardship ethics were also the explicit theme of development as the scientific management of resources for the benefit of society in the philosophy and practice of Gifford Pinchot and others early in [the twentieth century]. And in fact much sustainable-development discussion at the UN and among NGOs today moves in this orbit."

The default meaning of stewardship in America, it seems to me, is inextricably bound up with such cultural assumptions, above all, the drive to amass wealth, by being wise stewards of the bounties of God.

That a recent scholarly article on stewardship by John L. Paterson ends up by distinguishing between "hard," "soft," and "agricultural" stewardship shows how difficult it is make any clear and positive use of the construct.[9] Likewise for R. J. Berry's edited compendium of articles, *Environmental Stewardship: Critical Perspectives – Past and Present*: while its twenty-six chapters do not propose twenty-six different definitions of the term, the definitions used in this volume are manifold and sometimes contradictory.[10] This means that for the general reader, for sure, and perhaps for some scholarly readers as well, default meanings will probably trump specified meanings, since it is a huge challenge to make sense out of all the bewildering number of differing approaches to the subject.

The default meaning of stewardship, ironically, has also tended to inhibit the ongoing work of biblical scholarship. A number of scholars who themselves have apparently wanted to move beyond such default meanings still have tended, in the absence of other nomenclature, to use the term *stewardship*, which has inhibited the effectiveness of their arguments. This, for example, as far as I can see, is the only liability in William Brown's otherwise superb and illuminating study of Old Testament theology, *The Ethos of the Cosmos.*[11]

It is not without significance, moreover, that the popular literature on stewardship is enormous. Virtually all major religious publishing houses have their own stewardship books, films, study guides, or Web sites, as do many denominational and ecumenical centers. At least since the middle of the last century, moreover, most denominations have sponsored regular national and regional conferences on the matter and made available "stewardship experts" to meet with individual congregations and their leaders. Independent firms, which help churches raise money, frequently have their own literature and other media on stewardship that they provide pastors and congregations. Sunday school materials in virtually all denominations also find ways to push the stewardship theme.

More generally, something that a lot of people care about appears to be going on when this term is used. On one day, Google showed 16,200,000 hits for the word, which for an originally and fundamentally theological idea must surely be considered to be big-time. This shows, I surmise, that this is a cultural phenomenon of considerable importance, especially when compared with the interest in a major theological construct like "justification by faith," for which there were 1,700,000 hits. Stewardship is not yet as popular as Jesus Christ, for whom there were 30,700,000 hits, which may be reassuring to some. But stewardship appears to be at least half as popular as Jesus, about the meaning of which I will not speculate.

All of which is to say that the construct stewardship is fraught with ambiguities. We still await a major critical historical study of the subject. In the absence of such a study, I believe that it will be best to continue to avoid the term in any scholarly works and in church publications, too, insofar as that is humanly possible. I would advise parish pastors to do the same, perhaps restricting the word "stewardship" for use in financial contexts and invoking terms like "earthcare" in discussions of the ecojustice crisis. I would also recommend to all concerned to give serious consideration to the construct of "partnership" that I have proposed in this volume as a replacement for "stewardship."

On the other hand, I do not want to suggest that the construct stewardship is totally irredeemable. Serious theologians have taken stewardship seriously, and they should be given a hearing. In this connection, I will mention three works by two authors, each of which is of the highest quality, which may help readers to work their way through the jungle of materials available through church publishing houses. These works, more than any others I have read, make a strong case for a theologically informed usage of the construct, although I myself was not persuaded by them enough to abandon my reservations about the idea: Douglas John Hall's *The Steward: A Biblical Image Come of Age* and *Imaging God: Dominion as Stewardship*, and John Reumann's *Stewardship and the Economy of God*.[12]

Notes

Prologue: Come Walk with Me

1. James Nash, *Loving Nature: Ecological Integrity and Christian Responsibility* (Nashville: Abingdon; in cooperation with The Church's Center for Theology and Public Policy, Washington, D.C., 1991), 132–33.

1. The Making of a Theme: Ritualizing Nature

1. In this book, I am presupposing that there can be a *consonance* between the affirmations of theology and the findings of the natural sciences but that these disciplines proceed according to their own self-established methods. In this respect, I am depending on the work on "the dialogue between science and religion" accomplished by Ted Peters and his co-workers in a variety of writings. See especially *Cosmos as Creation: Theology and Science in Consonance,* ed. Ted Peters (Nashville: Abingdon, 1989).

2. For one accessible description of the postmodern spirit, understood as "a set of cultural circumstances," and a proposal for a theological response to those circumstances, see John Milbank, "The Gospel of Affinity," in *The Future of Hope: Christian Tradition Amid Modernity and Postmodernity*, ed. Miroslav Volf and William Katerberg (Grand Rapids: Eerdmans, 2004), 149–69. Milbank understands the postmodern spirit to mean, above all else, "the obliteration of boundaries" and "the confusion of categories" (p. 149). He also holds that Christianity "is the religion of the obliteration of categories," for example, rich and poor, male and female, Jew and Greek (p. 158). Yet he argues that Christianity offers an ordered freedom that transcends the cultural and spiritual chaos bequeathed to us by the postmodern spirit.

3. For some thoughtful reflections about the postmodern spirit and some tentative suggestions about an appropriate theological response that addresses our life in nature, see Mark I. Wallace, *Fragments of the Spirit: Nature, Violence, and the Renewal of Creation* (Harrisburg: Trinity Press International, 2002), chap. 1. Wallace develops what he thinks of as an "ecological pneumatology," focusing, as his title suggests, on the works of the Spirit, whom he thinks of as "the wounded Spirit." He summarizes his thinking in an essay, "The Wounded Spirit as the Basis for Hope in an Age of Radical Ecology," in *Christianity and Ecology: Seeking the Well-Being of Earth and Humans,* ed. Dieter T. Hessel and Rosemary Radford Ruether (Cambridge: Harvard University Press, 2000), 51–72.

For a self-consciously feminist response to the same postmodern trends, which is written from a pan-religious ecological perspective and which also focuses on the works of the Spirit, see Mary C. Grey, *Sacred Longings: The Ecological Spirit and Global Culture* (Minneapolis: Fortress Press, 2004), especially her summary statement (p. 86) about developing what she calls a "sacramental poetics," which, for her, appeals to our basic encounter with nature, "in word and symbol, prayer and gesture," thus awakening "a depth dimension and an experience of the sacred."

The postmodern spirit should surely be taken seriously, not only by those who write from a pneumatalogical perspective, as do Wallace and Grey, but also by those, such as myself, who write from a more particularistic, christological perspective. The postmodern spirit is a part of all of us in the West, in one way or another. But the postmodern spirit should not be taken too seriously. Indeed, what is perhaps the most fundamental theme of postmodern thought, that there is no metanarrative, itself needs to be deconstructed. To this end, see the pointed, short essay by Robert Jenson, "How the World Lost Its Story," *First Things* 38 (October 1993): 19–24. All of which is to suggest that the theologians and preachers of the church today appear to have before them in these times a countercultural challenge of profound proportions, discerning how to address this particular culture that has lost its story. This could well be a historic, kerygmatic opportunity, reminiscent of the apostolic era, to "tell the old, old story" *in a fresh way* that will engage those who think and live under the grips of the postmodern spirit.

I accent the words "in a fresh way," since the new telling of the grand narrative of faith that I have in mind will have to be like new wine in new wineskins. A fresh kind of theological rhetoric will be required for this new narrative theology, perhaps more in the tradition of Søren Kierkegaard and his "Paradoxical Religion B" than in the tradition of that great philosopher-theologian of the nineteenth century, whom Kierkegaard so passionately criticized, Georg Wilhelm Friedrich Hegel, and the many theologians over whom Hegel cast his shadow well into the twentieth century, who espoused what Kierkegaard thought of as "General Religion A."

4. I have argued this case in a variety of publications since 1970 and extensively in my 1985 book, *The Travail of Nature: The Ambiguous Ecological Promise of Christianity* (Minneapolis: Fortress Press, 1985). As far as I know, the basic thesis of this widely reviewed and oft-cited study has never been refuted.

5. Those familiar with my writings, especially *The Travail of Nature*, will immediately recognize that *Ritualizing Nature* adds a needed historical balance. I have hitherto been preoccupied with the teachings about nature of the great doctors of the church—people like Irenaeus, Augustine, Luther, Calvin, Barth, and Teilhard de Chardin—not with the formative power of the church's historic rituals. I have regularly alluded to and presupposed the existential importance of the church's worship for its theology of nature, as for everything else, but this is the first time I have written extensively on the matter.

6. I consider the Worldwatch publications published annually by Norton Press (New York) the single best treatment of our global ecological crisis. Speth's volume is published by Yale University Press (New Haven).

7. The most flagrant contributor to this well-funded disinformation campaign in the early years of this century has been ExxonMobil (other oil companies, like BP and Shell, have conceded the need to do something about global warming), called by *New York Times* columnist Paul Krugman an "enemy of the planet" ("Enemy of the Planet," *New York Times*, April 17, 2006, A25). ExxonMobil, Krugman points out,

has lavished grants "that have supported an alternative universe of global warming skeptics." Krugman also observes, soberingly, that given the press's general policy of providing "equal time" to both sides of any issue, major newspapers "gave the skeptics—a few dozen people, many if not most receiving direct financial support from ExxonMobil—roughly the same amount of attention as the scientific consensus, supported by thousands of independent researchers." Interestingly, early in 2007, even Exxon began to show some signs that the leadership of that company was recognizing global warming as an issue that had to be addressed. Whether, however, this was more than a mere public-relations action, in keeping with Exxon's longstanding practices in this respect, remains to be seen.

8. For example, a 2006 government report by the U.S. Climate Change Science Program, an interagency body, concluded that humans are driving the warming trend through greenhouse gas emissions, noting in the official press release that "the observed patterns of change over the past 50 years cannot be explained by natural processes alone, nor by the effects of short-lived atmospheric constituents such as aerosols and tropospheric ozone alone." (From a *Washington Post* story, carried by the *Boston Globe*, May 3, 2006, A16.)

9. Noah J. Toly, "Climate Change and Climate Change Policy as Human Sacrifice: Artifice, Idolatry, and Environment in a Technological Society," *Christian Scholar's Review* 35, no. 1 (Fall 2005): 63–78.

10. *Grist* magazine, May 30, 2006, http://www.grist.org/, accessed March 25, 2008.

11. See the article by Jeff Rickert, "Climate Change Comes to D.C.," *TomPaine.com,* http://www.tompaine.com/articles/2007/02/26/climate_change_comes_to_dc.php, accessed January 25, 2008.

12. Scripture quotation is from the Revised Standard Version of the Bible, copyright © 1946, 1952, 1971 National Council of the Churches of Christ in the USA. Used by permission. All rights reserved.

13. Paul Tillich, *Systematic Theology* I (Chicago: University of Chicago Press, 1951), 49.

14. Walter Wink, *Unmasking the Powers: The Invisible Forces That Determine Human Existence* (Minneapolis: Fortress Press, 1986).

15. Walter Wink, *Cracking the Gnostic Code: The Powers in Gnosticism,* Society of Biblical Literature Monograph Series 46 (Atlanta: Scholars, 1993), 30.

16. Ibid., 4.

17. Ibid., 6.

18. Reinhold Niebuhr, *The Nature and Destiny of Man: A Christian Interpretation* (New York: Scribner, 1946), and *Moral Man and Immoral Society: A Study in Ethics and Politics* (New York: Scribner, 1960).

19. Herman E. Daly and John Cobb Jr., *For the Common Good: Redirecting the Economy Toward Community, the Environment, and a Sustainable Future* (Boston: Beacon, 1989).

20. Cynthia D. Moe-Lobeda, *Healing a Broken World: Globalization and God* (Minneapolis: Fortress Press, 2002), 1.

21. David Pfrimmer, "The Changing Public Discourse on Ecology," *Journal of Lutheran Ethics* 3 (November 2003): 11, www.elca.org/scriptlib/dcs/jle, accessed January 25, 2008.

22. Larry Rasmussen, "Global Eco-Justice: The Church's Mission in Urban Society," in *Christianity and Ecology*, ed. Hessel and Ruether, 515–30; the quotations are from p. 520.

23. Holmes Ralston III, "Science, Religion, and the Future," in *Religion and Science: History, Method, Dialogue*, ed. Mark Richardson and Wesley Wildman (New York: Routledge, 1996), 79, cited by John F. Haught, "Theology and Ecology in an Unfinished Universe," in *Franciscans and Creation: What Is Our Responsibility?* Washington Theological Union Symposium Papers 2003, ed. Elise Saffau (St. Bonaventure, N.Y.: The Franciscan Institute, 2003), 1.

24. William McKibben, *The Death of Nature* (New York: Random House, 1989). This metaphor has been in the public domain at least since Carolyn Merchant published her study of the fate of nature in the modern period, *The Death of Nature: Women, Ecology, and the Scientific Revolution* (New York: Harper & Row, 1980). In that study, she argued that the philosophy and science of mechanism objectified nature and, in effect, handed it over to industrial society to be exploited. Which, for her, was the death of nature.

25. "God's Earth is Sacred: An Open Letter to Church and Society in the U.S.," National Council of Churches of Christ, February 14, 2005, http://www.ncccusa.org/news/14.02.05theologicalstatement.html, accessed January 25, 2008.

26. H. Paul Santmire, *Brother Earth: Nature, God, and Ecology in a Time of Crisis* (New York: Thomas Nelson, 1970).

27. It appears that the issues we are identifying here, which, in their severity, drive us to confront the threats of apocalyptic uncertainty, have been emerging for some time, although unobserved by many. For insight into these matters, it will be helpful to revisit the writings of an apocalyptic seer from an earlier era, William Stringfellow, to help us to grasp some deeper dimensions of our situation. See especially his book, *An Ethic for Christians and Other Aliens in a Strange Land* (Waco: Word, 1973).

28. For a review and critique of these novels, which draw extensively and often mistakenly on the Book of Revelation, see Barbara Rossing, *The Rapture Exposed: The Message of Hope in the Book of Revelation* (Boulder: Westview, 2004).

29. See the review of *The Road* (New York: Knopf, 2006), by William Kennedy, "Left Behind," *New York Times Book Review*, October 8, 2006, 1, 10. That *The Road* won a Pulitzer Prize in 2007 and was chosen in the same year by the immensely popular TV talk-show host, Oprah Winfrey, for her book club, thereby assuring that it would achieve an instant best-seller status, may also say something about the resonance of the book's message for the popular mind.

30. Michelle Huneven, *Jamesland* (New York: Random House, 2003), 304–5.

31. *New York Times,* February 17, 2004, D1. A more recent story from the front page of the *Times* Science section focused on the Earth alone, with the same Doomsday tonality: "In the end, there won't even be any fragments. . . . [A]bout 7.59 billion years from now Earth will be dragged from its orbit by an engorged red Sun and spiral to a rapid vaporous death" (*New York Times*, March 11, 2008, D1).

32. John Updike, "The Accelerating Expansion of the Universe," *Harper's* 309, no. 1853 (October 2004): 71.

33. It is striking that the widely respected natural scientist, Edward O. Wilson, a card-carrying "secular humanist," has now issued an urgent appeal to churches to address the global ecojustice crisis, the assumption being that what the churches say

matters publicly. See his book *The Creation: An Appeal to Save Life on Earth* (New York: Norton, 2006).

34. Thomas Berry, *The Great Work: Our Way Into the Future* (New York: Bell Tower, 1999). Here following Larry L. Rasmussen, "Sightings of Primal Visions: Community and Ecology," in *Character and Scripture: Moral Formation, Community, and Biblical Interpretation*, ed. William P. Brown (Grand Rapids: Eerdmans, 2002): "The great work ahead, [according to Berry] . . . , is to effect the transition from a period of 'the human devastation of the Earth to a period when humans [are] present to the planet in a mutually beneficial manner.' If we grant Berry's conclusion, it goes without saying that any such great work means changed cosmologies and moral universes, together with altered institutions and different habits. It means different inner disciplines as well as outward arrangements, different languages of understanding as well as different religious, cultural, and moral imagination. Like past 'great works,' these will be decades long, perhaps centuries long, in the making" (pp. 391–92).

35. See Steven C. Rockefeller, "Global Interdependence, the Earth Charter, and Christian Faith," in *Earth Habitat: Eco-Injustice and the Church's Response*, ed. Dieter T. Hessel and Larry Rasmussen (Minneapolis: Fortress Press, 2001), chap. 6.

36. It is, of course, difficult to say with precision how many organized ecojustice initiatives are effectively engaged in this global human effort. But the leading environmental activist, Paul Hawken, has made a good case that they number in the millions. See his article "A Global Democratic Movement Is About To Pop" in *AlterNet*, May 1, 2007, http://www.alternet.org/envirohealth/51088/?page=1, accessed January 25, 2008 (from *Orion* magazine).

37. See the essay by Mary Evelyn Tucker and John Grim, editors of the Harvard University book project on world religions and ecology, "The Greening of the World's Religions," *Chronicle of Higher Education: The Chronicle Review* 53, no. 23 (February 9, 2007): B9; and Gary T. Gardner, *Inspiring Progress: Religions' Contributions to Sustainable Development* (Washington, D.C.: Worldwatch Institute, 2006).

38. See Max Oelschlaeger, *Caring for Creation: An Ecumenical Approach to the Environmental Crisis* (New Haven: Yale University Press, 1994).

39. See, for example, Larry L. Rasmussen, *Earth Community Earth Ethics* (Maryknoll, N.Y.: Orbis, 1997).

40. See "Partnership for the Environment Among U.S. Christians: Reports from the National Religious Partnership for the Environment," in *Christianity and Ecology*, ed. Hessel and Ruether, 573–90.

41. Larry Rasmussen, "Eco-Justice: Church and Community Together," in *Earth Habitat*, ed. Hessel and Rasmussen, 7.

42. In so framing my confessional method, I mean to distance myself from a method in liturgical theology that presupposes the normative character of the theology that is given in the practices of the liturgy, sometimes called the *theologia prima*, which is then contrasted with, and given authority over, the discursive kind of theology developed by official interpreters of the tradition, the so-called *theologia secunda*. In this connection, some theologians then identify the oft-cited statement that "the law of praying is the law of believing" (*lex orandi, lex credendi*) as their highest methodological principle. Cf. David W. Fagerberg, *What Is Liturgical Theology? A Study In Methodology* (Collegeville, Minn.: Liturgical Press, 1992), 211: "Theology is influenced by the liturgy, yes; but leitourgia establishes theology because the

grammar of *lex orandi* precedes (normatively) the lex *credendi* of the community and the individual."

In contrast, the confessional method I am adopting here presupposes that, while the liturgy carries the kerygmatic witness of the church—often creatively and powerfully, and always indispensably—the Scriptures and the creedal tradition of the church are the primary and secondary theological authorities. For an illuminating exploration of some of these issues, which addresses the aforementioned *theologia prima/secunda* discussion in recent liturgical theology, see Michael B. Aune, "Liturgy and Theology: Rethinking the Relationship," *Worship* 81, no. 1 (January 2007): 46–68.

43. For reflections about this kind of theological thinking, see Christopher R. Seitz, ed., *Nicene Christianity: The Future for a New Ecumenism* (Grand Rapids: Brazos, 2001).

44. I regard my theological memoir, *South African Testament: From Personal Encounter to Theological Challenge* (Grand Rapids: Eerdmans, 1987), as the most focused work in confessional theology I have thus far written, in the first, personal sense of that expression, and my books *Brother Earth* and *The Travail of Nature* as most clearly the products of the confessional method in its second, discursive sense. My book *Nature Reborn: The Ecological and Cosmic Promise of Christian Theology* (Minneapolis: Fortress Press, 2000) and this current volume explicitly bring together elements of both the personal and the discursive.

45. Helmut Koester describes the first stages of the process by which this early Christian dialectic of the church's liturgy carrying the church's proclamation traditions, which proclamation traditions, later, in the form of the canonical New Testament writings, became the criterion for measuring the church's liturgy, in his seminal article, "The Memory of Jesus' Death and the Worship of the Risen Lord," *Harvard Theological Review* 91, no. 4 (1998): 335–50.

46. For a discussion of questions like the inspiration of Scripture and principles of interpretation of Scripture (hermeneutics), I refer the reader to Braaten's discussion of his summary statement. Carl E. Braaten, "The Holy Scriptures," in *Christian Dogmatics,* ed. Carl E. Braaten and Robert W. Jenson, et al. (Philadelphia: Fortress Press, 1984), vol. 1, 61–78.

47. For a description of the various terms Christians use about their worship, see James F. White, *Introduction to Christian Worship*, rev. ed. (Nashville: Abingdon, 1990), 31–37.

48. The complexities of this definitional issue are illustrated by a recent attempt to address it in thirty-two tightly argued pages: W. David Hall, "Does Creation Equal Nature? Confronting the Christian Confusion about Ecology and Cosmology," *Journal of the American Academy of Religion* 73, no. 3 (September 2005): 780–812.

49. For thoughtful probing of such questions, see the short but intense study by Neil Evernden, *The Social Creation of Nature* (Baltimore: Johns Hopkins University Press, 1992), 109, 116, 123 [italics in text], 110. Evernden traces the understanding of nature (or Nature) from medieval times through and to what might be called the end of modernity. He argues that "the entity which we take for granted as an objective reality has, in fact, a complex origin as a social creation." He further maintains that we moderns have become the captives of that, our very own social creation. In the process of creating our own "Nature," he suggests, we have lost touch with that mysterious *other* that premoderns encountered as "nature." We lose "nature," and gain ourselves:

"The more we come to dwell in an explained world, a world of uniformity and regularity, a world without the possibility of miracles, the less we are able to encounter anything else but ourselves." This means, in turn, that we are facing today much more than an "environmental crisis." We are confronted with a fundamental crisis in the way that we Westerners typically encounter the world. Hence, "the so-called environmental crisis demands not the inventing of solutions, but the re-creation *of the things themselves*." By this Evernden intends to adopt the adage of the French phenomenologist Maurice Merleau-Ponty: "To return to things themselves is to return to that world that precedes knowledge." Instructive as Evernden's discussion may be, it further illustrates the difficulties we face when we seek to define nature.

2. Counterculture, Simplicity, Ecstasy: Liturgy at First Glance

1. Frank C. Senn, *Christian Liturgy: Catholic and Evangelical* (Minneapolis: Fortress Press, 1997).

2. See the works by Gordon W. Lathrop, *Holy Things: A Liturgical Theology* (Minneapolis: Fortress Press, 1998); *Holy People: A Liturgical Ecclesiology* (Minneapolis: Fortress Press, 1999); *Holy Ground: A Liturgical Cosmology* (Minneapolis: Fortress Press, 2003).

3. For instructive and complementary reviews of Hauerwas's thought, see first the article by R. R. Reno in *The Blackwell Companion to Political Theology*, ed. Peter Scott and William T. Cavanaugh (Malden, Mass.: Blackwell, 2004), chap. 21, and then the essay by Reinhard Huetter, "The Ecclesial Ethics of Stanley Hauerwas," *dialog* 30, no. 3 (Summer 1991): 231–41.

4. See the succinct critique of Hauerwas's works by Jeffrey Stout, "Not of This World: Stanley Hauerwas and the Fate of Democracy," *Commonweal* 130, no. 17 (October 10, 2003): 14–20.

5. George Lindbeck, *The Nature of Doctrine: Religion and Theology in a Postliberal Age* (Louisville: Westminster John Knox, 1984).

6. Ibid., 32.

7. Ibid. 35.

8. Bernhard A. Eckerstorfer, "The One Church in the Postmodern World: Reflections on the Life and Thought of George Lindbeck," *Pro Ecclesia*, 13, no. 4 (Fall 2004): 421 (the foregoing quotes from Lindbeck are cited by Eckerstorfer, p. 410).

9. See his article, "Sacramental Lutheranism at the End of the Modern Age," *Lutheran Forum* 34, no. 4 (Winter 2000): 6–16, esp. p. 7, which I quote here.

10. Lathrop, *Holy Ground*; also see my review of this work published in *dialog* 45, no. 3 (Fall 2006): 303–08.

11. Justin Martyr, *Apology,* I, 65, 67 (*The First and Second Apologies* [New York: Paulist, 1997]).

12. There is some evidence that the mixing of water with wine also became a practice when traditions from different assemblies were combined (for the latter, see "The Apostolic Tradition," in *The Oxford History of Christian Worship*, ed. Geoffrey Wainwright and Karen B. Westerfield Tucker [New York: Oxford University Press, 2006], 48). Some communities apparently used bread and *water* for their meals, others bread

and *wine*. Then those traditions merged—that is the hypothesis. But even if this were the case, that does not yet explain *what that mixing meant* to those communities that used both the wine and the water, as well as the bread.

13. Here following the analysis of Bernd Wannenwetch, "The Liturgical Origin of the Christian *Politeia*: Overcoming the Weberian Temptation," in Christoph Strumpf and Holger Zaborowski, eds., *Church as* Politeia: *The Political Self-Understanding of Christianity* (New York: Walter de Gruyter, 2004), 331–34. More generally, see the previously cited article by Helmut Koester, "The Memory of Jesus' Death and the Worship of the Risen Lord," *Harvard Theological Review* 91, no. 4 (1998): 335–50.

14. For a general discussion of the social setting of the early Christian assemblies, see Senn, *The People's Work*, chaps. 1, 2. In particular, cf. the illuminating observation of William T. Cavanaugh, *Theopolitical Imagination* (New York: T&T Clark, 2002), 86–87: "The early Christians borrowed the term *ekklesia* or 'assembly' from the Greek city-state, where *ekklesia* meant the assembly of all those with citizen rights in a given city. The early Christians thus refused the available language of guild or association (e.g. *koinon, collegium*) and asserted that the church was not gathered around particular interests, but was interested in all things; it was an assembly of the whole. . . . [Yet] the ultimate source for the language of *ekklesia* is not the Greek city-state but the assembly of Israel at Sinai. . . . In using the term *ekklesia* the church understood itself as the eschatological gathering of Israel. In this gathering those who are by definition excluded from being citizens of the *polis* and consigned to the *oikos*—women, children, slaves—are given full membership through Baptism."

15. Cf. the important explanatory and qualifying words of David S. Yeago, "Messiah People: The Culture of the Church in the Midst of the Nations," *Pro Ecclesia* 6, no. 2 (Spring 1997): 152: ". . . the notion of 'culture' is being used analogically here, for one could point out all sorts of ways in which the church is a 'culture' in a rather different way than the nations are: for example, the culture of the church is not rooted in a shared natural language. . . . [Further, T]he culture of the church is always involved in absorbing and transforming and reshaping elements of the cultures of the nations which its members, so to speak, bring with them." And, more particularly, with regard to Paul: "Paul's Gospel, I want to argue, is not an abstract message or 'word-event' addressed to individuals in their existential inwardness; on the contrary, the Gospel is the proclamation that the God of Israel is now calling Gentiles to gather with Jews in the eschatological assembly of those 'sanctified in the Messiah Jesus, called to be holy ones' (I Cor. 1:2), the people of God in the last days. Recent New Testament research has shown us that ecclesiological issues, questions about the identity and integrity of the *ekklesia*, are far more central to Paul's thought than the problems of individual salvation that have often controlled our exegesis."

16. Cf. Arland J. Hultgren, "The Church as the Body of Christ: Engaging an Image in the New Testament," *Word and World*, 23, no. 2 (Spring 2002): 129: "There are few analogies in antiquity, if any at all, of the amount of correspondence flowing among early Christian communities, which in itself shows how the members of these communities had a sense of mutual care and accountability. . . . Generally it can be said that religious associations and cult groups in antiquity had an 'inward focus,' while the Christian communities had an 'international scope.'"

17. Lathrop, *Holy People*, 188.

18. Robert Jewett, "The Corruption and Redemption of Creation: Reading Romans 8:18-23 Within the Imperial Context," in *Paul and the Roman Imperial Order*,

ed. Richard A. Horsley (Harrisburg: Trinity Press International, 2004); Barbara R. Rossing, "River of Life in God's New Jerusalem: An Eschatological Vision for Earth's Future," in *Christianity and Ecology: Seeking the Well-Being of Earth and Humans*, ed. Dieter T. Hessel and Rosemary Radford Ruether (Cambridge: Harvard University Press, 2000), 205–26.

19. Quoted by Jewett, "The Corruption and Redemption of Creation," p. 39.

20. Aelius Aristedes, *Orations* 26:12, quoted by Rossing, "River of Life in God's New Jerusalem," 211.

21. Relevant materials concerning these matters are also reviewed by Helmut Koester in "The Memory of Jesus' Death and the Worship of the Risen Lord."

22. I can only give the most general kind of report of Jewett's complex exegetical argument here. But I do believe I can do justice to the substance of his exegesis. Beyond this, Jewett's article itself has been subjected to criticism (in the previously cited volume edited by Horsley) by historian of the Roman Empire Simon R. F. Price. Still, in my judgment, the fundamental lines of Jewett's interpretation still are valid and insightful. For a review of a whole spectrum of related issues, see Richard A. Horsley's introduction to *Paul and the Roman Imperial Order*.

23. This reading of Romans 8 in terms of its imperial setting, I believe, is a necessary reading. But I also believe that it cannot stand alone. Paul was not only writing over against the Roman imperium in Romans 8, he was also writing—self-consciously, it appears—in continuity with the witness of the Old Testament, particularly Genesis, but also the prophet Isaiah. For a careful reading of Romans 8 in those terms, see the thorough and insightful article by Laurie J. Braaten, "All Creation Groans: Romans 8:22 in Light of the Biblical Sources," *Horizons in Biblical Theology* 28 (2006): 131–59.

24. Quoted by Jewett, "The Corruption and Redemption of Creation," 51.

25. Lathrop, *Holy Things*.

26. Cynthia D. Moe-Lobeda has explored the transformative power of the liturgy insightfully in her essay, "Liturgy Reshaping Society," in *Ordo: Bath, Word, Prayer, Table—A Liturgical Primer in Honor of Gordon W. Lathrop*, ed. Dirk G. Lange and Dwight W. Vogel (Akron: OSL Publications, 2005), 164–87.

27. For this reading of St. Francis, see my essay "The Spirituality of Nature and the Poor: Revisiting the Historic Vision of St. Francis," in *Tending the Holy: Spiritual Direction Across Traditions*, ed. Norvene Vest (Harrisburg: Morehouse, 2003), chap. 9, and, more generally, my discussion of Francis in *The Travail of Nature: The Ambiguous Ecological Promise of Christianity* (Minneapolis: Fortress Press, 1985), 106–19. In the aforementioned essay, I draw on the research of Eloi Leclerc, *Francis of Assisi: Return to the Gospel*, trans. Richard Arnandez (Chicago: Franciscan Herald Press, 1983).

28. A more extended treatment of these trends would also have to be more nuanced and appreciative of the challenges the church had to face during the era of "Christendom." Cf. the comments of William T. Cavanaugh, "Church," in *The Blackwell Companion to Political Theology*, 397: "Constantine does not represent the mere 'fall' of the church from some pristine state of righteousness, nor does Christendom represent an unfortunate intermingling of two essentially distinct things—theology and politics, church and state—that we enlightened people of modernity have finally managed properly to sort out and separate. What is lumped together under the term 'Christendom' is in fact a very complex series of attempts to take seriously the inherently political nature of the church and its instrumental role in the integral salvation of the world in Jesus Christ."

On the other hand, there surely were times in the post-Constantinian history of Christianity when the countercultural character of the liturgy was virtually lost. Cf. this judgment by Martin D. Stringer, *A Sociological History of Christian Worship* (Cambridge: Cambridge University Press, 2005), 139–40. He talks about "cosmological Christianity" at the turn of the first millennium, in particular about the liturgy practiced at the Salisbury Cathedral: "The Christian community had come a long way from the small group of Spirit-filled individuals meeting in Corinth under Paul's leadership. Here was a Christianity that spoke less about individual conversion and concerns about the end of the world, and more about the maintenance of the world and being drawn up into the glory of God. . . . This is worship undertaken by a clerical elite, worship with fully detailed and carefully controlled ceremonial and ritual, worship whose sole function is the maintenance of the world as it is. Without this worship, demanded of us by God, then the whole of creation would groan and grind to a halt."

The divide between the pre- and post-Constantinian eras was also marked in the theology of the church by a shift from the communal, world-historical, and cosmic vision of the salvation wrought by Christ to a focus on the dynamics of sin and forgiveness in the lives of individual believers. This was a shift of emphasis to be sure, but it was fraught with implications for Christians' understanding of their place in the social order. Cf. the provocative observation by Walter Wink, *Cracking the Gnostic Code: The Powers in Gnosticism,* Society of Biblical Literature Monograph Series 46 (Atlanta: Scholars, 1993), 28–29: "It was only a matter of time . . . until the social theory of the atonement, so powerfully depicted in the Christus Victor imagery of Colossians 2:15, was discarded for more individualistic theories based on sin and guilt. Once the Gospel had been the proclamation of release of those who were formerly deluded and enslaved by the Domination System and its driving spirit, Satan. Now Christ's death came to be seen solely as a personal transaction between the believer and God. . . . The sin-forgiveness model of theology no longer portrayed a cosmic-historical-political-psychic conflict between Christ and the Powers on earth, but rather the struggle between the individual and the Devil, with the Devil representing . . . *rebellion against church and state* and all their laws, civil, criminal, and moral, regardless of how unjust, inhumane, degrading or oppressive they might be. *What the early Christians would have called 'kneeling to Caesar' or 'complicity with Satan' now became the very essence of faithfulness"* (italics in text)."

29. The eminent historian Peter Brown has argued that Christianity "invented" the idea of ministering to the poor and so worked to transvalue the society of the later Roman Empire, particularly through the work of its bishops. See Walter Brueggemann's review of Brown's book, *Poverty and Leadership in the Later Roman Empire* (Waltham, Mass.: Brandeis University Press, 2001), in *Christian Century* 120, no. 12 (June 14, 2003): 30–31.

30. The ground-breaking liturgical theology of Gordon W. Lathrop is predicated precisely on this assumption. See especially his *Holy Ground.*

31. Gordon W. Lathrop, "Bath, Word, Prayer, Table: Reflections on Doing the Liturgical Ordo in a Postmodern Time," in *Ordo: Bath, Word, Prayer, Table,* 224ff.

32. See I. Howard Marshall, "New Testament Worship," *A New Dictionary of Liturgy and Worship,* ed. J. G. Davies (London: SCM, 1986).

33. A more complete account of this liturgical *simplicity* would explain the importance of the qualifier: that liturgy is a *relatively* simple set of ritual practices. A distinction

would have to be made between the liturgical and the ceremonial. To this end, following Ronald Grimes, Gordon W. Lathrop writes in *Holy Things* (p. 176): "Both liturgy and ceremony are necessary rituals in human life. Unlike liturgy, however, ceremony expresses a value unambiguously, without any expression of its contrary. A graduation is a ceremony. . . . There is no reflection on class and wealth and on the poverty that has no education. There is no sense that this education may, in important matters, be rank ignorance. . . . The Christian liturgy, in contrast, embraces contraries: life and death, thanksgiving and beseeching, this community and the wide world. . . . In Christian use this ambiguity is not simply a general devotion to contrary principles as a way to truth. . . . The mystery of God is the mystery of life conjoined with death for the sake of life. . . . The contraries of the liturgy are for the sake of speaking this mystery." Which is why I am noting here that the liturgy is a *relatively* simple set of ritual practices.

34. For a critical review of modern liturgical scholarship focusing on those scholars who have use terms like "shape" or "pattern" or *"ordo,"* see Michael B. Aune's essay, "Liturgy and Theology: Rethinking the Relationship," *Worship* 81, no. 1 (January 2007): 46–68. Aune tends to see the thought of anyone who uses constructs like *ordo* as suspect—even though he himself, in a subsequent article, uses the construct "building blocks" of the liturgy, which sounds like the same idea all over again (Aune, "Liturgy and Theology: Rethinking the Relationship," *Worship* 81, no. 2 [March 2007]: 143). In any case, in my view, while Aune's review of the trajectory of the theological use of the concept *ordo* is generally insightful, his particular critique of Gordon Lathrop's careful employment of the idea is over-simplified and therefore not convincing. So we can follow Lathrop's interpretations, as I do here, with some confidence, which is a conclusion also reached by Maxwell E. Johnson in his essay, "The Apostolic Tradition," in *The Oxford History of Christian Worship*, chap. 2.

Further, Aune's critique of Lathrop's liturgical theology as not sufficiently emphasizing the initiative of *God* in the liturgy (see Aune's second article, pp. 156–57) represents, in my judgment, a misreading of Lathrop's argumentation, which is profoundly shaped by a classical Lutheran theology of the cross and is developed in a paradoxical style of discourse reminiscent of Kierkegaard. Lathrop's apophatic modesty in discussing the works of God in the liturgy should not be read as a failure to take the divine initiative seriously.

35. This point is argued forcefully and in great detail by Johnson in "The Apostolic Tradition."

36. Lathrop, *Holy Things*, 46–47.

37. *Book of Common Prayer* (New York: Seabury, 1979), 400–401, cited by Lathrop, *Holy People,* 154–55). Compare the very similar statement by the Evangelical Lutheran Church in America, in *The Use of the Means of Grace*, Application 4b (Minneapolis: Augsburg Fortress Press, 2002), 124: "We gather in song and prayer, confessing our need of God. We read the Scriptures and hear them preached. We profess our faith and pray for the world, sealing our prayers with the sign of peace. We gather an offering for the poor and for the mission of the Church. We set our table with bread and wine, give thanks and praise to God, proclaiming Jesus Christ, and eat and drink. We hear the blessing of God and are sent out in mission to the world."

38. See Jamie Smith, "The Emerging Church: A Guide for the Perplexed," *Reformed Worship* 77 (Advent; September 2005), 40–41; and Jason Byassee, "Emerging Model: A Visit to Jacob's Well," *Christian Century* 123, no. 19 (September 19, 2006): 20–24.

39. See http://jacobswellchurch.org/worship, accessed February 1, 2008.

40. Martin Luther, *Lectures on Genesis, Chapters 1–5*, Luther's Works 1 (hereafter LW), trans. George V. Schick, ed. Jaroslav Pelikan (St. Louis: Concordia, 1958), 94.

41. If I had more space to expand on these impressionistic phenomenological observations concerning this communal ecstasy, it surely would be illuminating to draw on the historical findings of Victor and Edith Turner. The Turners "suggested in their discussions of pilgrimages and sacred places that these created what they called *communitas*. This was a special temporary state in which conventional social or other distinctions are transcended in a spontaneous sharing of experience." (Philip Sheldrake, *Spaces for the Sacred: Place, Memory, and Identity* [Baltimore: Johns Hopkins University Press, 2001], 5). See, for example: Victor Turner, et al., *Worship and Ritual in Christianity and Other Religions* (Rome: Gregorian University Press, 1974). Turner's thought is helpfully summarized by Carl F. Starkloff, "The Church As Structure and Communitas: Victor Turner and Ecclesiology," *Theological Studies* 58, no. 4 (December 1, 1997): 643–69. For a more general theory of ritual in human life, see Randall Collins, *Interaction Ritual Chains* (Princeton: Princeton University Press, 2004). Collins talks about the emotional power of ritual in all its social forms, from sexuality to political movements to religious rites, as "collective effervescence."

This general phenomenological usage of the term *ecstasy*, I hasten to add, should be distinguished from the particular ways the word is used in the New Testament itself, which vary markedly from one context to another. For this, see the article "*ekstasis*," in the *Theological Dictionary of the New Testament*, ed. Gerhard Kittel, trans. Geoffrey W. Bromiley (Grand Rapids: Eerdmans, 1964), II, s.v.

42. Mark Searle, "Ritual," in *The Study of Liturgy*, rev. ed., ed. Cheslyn Jones, et al. (New York: Oxford University Press, 1992), 56. The theme of liturgy as performance that Searle brings to the fore here is the focus of an instructive study by Richard D. McCall, *Do This: Liturgy as Performance* (Notre Dame: University of Notre Dame Press, 2007).

43. These emotions are, of course, deeply rooted in biblical experience. For a rich study of their Old Testament expressions, see Gary A. Anderson, *A Time to Mourn, A Time to Dance: The Expression of Grief and Joy in Israelite Religion* (University Park: Pennsylvania State University Press, 1991). That lamentation and exultation were given different expressions in early Christianity and, indeed, through every era of the church's life virtually goes without saying. Yet the reverse is also true. Old Testament faith apperceptions also deeply influenced those subsequent eras as well, especially by the liturgical and devotional use of the psalms.

44. Geoffrey Wainwright, "The Language of Worship," in *The Study of the Liturgy*, 527.

45. For this material on the book of Revelation, see Richard Bauckham, *The Theology of the Book of Revelation* (Cambridge: Cambridge University Press, 1993), 3.

46. Deeper and more illusive issues are also at stake here, which would take us much too far afield were we to pursue them. But I do want to acknowledge these issues here, if for no other reason than to assure the reader that I am aware of them. I have already pointed to the cosmic nihilism of our time. I want to sharpen that observation here, in the form of a single, existential question. Tillich called this kind of question the "shaking of the foundations." *In this postmodern, post-Holocaust world, is faith in God possible anymore?* Call this the primordial dissonance of faith in these times.

With many sophisticated theologians and countless simple believers who have wrestled with this question, I believe that faith in the God attested by the liturgy *is* possible but only after those who aspire to believe allow themselves to "live with the question" (Rainer Maria Rilke), which means living in the world "as if God did not exist" (Dietrich Bonhoeffer). Only then can the experience announced by Friedrich Nietzsche, when he claimed that "God is dead," be overcome—by grace alone, through faith, as I am claimed by the church's liturgy which itself is shaped by both the brokenness of the Cross and the healing power of the resurrection.

So, as I participate in the liturgy, the work of the people, I can affirm my faith in God in these times of cosmic nihilism, notwithstanding my unfaith. And when I do, I do so in the spirit of Martin Luther, who once likened the life of faith to taking the hand of a guide while blindfolded, and following the guide over a high and narrow bridge. Or, again, in the spirit of Luther's oft-quoted words, when I do write as a theologian, I always write with fragmentary testimony, because: "A theologian is made by living, indeed by dying and being damned, not by understanding, reading, and speculating." (Martin Luther, *Werke,* Weimar Ausgabe [hereafter WA] 5:163, 20–30, quoted by Paul Rorem, "Martin Luther's Christocentric Critique of Pseudo-Dionysian Spirituality," *Lutheran Quarterly* 11, no. 3 [Autumn 1997]: 296).

The reader who wishes to pursue this kind of exploration of the cosmic nihilism of our time and the challenge of faith in God is encouraged to begin with the illuminating historical and systematic study by Daniel J. Peterson, "Speaking of God After the Death of God," *dialog* 44, no. 3 (Fall 2005): 207–26. Peterson explores the traditional, modern, and postmodern theme of *the hiddenness of God* in conversation with Luther, Karl Barth, Paul Tillich, David Tracy, Gustavo Gutiérrez, Elizabeth Johnson, Richard Rubenstein, and Martin Buber. For an example of a theologian who holds that the classical trinitarian faith in a personal God, presupposed by the liturgy, is *no longer tenable* in our postmodern, post-Holocaust era, consult Gordon D. Kaufman's study *In The Face of Mystery: A Constructive Theology* (Cambridge: Harvard University Press, 1993).

3. The Cognitive Dissonance: Liturgy and Nature

1. Ken Johnson, "Generating the Transcendent," *Harvard Divinity Bulletin,* 24, no. 1 (Winter 2006): 73–79.

2. For a more thorough examination of these phenomena, see the illuminating study by Owen C. Thomas, "Spiritual But Not Religious: The Influence of the Current Romantic Movement," *Anglican Theological Review* 88, no. 3 (Summer 2006): 397–416.

3. For a review of Thoreau's thought, see H. Paul Santmire, *Brother Earth: Nature, God, and Ecology in a Time of Crisis* (New York: Thomas Nelson, 1970), chap. 1.

4. I am reading Thoreau here as a representative figure. American intellectual history has been rife with the perspective that Thoreau exemplifies. For a helpful survey of these trends, see Roger Lundin, "'To the Unknown Gods': Pragmatism, Postmodernity, and the Theology of Experience," *Books and Culture* 12, no. 3 (May/June 2006): 10–15.

5. For a balanced theological evaluation of the New Age movement, see Ted Peters, *The Cosmic Self: A Penetrating Look at Today's New Age Movement* (San Francisco: HarperSanFrancisco, 1991).

6. Edward Schillebeeckx, "Towards a Rediscovery of the Christian Sacraments: Ritualizing Religious Elements in Daily Life," in *Ordo: Bath, Word, Prayer, Table—A*

Liturgical Primer in Honor of Gordon W. Lathrop, ed. Dirk G. Lange and Dwight W. Vogel (Akron: OSL Publications, 2005), 8.

7. See H. Paul Santmire, *South African Testament: From Personal Encounter to Theological Challenge* (Grand Rapids: Eerdmans, 1987), for this full story.

8. As I write this, Rasmussen (now Reinhold Niebuhr Professor of Social Ethics emeritus at Union Theological Seminary, New York) has yet to publish a full account of his explorations. He alludes to them suggestively, however, in an essay, "Sightings of Primal Visions: Community and Ecology," in *Character and Scripture: Moral Formation, Community, and Biblical Interpretation*, ed. William P. Brown (Grand Rapids: Eerdmans, 2002), 389–409.

9. See the short essay by Lukas Fischer, "The Making of Taizé," *Christian Century* 122, no. 19 (September 20, 2005): 8–9.

10. See H. Paul Santmire, *The Travail of Nature: The Ambiguous Ecological Promise of Christian Theology* (Minneapolis: Fortress Press, 1985), chaps. 7, 8.

11. For a critical review of Matthew Fox's thought, see H. Paul Santmire, *Nature Reborn: The Ecological and Cosmic Promise of Christian Theology* (Minneapolis: Fortress Press, 2000), chap. 2.

12. This analysis reflects the interpretation in the encyclopedia article by H. Paul Santmire and John B. Cobb Jr., "The World of Nature According to the Protestant Tradition," in *The Oxford Handbook of Religion and Ecology*, ed. Roger S. Gottlieb (New York: Oxford University Press, 2006), chap. 4. See also the account of the WCC's theological approaches to nature by Wesley Granberg-Michaelson, "Creation in Ecumenical Theology," in *Ecotheology: Voices from South and North*, ed. David G. Hallman (Maryknoll, N.Y.: Orbis, 1994), 96–106.

13. Cited by Granberg-Michaelson, "Creation in Ecumenical Theology," 96.

14. This is not to say that ecumenical theologians did not discuss the theology of creation. There was indeed much discussion of that theme during the second half of the twentieth century. But, ironically, much of that discussion had little to do with the theology of nature. Discussions of creation often focused on the relationship between redemption and creation (typically anthropocentrically construed) or on disputes regarding "natural revelation" in the world of creation. For a chronicle of those sometimes convoluted discussions (through 1989), see Per Loenning, *Creation—An Ecumenical Challenge? Reflections Issuing from a Study by the Institute for Ecumenical Research* (Macon: Mercer University Press, 1989).

As late as 1991 in the WCC meeting in Canberra, moreover, when delegates had the opportunity at least to temper the then-reigning anthropocentric theological perspective, they specifically excised statements in prepared documents that would have moved in that direction. The latter story is told by Larry Rasmussen, who was deeply involved in the Canberra discussions (and who may have been the writer of those excised paragraphs) in *Earth Community Earth Ethics* (Maryknoll, N.Y.: Orbis, 1997), 234ff.

15. Paulos Gregorios, *The Human Presence: An Orthodox View of Nature* (Geneva: World Council of Churches, 1978). The following quotations are from pp. 85 and 84 respectively.

16. See John Zizioulas (Metropolitan John of Pergamon), "Preserving God's Creation: Three Lectures on Theology and Ecology," *King's Theological Review* 12 (1989). Zizioulas summarized his position succinctly in his foreword to the volume *Cosmic Grace: Humble Prayer: The Ecological Vision of the Green Patriarch Bartholomew I*, ed.

John Chryssavgis (Grand Rapids: Eerdmans, 2003), viii: ". . . the human being is the *Priest of Creation* called to take in his or her hands the world as gift and refer it back to the Giver with thankfulness (*eucharistia*). As the world passes through human hands it is, of course, transformed and cultivated: this is what human labor, including science, art, economy, and so on, does to nature. But in a eucharistic approach, all this labor is justified only insofar as (a) it is *shared* in love with all human beings (= *koinonia*, communion) and (b) it is *referred* back to the Creator with the acknowledgment that human beings are not the possessors of nature, but an organic part of it endowed with the call to lift it up to the One who can give it eternal meaning and life" (italics in original). The fundamentally anthropocentric character of this theological perspective is revealed later in the same volume (p. 54) in a 1998 encyclical letter by Patriarch Bartholomew: *"Even though the human being, either as an isolated individual or as collective humanity, is only a minuscule speck in the face of the immense universe, it is a fact that the entire universe is endowed with meaning by the very presence of humanity within it . . . , meaning that . . . came about and exists for the sake of humanity"* (italics in original).

17. Regarding "stewardship," see this book's appendix.

18. Thomas Derr, *Ecology and Human Need* (Philadelphia: Westminster, 1973).

19. The most accessible place to find this oft-cited address is Joseph Sittler, *Evocations of Grace: Writings on Ecology, Theology, and Ethics*, ed. Steven Bouma-Prediger and Peter Bakken (Grand Rapids: Eerdmans, 2000), 38–50.

20. See my review, *Word and World* 26, no. 3 (Summer 2006): 340–44.

21. Gordon W. Lathrop, *Holy Ground: A Liturgical Cosmology* (Minneapolis: Fortress Press, 2003).

22. Leonardo Boff, *Cry of the Earth, Cry of the Poor* (Maryknoll, N.Y.: Orbis, 1997).

23. Rasmussen, *Earth Community Earth Ethics,* 247.

24. Steven Bouma-Prediger, *For the Beauty of the Earth: A Christian Vision of Creation-Care* (Grand Rapids: Baker Academic, 2001). The Evangelical Environmental Network declaration is available online at http://www.creationcare.org/resources/declaration.php, accessed February 6, 2008.

25. "Climate Change: An Evangelical Call to Action" is available online at http://www.christiansandclimate.org/statement, accessed February 6, 2008.

26. Available as an appendix in Drew Christiansen and Walter Grazer, eds., *"And God Saw That It Was Good": Catholic Theology and the Environment* (Washington, D.C.: United States Catholic Conference, 1996).

27. Denis Edwards, *Jesus and the Wisdom of God* (Maryknoll, N.Y.: Orbis, 1995).

28. John F. Haught, *God after Darwin: A Theology of Evolution* (New York: Westview, 1999).

29. Christiansen and Grazer, eds., *"And God Saw That It Was Good."*

30. John Vidal and Tom Kington, "Protect God's creation: Vatican issues new green message for world's Catholics," *The Guardian*, April 27, 2007.

32. "Pope Benedict XVI's Address to the U.N. General Assembly," *New York Times,* April 19, 2008, http://www.nytimes.com/2008/04/19/nyregion/18popeatun.html?_r=1&oref=slogin (accessed April 22, 2008).

32. See Chryssavgis, ed., *Cosmic Grace.*

33. "Address of His All Holiness Patriarch Bartholomew at the Environmental Symposium, Saint Barbara Greek Orthodox Church, Santa Barbara, California,

November 8, 1997," available online at http://www.religionandnature.org, accessed February 6, 2008.

34. See the WCC press release and reports about the Brazil meeting online at http://www.wcc-assembly.info/en/theme-issues/assembly-documents, accessed February 6, 2008.

35. For a short but detailed chronicle of the Orthodox response to the ecological crisis, begun in earnest in the 1990s, see Vasilios N. Makrides, http://www.clas.ufl .edu/users/bron/PDF—Christianity/Makrides—Christianity—Greek%20Orthodox% 20(contemporary).pdf, accessed February 6, 2008.

36. See especially: Jürgen Moltmann, *The Future of Creation*, trans. Margaret Kohl (Philadelphia: Fortress Press, 1979), and John B. Cobb Jr., *Is It Too Late? A Theology of Ecology* (Beverly Hills: Bruce, 1972). In addition to this kind of substantive reflection, major thinkers have been joined by hundreds, perhaps thousands, of writers of secondary importance. For a review of some of the richness of this field through 1995 only, much of it unheralded in the larger ecumenical world, see Peter Bakken, et al., eds., *Ecology, Justice, and Christian Faith: A Critical Guide to the Literature* (Westport, Conn.: Greenwood, 1995). Since 1995 this secondary literature has continued to grow, with apparently no bounds in sight.

37. See especially Ruether, *Gaia and God*, and McFague, *The Body of God*.

38. James A. Nash, *Loving Nature: Ecological Integrity and Christian Responsibility* (Nashville: Abingdon ; in cooperation with The Church's Center for Theology and Public Policy, Washington, D.C., 1991).

39. John B. Cobb Jr. and Charles Birch, *The Liberation of Life: From Cell to Community* (Cambridge: Cambridge University Press, 1981).

40. The theology, ecology, and ecojustice literature has now become something of a torrent of publications. The emergence of this stream of publications was already evident some thirteen years ago, when Peter W. Bakken, Joan Gibb Engel, and J. Ronald Engle edited and introduced *Ecology, Justice, and Christian Faith* (Westport, Conn., 1995), a bibliography with 511 entries. A more recent, albeit shorter bibliography of the field, compiled by Peter Bakken, can be found in, *Christianity and Ecology: Seeking the Well-Being of Earth and Humans*, ed. Dieter T. Hessel and Rosemary Radford Ruether (Cambridge: Harvard University Press, 2000), 615–37. A still more recent, but also shorter bibliography is available in the essay collection, *Environmental Stewardship: Critical Perspectives Past and Present*, ed. R. J. Berry (London: T&T Clark, 2006), 318–38.

4. The Heart of the Matter: The Liturgical Assembly

1. This formulation leaves open the question about "the rite" that forms what for the sake of convenience can be called "nonliturgical" assemblies. That is for spokespersons from those traditions to identify. That a Friends' Meeting, for example, is highly ritualized, albeit mostly in silence, is a thought that could be explored by someone familiar with that particular tradition. Likewise for the "services of the Word" that are the most common form of worship in a variety of Protestant traditions.

2. Robert Jenson, *Visible Words: The Interpretation and Practice of the Christian Sacraments* (Philadelphia: Fortress Press, 1978), 42.

3. Martin Luther, LW 41:150, quoted by Gordon W. Lathrop and Timothy J. Wengert, *Christian Assembly: Marks of the Church in a Pluralistic Age* (Minneapolis: Fortress Press, 2004), 40.

4. Gordon W. Lathrop, *Holy People: A Liturgical Ecclesiology* (Minneapolis: Fortress Press, 1999), 21.

5. Here following ibid., 29ff.

6. Helmut Koester, "The Memory of Jesus' Death and the Worship of the Risen Lord," *Harvard Theological Review* 91, no. 4 (1998): 335–50.

7. See John Koenig, *New Testament Hospitality: Partnership with Strangers as Promise and Mission,* Overtures to Biblical Theology (Minneapolis: Fortress Press, 1985).

8. Terence L. Donaldson, *Jesus on the Mountain: A Study of Matthean Theology,* JSNT Supplements 8 (Sheffield: JSOT Press, 1985), esp. p. 197: "In Matthean perspective, therefore, it is when Jesus is 'on the mountain' that his significance and the nature of his mission are most clearly seen. Consequently it can be said that mountains in Matthew function not primarily as places of revelation or isolation but as eschatological sites where Jesus enters into the full authority of his Sonship, where the eschatological community is gathered, and where the age of fulfillment is inaugurated." For a complementary history-of-religions approach to the theme of mountains in the Gospel of Matthew, see K. C. Hanson, "Transformed on the Mountain: Ritual Analysis and the Gospel of Matthew," *Semeia* 67 (1994): 147–70.

9. Cf. the comments of Robert L. Cohn, *The Shape of Sacred Space: Four Biblical Studies* (Chico, Calif.: Scholars, 1981), 41, concerning "the futuristic visions" of Ezekiel and Zechariah: both "stress the fertility that flows from the new Jerusalem just as they report its elevation. Ezekiel sees a river extending from Jerusalem to the Dead Sea, carrying life-giving water to the desert (Ez. 47:7-12). This river, issuing from beneath the temple situated on the 'very high mountain,' transforms the Dead Sea into a fresh water lake and the wilderness in to a lush land whose trees produce fresh fruit every month. Zechariah speaks of a similar Edenic new creation. Here, however, rivers of 'living water' flow both eastward and westward from the new Jerusalem (Zech. 14:8). Furthermore, continuous day reigns . . . 'on that day' when Yahweh reigns over the earth . . ."

10. Rodney Stark, *Cities of God: The Real Story of How Christianity Became an Urban Movement and Conquered Rome* (San Francisco: HarperSanFrancisco, 2006), 129, citing works by the New Testament scholars E. A. Judge and Abraham A. Malherbe.

11. Krister Stendahl, "The Apostle Paul and the Introspective Conscience of the West," *Harvard Theological Review* 66, no. 3 (July 1963): 199–216. This article set the stage for what is now regarded as the "new perspective on Paul" and for scholarly developments that then go beyond that perspective, while presupposing it. For the significance of Stendahl's contributions, see Douglas Harink, *Paul Among the Postliberals: Pauline Theology Beyond Christendom and Modernity* (Grand Rapids: Brazos, 2003), 13–16.

12. Douglas Harink helpfully sets forth this contrast in his article, "Doing Justice to Justification: Setting It Right," *Christian Century,* 122, no. 12 (June 14, 2005): 20. In saying this much, however, I do not intend to suggest that discussion of a whole range of issues in Pauline studies should be foreclosed. Thus, I do not regard the "new perspective" as it is championed by N. T. Wright, for example, as the last word about Paul's theology (see Wright's *Paul: In Fresh Perspective* [Minneapolis: Fortress Press, 2005]), although it appears to me that discussions of Paul's theology cannot bypass that approach. If anything, rightly, the challenge for interpreters of Paul is to go *through and beyond* that "new perspective." For those who wish to pursue these matters, cf. Karl Paul Donfried, *Paul, Thessalonica, and Early Christianity* (Grand Rapids: Eerdmans, 2002, esp. chap. 1, "Shifting Paradigms: Paul, Jesus, and Judaism"

and Richard A. Horsley, ed, *Paul and Politics: Ekklesia, Israel, Imperium, Interpretation* (Harrisburg: Trinity Press International, 2000).

13. Harink, "Doing Justice to Justification," 20. More generally, on the new perspective on Paul, see Wright, *Paul: In Fresh Perspective*. Harink develops his interpretation of Paul extensively and also takes issues with some of Wright's findings, in Harink's study, *Paul Among the Postliberals*.

14. Lathrop, *Holy People*, 188.

15. Cf. ibid., 190: "Echoing the Jewish meal prayers which speak of the 'kingdom of God,' the meals of Jesus enacted a prophetic sign of the profoundly needed nearness of the reign of the *melech ha-olam*. So in Mark 2:18-20, Jesus and his company do not fast but rather feast, in celebration of the presence of the 'bridegroom,' an old prophetic image for the presence of God in Israel. And the petition of Jesus' prayer for 'daily bread' may well be a way in which he sees the hoped for 'day of God' already imaged in the shared meals of his company. It is as if the company around Jesus is already the *assembly* of the end times."

16. Ibid., 191.

17. For a brief but suggestive introduction to the scope of contemporary ritual studies, see Edward Schillebeeckx, "Towards a Rediscovery of the Christian Sacraments: Ritualizing Religious Elements in Daily Life," in *Ordo: Bath, Word, Prayer, Table—A Liturgical Primer in Honor of Gordon W. Lathrop*, ed. Dirk G. Lange and Dwight W. Vogel (Akron: OSL Publications, 2005), 10–17.

18. Here drawing on the discussion by Gary A. Anderson, *A Time to Mourn, A Time to Dance: The Expression of Grief and Joy in Israelite Religion* (University Park: Pennsylvania State University Press, 1991), 3ff.

19. Ibid., 5ff.

20. Erik H. Erikson, "The Development of Ritualization," in *The Religious Situation*, ed. Donald R. Cutler (Boston: Beacon, 1968), 711–33.

21. Cf. this representative statement by Gregor T. Goethals in "Ritual: Ceremony and Super Sunday," *The TV Ritual: Worship at the Video Altar* (Boston: Beacon, 1981), 5: "Ritual action, the dramatization of a significant event, is a major means of social integration. At its most fundamental level, ritual is the enactment of myth. In the past, religious and political myths gave the members of a community a sense of their origins and destiny. In our present technological society, churches and synagogues often provide this kind of attunement to communal principles. For those who genuinely participate, the rituals offer occasions for identity and renewal. . . . Although the mythic and aesthetic forms of ritual differ from culture to culture, its function remains the same—to provide an immediate, direct sense of involvement with the sacred, confirming the worldview, indeed the very being of the participant." Many of the essays in the volume *The Roots of Ritual*. ed. James D. Shaughnessy (Grand Rapids: Eerdmans, 1973), come to similar conclusions.

The work that appears to have set the standard for all future discussions of the centrality of ritual in human life is Roy A. Rappaport, *Ritual and Religion in the Making of Humanity* (Cambridge: Cambridge University Press, 1999). Cf. his summary statement concerning ritual's function in human history: ". . . *the performance of more or less invariant sequences of formal acts and utterances not entirely encoded by the performers logically entails the establishment of convention, the sealing of social contract, the construction of . . . integrated conventional orders . . . , the investment of whatever it encodes with morality, the construction of time and eternity: the representation of a paradigm of creation, the generation of the concept of the sacred and the sanctification of the conventional order . . . and the construction of orders of meaning transcending the semantic,*" p. 27 (italics his).

For a helpful overview of these developments in the phenomenology of religion, from A. R. Radcliffe-Brown and Emile Durkheim to Clifford Geertz and George Lindbeck, see the aforementioned work of Anderson, *A Time to Mourn, A Time to Dance*, 1–9.

22. Cf. Lindbeck's summary statement in *The Nature of Doctrine: Religion and Theology in a Postliberal Age* (Philadelphia: Westminster, 1984), 33: "Like a culture or language, [religion] is a communal phenomenon that shapes the subjectivities of individuals rather than being primarily a manifestation of those subjectivities. It comprises a vocabulary of discursive and non-discursive symbols together with a distinctive logic or grammar in terms of which this vocabulary can be meaningfully deployed. Lastly, just as a language. . . . is correlated with a form of life, and just as a culture has both cognitive and behavioral dimensions, so it is also in the case of a religious tradition. Its doctrines, cosmic stories or myths, and ethical directives are integrally related to the rituals it practices, the sentiments or experience it evokes, the actions it recommends, and the institutional forms it develops." Quoted by Anderson, *A Time to Mourn, A Time to Dance*, 6ff. See also the discussion of Lindbeck's work above, pp. 35–36.

23. I first argued this point more than thirty-five years ago. See H. Paul Santmire, "The Mission of the Church: Reflections Along the Way," *Lutheran Quarterly* 23, no. 4 (November 1971): 366–87. In recent years the theme that the mission of the church is to be the church has become a theological commonplace, thanks to the works of Stanley Hauerwas.

24. For one suggestive and well-argued treatment of the importance of "practices," see Martha Ellen Stortz, "Practicing Christians: Prayer as Formation," in *The Promise of Lutheran Ethics*, ed. Karen L. Bloomquist and John R. Stumme (Minneapolis: Fortress Press, 1998), chap. 4, and also her unpublished lecture, "Discerning Practices" http://www.plts.edu/articles/stortz/discerning, accessed February 7, 2008. But there are practices and there is *the* practice. The Eucharist is *the* practice, in my view, "first among equals," as the ecclesial body of Christ is the whole that is greater than the sum of all the individual members. When things are not right with *this* practice, everything else is at risk. Hence a study like Daniel G. Deffenbaugh's *Learning the Language of the Fields: Tilling and Keeping as Christian Vocation* (Cambridge: Cowley, 2006), which seeks to develop a new spirituality of the earth by focusing on gardens as "our sanctuaries," cannot stand alone—particularly since Deffenbaugh announces at the outset that it is not his intention to try to change Christian worship, which takes place "in some building" (p. ix). Regarding the formative power of liturgy more generally, see Philip H. Pfatteicher, *The School of the Church: Worship and Christian Formation* (Valley Forge: Trinity Press International, 1995).

5. The Ambiguities of the Gothic Vision: The Theology of Ascent

1. I first began to put in place some of the rudiments for the discussion in this chapter in an essay "How Does the Liturgy Relate to the Cosmos and Care for the Earth," in the small book *What Are the Ethical Implications of Worship?*, ed. Gordon Lathrop (Minneapolis: Fortress Press, 1996), 14–21.

2. Erwin Panofsky, *Gothic Architecture and Scholasticism* (New York: Meridian, 1957).

3. Ibid., 44–45.

4. Arthur Lovejoy, *The Great Chain of Being: A Study of the History of an Idea* (New York: Harper & Brothers, 1936).

5. Otto von Simpson, *The Gothic Cathedrals: Origins of Gothic Architecture and the Medieval Concept of Order*, Bollingen Series 48 (Princeton: Princeton University Press, 1956), chaps. 3 and 4.

6. Ibid., 103.

7. George Duby, *The Age of the Cathedrals: Art and Society, 980–1420*, trans. Eleanor Levieux and Barbara Thompson (Chicago: University of Chicago Press, 1981), 99.

8. H. Paul Santmire, *The Travail of Nature: The Ambiguous Ecological Promise of Christian Theology* (Minneapolis: Fortress Press, 1985).

9. Duby, *Cathedrals*, 100.

10. See Santmire, *Travail of Nature*, chap. 5.

11. *The Dialogues of Gregory the Great* 4.58, trans. P. W. (London, 1911), cited by Elizabeth C. Parker, "Architecture as Liturgical Setting," in *The Liturgy of the Medieval Church*, ed. Thomas J. Heffernan and E. Ann Matter (Kalamazoo: Medieval Institute Publications, 2001), 274.

12. Ibid., chap. 6.

13. Martin R. Dudley, "Sacramental Liturgies in the Middle Ages," in *The Liturgy of the Medieval Church*, ed. Heffernan and Matter, 227.

14. Helmar Junghans, "Luther on the Reform of Worship," in *Harvesting Martin Luther's Reflections on Theology, Ethics, and the Church* (Grand Rapids: Eerdmans, 2004), 213.

15. See my discussion of Augustine in *The Travail of Nature*, chap. 4.

16. Barbara Nolan, *The Gothic Visionary Perspective* (Princeton: Princeton University Press, 1977), 4.

17. Richard of St. Victor, *Benjamin Major* v, 5, quoted in ibid., 32.

18. Nolan, *The Gothic Visionary Perspective*, 41.

19. See Frank C. Senn, *Christian Liturgy: Catholic and Evangelical* (Minneapolis: Fortress Press, 1997), chap. 7.

20. See Santmire, *Travail of Nature*, chap. 6.

21. For documentation of this observation, see my discussion in ibid., 77–84, which draws, in part, on the findings of M. D. Chenu, *Nature, Man, and Society in the Twelfth Century: Essays on New Theological Perspectives in the Latin West*, ed. and trans. Jerome Taylor and Lester K. Little (Chicago: University of Chicago Press, 1968).

22. Lynn White Jr., "Natural Science and Naturalistic Art in the Middle Ages," in *Religion and Technology: Collected Essays* (Berkeley: University of California Press, 1978), 33; quoted by Senn, *Christian Liturgy*, 241.

23. I hasten to add that I am not speaking about *all* the modern and current traditions of Roman Catholicism. I have already referred to the works of Denis Edwards, *Jesus and the Wisdom of God* (Maryknoll, N.Y.: Orbis, 1995), and John Haught, *God after Darwin: A Theology of Evolution* (New York: Westview, 1999), which move in markedly different directions. See also Cho Hyun-Chul, *An Ecological Vision of the World: Toward a Christian Ecological Theology for Our Age* (Rome: Gregorian University Press, 2004).

24. See Santmire, *Travail of Nature*, chap. 8.

25. Louis Bouyer, *Cosmos: The World and the Glory of God*, trans. Pierre De Font-nouvelle (Petersham, Mass.: St. Bede's, 1988), 200.

26. Ibid., 208–9.

27. Ibid., 231. Cf. p. 225: "The universe will henceforth be entirely seized by mankind and returned to the praise of its creator, Father, Son, and Holy Spirit."

28. This notion Bouyer seems to claim from the thought-patterns of Dionysius. Cf. the exposition of Dionysius's thinking in this respect by Denys Rutledge, *Cosmic Theology: The Ecclesiastical Hierarchy of Pseudo-Denys: An Introduction* (London: Routledge and Kegan Paul, 1964), 17, a work that Bouyer himself cites with approval: "Man possesses the world in its 'microcosmic' form; its essence is an aspect of his own being and, some would say, his consideration of what he has *is* its projection in material form. It is, in any case, an inevitable consequence of man's nature, of his place in the hierarchy of being, that the material world should continue to be projected through him as a picture is projected through a film by the light shining through it; that we carry our world always with us, our own world with its own special characteristics, the slant given it by our own personality, and that there will follow us our own world of earth, sky and sea, of birds and animals, plants and flowers, that this final, perfect subjection of the material to the spiritual will, in fact, be the 'new heavens and new earth' we look for."

29. Bouyer, *Cosmos*, 230.

30. The resurrected elect, the chosen humans, and the glory that surrounds them—that is the picture of God's eternal consummation of all things that Bouyer eloquently projects, not a totally renovated creation of humans *and* many other creatures of nature: "The elect have left the world where time slips away, and all together have reached the other shore, where everything endures. The transfigured universe, all around the resurrected bodies, is swathed in a kind of rainbow in which the indivisible glory of God shines forth, and in which the sparkles are as numerous as the elect. . . . In an endless procession, the angels descend and rise again with the Son of Man, who comes down alone from the Father and returns to him with his Bride [the elect], who is in perfect union with the Son through the very unity of the Spirit which eternally connects the Son to the Father. . . . [T]he elect sing forever the hymn . . . of enthronement of the King who finally takes possession of his Kingdom only by also allowing all his children to take part in it through his only-begotten Son." Bouyer, *Cosmos*, 232–33.

31. Christian Copyright Licensing International reports that it was the most frequently used American hymn from 1997 to 2005 and that it has remained in the top ten of the most popular hymns since then. It is likewise popular in the UK and Australia.

32. Ronald P. Byars, *Lift Your Hearts on High: Eucharistic Prayer in the Reformed Tradition* (Louisville: Westminster John Knox, 2005). Readers are not told, in so many words, where the title comes from; we are left to discover that this is a quotation from the sixteenth-century Strassbourg reformer Martin Bucer (p. 27).

33. These tendencies are quite evident in the highly regarded study by Douglas Farrow, *Ascension and Ecclesia: On the Significance of the Doctrine of the Ascension for Ecclesiology and Christian Cosmology* (Grand Rapids: Eerdmans, 1999). Much of this kind of emphasis on the ascension can traced back to Calvin himself. This is well documented by Randall C. Zachman in his excellent study, *Image and Word in the Theology of John Calvin* (Notre Dame: University of Notre Dame Press, 2007), see particularly pp. 8, 15, 261, 274–75, 307, 308, 337.

34. Max Weber, *The Protestant Ethic and the Spirit of Capitalism*, trans. Talcott Parsons, with an introduction by Anthony Gidden, 2d ed. (New York: Routledge, 2001).

35. On the "de-naturing" of modern Protestantism more generally, see my discussion in *The Travail of Nature*, 133–44.

36. See my discussion of Gnosticism in *The Travail of Nature*, 32–35, 55–56.

37. Harold Bloom, *The American Religion: The Emergence of the Post Christian Nation* (New York: Simon & Schuster, 1992).

38. For that, see the review of *The American Religion* by Martin E. Marty, *Christian Century* 109, no. 18 (May 20–27, 1992): 545–48. Marty writes (p. 545), "That Gnosticism is pervasive in many American subcultures is a common observation. Many contend that it forms the basis of what the sociologists call the individualized, privatized, 'invisible' religion of noninstitutionally religious Americans. Gnosticism is largely at the core of the 'spiritual search' and the 'spirituality' that are such great market items in the 1990s. And it takes no daring to generalize that Gnosticism is a feature of New Age and other alternative religions which lure many in an age that was supposed to have been secular."

39. See Philip J. Lee, *Against the Protestant Gnostics* (London: Oxford University Press, 1986).

40. For a thorough and historically informed review of the release of the *Gospel of Judas*, its historical meaning, and its meaning today, see N. T. Wright, *Judas and the Gospel of Jesus: Have We Missed the Truth About Christianity?* (Grand Rapids: Baker, 2006).

41. Herbert Krosney, quoted by N. T. Wright, *Judas*, 133.

42. For a review of both the theology of the book of Revelation and the markedly different theology of the "Left Behind" novels, see the work of Barbara R. Rossing, *The Rapture Exposed: The Message of Hope in the Book of Revelation* (Boulder: Westview, 2004).

43. Strikingly, Lee, in *Against the Protestant Gnostics*, pp. 269ff., makes a plea for "the restoration of ritual" in American Protestant churches as a viable way for these churches to overcome the anti-nature, anti-material theology of Gnostic inwardness, which he believes permeates American Protestantism.

6. A Revolutionary Vision of Divine Immanence: The Theology of Descent

1. Luther cites this text from Jeremiah in his important sacramental discussion with Zwingli about God's omnipresence. See "That These Words of Christ, 'This Is My Body,' Etc. Still Stand Firm Against the Fanatics," *Luther's Works*, ed. Robert H Fischer (Philadelphia: Muhlenberg, 1961), 37:62.

2. The terms *sacramental* and *sacral* are sometimes conflated in current discussions, as James Nash does when he writes that "Christian sacramentality sacralizes but does not divinize nature." *Loving Nature: Ecological Integrity and Christian Responsibility* (Nashville: Abingdon, 1991), 115.

3. Elizabeth A. Johnson, "Heaven and Earth Are Filled with Your Glory," in *Finding God in All Things: Essays in Honor of Michael J. Buckley, S.J.* (New York: Crossroad, 1996), chap. 6. I also have some reservations about Johnson's use of the metaphor of "participation" in this context; but that is a topic for discussion some

other time. Johnson instances the following theologians as seeing the earth in terms of sacrament: Sallie McFague, Jürgen Moltmann, John Haught, Michael J. Himes, Kenneth R. Himes, and Denis Edwards. Perhaps the most representative and at the same time most accessible of many of these studies is John Hart's *Sacramental Commons: Christian Ecological Ethics* (Lanham, Md.: Rowman & Littlefield, 2006). For a positive appreciation of this approach, in comparison with others, see Larry L. Rasmussen, *Earth Community Earth Ethics* (Maryknoll, N.Y.: Orbis, 1997), 227–47. For an Orthodox treatment of the earth as sacrament, see John Chryssavgis, "The Earth as Sacrament: Insights from Orthodox Christian Theology and Spirituality," in *The Oxford Handbook of Religion and Ecology*, ed. Roger S. Gottlieb (New York: Oxford University Press, 2006), chap. 3.

4. Thus in Hart's *Sacramental Commons*, the idea of a "sacramental universe" more or less swallows up the particular meaning of the church's sacraments. Cf. Hart's comparison of the two (p. 15): "Church sacraments are symbols that signify their role of mediation [of the Divine Spirit] in a special way, ordinarily through the actions of a priest. The universe, the creation of God-transcendent permeated by God-immanent, provides countless means and moments of mediation when people reflectively commune with individual creatures or reflect on the beauty of Earth's vistas or other visible parts of the cosmos."

5. Rosemary Radford Ruether, "Conclusion: Eco-Justice at the Center of the Church's Mission," in *Christianity and Ecology: Seeking the Well-Being of Earth and Humans*, ed. Dieter T. Hessel and Rosemary Radford Ruether (Cambridge: Harvard University Press, 2000), 610.

6. Thus, in his article, "Martin Luther's Christocentric Critique of Pseudo-Dionysian Spirituality," *Lutheran Quarterly* 11, no. 3 (Autumn 1997): 291–307, Paul Rorem has instructively explored Luther's critique of Dionysian spirituality and interpreted that critique essentially in christological terms, which probably was the driving theological force that set Luther against the Dionysian way. Rorem leads off his discussion with a striking quote from Luther's 1520 treatise, "The Babylonian Captivity" (in LW 36, ed. Jaroslav Pelikan and Helmut Lehmann [Philadelphia: Fortress Press, 1955], 109): "But in his *Theology*, which is rightly called *Mystical*, of which certain very ignorant theologians make so much, he is downright dangerous, for he is more of a Platonist than a Christian. . . . Let us rather hear Paul, that we may learn Jesus Christ and him crucified [I Cor. 2:2]. He is the way, the life, and the truth; he is the ladder [Gen. 28:12] by which we come to the Father, as he says: 'No one comes to the Father, but by me. [John 14:6].'" But Rorem does not explore—or even hint at—the implications for this kind of christocentric reversal for Luther's theology of creation, in general, and Luther's theology of the divine immanence, in particular.

For his part, in his article "Luther and the Ascent of Jacob's Ladder," *Church History* 55, no. 2 (June 1986): 179–92, David G. Steinmetz has made much of Luther's interpretation of that single biblical theme. In one particular lecture that touches on Jacob's ladder, Steinmetz observes, "Luther does not appear to be repelled by what he calls the 'godly speculations' of medieval commentators" about this theme. Further, says Steinmetz: "There is not a hint in his lecture that he disapproves of the idea that Christians ascend and descend Jacob's ladder. The problem is not with the metaphor of ascent and descent but with the notion that the ascent is helped along by the merit of good works. Good works belong to the descent and not to the ascent of the ladder.

Christians ascend Jacob's ladder by the imputation of Christ's merits" (both refs. p. 190). The agenda for Luther's interpretation in this respect, Steinmetz concludes, was set by the medieval exegesis that Luther inherited.

On the basis of Steinmetz's findings, *that* seems perfectly clear. But it also seems perfectly clear that this is one of these very familiar instances where Luther is writing, in a focused way, as an exegete and not as a systematic thinker. Steinmetz has no real basis to *generalize* about Luther's theological thought about the ladder, in this respect, especially in light of Luther's more self-consciously theological rejection of Dionysian spirituality (see Rorem) and of Luther's identification of "the ladder" with *Christ* in "The Babylonian Captivity" passage quoted above. Which Christ? For Luther, in his mature writings, this Christ is always God-with-us in the flesh, available to us in, with, and under the ministrations of the church. It makes no sense, according to this way of thinking, even to imagine that the Christian, in faith, somehow ascends to this Christ. Which leads one to ask: has perhaps Steinmetz overstated his case, even regarding Luther's focused, exegetical treatment of the ladder theme?

7. Martin Luther, *Werke*, WA 5:503, 10–11, quoted by Rorem, "Martin Luther's Christocentric Critique," 291.

8. Martin Luther, "That These Words of Christ . . . ," LW 57, ed. Helmut Lehmann (Philadelphia: Fortress Press, 1961), 57–58. See H. Paul Santmire, *The Travail of Nature: The Ambiguous Ecological Promise of Christian Theology* (Minneapolis: Fortress Press, 1985), chap. 7.

9. Luther, *Werke*, WA 23:134.34–23:136.36, quoted by Heinrich Bornkamm, *Luther's World of Thought*, trans. Martin Bertram (St. Louis: Concordia, 1958), 189. Cf. this remark by Luther in a Lenten sermon, clearly addressed to those, including theologians, who, Luther believed, held to the notion (influenced by Aristotle's metaphysics) of a *Deus otiosus* (an idle deity): "For God is wholly present in all creation, in every corner, he is behind you and before you. Do you think he is sleeping on a pillow in heaven?" ("Two Lenten Sermons, 1518," *Luther's Works*, ed John W. Doberstein [Philadelphia: Muhlenberg, 1959] 51:43.)

10. Robert Jenson, *Visible Words: The Interpretation and Practice of the Christian Sacraments* (Philadelphia: Fortress Press, 1978).

11. I have developed the rudiments of a "cosmic christology" in my book *Nature Reborn: The Ecological and Cosmic Promise of Christian Theology* (Minneapolis: Fortress Press, 2000), chap. 4, drawing on the thought of Pierre Teilhard de Chardin, appropriately revised in order to factor out his dominating anthropocentrism and his heavy accent on the mastery of nature. I have developed these thoughts further in my essay: "'So That He Might Fill All Things': Comprehending the Cosmic Love of Christ," *dialog* 42, no. 3 (Fall 2003): 257–78. For a different kind of approach to this theme, see the instructive study by George L. Murphy, *The Cosmos in Light of the Cross* (Harrisburg: Trinity Press International, 2003).

12. Here I am speaking about Sittler's call for a cosmic Christology as an event of public theological significance. Sittler himself, in that address, acknowledged his debt to patristic writers, in this regard, and also to a groundbreaking modern work, which, by Sittler's time, had not had a widespread impact in ecumenical circles. See Allan D. Galloway, *The Cosmic Christ* (New York: Harper & Bros., 1951). This work is now virtually forgotten.

13. Martin Luther, *Sermons on the Gospel of John, Chapters 1-4*, Luther's Works, ed. Jaroslav Pelikan, trans. Martin H. Bertram (St. Louis: Concordia, 1957), 22:28.

14. Thus, Jan D. Kingston Siggins, in his lengthy study, *Martin Luther's Doctrine of Christ* (New Haven: Yale University Press, 1970), mentions Luther's understanding of the ubiquity of Christ only once, and that in passing.

15. Among Luther's many critics in this regard, perhaps the most influential has been Thomas F. Torrance. See especially his study *Space, Time, and Resurrection* (Grand Rapids: Eerdmans, 1976). Although Torrance distinguished himself as an interpreter of Reformation theology in other contexts, his treatment of Luther's view of ubiquity in this volume and elsewhere in his own writings generally shows a remarkable lack of attention to the details of Luther's thought, resulting in interpretations that are frequently misleading if not altogether inaccurate. But this is a critique that it would take us too far afield to document here.

16. In his otherwise instructive exposition of Luther's sacramental theology, David C. Steinmetz, in his essay, "Scripture and the Lord's Supper in Luther's Theology," in *Luther in Context* (Bloomington: Indiana University Press, 1986), esp. 78–82, does not sufficiently emphasize the theological use of paradox in Luther's thought at this point. Rather, Steinmetz is content to reproduce Luther's occasional and rather wooden use of a philosophical distinction between three different kinds of "being present" that Luther learned from the teachings of William of Occam. That surely is one of the approaches Luther takes to the theology of divine immanence; but it appears to me to be secondary to his passionate and frequent reference to the presence of God and Christ by the paradoxical use of prepositions.

17. Karl Barth attempted to go beyond the dispute between the Lutheran theologians, who affirmed, as Luther did, that the right hand of God is everywhere, hence that the ascended Christ is everywhere, and the Calvinist theologians, who affirmed, following Calvin, that the right hand of God, where the ascended Christ resides, is a "local presence." See *Church Dogmatics, II:1: The Doctrine of God*, ed. G. W. Bromiley and T. F. Torrance (Edinburgh: T&T Clark, 1957), 489–90, where Barth invokes what might be thought of as his *theocentric view of space*: "If God's presence in Jesus Christ is God's proper presence in the world, and we are therefore to understand that in Jesus Christ the space of God himself (in the strictest original sense of the concept, the throne of God) has become identical with creaturely human space, then it is at once apparent (as the Reformed saw against the Lutherans) that both the corporeality of the historical and exalted Jesus Christ and also the right hand of God as his place must have a definiteness and distinctiveness from other spaces, and this must not be denied for the sake of the truth of Jesus Christ's humanity. But it is also apparent (as the Lutherans saw against the Reformed) that there is not only an omnipresence of Jesus Christ in accordance with his divinity. There is also a human corporeal omnipresence of Jesus Christ. In virtue of the proper and original presence of God on His supra-heavenly throne, in which in Jesus Christ even human nature in its corporeality has a part, there does exist also a relative but real presence of God on his supra-heavenly throne, in which in Jesus Christ even human nature in its corporeality has a part, there does exist also a relative but real presence in the world (both in particular and in general), not only of God, but also of man united with God in Jesus Christ."

What Barth does with the theme of the ubiquity of Jesus Christ, particularly with regard to the theology of nature is something else. Cf. my unpublished doctoral dissertation, *Creation and Nature: A Study of the Doctrine of Nature with Special Attention to Karl Barth's Doctrine of Creation* (Th.D. diss., Harvard University, 1966).

18. Luther, *WA* 23.134.34-23.136.36 (cited by Heinrich Bornkamm, *Luther's World of Thought*, trans. Martin H. Bertram (St. Louis: Concordia, 1958), 189.

19. On the omnipresence of the right hand of God, cf. Luther in his sacramental discussions: ". . . if [God's] power and Spirit are present everywhere and in all things to the innermost and outermost degree, through and through, as it must be if he is to make and preserve all things everywhere, then his right hand, nature, and majesty must be everywhere" ("That These Words of Christ, 'This is my Body,' Etc. Still Stand Against the Fanatics," *Luther's Works*, ed. Robert H. Fischer (Philadelphia: Muhlenberg, 1961), 37:62.

20. Luther's teaching about the ubiquity of the ascended and resurrected Christ should be distinguished from the reformer's closely related discussions of the person of Christ. In the latter context—for some of the same reasons that prompted Luther to project the ubiquity doctrine—Luther goes to some length in various contexts to underscore the closeness of the relationship between the divine and human natures of Jesus Christ. Luther stresses, indeed, that properties of those individual natures are communicated to each other (*communicatio idiomatum*). This meant that Luther bequeathed to his more systematically minded successors the challenge not only of dealing with his ascension theology, but also with questions whether the *human* Christ was omniscient, omnipotent, etc. I am *not* arguing here in behalf of the *communicatio idiomatum* doctrine. On the contrary, that teaching may bring with it more problems than viable insights. For a discussion of these matters, see the sympathetic treatment of Luther's struggles with the *communicatio idiomatum* theology by Marc Lienhard, *Luther: Witness to Jesus Christ—Stages and Themes of the Reformer's Christology* (Minneapolis: Augsburg, 1982), 335–46. Lienhard, however, fails to distinguish between Luther's teaching about the ascension, on the one hand, and Luther's teaching about the person of Christ, on the other.

Still, without further study, it is difficult not to agree with Lienhard's negative response to Luther's *communicatio idiomatum* teachings. Lienhard says that he agrees with the negative response to those teachings voiced by the conservative Lutheran systematic theologian Paul Althaus, whom Lienhard quotes: "A man with the divine properties of omnipotence and omniscience is no longer a man. The mystery of the person of Jesus finds itself rationalized [by Luther] by a metaphysical construct which destroys the real humanity. It is in total contradiction to the picture of Jesus in the Gospels."

21. In this discussion, I believe that I am following the baselines of the argument Karl Barth set forth about these questions. See n. 17 above.

22. Cf. David F. Ford, who states: "There was a danger that the Lutheran affirmation of the ubiquity of Christ would compromise the continuing particularity of his humanity." "What Happens in the Eucharist," *Scottish Journal of Theology* 48, no. 3 (1995): 377 n. 33.

23. Luther is self-conscious about the theological task at this point: theological language, if it is to be authentic, *requires* the employment of paradox. Luther's critics at this point, on the other hand, seem to assume that theological discourse is somehow *literal*: that that place at the right hand of the eternal God is a place like any other place we know.

24. In this process of considering the theological use of paradox, Paul Tillich's contributions to the discussion should be given serious attention; see *Systematic Theology*, I (Chicago: University of Chicago Press, 1951), 56–57, 150–52. Cf. esp. p. 57: "Paradoxical means 'against the opinion,' namely, the opinion of finite reason. Paradox points to the fact that in God's acting finite reason is suspended but not annihilated; it expresses this fact in terms that are not logically contradictory but which are supposed to point beyond the realm in which finite reasons is applicable. . . . The acceptance of . . . paradox is not the acceptance of the absurd, but it is the state of being grasped by the power of that which breaks into our experience from above it. Paradox in religion and theology does not conflict with the principle of logical rationality. Paradox has its logical place."

25. Ford, "What Happens in the Eucharist," 377 n. 33.

26. H. Paul Santmire, "I-Thou, I-It, I-Ens," *Journal of Religion* 48, no. 3 (July 1968): 260–73.

27. Joseph Sittler, "Ecological Commitment as Theological Responsibility," *Zygon* 5 (June 1970): 175, quoted by Steven Bouma-Prediger, "Sittler the Pioneering Ecological Theologian," in Joseph Sittler, *Evocations of Grace: Writings on Ecology, Theology, and Ethics*, ed. Steven Bouma-Prediger and Peter Bakken (Grand Rapids: Eerdmans, 2000), 229.

28. From a personal conversation with Sittler, 1976.

29. Luther was by no means alone with kind of apperception of nature. For many in the Western Middle Ages nature was not a friendly place. See the discussion by Jonathan Sumption, *The Age of Pilgrimage: The Medieval Journey to God* (Mahwah, N.J.: HiddenSpring, 2003), 9–13.

30. In another essay, I have attempted to work out the implications of this kind of apperception of Christ and nature in much more comprehensive terms. See H. Paul Santmire, "'So That He Might Fill All Things': Comprehending the Cosmic Love of Christ," *dialog* 42, no. 3 (Fall 2003): 257–78.

31. Cited by Carl A. Volz, "Holy Communion in the Lutheran Confessions," *Word and World* 17, no. 1 (Winter 1997): 10.

32. Cf. Gordon Lathrop's discussion of the trinitarian shape of the liturgy in *Holy Ground: A Liturgical Cosmology* (Minneapolis: Fortress Press, 2003), 139, a discussion he concludes with these words: "One could even say that 'Trinity' is what Christians have found they must say about God; it is the dogma that is the 'soul' of the liturgy."

33. Such a focus on Christ—this "christocentrism"—is, of course, not new in modern theology. It was championed most memorably in the last century by Karl Barth, although Barth was not alone in this respect by any means. Also, be it noted that christocentrism can go hand in hand with a thoroughgoing trinitarianism, as the case of Barth shows.

34. The argument of this book, in this respect, stands in a certain tension—I think of it as a creative tension—with the approach to the theology of nature championed by a range of prominent ecological theologians, whose point of departure is more pneumatalogical than christological. Call them ecological theologies of the Third Person, the Spirit of God. In this group I would include Larry Rasmussen, *Earth Community Earth Ethics*; Mark Wallace, *Fragments of the Spirit: Nature, Violence, and the Renewal of Creation* (Harrisburg: Trinity Press International, 2002); and Mary Grey, *Sacred Longings: The Ecological Spirit and Global Culture* (Minneapolis: Fortress Press, 2004).

35. The challenge of developing an explicit, fully scripted cosmic pneumatology can already be found in the extensive work of two major modern theologians of nature, Paul Tillich and Jürgen Moltmann, although in quite different ways. See Paul J. Tillich, *Systematic Theology*, III: *Life and the Spirit; History and the Kingdom of God* (Chicago: University of Chicago Press, 1963); Jürgen Moltmann, *God in Creation: A New Theology of Creation and the Spirit of God*, trans. Margaret Kohl (New York: Harper & Row, 1985).

36. For one entry into the world of the classic Celtic saints, see my discussion in *Nature Reborn*, chap. 7.

37. Jürgen Moltmann, "Progress and Abyss: Remembrances of the Future of the Modern World," in *The Future of Hope: Christian Tradition Amid Modernity and Postmodernity*, ed. Miroslav Volf and William Katerberg (Grand Rapids: Eerdmans, 2004), 15.

38. But, of course, other eras *have* known the force of the theodicy question. One striking example is the journals of the extraordinary French parish priest, Jean Meslier (1678–1733), some of which were published by Voltaire, d'Holbach, and Diderot. Meslier's savage attack on Christianity prefigured most of points that would later be made not only by Enlightenment critics but also by philosophers like Nietzsche and his successors. See Will and Ariel Durant, *The Age of Voltaire: A History of Civilization in Western Europe from 1715 to 1756, with Special Emphasis on the Conflict between Religion and Philosophy* (New York: Simon & Schuster, 1965), 611–17.

39. For a single, promising entry into this theological wilderness, see the short but insightful article by Lois Malcolm, "The Crucified Messiah and Divine Suffering in the Old Testament," in *"And God Saw That It Was Good": Essays on Creation and God in Honor of Terence E. Fretheim, Word and World* Supplement Series, 5, ed. Frederick J. Gaiser and Mark A. Throntveit (St. Paul: Luther Seminary, 2006), 136–44. Malcolm summarizes the argument of the seminal work by Paul Ricoeur, *The Symbolism of Evil* (Boston: Beacon, 1967), and then offers further reflections of her own, in response to the works of Fretheim, especially his study *The Suffering of God: An Old Testament Perspective*, Overtures to Biblical Theology (Philadelphia: Fortress Press, 1984).

40. At least the image of the ubiquitous Christ, suffering with the dying, however fragile this thought may be, has the advantage of allowing us to envision *God as somehow engaged with human suffering "on the ground,"* as it were, in contrast to the image of Christ sitting in regal splendor in the heavens at the right hand of God, even as *absent* from our world, as some interpreters of the ascension of Christ maintain.

41. Cited by James Hamilton, *Turner: The Late Seascapes* (New Haven: Yale University Press, 2003), 39.

7. Baptism, Proclamation, Offertory: Framed by the Theology of Descent

1. See my discussion of root metaphors in *The Travail of Nature*, 14–17. The notion of "framing" is also used in other (related) ways by both psychologists, like Erving Goffman (*Frame Analysis: An Essay on the Organization of Experience* [Boston: Northeastern University Press, 1986], and by linguists, such as the popularizing work of George Lakoff (*Don't Think of An Elephant: Know Your Values and Frame the Debate* [White Mountain Junction, Vt.: Chelsea Green, 2004]).

2. For a concise but strong ecumenical statement of the general meaning of baptism, see *Baptism, Eucharist, and Ministry,* Faith and Order Paper 111 (Geneva: World Council of Churches, 1982), 2–9.

3. Contrast the impression of baptism that Mary Grey conveys as normative. As I have noted, she seeks to create "a sacramental poetics of water." She wants to "widen the dimensions and understanding of sacrament beyond" what she thinks of "its limited ritualistic church setting," which, in her view, is a "celebration that mostly ignores sensuous experience . . ." (Mary Grey, *Sacred Longings: The Ecological Spirit and Global Culture* [Minneapolis: Fortress Press, 2004], 86). Has Grey really encountered the fullness of the church's baptismal practices in our time? Later, indeed, she shows high regard for the use of water in the church's Easter Vigil (p. 97). It is not clear what "church setting" she really has in mind.

4. *Lutheran Book of Worship* (Philadelphia: Board of Publication, Lutheran Church in America/Minneapolis: Augsburg, 1978), 122.

5. For these historical materials and for some insightful explorations of the meaning of this prayer, see Benjamin Stewart, "Flooding the Landscape: Luther's Flood Prayer and Baptismal Theology," *CrossAccent* 13, no. 1 (January 2005): 4–14.

6. For a suggestive, liturgically informed way to deal with this problem of "taking time," see Dorothy C. Bass, *Receiving the Day: Christian Practices for Opening the Gift of Time* (San Francisco: Jossey-Bass, 2000).

7. Benjamin M. Stewart, *A Tree Planted by Water: Ecological Orientation at the Vigil of Easter,* unpublished master's thesis, Lutheran Theological Seminary, Philadelphia, 2004.

8. This is why it makes profound liturgical sense for baptism, whenever possible, to be an integral part of the liturgy, as in the Easter Vigil, and not in any sense "a private ceremony," reserved only for invited guests.

9. For Catholic social teaching, see *Option for the Poor: A Hundred Years of Vatican Social Teaching,* rev. ed., ed. Donal Dorr (Maryknoll, N.Y.: Orbis, 1992). See the editor's introduction for a concise overview of this tradition, pp. 1–12. For a single, compelling statement, see Norbert F. Lohfink, *Option for the Poor: The Basic Principle of Liberation Theology in Light of the Bible,* trans. Linda M. Maloney, ed. Duane L. Christensen (North Richland Hills, Tex.: BIBAL, 1987).

10. See my longer discussion of these matters in *Brother Earth: Nature, God, and Ecology in a Time of Crisis* (New York: Thomas Nelson, 1970), chaps. 1 and 2.

11. Martin Luther, "A Brief Introduction on What to Look For and Expect in the Gospels," in LW 35 (Philadelphia: Fortress Press, 1960), 121, quoted by Gordon W. Lathrop, "Preaching in the Dialogue of Worship with Culture," in *Baptism, Rites of Passage, and Culture,* ed. S. Anita Stauffer (Geneva: The Lutheran World Federation Department of Studies, 1998), 252.

12. Gordon W. Lathrop, "Preaching in the Dialogue of Worship with Culture," 250.

13. See the article by Martinus C. De Boer, "Paul, Theologian of God's Apocalypse," *Interpretation* 56, no. 1 (January 2002): 33: "The apocalyptic perspective of Paul cannot be reduced to a personal, mystical experience of the heavenly world or to the reception of heavenly secrets. It has little or nothing to do with travel up to heaven in a visionary experience or something similar . . . , but everything to do with the invasive action of God in this world to deliver human beings from this present age. . . . [For

Paul,] the whole of God's eschatological saving activity in Jesus Christ, from beginning to end is apocalyptic. This event involves a cosmic drama that God has begun and will bring to a conclusion in the [second coming of Christ]. The focus of Paul is the redemptive or liberating action of God in Christ, the Christ who is now proclaimed in the Gospel. . . . According to Paul, God has done this in the apocalyptic-eschatological event of Jesus Christ, who (so Paul claims) died for human beings and was raised by God. Paul presents himself primarily as a theologian of this revelation, this apocalypse, of God."

14. Cf. the quote by Robert Jenson, *Visible Words: The Interpretation and Practice of the Christian Sacraments* (Philadelphia: Fortress Press, 1978), 42.

15. Readers relatively new to such discussions can find helpful entry points in the following works: Donald E. Gowan, *Eschatology in the Old Testament* (Edinburgh: T&T Clark, 2000; Carl E. Braaten and Robert W. Jenson, eds., *The Last Things: Biblical and Theological Perspectives on Eschatology* (Grand Rapids: Eerdmans, 2002), especially the chapter by Arland J. Hultgren, "Eschatology in the New Testament: The Current Debate," 67–89; Geoffrey Wainwright, *Eucharist and Eschatology* (Akron: OSL Publications, 2002); John Koenig, *The Feast of the World's Redemption: Eucharistic Origins and Christian Mission* (Harrisburg: Trinity Press International, 2000). For a magisterial theological treatment of eschatology, consult the works of Jürgen Moltmann, above all *The Coming of God: Christian Eschatology*, trans. Margaret Kohl (Minneapolis: Fortress Press, 1996).

16. Thus, the Web of Creation coalition sponsored by the Lutheran School of Theology in Chicago has made available texts and other liturgical resources for a "Season of Creation" series, developed by the Australian biblical scholar Norman Habel. The 2006 schedule was as follows: September 3, Planet Earth Sunday; September 10, Humanity Sunday; September 17, Sky Sunday; September 24, Mountain Sunday; October 1, Blessing of the Animals. See http://www.webofcreation.org/SeasonofCreation/index.html, accessed February 12, 2008.

17. The Evangelical Lutheran Church in America lectionary leaflet series, *Celebrate*, has done this for several years. Congregational feedback has indicated that local churches have come to expect these petitions, once the petitions have become a weekly part of their public prayers.

18. A number of helpful resources are available to support good liturgical preaching, in this respect. Still very much worth consulting is the great sermon of Paul Tillich, "Nature, Too, Mourns for a Lost God," *The Shaking of the Foundations* (New York: Scribners, 1948). Many of Joseph Sittler's works also offer rich materials for homiletical reflection. See, for example, *The Care of the Earth and Other University Sermons* (Philadelphia: Fortress Press, 1964); and, more generally, *The Anguish of Preaching* (Philadelphia: Fortress Press, 1966). Ecojustice themes are highlighted in the volume edited by Dieter T. Hessel, *For Creation's Sake: Preaching, Ecology, and Justice* (Philadelphia: Geneva, 1985). George L. Murphy and his colleagues have provided ecologically and cosmically relevant exposition of the common lectionary of the church, in *Cosmic Witness: Commentaries on Science/Technology Themes* (Lima, Ohio: CSS, 1996), as has Jennifer M. Phillips, *Preaching the Creation throughout the Church Year* (Boston: Cowley, 2000). Cf. also J. Michael Scheid, *A Theology of Nature and Its Implications for Christian Worship,* unpublished dissertation, San Francisco Theological Seminary, 1997.

19. Cf. the comment by Alexander Olivar, "Reflections on Problems Raised by Early Christian Preaching," in *Preacher and Audience: Studies in Early Christian and Byzantine Homiletics*, ed. Mary B. Cunningham and Pauline Allen (Boston: Brill, 1998), 23, concerning second-century preaching: "Thanks to the preservation of these homilies, it is possible to form a real appreciation of the lively contact, almost a dialogue, that took place between the speaker and an enthusiastic congregation."

20. Ibid., 21.

21. Martin Luther, "Sermon at the Dedication of the Castle Church," *Luther's Works*, ed. John W. Doberstein (Philadelphia: Muhlenberg, 1959), 51:333.

22. On the biblical meaning of "flesh," cf. the words of N.T. Wright, *Paul: In Fresh Perspective* (Minneapolis: Fortress Press, 2005), 35, commentary that may also be read as reflecting a more general New Testament approach to this matter: "[For Paul,] humans were made to function in particular ways, with worship of the creator as the central feature, and those who turn away from that worship—that is, the whole human race, with a single exception—are thereby opting to seek life where it is not found, which is another way of saying that they are courting their own decay and death." "All this contextualizes one of Paul's key technical terms, *sarx*, normally translated 'flesh.' As is well known, Paul does not mean by 'flesh' simply physical substance. For that he normally uses *soma*, usually translated 'body.' For him, the word 'flesh' is a way of denoting material within the corruptible world and drawing attention to the fact that it is precisely corruptible, that it will decay and die. From that point Paul's usage expands one more level, to include the moral behavior which, consequent upon idolatry, is already a sign of, and an invitation to, that progressive corruption: hence 'the works of the flesh.' This analysis, seen from within an overall theology of the goodness of creation and the deconstruction of it through idolatry, is preferable to those accounts which approach the problem from other angles, for instance the early history of the word on the one hand or the assumptions of a dualist worldview on the other."

23. Irenaeus *Against the Heresies* 4.17.5, quoted by Paul F. Bradshaw, "The Offering of the First fruits of Creation: An Historical Study," in *Creation and Liturgy*, ed. Ralph N. McMichael Jr. (Washington, D.C.: The Pastoral Press, 1993), 34.

24. Jenson, *Visible Words*, 92.

25. Philip H. Pfatteicher, *Commentary on the Lutheran Book of Worship: Lutheran Liturgy in Its Ecumenical Context* (Minneapolis: Augsburg Fortress Press, 1990), 153.

26. For this history, see Thomas Phelan, "Offertory," *A New Dictionary of Liturgy and Worship*, ed. J. G. Davies (London: SCM, 1986), s.v.; Colin Buchanan, *The End of the Offertory: An Anglican Study*, Grove Liturgical Study, 14 (Bramcote Notts, UK: Grove, 1978).

27. Frank C. Senn, *A Stewardship of the Mysteries* (New York: Paulist, 1999), 74.

28. Martin Luther, *Formula Missae et Communionis* (1523), ed. Emil Sehling, *Die evangelische Kirchenordnungen des sechzehnten Jahrhunderts*, I (Leipzig: Reisland, 1902), 5, cited by Senn, *A Stewardship of the Mysteries*, 73.

29. Quoted by Carter Lindberg, "Luther's Concept of Offering," *dialog* 35, no. 4 (Fall 1996): 63.

30. Martin Luther, *Luther's Works* (Philadelphia: Fortress Press, 1959), 36:54, quoted by Senn, *A Stewardship of the Mysteries*, 79.

31. See my appreciation for and response to this critique in my article, "The Eclipse of the Offering?" *Lutheran Partners* (May/June 1998), 22–28.

32. See the appendix of this book on "Stewardship."

33. For introductory explorations of these issues, see the three lead articles in *dialog* 35, no. 4 (Fall 1996): Paul Rorem, "The End of All Offertory Processions," 247–50; Carter Lindberg, "Luther's Concept of Offering," 251–57; Gordon W. Lathrop, "Transforming Offering: A Response to Carter Lindberg and Paul Rorem," 258–62.

34. For another, quite different but still quite positive approach to the offertory, see Jenson, *Visible Words*, chap. 9.

35. Luther, *Sermons on the Gospel of John 1-4*, Luther's Works, ed. Jaroslav Pelikan (St. Louis: Concordia, 1957) 22:496.

36. Bernd Wannenwetsch, "Liturgy," in *The Blackwell Companion to Political Theology*, ed. Peter Scoot and William T. Cavanaugh (Malden, Mass.: Blackwell, 2004), 78.

37. Ibid., 81.

38. Cf. the comment of Senn, *A Stewardship of the Mysteries*, 73: "There is no doubt that the Offertory has become one of the major moments in the liturgy. It is certainly one of the most ceremonially complex rituals in the service."

39. This is why the increasingly common practice by Christian congregations to allow members to use credit cards for donations to the church is troublesome. It appears to be yet another way for the ownership economy—"paying the bills with my money"—to shape the life of assemblies. Thus the head of the Nilson Report, a California newsletter that follows the payments industry, recently said of church credit-card giving: "It's the same concept here that people use to pay their health club membership, quarterly insurance payments, and utilities" (Ross Kerber, "Bless You, We Take Visa," *Boston Globe* [January 29, 2007], D1). That congregants may "deposit" their credit-card receipts in the offering plates would not appear to change the ownership consciousness of the whole process. Liturgical and assembly leaders will have to wrestle with this issue, with a view to making it a teaching point in behalf of developing an offering consciousness on the part of the faithful.

40. For this, see Karl Paul Donfried, *The Dynamic Word: New Testament Insights for Contemporary Christians* (San Francisco: Harper & Row, 1981), 104.

41. Readers familiar with theological discussions of the liturgy, and with actual liturgical practices in some communions, will have noticed that I have *not* employed the language of "sacrifice" in my interpretation of the Offertory. Nor will I employ it in our explorations of the Eucharist in the next chapter. Whole books have, of course, been written on "eucharistic sacrifice" in particular, and about the meaning of that theme, in retrospect, for the Offertory. I obviously cannot adjudicate that complex and much contested issue in a few words here. But I do owe the reader an explanation of the course I have chosen to follow. I find that such language is too loaded with theologically unacceptable themes—such as "the church offers Christ"—to be helpful here, apart from extensive clarifying and critical discussion, which is not possible in a book like this. More particularly, the language of sacrifice is historically tied in with deeper issues of religious violence, which casts the very basis of this language into serious doubt. If the language of sacrifice is to be used at all, in my view, it would have to be in the sense employed by Gordon Lathrop, as a metaphorical reversal, suggesting that the church's sacrifice in the liturgy is no sacrifice at all. Beyond Lathrop's discussion, for an entry into the theological discussion of these issues from both Catholic and Protes-

tant perspectives, respectively, see Robert J. Daly, "Images of God and the Imitation of God: Problems with the Atonement," *Theological Studies* 68 (2007): 36–51, and S. Mark Heim, *Saved From Sacrifice: A Theology of the Cross* (Grand Rapids: Eerdmans, 2006), and the literature cited in both those studies.

8. Eucharist and Sending:
Framed by the Theology of Descent

1. For a short but thorough ecumenical statement of the general meaning of the Eucharist, see *Baptism, Eucharist, and Ministry*, Faith and Order Paper 111 (Geneva: World Council of Churches, 1982), 10–19.

2. This impressive renovation was shepherded by an ecumenical collaboration: Richard Giles, Dean of the Cathedral (see the reference to one of his books on such matters in the following note), Andrew Ciferni, a Canon regular at the Daylesford Abbey in Paoli, Pennsylvania, and Gordon Lathrop, a leading Lutheran liturgical theologian, whose works are referred to frequently in this book.

3. Richard Giles, *Re-Pitching the Tent: Re-ordering the Church Building for Worship and Mission*, rev. and exp. ed. (Collegeville, Minn.: Liturgical, 2004), 123.

4. For a brief review of the history of this dialogue, see Philip H. Pfatteicher, *Commentary on the Lutheran Book of Worship: Lutheran Liturgy in Its Ecumenical Context* (Minneapolis: Augsburg Fortress Press, 1990), 158–59.

5. Cf. the comment by Maxwell E. Johnson, "The Apostolic Tradition," in *The Oxford History of Christian Worship*, ed. Geoffrey Wainwright and Karen B. Westerfield Tucker (New York: Oxford University Press, 2006), 56: "One prayer that has captured the imagination of contemporary liturgists in the West, and that now appears in some form in the modern liturgical books of several different churches, Roman Catholic and Protestant alike, is the . . . model bipartite anaphora provided among the materials for the ordination of a bishop in the *Apostolic Tradition*."

6. This text is quoted by Frank C. Senn, *Christian Liturgy: Catholic and Evangelical* (Minneapolis: Fortress Press, 1997), 78, depending on a reconstruction by Gregory Dix.

7. The 1986 *Book of Worship* of the United Church of Christ *adds* to the accent on the theme of heights. We do meet the traditional words, "Lift up your hearts," with the response (the word *God* being substituted for *Lord*), "We lift them up to God." But the UCC dialogue continues *not* with traditional words such as these, "Let us give thanks to the Lord our God." In the UCC rite, the officiant says "Let us give thanks to God *Most High*" (italics added). This material is cited by Ronald P. Byars, *Lift Your Hearts on High: Eucharistic Prayer in the Reformed Tradition* (Louisville: Westminster John Knox, 2005), 61.

8. Byars, *Lift Your Hearts on High*, 27.

9. Romano Guardini, *The Spirit of the Liturgy*, trans. Ada Lane (New York: Crossroads, 1998), 48ff.

10. *Baptism, Eucharist, and Ministry*, par. 29.

11. Further historical reflection about these issues is surely required. One important question for such research to pursue would be, Does the theological focus on *the elements alone*, whether in the form of the doctrine of transubstantiation or in the form of the more Lutheran paradoxical teaching of "in, with, and under," go hand in

hand with a theology that is shaped overall by the metaphor of ascent? According to this way of thinking, the divine purpose of the real presence, however that is understood, is for God graciously to reach down to sinners, as it were, and then to elevate them to heaven, by their reception of the bread and wine as the true body and blood of Christ. The theology of Christ *as host*, however, as distinct from the more narrow focus on the elements, tends to accent the divine purpose as the restoration and salvation of the world, here and now, through the present Christ.

12. I first began making this proposal for a revision of the *Sursum Corda* in publications around the year 2000. It was only in reading Byars's *Lift Your Hearts on High* in 2006 that I discovered (p. 66) that the United Church of Canada had already adopted similar language in its 2000 worship book, *Celebrate God's Presence: A Book of Services for the United Church of Canada* (Etobicoke, Ontario: United Church Publication House, 2000), 244: "Let us open our hearts to God," with the response, "We open them to God and to one another."

13. For a historical review of the eucharistic prayer, see W. Jardine Grisbrooke, "Anaphora," in *A New Dictionary of Liturgy and Worship*, ed. J. G. Davies (London: SCM, 1986), s.v.

14. Byars, *Lift Your Hearts on High*, 21, 25.

15. Martin Luther, LW 35:82, cited by Helmar Junghans, "Luther on the Reform of Worship," in *Harvesting Martin Luther's Reflections on Theology, Ethics, and the Church*, ed. Timothy J. Wengert (Grand Rapids: Eerdmans, 2004), 210.

16. For this, see Junghaus, "Luther on the Reform of Worship," 207–25.

17. Robert Jenson, *Visible Words: The Interpretation and Practice of the Christian Sacraments* (Philadelphia: Fortress Press, 1978), 69.

18. See Ray Carlton Jones Jr., "The Lord's Supper and the Concept of *Anamnesis*," *Word and World* 6, no. 4 (Fall 1986): 434–45. Jones works around the hotly contested issue whether or not the Last Supper was a Passover celebration by arguing that, however one resolves that question, the fact remains that "the institution of the Lord's supper was comprehensible for the disciples because of their knowledge of the Passover. . . . [Accordingly, in terms of the theology of the Passover,] *anamnesis* means that we are drawn into the history of salvation: 'In every generation let each man looks on himself as if he came out of Egypt.' . . . *Amamnesis* means that the entire history of salvation is remembered and re-experienced—from creation to the return of Christ. The bread in the Passover meal points back in time to creation and liberation; the wine points forward in time to the Day of the Lord and the coming of the Messiah. This is the eschatological aspect of the Passover—an aspect which is also true for the Lord's Supper."

19. At a theological conference, I once heard this fine petition caricatured as "the Star Wars Prayer." Such comments only reveal how necessary such petitions are in the life of the church today.

20. Eucharistic Prayer VII, *Evangelical Lutheran Worship* (Minneapolis: Augsburg Fortress Press, 2006).

21. Ibid.

22. For a forceful, and accessible, statement of the Roman Catholic understanding of "transubstantiation" today, by a respected theologian, see Terence L. Nichols, "'This Is My Body': How to Understand Transubstantiation," *Commonweal* 132, no. 17 (October 7, 2005): 12–14. Nichol's approach, as he indicates, is ripe with ecumenical

implications, particularly for those who take seriously Luther's approach to the real presence, in his terms of "in, with, and under." See also Terence L. Nichols, "Transubstantiation and Eucharistic Presence," *Pro Ecclesia* 11, no. 1 (Winter 2002): 57–75. For a summary of recent, convergent ecumenical discussion of the real presence, see Robert W. Jenson, *Unbaptized God: The Basic Flaw in Ecumenical Theology* (Minneapolis: Fortress Press, 1992), 26–33.

23. On Zwingli, see David C. Steinmetz, *Luther in Context* (Bloomington: Indiana University Press, 1986), 76–77.

24. Dietrich Bonhoeffer, in his own terms, affirmed the Zwinglian point that the church *is* the body of Christ. See *Christ the Center*, trans. Edwin H. Robertson (San Francisco: Harper & Row, 1978), 58–59: "Just as Jesus Christ is present as Word in the Word, as Sacrament and in Sacrament, so he is also present as Church and in the Church. . . . The Church is the body of Christ. Here body is not only symbol. The Church *is* the body of Christ, it does not *signify* the Body of Christ. When applied to the Church, the concept of body is not only a concept of function which refers only to the members of his body. It is a comprehensive and central concept of the mode of existence of the one who is present in his exaltation and humiliation." For a review of Bonhoeffer's fundamental christological insights in this connection, see Clifford J. Green, *Bonhoeffer: A Theology of Sociality*, rev. ed. (Grand Rapids: Eerdmans, 1999).

25. Although Luther's thought is replete with a certain "Christ mysticism," a vision of the indwelling Christ in believers' hearts, and although, in this respect, Luther's understanding of justification by faith was therefore not merely forensic in character, but personal and participatory and communal, he does not appear to have developed this theology of *christic presence in the worshiping ecclesial body* in any extended or discursive way. He apparently was preoccupied with other issues. For a suggestive and historically informed contemporary exposition of the meaning of the presence of the risen Christ, see Gerald O'Collins, *Christology: A Biblical, Historical, and Systematic Study of Jesus* (New York: Oxford University Press, 1955), chap. 14.

26. Ernst Käsemann, *New Testament Questions of Today*, trans. W. J. Montague (Philadelphia: Fortress Press, 1969), 132.

27. The enormously popular hymn, "How Great Thou Art," was written by the Swedish composer, Carl Boberg (d. 1940) and set to a Swedish folk tune.

28. Martin Luther, *Werke: Tischreden*, WA 1:1160, cited and trans. by Heinrich Bornkamm, *Luther's World of Thought*, trans. Martin H. Bertram (St. Louis: Concordia, 1958), 184. Luther, to be sure, was preoccupied with coming to faith in Christ, not so much with what later theologians were to think of the sanctified life in Christ. Luther's major struggle was to overcome the notion that humans can do something, anything, to ascend into God's presence. Hence, Luther accented the wrath of God in the creation, the hiddenness of God in this negative sense, as in this statement: "Begin your search with Christ and stay with him and cleave to him, and if your own thoughts and reason, or another man's, would lead you elsewhere, shut your eyes and say: I should and will know of no other God than Christ, my Lord. . . . For apart from Christ, nature can neither perceive nor attain the grace and love of God, and apart from Him is nothing but wrath and condemnation" (LW 37:79, cited by Steinmetz, *Luther in Context*, 27). This is *not* to suggest that Luther was *not* interested in the sanctified life, that, more particularly, he did not want *believers* to see the whole creation in more positive terms. Rather, it was a matter of emphasis. As the statement from his commentary on

John (cited in the text above) shows, Luther was not without his moments of celebrating Christ *and* the whole creation as well.

29. I refer again to Ted Peters's work, especially as it appears in the volume *Cosmos as Creation: Theology and Science in Consonance*, ed. Ted Peters (Nashville: Abingdon, 1989).

30. Robert Barron, *Bridging the Great Divide: Musings of a Post-Liberal, Post-Conservative Evangelical Catholic* (New York: Rowman & Littlefield, 2004), 77.

31. For the history of "the dismissal," see Pfatteicher, *Commentary on the Lutheran Book of Worship*, 195–96.

32. For a short but thoughtful discussion of the sending as an integral part of the liturgy, see Dirk G. Lange, "Eating, Drinking, Sending: Reflections on the Juxtaposition of Law and Event in the Eucharist," in *Ordo: Bath, Word, Prayer, Table—A Liturgical Primer in Honor of Gordon W. Lathrop*, ed. Dirk G. Lange and Dwight W. Vogel (Akron: OSL Publications, 2005), 84–97, esp. 96–97.

33. Here I am following the exegesis of Ernst Käsemann, *Commentary on Romans*, trans. and ed. Geoffrey W. Bromiley (Grand Rapids: Eerdmans, 1980), 323–31. See especially p. 327 (trans. slightly altered): "What was previously cultic is now extended to the secularity of our earthly life as a whole. . . . Naturally this does not mean any disparagement of worship and the sacraments. Nevertheless, these events are no longer, as in cultic thinking, fundamentally separated from everyday Christian life. . . . Either the whole of Christian life is worship, and the gatherings and sacramental acts of the community equip and instruct for this, or these gatherings and acts lead in fact to absurdity."

34. On Romans 12:1ff., see, further, the discussion of Calvin J. Roetzel, "Sacrifice in Romans 12–15," *Word and World* 6, no. 4 (Fall 1986): 410–19, esp. pp. 418–19: "In 12:3–15:13, Paul views daily conduct through the cultic metaphor as 'daily sacrifice' (12:1-2). In what follows Paul does not present an ethical system or even a summary of an ethical system. Instead he provides instances of sacrificial obedience consistent with his gospel of grace and the imminent [return] of Christ. . . . Paul argues [that] life in Christ should lead to sacrifice for others expressed in service to the body of Christ (12:3-8), to genuine love for each community member (12:9-13), and to the renunciation of hatred for, and retaliation toward, the oppressor (12:14-21). The gospel of grace or participation in the rule of God exempts no one from civic duty (13:1-7), and love, the supreme charism of the New Age, does not abrogate the law but fulfils it, does not relax the moral demand, but intensifies it (13:8-10). . . . Paul's gospel of grace promotes a heightened level of commitment, solidarity, and love for the insider and the outsider, not the immoral behavior, heedless individualism, destructive and insensitive acts of freedom or arrogant and greedy acts that degrade both their victim and their doer."

35. For a discussion of Bonhoeffer's construct of the "discipline of the secret," see Ralf K. Wuestenberg, "'Religionless Christianity': Dietrich Bonhoeffer's Tegel Theology," in *Bonhoeffer for a New Day: Theology in a Time of Transition*, ed. John W. de Gruchy (Grand Rapids: Eerdmans, 1997), 57–71, esp. 59–61.

36. For these reflections, see Dietrich Bonhoeffer, *Letters and Papers from Prison*, the enlarged edition, ed. Eberhard Bethge (New York: Macmillan, 1971), 299–300.

37. Aidan Kavanagh, "Seeing Liturgically," in *Time and Community*, ed. J. Neil Alexander (Washington, D.C.: Pastoral, 1990), 258. The history of processions is much more complex than I can indicate here. In the period to which Kavanagh refers and

beyond, processions were often deeply integrated into the power politics of their time and functioned to reenforce social stratification. For this, see Martin D. Stringer, *A Sociological History of Christian Worship* (Cambridge: Cambridge University Press), 63–68, 173–74.

38. For good introductions to the growing theological literature on animals, see Andrew Linzey, *Animal Gospel* (Louisville: Westminster John Knox, 1998) and Andrew Linzey and Tom Regan, eds., *Animals and Christianity: A Book of Readings* (New York: Crossroad, 1988).

39. The idea of such a march on Washington is, at this time of writing, a hopeful fantasy but not impossible. On the other hand, the more pedestrian idea about church statements and political advocacy in behalf of the positions taken by the statements is quite common in American church life. And, by most accounts, such church advocacy efforts have become an important force in American politics. For a representative church ecojustice statement, see *Caring for Creation: Vision, Hope, and Justice* (Chicago: ELCA, 1993). For an example of an ecojustice statement directed to a particular issue, see *The Columbia River Watershed: Caring for Creation and the Common Good*, issued by twelve Roman Catholic bishops in the Pacific Northwest (Seattle: Columbia River Pastoral Letter Project, 2001).

9. The Habits of Awe and Serving: Our Walk with Nature Ritualized

1. For a theological discussion of habits of faith, understood as a Christian "virtue-ethic" see Stanley Hauerwas, *Christians Among the Virtues: Theological Conversations with Ancient and Modern Ethics* (Notre Dame: University of Notre Dame Press, 1997) and the works on Hauerwas cited above, chap. 2, note 3. For a short account of the topic, see Lisa Fullam, "Virtue Ethics: An Introduction," *Journal of Lutheran Ethics*, December 7, 2006, http://www.elca.org/jle/article.asp?k=687, accessed February 14, 2008.

2. Hundreds of books, it seems, have been written on the topic Christian spirituality and nature in recent years, with mixed results. For entry into this discussion, see my critique of the writings of one of the most renowned writers in this arena, Matthew Fox, on the one hand, and my account of an encounter with the spirituality of the classic Celtic saints, on the other hand, in *Nature Reborn: The Ecological and Cosmic Promise of Christian Theology* (Minneapolis: Fortress Press, 2000), chaps. 2 and 7, respectively. See also my discussion of St. Francis, "The Spirituality of Nature and the Poor: Revisiting the Historic Vision of St. Francis," in *Tending the Holy: Spiritual Direction Across Traditions,* ed. Norvene Vest (Harrisburg: Morehouse, 2003), chap. 9. Scores of books have also been written about Christian faith and the ethics of nature. Among these, as I have already indicated, I regard the work by James Nash, *Loving Nature: Ecological Integrity and Christian Responsibility* (Nashville: Abingdon, 1991), to be a highly reliable guide.

3. For a brief history of the Sanctus, see Philip H. Pfatteicher, *Commentary on the Lutheran Book of Worship: Lutheran Liturgy in Its Ecumenical Context* (Minneapolis: Augsburg Fortress Press, 1990), 161ff. For an exhaustive account of the textual history of the Sanctus, see Bryan D. Spinks, *The Sanctus in the Eucharistic Prayer* (Cambridge: Cambridge University Press, 1991).

4. This text is from *the Lutheran Book of Worship* (Philadelphia: Board of Publication, Lutheran Church in America/Minneapolis: Augsburg, 1978), 69.

5. Elizabeth A. Johnson, "Heaven and Earth Are Filled with Your Glory," in *Finding God in All Things: Essays in Honor of Michael J. Buckley*, ed. Michael J. Himes and Stephen J. Pope (New York: Crossroad, 1996), 91.

6. The material I am touching on here is representative of major themes in Old Testament theology, two extensive and too complex to explore in this context. Implicit in Isaiah's vision, seen in its broader Old Testament context, are the rich theological images of the temple as the mountain of God and of the whole creation as a kind of temple of God, the dwelling of God. A still deeper motif is the image of the cosmic mountain as the navel of the world, a motif known both in ancient Israel and in the worldviews of its neighbors. For a thorough discussion of these matters, see Jon D. Levenson, *Sinai and Zion: An Entry into the Jewish Bible* (New York: Harper & Row, 1985).

7. See Susan E. Schreiner, *The Theater of His Glory: Nature and the Natural Order in the Thought of John Calvin* (Grand Rapids: Baker, 1991).

8. William P. Brown, "'Night to Night,' 'Deep to Deep': The Discourse of Creation in the Psalms," at the Annual Meeting of the Society of Biblical Literature, Washington, D.C., November 19, 2006 (unpublished). Brown's interpretation of the deep waters theme marks a departure from standard interpretations, which generally see the waters as threatening, even chaotic. But his case is convincing. "Psalm 42," he observes, "by attributing the formidable power of cascading waters to God rather than to the speaker's enemies, resists demonizing (or better "chaosizing") the waters." (My thanks to William Brown for a copy of his lecture, which will be published.)

9. Translation by William B. Brown.

10. The theme of the two temples also appears in the creation narrative of Genesis 1, almost architecturally in parallel. For this, see S. Dean McBride Jr., "Divine Protocol: Genesis 1:1–2:3 as Prologue to the Pentateuch," in *God Who Creates: Essays in Honor of W. Sibley Towner*, ed. William P. Brown and S. Dean McBride Jr. (Grand Rapids: Eerdmans, 2000), 11–15.

11. See Terence E. Fretheim, *God and World in the Old Testament: A Relational Theology of Creation* (Nashville: Abingdon, 2005). See also my review in *Word and World* 26, no. 3 (Summer 2006), 33-39.

12. On Genesis 1 and Psalm 104, see Santmire, *Nature Reborn*, chap. 3.

13. See H. Paul Santmire, *Brother Earth: Nature, God, and Ecology in a Time of Crisis* (New York: Thomas Nelson, 1970), 133–39.

14. On these themes generally and the book of Job in particular, see my article, "Partnership with Nature According to the Scriptures: Beyond the Theology of Stewardship," *Christian Scholar's Review* 32, no. 4 (Summer 2003): 381–412.

15. For these materials, see Santmire, *The Travail of Nature: The Ambiguous Ecological Promise of Christian Theology* (Minneapolis: Fortress Press, 1985), chaps. 7, 8.

16. For Thomas, see ibid., 84–95.

17. Following the aforementioned theme that a confessional theology of the kind I am developing here can be the occasion for the discovery of a certain consonance between theological and natural scientific statements, it is interesting to note here that the theological notion of God reflecting the divine power, vitality, and personal intimacy in God's communication of Godself to material nature, to life, and to humans

seems to be consonant with some (at least) scientific construals of the cosmos that highlight emergence from matter to life to human self-consciousness. For an entry into this discussion, see Ian G. Barbour, "Evolution and Process Thought," *Theology and Science* 3, no. 2 (July 2005): 161–78.

18. Here drawing on Tillich's discussion in his *Systematic Theology*, I (Chicago: University of Chicago Press, 1951), 16–18.

19. For an accessible introduction to the evolution of Barth's theology in its historical context, see the instructive essay by Clifford Green in the volume of selections from Barth's writings, *Karl Barth: Theologian of Freedom* (London: Collins Liturgical, 1989), 11–45.

20. I argued this case in my 1966 Harvard Divinity School doctoral dissertation (unpublished) on Karl Barth's theology of nature. The results of that study are summarized in my book *The Travail of Nature*, chap. 8.

21. I am instancing Thoreau and Muir here as figures whose visions were popularized. Their own views were more complex than I can indicate here. See my discussion in *Brother Earth*, chaps. 1, 2.

22. Translation by William P. Brown.

23. Joseph Sittler, *Essays on Nature and Grace* (Philadelphia: Fortress Press, 1972), 42.

24. Tillich talked about this experience on more than one occasion in his lectures at Harvard Divinity School, when he was teaching there.

25. See my discussion of the issue of a cosmic fall, in *Brother Earth*, 192–200. This approach has been reaffirmed by Fretheim, *God and World in the Old Testament*.

26. *Lutheran Book of Worship*, 92.

27. This story is told strikingly by Helmut Koester in his article, "The Memory of Jesus' Death and the Worship of the Risen Lord," *Harvard Theological Review* 91, no. 4 (1998): 335–50.

28. To speak of the work of Christ in this way, as having a twofold rationale, is, admittedly, to schematize the rich and diverse witness of the Scriptures and the liturgy. But some kind of schematization like this is unavoidable; even the decision not to decide is a decision. For a systematic discussion of this topic, see my study, *Brother Earth*, chap. 8, and, in particular, this comment by Jürgen Moltmann: "According to Paul, Christ was not merely 'delivered for our offenses' but was also 'raised for our justification' (Rom. 4:25). This is the way Paul expresses the imbalance between sin and grace and the *added value* of grace. The surplus of grace over and above the forgiveness of sins and the reconciliation of sins represents the power of the new creation which consummates creation-in-the-beginning. It follows that the Son of God did not become man simply because of the sin of men and women, but rather for the sake of perfecting creation." *The Trinity and the Kingdom: The Doctrine of God* (New York: Harper & Row, 1981), 116.

29. I refer the reader again to my article, "So That He Might Fill All Things: Comprehending the Cosmic Love of Christ," dialog 42:3 (fall 2003), pp. 257-278, for a more comprehensive treatment of the subject, and to the well-argued study by George Murphy, *The Cosmos in Light of the Cross* (Harrisburg: Trinity Press International, 2003).

30. Russell Bradner Norris Jr., "Logos Christology as Cosmological Paradigm," *Pro Ecclesia* 5, no. 2 (Spring 1996): 189–90.

31. See the discussion by Raymond E. Brown, *The Gospel According to John, I–XII*, Anchor Bible (Garden City, N.Y.: Doubleday, 1966), Appendix IV (EGO EIMI—"I AM"), 533–38.

32. For a survey of the rich symbolism of "the shepherd" in biblical times, much of that symbolism having royal, even cosmic meanings, see the article by Joachim Jeremias in *Theological Dictionary of the New Testament*, ed. Gerhard Friedrich, trans. and ed. Geoffrey W. Bromiley (Grand Rapids: Eerdmans, 1968), 6:485–502.

33. Cf. Moltmann, *The Way of Jesus Christ: Christology in Messsianic Dimensions*, trans. Margaret Kohl (London: SCM, 1990), 290–91: "God preserves his creation from corruption because, and inasmuch as, he has patience with what he has created. His patience creates time for his creatures. His longsuffering leaves them space. His patience, which is prepared to suffer, and his waiting forbearance are virtues of his hope for the turning back and the homecoming of his creatures to the kingdom of his glory."

34. On the motif of God's "bearing with," see the discussion of Second Isaiah by Frederick J. Gaiser, "'I will carry and will save': The Carrying God of Isaiah 40–66," in *And God Saw That It Was Good: Essays on Creation and God in Honor of Terence E. Fretheim*, Word & World Supplement Series 5, ed. Frederick J. Gaiser and Mark A. Throntveit (St. Paul: Word & World, 2006), 94–102.

35. Again, I must take note of the fact that a more systematic discussion here would highlight the work of the Holy Spirit. I would want to explore the vision of the cosmic shepherd in relationship with what must also be an equally comprehensive vision of the cosmic vocation of the Holy Spirit. Such explorations would find a rich store of theological discourse about the works of the Spirit in the already cited writings of Moltmann. As a down payment on that kind of reflection, cf. Moltmann's statement in *The Way of Jesus Christ*, 289–90: "The New Testament writings do not make any systematic distinction . . . between Word and Spirit in creation. The two together circumscribe the mystery of God in the world and stress Christ's mediatorship in creation, out of which all things receive both the fellowship that binds them and their own unique character. The two aspects also make it clear that creation is not merely a 'work' of 'God's hands', but that through his ceaselessly uttering and creating Word he is the foundation and continuance of all things. God is the innermost life of the world."

36. Hiebert, "Rethinking Traditional Approaches to Nature in the Bible," in *Theology for Earth Community: A Field Guide*, ed. Dieter T. Hessel (Maryknoll, NY: Orbis Books, 1996), 28f.

37. Ibid., 28.

38. Cf. Brigitte Kahl, "Fratricide and Ecocide: Rereading Genesis 2–4," in *Earth Habitat: Eco-Justice and the Church's Response*, ed. Dieter T. Hessel and Larry Rasmussen (Minneapolis: Fortress Press, 2001), 55: "We might expect God to lean back and watch his creature taking up the spade to start digging and planting. . . . But instead we see God taking the spade and planting the trees in the garden, definitely hard and dirty manual work. . . . Adam's task is simply to serve and preserve the garden. Wherever humans touch the soil, God's footmarks and fingerprints are already there."

39. See Leslie Sauer, "Bring Back the Forests: Making a Habit of Reforestation, Saving the Eastern Deciduous Forest," *Wildflower* (Summer 1992), 27–34.

40. See George W. Ramsey, "Is Name-Giving an Act of Domination in Genesis 2:23 and Elsewhere?," *Catholic Biblical Quarterly* 50, no. 1 (January 1988): 24–35.

41. William P. Brown, *The Ethos of Cosmos: The Genesis of Moral Imagination in the Bible* (Grand Rapids: Eerdmans, 1999), 141, seems to adhere to the older view, but this appears to be inconsistent with his overall approach to the theology of the Yahwist.

42. Note that Adam names only the living things, not all things. Cf. Claus Westermann, *Genesis 1–11: A Commentary*, trans. John J. Scullion (Minneapolis: Augsburg, 1984), 229: "Names are given first to living thing things, because they are closest to humans." Cf. also the remarks of Fretheim, *The Suffering of God: An Old Testament Perspective*, Overtures to Biblical Theology (Philadelphia: Fortress Press, 1984), 100, regarding the meaning of "naming" more generally in the Old Testament: "Giving the name opens up the possibility of, indeed admits a desire for, a certain intimacy in relationship. A relationship without a name inevitably means some distance. Naming the name is necessary for closeness."

43. For a balanced entry into the field of what might be called agrarian theology, see Norman Wirzba, *The Paradise of God: Renewing Religion in An Ecological Age* (New York: Oxford University Press, 2003).

44. See my essay, "The Spirituality of Nature," in *Tending the Holy*, ed. Vest, chap. 9.

45. Cf. Larry Rasmussen, *Earth Community Earth Ethics* (Maryknoll, N.Y.: Orbis, 1997), 2, on "creation-loving asceticism": "An asceticism that loves earth fiercely in a simple way of life is desperately needed, above all among the wealthy of the world and others habituated to unsustainable consumption as a lifestyle." James Nash is the ethicist who has perhaps developed this theme most pointedly, under the rubric of "voluntary frugality." See his discussion in *Loving Nature*, 64.

46. See, for example, Duane Elgin, *Voluntary Simplicity: Toward a Way of Life That Is Outwardly Simple and Inwardly Rich*, rev. ed. (New York: William Morrow, 1993), and Richard A. Horsley, *The Liberation of Christmas: The Infancy Narratives in a Social Context* (New York: Continuum, 1993).

47. See, for example, Margaret R. Miles, *Fullness of Life: Historical Foundations for a New Asceticism* (Philadelphia: Westminster, 1981).

48. The Evangelical Lutheran Church in America has taken the lead in developing this kind of thinking about the role of assemblies and of wider church bodies in responding to the groaning of the creation.

49. Theological reflection about the value of animals or "animal rights" is, by now, generally highly sophisticated. A very helpful entry point into this whole discussion is the work by John B. Cobb Jr. and Charles Birch, *The Liberation of Life: From Cell to Community* (Cambridge: Cambridge University Press, 1981).

10. The Habit of Partnering: Our Walk with Nature Ritualized

1. The promise of the metaphor of "partnering" for this kind of theology-of-nature project dawned on me when I was doing the research for my article, "Partnership with Nature According to the Scriptures: Beyond the Theology of Stewardship," *Christian Scholar's Review* 32, no. 4 (Summer 2003): 381–412. By coincidence at that time I happened to notice Letty's Russell's book *Growth in Partnership* (Philadelphia: Westminster, 1981) on my shelf (which, I hasten to add, is not about the theology of nature), and it all fell together. Later, I realized that the term had also been in the back of my mind from many years' study of Karl Barth's theology, where the

expression "covenant partner" is of major significance, and perhaps also from a more recent reading of Larry L. Rasmussen's book, *Earth Community Earth Ethics* (Maryknoll, N.Y.: Orbis, 1997), esp. 236–42. It also occurred to me, after I had concluded most of the chapters of this book that the idea of a "partnership society" figures significantly in the discussions of Walter Wink about the "principalities and powers." Wink indeed envisions the partnership society as being the viable biblically inspired alternative to the "domination system" that has had most of "civilized" human history in its grasp for aeons. See Wink's study, already referred to, *Engaging the Powers: Discernment and Resistance in a World of Domination* (Minneapolis: Fortress Press, 1992), esp. 37–45.

The New Testament uses the root word for partnering (*koinon*) explicitly and powerfully regarding the believer's relationship with Christ, particularly in the Eucharist, and also regarding believers' relationship with one another "in Christ." (See Friedrich Hauck, "*koinon*," in *Theological Dictionary of the New Testament*, ed. Gerhard Kittel, trans. Geoffrey W. Bromiley [Grand Rapids: Eerdmans, 1965], 3:804–09.) But this by no means precludes a more comprehensive *theological* use of the term, as in this book, which understands the word against the background of the entire biblical narrative, from Genesis to Revelation. In this respect, the New Testament usage, which accents mutuality and respect and communion, can also exercise a kind of anchor of meaning, keeping the word from slipping willy-nilly in readers' minds toward more objectifying and legalizing nuances (as in the case of some "business partnerships").

2. *Baptism, Eucharist and Ministry*, Faith and Order Paper 111 (Geneva: World Council of Churches, 1982), 16.

3. This twofold character of the redemption wrought by Christ is described at length in my book, *Brother Earth: Nature, God, and Ecology in a Time of Crisis* (New York: Thomas Nelson, 1970), chap. 8.

4. L. E. Phillips, *The Ritual Kiss in Early Christian Worship* (Nottingham, UK: Grove, 1996), 12, cited by Martin D. Stringer, *A Sociological History of Christian Worship* (Cambridge: Cambridge University Press, 2005), 11.

5. Bernard W. Anderson, "Introduction: Mythopoeic and Theological Dimensions of Biblical Creation Faith," in *Creation in the Old Testament* (Philadelphia: Fortress Press, 1984) 11, following Paul Humbert, *La relation de Genese 1 et du Psaume 104 avec la liturgie du Nouvel-An Israelite*," in *Opuscules d'un hebraisant* (Neuchatel: Universite de Neuchatel, 1958), 60-83.

6. For a suggestive interpretation of this psalm, see William P. Brown, "Joy and the Art of Cosmic Maintenance: An Ecology of Play in Psalm 104," in *"And God Saw That It Was Good": Essays on Creation and God in Honor of Terence E. Fretheim*, Word & World Supplement Series 5, ed. Frederick J. Gaiser and Mark A. Throntveit (St. Paul: Word & World, 2006), 23–32.

7. For these materials, see my article "Partnership with Nature," 381–412. Some of the most insightful exegesis of the Genesis creation accounts is to be found in William P. Brown's *The Ethos of Cosmos: The Genesis of Moral Imagination in the Bible* (Grand Rapids: Eerdmans, 1999), chaps. 2 and 3. Also see Terence Fretheim, "Creator, Creature, and Co-Creation in Genesis 1–2," in *All Things New: Essays in Honor of Roy A. Harrisville*, Word & World Supplement Series 1 (St. Paul: Word & World, 1992), 11–20, and my article "The Genesis Creation Narratives Revisited: Themes for a Global Age," *Interpretation* 45, no. 4 (October 1991): 366–79.

8. I first espoused the construct of "the integrity of nature" in my 1970 study, *Brother Earth*, chap. 7.

9. Discerning the meaning of the "image of God" (*imago Dei*) language in Genesis 1 has preoccupied biblical writers, theologians, scholars and others for centuries. The literature on the subject is enormous, including one recent, well-regarded study: J. Richard Middleton, *The Liberating Image: The Imago Dei in Genesis 1* (Grand Rapids: Brazos, 2005). This book was positively reviewed by W. Sibley Towner in *Interpretation* 59, no. 4 (October 2005): 408–10. The single best entry into this jungle of exegetical richness is a short article by the same W. Sibley Towner, "Clones of God: Genesis 1:26-28 and the Image of God in the Hebrew Bible," in the same issue of *Interpretation*, 344–57.

10. Brown, *Ethos*, 43–44.

11. It is beyond the scope of this study to probe deeply into the discussion concerning the distinctiveness of the human creature in relationship with other animal creatures. That humans are animals Genesis 1 and 2 takes for granted. Humans and the other animals are created on the same day (Genesis 1); humans and the other animals are made of the same arable soil and each one is a "living soul" (*nephesh hayya*) (Genesis 2). On the other hand, only humans are created according to the image of God (Genesis 1). The human (Adam) only bonds most deeply with another human (Eve), and only the human is personally addressed by God (Genesis 2). I understand this as a profound quantitative continuity between humans and other animals, which quantitative continuity at some point becomes qualitative.

Teilhard de Chardin once observed of the emergence of the human creature in the midst of the long history of evolution: humanity "came silently into the world." By this Teilhard meant that by every criterion at the time of human emergence there was virtually no distinguishable difference between pre-humans and humans. Teilhard also believed that, in retrospect, with the long history of human life in view, there was at some point, in the midst of vast continuities, a qualitative step forward to something new, the emergence of the human animal. Teilhard expected that that point of transition, however, would in all likelihood forever remain unknown. But such thoughts can only be entertained as suggestive here. For detailed explorations of such issues, see Philip Hefner, *The Human Factor: Evolution, Culture, and Religion* (Minneapolis: Fortress Press, 1993).

12. For more exegetical details, see S. Dean McBride Jr., "Divine Protocol: Genesis 1:1-2:3 as Prologue to the Pentateuch," in *God Who Creates: Essays in Honor of W. Sibley Towner*, ed. William P. Brown and S. Dean McBride Jr. (Grand Rapids: Eerdmans, 2000), 3–41.

13. Cf. Brown, *Ethos*, 42: "Given the rich ancient Near Eastern background behind the so-called *Chaoskampf*, the archetypal conflict between the Deity and chaos, the Priestly cosmologist boldly divests all intimations of conflict from divine creation."

14. Cf. the discussion of this point by Fretheim, *The Suffering of God: An Old Testament Perspective*, Overtures to Biblical Theology (Philadelphia: Fortress Press, 1984) 73.

15. Ibid., 78.

16. Cf. Keith Whitelam, "Israelite Kingship: The Royal Ideology and Its Opponents," in *The World of Ancient Israel*, ed. Ronald Clements (Cambridge: Cambridge University Press, 1989), 121: "Royal ideology provided a justification for the control of

power and strategic resources; it proclaimed that the king's right to rule was guaranteed by the deities of the state. A heavy emphasis was placed on the benefits of peace, security and wealth for the population of the state which flowed from the king's position in the cosmic scheme of things." Quoted by Norman Habel, *The Land Is Mine: Six Biblical Land Ideologies* (Minneapolis: Fortress Press, 1995), 17.

17. See Habel, *The Land is Mine*, chap. 2.

18. Cf. further James Limburg, "The Responsibility of Royalty: Genesis 1–11 and the Care of the Earth," *Word & World* 11, no. 2 (Spring 1991): 124–30.

19. Walter Brueggemann, *Genesis,* Interpretation: A Bible Commentary for Teaching and Preaching (Atlanta: John Knox, 1982), 32.

20. So Brown, *Ethos*, 44. See also Mark G. Brett, "Earthing the Human in Genesis 1–3," in *The Earth Story in Genesis*, ed. Norman C. Habel and Shirley Wurst (Cleveland: Pilgrim, 2000), 77: "The characteristic association of the phrase 'image of God' with Mesopotamian kings and Egyptian pharaohs has been long observed, but the implications of this comparison have often been under-analyzed. If the health of the created order does not depend upon kings, then the democratizing tendency of Gen. 1:27-28 can be seen as anti-monarchic. Indeed, there is an anti-monarchic tone to Genesis, which begins in Genesis 1 but extends into the second creation story and beyond. The polemical intent is subtle, but the evidence for it accumulates as the narrative unfolds."

21. Cf. Fretheim, *The Suffering of God*, 128: "God is thus portrayed not as a king dealing with an issue at some distance, nor even as one who sends a subordinate to cope with the problem, nor as one who issues an edict designed to alleviate suffering. God sees the suffering from the inside; God does not look at it from the outside, as through a window. God is internally related to the suffering of the people. God enters fully into the hurtful situation and makes it his own. Yet, while God suffers with the people, God is not powerless to do anything about it; God moves in to deliver, working in and through leaders, even Pharaoh, and elements of the natural order."

22. Although, cf. the caveat of Theodore Hiebert, "Re-Imaging Nature: Shifts in Biblical Interpretation," *Interpretation* 50:1 (January 1996), 42. "In the preindustrial age of biblical Israel, it is impossible that the Priestly writer had more in mind in these concepts of dominion and subjection than the human domestication and use of animals and plants and the human struggle to make the soil serve its farmers."

23. Brown, *Ethos*, 45.

24. Ibid. Brown is using the word *command* here in a more positive sense than I have used it above, in my discussion of the authoritarian character of Babylonian rule.

25. For my ambivalence about the construct *stewardship*, see the appendix below.

26. Brown, *Ethos*, 60.

27. Cf. T. J. Gorringe, *A Theology of the Built Environment: Justice, Empowerment, Redemption* (Cambridge: Cambridge University Press, 2002), 6: "In imaging God as Creator the Hebrew Bible conceives of the whole cosmos as the proper territory for acts of artifice and intelligence. These are not autonomous, but represent responses to the Creator Spirit."

28. Cf. Brueggemann, *Genesis,* 37, regarding creation as "good": "The 'good' used here does not refer primarily to a moral quality but to an aesthetic quality. It might better be translated 'lovely, pleasing, beautiful' (cf. Eccles. 3:11)."

29. Cf. Brown, *Ethos*, 50–51: "A stable creative order prevails in this cosmos, accomplished not through conflict and combat but by coordination and enlistment.

Each domain, along with its respective inhabitants, is the result of a productive collaboration between Creator and creation. The final product is a filled formfulness. Form is achieved through differentiation, the mark of goodness. While differentiating the various cosmic components, the process of separation, paradoxically, serves to hold the cosmic order together. Creation's 'filledness' is achieved by the production of life. From firmaments to land, boundaries maintain the integrity of each domain as well as provide the cement that finds the cosmos as a whole."

30. Some theologians have wanted to push the discussion further at this point by affirming what appears to be a speculative insight promulgated by some cosmological physicists and philosophers: the so-called "anthropic principle." This is the idea that the emergence of humanity on planet Earth was in some sense, either blindly ("the weak" anthropic principle) or intentionally ("the strong" anthropic principle), ordained from the very beginning, the "big bang," since the end result, the emergence of humanity on Earth, could only have happened, physically and biologically, if a particular and infinitely complicated set of physical variables were in place right from the beginning.

In my view, the anthropic principle should be left to the cosmological physicists and the philosophers. If by their own criteria, they can make a case for it, then it might be possible to explore what it would mean to compare the anthropic principle to the biblical witness to creation in order to see what kind of consonance between the two might be identified, if any. For a helpful review of these issues, see George Murphy, *The Cosmos in Light of the Cross* (Harrisburg: Trinity Press International, 2003), 178–84.

31. Gorringe, *A Theology of the Built Environment*, 139.

32. Writing in 2002, Gorringe, *A Theology of the Built Environment*, 23, observed: "We have to come to terms with a world population which has doubled in [the last] fifty years to top 6 billion, and which has to be not just fed, but housed. We have to come to terms with a change in the balance of human settlements which has profound psychic and spiritual consequences for us. Deep into the twentieth century villages have been home to most of the human race, but in the last decade of that century the proportion of people in cities finally exceeded fifty per cent, and the trend to urbanization continues, despite what is called 'counter urbanization' in some parts of the First World."

33. For a sobering yet hopeful report on global urbanization trends, see *State of the World 2007: Our Urban Future* (Washington, D.C.: Worldwatch Institute, 2007).

34. Douglas Foy and Robert Healy, "Cities Are the Answer," *Boston Globe*, April 4, 2007, A7.

35. For an entry into this whole dynamic and complicated discussion, see John B. Cobb Jr., *Sustainability: Economics, Ecology, and Justice* (Maryknoll, N.Y.: Orbis, 1992).

36. Scripture is taken from *The New King James Version*, copyright © 1979, 1980, 1982 Thomas Nelson, Inc. Used by permission. All rights reserved.

37. Gorringe, *A Theology of the Built Environment*.

Epilogue: "Come and See"

1. This, according to the Hartford Institute for Religious Research: http://hirr.hartsem.edu/research/fastfacts/fast_facts.html#growlose (accessed March 13, 2008).

2. Dieter T. Hessel, "The Church Ecologically Reformed," in *Earth Habitat: Eco-Injustice and the Church's Response*, ed. Dieter T. Hessel and Larry Rasmussen (Minneapolis: Fortress Press, 2001), 186.

Appendix: On the Ambiguities of Stewardship

1. Much of my discussion, in this respect, is based on the research I did for my article, "Partnership with Nature According to the Scriptures: Beyond the Theology of Stewardship," *Christian Scholar's Review* 32, no. 4 (Summer 2003): 381–412.

2. I already expressed some of these reservations in my book, *Nature Reborn: The Ecological and Cosmic Promise of Christian Theology* (Minneapolis: Fortress Press, 2000), 120.

3. Larry L. Rasmussen, *Earth Community Earth Ethics* (Maryknoll, N.Y.: Orbis, 1997), 230–36.

4. Paul Krugman, "Enemy of the Planet," *New York Times*, April 17, 2006, A25.

5. *The Living Pulpit* 15:3 (July-September 2006).

6. Marian E. Renan, "The Stewardship Model of Christian Environmentalism," ibid., 18–19.

7. Rasmussen, *Earth Community Earth Ethics*, 235 n. 18.

8. Rasmussen refers the reader here to: Carolyn Merchant, *Radical Ecology: The Search for a Liveable World* (New York: Routledge, 1992), p. 72.

9. John L. Paterson, "Conceptualizing Stewardship in Agriculture within the Christian Tradition," *Environmental Ethics* 25, no. 1 (Spring 2003): 43–58.

10. R. J. Berry, *Environmental Stewardship: Critical Perspectives—Past and Present* (New York: T&T Clark, 2006. This volume includes a shortened version of my article on stewardship and partnership referred to above.

11. William P. Brown, *The Ethos of Cosmos: The Genesis of Moral Imagination in the Bible* (Grand Rapids: Eerdmans, 1999)

12. Douglas John Hall, *The Steward: A Biblical Image Come of Age*, rev. ed. (Grand Rapids: Eerdmans, 1990); Douglas John Hall, *Imaging God: Dominion as Stewardship*, Commission on Stewardship, National Council of Churches of Christ in the U.S.A. (Grand Rapids: Eerdmans, 1986); John Reumann, *Stewardship and the Economy of God*, The Ecumenical Center for Stewardship Studies, Indianapolis (Grand Rapids: Eerdmans, 1992).

Index

Ambrose of Milan, 226
Anderson, Bernard W., 300n5
Anderson, Gary A., 270n43, 276n18,
   277nn21–22
Animals
   as human kin, 206–7, 212–13
   blessing of, 178–79
Anselm of Canterbury, 144, 195
"Anthropic principle," 303n30
Apocalyptic vision, 21–23
   and hope, 23–26
Aristides Aelius, 41, 267n20
Augustine of Hippo, 27, 28, 29, 32,
   81, 97, 102, 108, 111, 114, 117,
   260n5, 278n15
Augustus, 40
Aune, Michael B., 264n41, 269n34
Aquinas, Thomas. *See* Thomas Aquinas
Awe of nature, habit of, 185–95

Bach, J. S., 60
Bakken, Peter, 274n40
Baptism, 132–136
   and the baptistery, 133, 135
Barbour, Ian, 297n17
Barron, Robert, 173, 294n30
Barth, Karl, x, 28, 29, 30, 31, 81, 114,
   145, 189, 191, 192, 242, 260n5,
   271n46, 283n17, 284n21,
   285n33, 297n20, 300n1
Bartholomew, Ecumenical Patriarch,
   74, 273n31
Bass, Dorothy C., 287n6
Bauckham, Richard, 270n45

Benedict XVI, Pope, 74
Bente, Paul F., 13
Berger, Peter, 6
Bernard of Clairvaux, 46
Berry, R. J., 255, 274n39, 304n10
Berry, Thomas, 24, 262n34
Birch, Charles W., 75, 274n37, 299n49
Blake, William, 170
Bloom, Harold, 103, 280n37
Boberg, Carl, 293n27
Boff, Leonardo, 73, 273n22
Bonhoeffer, Dietrich, 27, 175, 176, 241,
   270n46, 293n24, 294nn35–36
Bornkamm, Heinrich, 282n9
Boulding, Kenneth, 235
Bouma-Prediger, Steven, 273n24, 285n27
Bouyer, Louis, 99–100, 279nn25, 28–29
Braaten, Carl E., 30, 264n46
Braaten, Laurie J., 267n22
Bradshaw, Paul F., 289n23
Brancusi, Constantin, 174
Brett, Mark G., 302n20
Brooks, David, 13
Brown, Norman O., 193
Brown, Peter, 268n29
Brown, Raymond E., 298n31
Brown, William P., 186, 227, 231, 256,
   263 n. 33, 296nn8, 9, 297n22,
   299n41, 300nn6–7, 301nn10, 13,
   302nn20, 23, 26, 303n29, 304n11
Brunner, Emil, 145, 170, 189
Buber, Martin, 119, 120, 146, 271n46
Bucer, Martin, 161
Buchanan, Colin, 289n26

271n46, 274n3, 280n1, 281n6,
282nn7–8, 282n9, 283n15,
283n16, 284nn18–20, 285n29,
287n11, 289n21, 289n28,
289n30, 290n35, 292n15, 293n28
on the *communicatio idiomatum*,
284n20
on the immanence of God. *See*
Theology of descent
and the theological use of paradox,
113–15, 283n16
and the theology of ascent, 281–
82n6
on the ubiquity of Christ, 116–18
and "wrath" in nature, 293–94n28

Malcolm, Lois E., 286n39
Marshall, I. Howard, 268n32
Marty, Martin E., 280n38
Marx, Karl, 37
McBride, S. Dean, Jr., 296n10, 301n12
McCall, Richard D., 270n42
McCarthy, Cormac, 22
McClurkin, Donnie, 100
McFague, Sallie, 75, 274n35, 281n3
McKibben, Bill, 20, 262n24
Melanchthon, Phillip, 27, 112
Merchant, Carolyn, 304n8
Middleton, Richard, 301n9
Merleau-Ponty, Maurice, 265n48
Meslier, Jean, 286n38
Metaphors, root, 132
Milbank, John, 259n2
Miles, Margaret R., 299n47
Moe-Lobeda, Cynthia, 19, 261n20,
267n26
Moltmann, Jürgen, 75, 129, 201, 228,
274n34, 281n3, 286n37, 288n15,
297n28, 298nn33, 35
Mozart, Wolfgang, 53
Muir, John, 120, 193, 297n21
Murphy, George L., 282n11, 288n18,
297n29, 303n29

Nash, James, xv, xvi, 75, 259n1, 274n38,
280n2, 295n2
Nature

and anthropocentrism, 7, 218, 227–33
and the city, 233–36, 239, 243–44
cognitive dissonance of nature and
liturgy, 57–76
in crisis, xiv, 8–16
death of, 20–21
defined, 31–33
dominion over, human, 204, 216–17,
222–23, 230–32
eclipse of in modern theology,
69–72
emergence of in recent ecumenical
theology, 73–74
and eschatology, xii
ethics of, 183, 211–12, 242, 295n2
and human fallenness, 198–99
integrity of, 228–29
life of its own with God, 187–90
mastery of. *See also* Nature,
dominion over, 92–97
partnership with. *See* Partnership,
habit of
redemption of (cosmic redemption),
xv–xvi
ritualizing of, 4–6, 180–81
as not fallen, 151, 198–99
as sacral, 107–11
as sacramental, 107–11
sacrality of and the ubiquitous
Christ, 119–23
serving. *See* Serving nature, the
habit of
as a "social creation," 264n48
spirituality of. *See* Spirituality
wild, cultivated, fabricated, 32–33
Nichols, Terence L., 292n22, 293n22
Niebuhr, Reinhold, 8, 18, 261n18
Nietzsche, Friedrich, 271n46
Nolan, Barbara, 97, 278n16
Norris, Russell Bradner, Jr., 202, 297

O'Collins, Gerald, 293n25
Oelschlaeger, Max, 263n38
Offertory, 146–53
as embodied response, 146n49
and money, 149, 152
promise of the, 150n53